D1593308

Remorse

Remorse

A Christian Perspective

Anthony Bash

FOREWORD BY
Martyn Percy

CASCADE *Books* · Eugene, Oregon

REMORSE
A Christian Perspective

Cascade Books
An Imprint of Wipf and Stock Publishers
199 W. 8th Ave., Suite 3
Eugene, OR 97401

www.wipfandstock.com

PAPERBACK ISBN: 978-1-7252-7234-7
HARDCOVER ISBN: 978-1-7252-7235-4
EBOOK ISBN: 978-1-7252-7236-1

Cataloguing-in-Publication data:

Names: Bash, Anthony, author. | Percy, Martyn, foreword.

Title: Remorse : a Christian perspective / by Anthony Bash ; foreword by Martyn Percy.

Description: Eugene, OR: Cascade Books, 2020 | Includes bibliographical references and index.

Identifiers: ISBN 978-1-7252-7234-7 (paperback) | ISBN 978-1-7252-7235-4 (hardcover) | ISBN 978-1-7252-7236-1 (ebook)

Subjects: LCSH: Remorse | Guilt | Theology, Practical | Forgiveness—Biblical teaching

Classification: BT790 B374 2020 (print) | BT790 B374 (ebook)

Manufactured in the U.S.A.   09/29/20

To Melanie

Remorse: A Fragment

Of all the numerous ills that hurt our peace,
That press the soul, or wring the mind with anguish
Beyond comparison the worst are those
By our own folly, or our guilt brought on:
In ev'ry other circumstance, the mind
Has this to say, "It was no deed of mine:"
But, when to all the evil of misfortune
This sting is added, "Blame thy foolish self!"
Or worser far, the pangs of keen remorse,
The torturing, gnawing consciousness of guilt—
Of guilt, perhaps, when we've involved others,
The young, the innocent, who fondly lov'd us;
Nay more, that very love their cause of ruin!
O burning hell! in all thy store of torments
There's not a keener lash!
Lives there a man so firm, who, while his heart
Feels all the bitter horrors of his crime,
Can reason down its agonizing throbs;
And, after proper purpose of amendment,
Can firmly force his jarring thoughts to peace?
O happy, happy, enviable man!
O glorious magnanimity of soul!

—Robert Burns

Contents

Foreword

The Very Revd Professor Martyn Percy,
Dean of Christ Church, Oxford.

THE SAMARITANS IS AN organization founded in 1953 by the Reverend Chad Varah, who at the time was a young curate in the city and diocese of Lincoln. It is no exaggeration to say that the Samaritans—which is now international and counsels the lonely, the depressed, and the suicidal—grew out of a particular encounter that Varah had with shame and remorse. Cycling back to his clergy lodgings one day, he was greeted by the housekeeper at the door, who told him that his Rector was ill, so he would need, at the last minute, to take a funeral. He cycled off to the cemetery, cassock flapping in the breeze.

When Varah arrived at the cemetery gates, the funeral was about to start. At this point, he did not know the name of the deceased, but was curious about why the body was laid to rest in an unmarked plot, and in the part of the cemetery that was not consecrated for burial. He finished the funeral, and then began to ask some questions. Varah ascertained that he had just presided over the funeral of a girl, aged thirteen years, who had killed herself because she had begun menstruating. Mortified that the girl had to be buried in unconsecrated ground, with parts of the burial liturgy redacted as the death was a suicide, Varah felt his own remorse. The girl's family was there too—and no less remorseful. Shame and guilt lay thick in the air, held together with the collective remorse of the mourners.

Varah's response to his remorse, and the guilt and shame of the mourners, was constructive and imaginative. He became concerned about the state of sex education for teenagers in the city, and so started to work with young people, especially listening to those who were contemplating suicide. Varah's Samaritan movement grew rapidly when he subsequently moved to London. Within ten years, the Samaritans was a sizable charity, offering a supportive and empathic listening service that is not political or religious.

I am writing this foreword to the very fine book by Anthony Bash in a week when I have learned that an old friend of mine from school days has taken his own life. His father is a bishop; his older brother a priest, and his sister married to a priest. My friend was married, with grown-up children. They were a clergy family through-and-through, deeply embedded in faith and love, and in the hope and grace of the gospel. And yet, and yet . . . .

My friend took his life after a prolonged period struggling with depression. The cycle of shame, remorse, and depression pulled him ever-downwards—though ultimately into the everlasting arms of God. The days when mourners were left with remorse from the stigma of family members who take their own lives are, thankfully, mostly gone. We now speak differently of these deaths. For we understand the power of remorse to cause deep damage to individuals and to families, communities, and nations.

It is only in recent times that we have begun to understand quite why so many German citizens took their own lives as the Second World War ended. For a few, it was their Nazi zeal, and not wanting to live in a world without their Fürher-leader, and where the Reich was destroyed. For many, however, it was their own multiple overwhelmings of shame and remorse that did for them. The raped; the silent witnesses and bystanders who had watched the trains trundling to the camps (and always leaving empty) but who had said nothing; those who had saved their own lives and betrayed others, only in order to save themselves. Indeed, many chose to symbolize that sense of being swamped by their individual and collective sins by drowning themselves and their children.[1]

The Scriptures are full of remorseful characters, and they pepper the Old Testament and the New Testament with their biographies. Lives lived out of regret are painful to engage with, and the Scriptures give us plenty of insight into this, yet as part of the overall ecology of salvation.

The Gospels often chide the church for trying to act as a kind of "Border Agency Police" for heaven, and chide Christians for offering their well-meaning services to Jesus as self-appointed "Immigration Control Officers" for paradise. But Jesus is not impressed with these proposals to police his kingdom. Hence, the Gospels offer extreme cases of God saying, "Let it be," or "Let them come to me." The dying thief on the cross is an obvious example

---

1. On this, see the fine study by Christian Goeschel, *Suicide in Nazi Germany* (Oxford: Oxford University Press, 2009).

Acknowledgments

THIS BOOK HAS ITS origins from reading J. K. Rowling's *Harry Potter* books, first to my children when they were younger, and latterly also for my own pleasure. I noticed that in Rowling's books there is next to nothing about forgiveness—a subject on which I have written for several years—but there is a great deal about remorse. Clearly, Rowling is interested in remorse. But what is remorse, and where is its place in the Judeo-Christian quartet of wrongdoing, repentance, forgiveness, and reconciliation? At first, I was not sure, and this book is the result of a long period of thought.

As I wrote this book, many people have shaped my thinking and given generously of their expertise. I thank Dr Anthony Atkinson, Dr Stephen B. Barton, Fr Andrew Downie, Professor John Gaskin, Dr Stephen Humphreys, Professor R. Walter L. Moberly, His Honour Judge Christopher Prince, Richard G. Rohlfing Jr, and Professor Peter J. Rhodes. They have read or talked to me about parts of earlier drafts of this book. Much of what I have written bears the imprint of Professor Geoffrey F. Scarre's insightful comments and I warmly thank him. Dr Hugh Firth and David Sheard have helped me to think carefully about ways to articulate Christian ethics and morality in a contemporary setting. The Very Revd Professor Martyn Percy, a good friend for many years, generously wrote the Foreword. Hannah Bash, Simeon Bash, and Matthias Bash have each contributed to this book, either by reading or commenting on parts or by talking to me and honing my thinking. Matthias has especially helped with proofreading. Last of all, I thank my wife, Melanie. Her love and support enable me to think and write in ways that I would not (and could not) without her. This book is, of course, dedicated to her, with love and gratitude.

List of Abbreviations

ABD
: *The Anchor Bible Dictionary*. 6 vols. Edited by David Noel Freedman. New York: Doubleday, 1992.

BAGD
: Walter Bauer, Frederick W. Danker, W. F. Arndt, and F. W. Gingrich. *Greek-English Lexicon of the New Testament and Other Early Christian Literature*. 3rd ed. Chicago: University of Chicago Press, 2000.

BCP
: The *Book of Common Prayer*, Oxford: Oxford University Press.

BDB
: Francis Brown, S. R. Driver, and Charles A. Briggs, 2005. *Hebrew and English Lexicon of the Old Testament*. Oxford, Clarendon, 1907.

CW-CI
: *Common Worship. Christian Initiation*. London: Church House, 2006.

CW-SP
: *Common Worship. Services and Prayers for the Church of England*. London: Church House, 2000.

EE
: Aristotle, *Eudemian Ethics*

ESV
: *Holy Bible. English Standard Version. Containing the Old and New Testaments*. London: Collins, 2002.

LCL
: Loeb Classical Library

LSJ   Henry George Liddell, Robert Scott, and Henry Stuart Jones. *A Greek-English Lexicon, with a Revised Supplement.* 9th ed. Oxford: Clarendon, 1996.

LXX   *Septuaginta. Id est Vetus Testamentum graece iuxta LXX interpretes edidit Alfred Rahlfs, Duo Volumina in uno.* Stuttgart: Deutsche Bibelgesellschaft, 1979.

MED   *Middle English Dictionary.* 1952–2001. Edited by Robert E. Lewis et al. Ann Arbor, MI: University of Michigan Press, 2001–18.

MT   Masoretic Text.

NE   Aristotle, *Nicomachean Ethics*

NIDOTTE   *New International Dictionary of Old Testament Theology and Exegesis.* Edited by Willem A. VanGemeren. Carlisle, UK: Paternoster, 1997.

NIV   *Holy Bible. New International Version.* London: Hodder & Stoughton, 2011.

NRSV   *Holy Bible: New Revised Standard Version (NRSV) Anglicized.* London: Collins, 1995.

OED   *Oxford English Dictionary.* 20 vols. 2nd ed. Oxford: Clarendon, 1991.

Rhet.   Aristotle, *Art of Rhetoric*

ST   Thomas Aquinas, *Summa Theologiae*

Chapter 1

Remorse

WHY A BOOK ON REMORSE? Søren Kierkegaard (1813–55) wrote that being remorseful is part of what it means to be pure in heart. "So wonderful a power is remorse, so sincere its friendship," he says, "that to escape it entirely is the most terrible thing of all." He adds that remorse is "a concerned guide," a "sincere and faithful friend" who protects from "delusion."[1] He describes remorse as the guide that helps people to look back and, in his florid, traditional language, says that remorse "calls man back from evil."[2] Both repentance and remorse are "eternity's emissaries"; remorse and its "call" teach people to "know the way" and they lead to "purity of heart."[3] In contemporary language, remorse leads to the sort of virtue that is—or should be—characteristic of Christian discipleship and spirituality. It is a constituent of "moral passion," that is, one of the "essential features of genuinely moral behavior."[4]

Christian theology has a well-developed theology of remorse towards God about sin. So, when people do wrong, they may express to God their remorse about what they have done, because they believe that they have sinned against God. They may believe that if they wrong people, they also sin against God, and so should express remorse to God about the wrong they have done to such people. However, and as we shall see in this book,

---

1. Kierkegaard, *Purity*, 10.

2. In contrast, repentance causes people to look forward (Kierkegaard, *Purity*, 11).

3. Kierkegaard, *Purity*, 11. The last three words of the quotation are taken from the title of three works in *Upbuilding Discourse in Various Spirits* (1847). The work is addressed to "an individual" as a spiritual preparation for the office of confession. The same discourse is translated in Kierkegaard, *Upbuilding*, Part One, 7–154.

4. Gill, *Moral Passion*, 10.

1

Christian theology has not often emphasized that it is important for wrong-doers in such situations also to express remorse to the people they have wronged. In other words, Christian theology appears to have an under-developed theology of interpersonal remorse.

Of course, many thoughtful, decent people put right the wrongs they have done to other people before or as part of the way they express remorse to God. In many traditional Christian liturgies, such a practice is implicit rather than enjoined. For example, the words of the Confessions in the *Book of Common Prayer* (1662) of the Church of England refer only to sin against God. True, those who come to receive Holy Communion must be "in love and charity" with their "neighbors." In contrast, those who sin against God say the more severe words in one of the Confessions that they "acknowledge and bewail" their "manifold sins and wickedness" against *God*, with no words of confession about wrongs against "neighbors," and no words commending remorse, repentance, and restitution for such wrongs. It is as if wrongs against other people are subordinated under the rubric of wrongs against God, with interpersonal wrongdoing seen as being in a subsidiary, and less grievous, category of wrongdoing. One of the aims of this book is to explore the reasons why such a theological approach to interpersonal remorse is under-developed.

Another deficiency this book attempts to address is lack of clarity about what interpersonal remorse is. The word "remorse" is often used loosely with words such as "repentance" and "regret," as if the three words mean much the same when understood from different perspectives. As we will see, the words are related but have distinct meanings, and the differences, as well as the points of overlap, are important. In this book, we attempt to give a clear and precise description of interpersonal remorse, and we explore its nature and form as an emotion.[5]

Describing what interpersonal remorse is does not, of course, ex-plain that to be remorseful and to behave appropriately as a result are virtuous. As we see in chapter 6, some think that remorse is pathological, "a product of old-time religion,"[6] and something to be thrown off as psy-chologically unhelpful. We set out in this book cogent, compelling reasons why remorse *can* be virtuous.

Outside the Christian tradition, there is important work in the fields of philosophy, psychology, law, and some of the sciences (such as psychol-ogy, neurology, and evolutionary biology), for example, that directly or in-directly influences the way we can (and sometimes should) think about and

---

5. Remorse is not an action-response in the way that repentance is, for example.

6. Hauck, "Remorseful Patient," 18.

understand interpersonal remorse. Much of this book is set in the context
of and in critical dialogue with some of the findings in these areas of understanding. We will see that secular writers and thinkers on the whole have
led and shaped contemporary work on remorse, with the church and Christian thinkers sometimes lagging behind and with the tradition of Christian
thought (such as it is) on the topic being largely ignored.[7] We will show that
Christian theology *does* have a significant contribution to make to contemporary, secular discussion about interpersonal remorse.

We hope to offer in this book a carefully articulated ethic of interpersonal remorse by drawing on both secular and Christian traditions, by developing a theological rationale of interpersonal remorse, and by critically
engaging with contemporary, secular discussion of remorse in the context
of its scientific, philosophical, and jurisprudential settings. We show that
the "logic" of the gospel commends interpersonal remorse as an appropriate ethic for those who have done wrong. It also commends particular
behaviors, such as repentance and restitution, which can result from interpersonal remorse. We show that interpersonal remorse is a long-neglected
virtue that is embedded in Judeo-Christian thought, though only in incho-
ate form. We also explore why interpersonal remorse has "come of age"
only in the contemporary period.

Gordon Graham observes that "[t]he intellectual position of Christianity in the modern world . . . is largely one of retreat" because "theologians and believers more generally have lost confidence in the relevance of
Christian theology to the explanatory endeavors of intellectual enquiry."[8]
This book seeks to contribute to stemming what Graham calls the "retreat"
through a vigorous, informed, and critical theological approach to ethics,
as well as through demonstrating that Christian ethics, especially when articulated in some of the language and categories of modern discourse, can
make a distinctive and important contribution to current debates. The result
will be, I hope, not only deepened understanding for all people but also,
for those within the Christian church, renewed motivation for vigorous,
thoughtful, and practical Christian discipleship and spirituality.

Remorse, Regret, and Repentance

As I said above, the words "remorse," "regret," and "repentance" are often
associated with one another. They can be said to "lack sharp boundaries"
and "[e]ach word can . . . be considered a label for a fuzzy set, defined as a

7. The Christian philosopher Robert C. Roberts is a notable exception.

8. Graham, *Evil*, 1.

class . . . in which there is a gradual but specifiable transition from membership to nonmembership."[9] More generally, each in a list of remorse, regret, sadness, disappointment, shame, guilt, and sorrow, for example, may have aspects of any of the others in the list, even though they are all regarded as discrete emotions.

Remorseful people regret what they have done and often are also repentant. "Remorse" and "regret" are sometimes even used interchangeably. An obvious example of this are the words "remorse" quoted above in the extract from Kierkegaard's writings: they are from a translation published in 2008[10]—and the same words are translated "regret" in a 1993 translation of the same work.[11] As we shall see, there are important differences between "remorse" and "regret," and in the contemporary period it is inaccurate to treat the words as interchangeable.

The word "regret" in modern English is a hypernym for the varieties of ways that people feel, recognize, and acknowledge that they feel sad, disappointed, and even repentant about something. Remorse is a species (or "variant")[12] of regret. According to the *OED*, remorse is "deep regret or guilt for doing something morally wrong." As we would expect with emotions that are related to one another, remorse bears only some of the characteristics of regret; it also bears characteristics of other emotions that are outside the ambit of regret. In other words, remorse is not regret only and regret is not the same as remorse.[13]

Of course, in everyday speech the word "remorse" is sometimes used more loosely than the way it is defined in the *OED*, and throughout this book we refer to the varieties of ways the word can be understood and to examples of more popular usage. One egregious example is of Jeff Skilling, former Chief Executive of Enron Corporation, who was sentenced to a lengthy prison sentence for fraud. He said of himself, "I can't imagine more remorse" but also said that day that he was "innocent of every one" of the charges against him.[14] By almost any mainstream description of remorse, it

9. Russell, "Circumplex," 1165.

10. Kierkegaard, *Purity.*

11. Kierkegaard, *Upbuilding.* The different ways to translate the same Danish word are reflected in the differing translations.

12. Roberts, *Essay*, 240.

13. This approach is based on "the prototype approach" to perceptual and semantic categories, with the categories of "regret" and "remorse" standing in a hierarchic relationship to one another in a basic category and a subordinate category respectively (Shaver et al., "Emotion Knowledge," 1062).

14. *Washington Post*, 24 October 2006.

is hard to see how one can be both remorseful and continue to assert that one is innocent of legal or moral wrongdoing.

Etymologically, the word "remorse" comes from the Latin verb *remordere*, which means "to bite back" or "to sting again." The word is first used in English in the late-fourteenth century.[15] *Remordere* can also mean "to vex persistently," "to gnaw," or "to nag." The word "regret" comes from the Old French verb *regreter*, meaning "to bewail" (usually the dead). Of course, I am not saying that the etymology of these words tells us what they mean today; I am no more than pointing out that in their origins (and, as we shall see, in their meanings today, too) the words refer to different, but related, emotions.

The remainder of this chapter is a preliminary overview of remorse as a form of regret. It provides the framework for chapters 2 to 5 that trace the history and development of remorse. In chapters 6 to 9, we explore the nature of contemporary remorse, In the last chapter, chapter 10, we draw together our findings and look at remorse in its form as a distinctively Christian ethic.

Regret

"Regret" is used in a range of contexts and is a word with a wide spectrum of meaning.[16] Robert C. Roberts regards regret as "a relatively indeterminate, all-purpose emotion type."[17] He defines regret as "X (occurrence, nonoccurrence, action, omission, state of affairs), which is contrary to my concern(s), might have been otherwise."[18] People do not always regret something for moral reasons,[19] and it is possible to regret doing the right thing or something

---

15. *MED, s.v.* "remorse."

16. On regret, see Thalberg, "Remorse," 547; Rorty, "Agent Regret"; Bittner, "Is It Reasonable?"; Kierkegaard, *Upbuilding*, 13–18; Landman, *Regret*; Zeelenberg, "The Use of Crying," 325; Tudor, *Compassion and Remorse*, 160–66; Miller, *Faking It*, 81–83; Roberts, *Essay*, 240–41; Betzler, "Sources," 215; Peijnenburg, "Is What Is Done Done?"; Smith, *I Was Wrong*, 67–74; Davison, "Regret"; Barnum-Roberts, "Apologizing"; Enoch "Being Responsible"; Wallace, *View*; McQueen, "When Should We Regret?" 609; Gilbert "Vain Regrets"; and most of issue 5 of the *International Journal of Philosophical Studies* (2017). For regret in the ancient world, see Fulkerson. "Metameleia," 244. On collective regret, see, Olick, *Politics*, 2007. Regret is an important area of study in social psychology: see Zeelenberg, "Regret," for example. On the psychology of regret, see Gilovich and Medvec, "Experience."

17. Roberts, *Essay*, 240

18. *Essay*, 241, with italics removed.

19. Betzler, Review of *The View From Here*.

that is not a wrong,[20] such as when a parent regrets having to discipline a recalcitrant child. It is also possible to be satisfied with the state of affairs one has brought about but regret the process that one initiated to bring it about. As for whether regret should be well-founded, Roy Sorensen argues that it need not,[21] but Cara Bagnoli argues that it should.[22]

Regret has been classified in at least four ways. "Agent regret" is when one regrets one's own part, however great it may be, in bringing about a state of affairs that one wishes were different. Bernard Williams points out that it is possible to regret the outcome of a correct moral choice.[23] We discuss in chapter 10 whether one can also be remorseful about such a choice. There are at least three other types of regret: spectator regret, character regret, and patient regret. "Spectator regret" is no more than when one observes and regrets a state of affairs that one has not caused or brought about.[24] Amélie Rorty additionally identifies "character regret," that is, regret for defects of character.[25] Last, Geoffrey Scarre suggests there can be "patient regret," that is, "instances where I am wholly non-responsible for something unfortunate that happened to me."[26] As these types of regret are not regret about one's wrongs, they cannot be remorse as well.

Regret is an "elastic" word and, in Rorty's words, can range from "passing light regret to dark and heavy regret." It can be no more than a wistful feeling, "relatively low keyed in comparison with remorse or guilt."[27] This sort of regret is sometimes thought of as a restrained or polite word, intended to be little more than a "social lubricant"[28] the purpose of which is "to keep oiled the wheels of civility and good manners,"[29] such as when one declines a dinner invitation. Often, with the passing of time, such regret ceases to be either sharp or painful.

Rorty's suggestion that "regret" can have such a wide range of meaning sometimes produces odd results. It would be clearer to use different words or phrases to describe each of "dark and heavy regret" about someone's suffering,

20. Cowley, "Regret," 630.

21. Sorensen, "Rewarding Regret."

22. Bagnoli, "Value in the Guise of Regret."

23. Williams, Problems, 166–86. Williams differentiates agent regret from remorse (Moral Luck, 29).

24. Williams, Moral Luck. See also Taylor, Pride, Shame, and Guilt, 98.

25. Rorty, "Agent Regret," 490.

26. Scarre, "'Constitutive Thought,'" 570.

27. Rorty, "Agent Regret," 493, 496.

28. Bovens, "Apologies," 219.

29. Murphy, Punishment, 144.

a deep sense of regret about having done wrong, and a relatively minor mishap, disappointment, or mistake. The words we choose should be appropriate to help differentiate the degree of the agent's affect, the nature of the harm or wrong, and the proportionality of the response to the harm or wrong, even if the words also presuppose and include regret.[30]

Perhaps surprisingly to the modern reader, the reaction of Herod to the death of John the Baptist, of which he was the unwilling (or, at least, unenthusiastic) agent, is akin to regret. Herod is said to have been "grieved" about having to order John's death (Matt 14:9). Herod's grief was regret that he had to keep a promise the outcome of which he feared would incite the people (Matt 14:5), not remorse about being the agent of John's death.

Remorse

Remorse is more limited in scope than regret, and we explore it carefully in the rest of this book. At this point, we can say that remorse is a strong, reactive emotion. As we have seen, the *OED* limits remorse to being "deep regret" or "guilt" about one's own wrongdoing.[31] The *OED* also limits remorse to situations where people have done "something morally wrong" and so excludes social lapses, solecisms, or shortcomings. Central to the *OED*'s approach to remorse are guilt and morality, and acknowledgment of personal responsibility and so moral accountability for what one has done.[32] One therefore cannot be remorseful, though one may regret, and even regret very much, that one has sold shares at a loss before the market rose, or that one missed a train and so is delayed for an important meeting, or that one interviewed badly for a new job. The *OED* definition also excludes being remorseful about what one might do, because one can only be remorseful about what one *has* done: a wrong one might do is no more than a contingency.[33] Irving Thalberg has said, "One cannot have remorse about one's character, but only how one acts. Of course, the actions may be *due* to one's character, but the remorse is for the results. . . . [I]t would be absurd to feel remorse prior to a

---

30. Proeve and Tudor, *Remorse*, 63; Taylor, *Pride, Shame, and Guilt*, 98; Hauck, "Remorseful Patient," 13; Greenberg and FitzPatrick, "Regret," 35–36; and Greenspan, *Practical Guilt*, 135.

31. Whether there can be "guilt-free morality," see Harman, "Guilt-Free Morality."

32. For an exploration of the relationship of responsibility and Christian ethics (but without considering regret, remorse, and repentance), see Schweiker, *Responsibility*.

33. In contrast, Rorty thinks one can regret what one intends to do or something one is convinced one is likely to do ("Agent Regret," 490).

misdeed."[34] In short, remorse involves recognizing and acknowledging—at least to oneself—that one has done wrong.

It is, of course, possible to be guilty but not feel a sense of guilt or remorse, for people may have cognitive knowledge that an act or omission is wrong but from their viewpoint disagree that the act or omission is wrong. They may think, as Mr. Bumble did when told that the law assumed his wife acted under his direction, that ". . . the law is a[n] ass—a[n] idiot. If that's the eye of the law, the law is a bachelor, and the worst I wish the law is that his eye may be opened by experience—by experience."[35]

Of course, one has to keep a sense of proportion when it comes to remorse. To speak of being remorseful because one forgot a lunch invitation with a friend whom one continues to see regularly is, I suggest, absurd, and suggests the neurosis of a self-absorbed, over-sensitive conscience. Raimond Gaita rightly calls such remorse "corrupt" and "egocentric" and says that "regret" would be a better way to describe how such a person feels.[36]

We can illustrate many of the observations above about regret and remorse from seven examples of Bella, who hates her spouse Caroline.

1. Bella may have no more than occasional thoughts about living without Caroline. She may feel guilty about her passing thoughts. She may also feel ashamed of herself for having such thoughts because of where they might lead. However, she cannot properly say she is remorseful, because one can only feel remorseful about a wrong one has done: passing thoughts are just thoughts, not moral acts. In Thalberg's words that I quoted above, there is no "result" of an "action" about which one could feel remorseful. Bella can properly say that she regrets the thoughts and is ashamed of them.

2. If Bella experiences more than passing thoughts about Caroline and chooses willfully and persistently to indulge in malevolent thoughts in a deliberate and focused way, and later deeply regrets the way she ruminated on them, we can say that her deep regret amounts to remorse if she believes that deliberately to feed malevolent thoughts is to do wrong. Here, again using Thalberg's words, the "result" of the "action" is a "misdeed," namely, nursing what is malign, even though the subject of what is malign are thoughts, not actions.[37] Jesus

34. Thalberg, "Remorse," 546.

35. Dickens, *Oliver Twist*, 354.

36. Gaita, *Good and Evil*, 47, 52.

37. Smith rightly allows for "the possibility of wronging another through an unexpressed attitude" ("Guilty Thoughts," 255).

says much the same about nursing thoughts in Matt 5:28 of those who look with lustful intent. It is not the seeing that is sin. Rather, according to Jesus, the sin of looking with lustful intent is to *keep* looking. This element of continuity is indicated by a present tense that points to continuity of action.

3. Suppose Bella kills Caroline by poisoning a gin and tonic Bella gives Caroline to drink. If Bella later deeply regrets what she has done because she realizes it is wrong, she may say she is remorseful.

4. If Caroline drinks the poisoned gin and tonic and dies, Bella may think, as some murderers do of their victims, that she is well rid of Caroline and she may deeply regret what she sees as the folly of having entered into a relationship with Caroline. Can Bella say that she is remorseful about the relationship with Caroline, even if she is not remorseful about having murdered her? I think not, because (so far as we know) she did not do wrong in marrying Caroline but made a choice the outcome of which (an unhappy partnership) she deeply regrets. The thought "I wish I'd never even met her," is deep regret, but not, in this instance, remorse.

5. If Bella is confronted with the fact that she had murdered Caroline (for example, if there were evidence incontrovertibly to point to her criminal guilt), the gravity and evil of what she has done may become apparent to her and she may be deeply remorseful. It is as if her viewpoint has changed from being glad of the end she brought about (to be rid of Caroline through murder) to regretting deeply the end and the means used.

6. Suppose Caroline did not consume the poisoned gin and tonic. If Bella later realizes the foolhardiness of what she had done (poisoning the gin and tonic and thereby attempting to kill Caroline), she may say she is remorseful about the intentions she attempted to carry out. Bella would be remorseful about how she had acted (as Thalberg suggests of remorse), even though (in this case) the intended outcome of her wrong actions (Caroline's death) was not realized. "Regret" seems too anodyne a description of Bella's likely emotions when she realizes how misguided she had been.

7. If Bella were tried and convicted of Caroline's murder, and imprisoned for the offence, she may continue to be glad to be rid of Caroline but lament that she was in prison for having murdered her. She may be sorry and deeply regret that she has been found out. This is not remorse at all but a form of pathological self-pity that is without moral perspective.

We should also add for completeness that people may be selective about what they deeply regret when it comes to a series of related, wrongful actions. For example, Bella may not regret the end she brought about (to be rid of Caroline) but be remorseful about the means she used (premeditated murder by poisoning). The same may be true of David who committed adultery with Bathsheba and who engineered the death of her husband (2 Sam 12:1–14). Nathan confronted David with what he had done, and as a result, David's moral outlook was restored and he was remorseful (2 Sam 12:13). But what was he remorseful about? He may have been remorseful because he had committed adultery and because he had engineered the death of Uriah in battle. Nevertheless, the fact that he remained married to Bathsheba (or at least did not separate from her)[38] suggests that David did not regret the end he brought about.

Words Akin to "Remorse"

People may express their deep regret or guilt for having done something morally wrong apart from by the word "remorse."

In former times, people may have said they felt *compunction*, that is, according to the *OED*, a "pricking or stinging of the conscience or heart; regret or uneasiness of mind consequent on sin or wrongdoing; remorse, contrition." The word "compunction" seems largely to have fallen out of modern use. We shall see in chapter 5 that "compunction" is the anglicized form of the Latin word *compunctio*, which means "remorse." When the word "compunction" is used today, it usually means no more than a slight or passing regret for wrongdoing, or a feeling of regret for some slight offence. As the word now means little more than "regret" on the rare occasions when it is now used, we will not consider the word further in this book, and we will regard it as a species of regret.

Contemporary people, if they use the word "penitent," tend to use it in ways that are divorced from its religious roots. They usually mean no more than regret for their wrongdoing, and that they want to hang their heads in shame and try to do better in the future. Some people baulk at using the word because of its religious associations, and instead choose to use more neutral language. Traditionally, the word presupposes the idea of remorse. We consider the words "penitent" and "penitence" in their use in traditions of Christian spirituality in chapter 5.

Lastly, according to the *OED*, the word "contrition" refers to the "condition of being bruised in heart" and to "sorrow or affliction of mind for

---

38. Compare 2 Sam 20:3.

some fault or injury done." Contrite people are usually remorseful and the two words—"contrition" and "remorse"—are essentially synonyms.[39]

More than "remorse," the word "contrition" tends to be used in a religious context and, in that context, means regret that is a thoroughgoing sorrow towards God for sin. An example of public contrition is from around the time of the millennium when Pope John Paul II publicly expressed contrition for the errors and mistakes of the Catholic Church at various times during the Church's history.[40]

Roberts regards contrition (along with joy, hope, and gratitude) as "emotion-virtues" that are "especially fitting ways to grasp the central Christian truths."[41] He writes:

> The Christian emotions [such as contrition] have a central and fundamental place in Christian knowledge because (a) they make essential use of the Christian propositions; (b) they are perceptions (yet without being sense perceptions), rather than mere beliefs or knowledge; and (c) they essentially embody the concerns that befit the Christian truths. No other type of mental state incorporates all these Christian epistemic virtues.[42]

Nick Smith has explored the idea of contrition in contemporary discussion about retributive punishment. He suggests that "categorically apologetic offenders" (that is, apologies by offenders who admit guilt, accept blame, refrain from further wrongdoing, and provide compensation or reparation) deserve less punishment if they are contrite because contrition can modify the very nature of the offence and so make it less bad, meriting less punishment.[43] This is a contentious view, and we discuss both this view and the place of remorse and contrition in a retributive model of criminal law and punishment in chapter 9.

In the remainder of this chapter, we introduce some of the ways remorse in its broadest sense intersects with emotions (such as guilt), behaviors (such as apologies), and language. We also return to these topics throughout the book.

---

39. This is not so in the thought of Aquinas, as we shall see in chapter 5.

40. See Kalbian, "The Catholic Church's." For a critical view, see Glendon, "Public Acts."

41. Roberts, *Spiritual Emotions*, 95.

42. Roberts, "Emotions as Access," 83.

43. Smith, "Dialectical Retributivism," 244.

Remorse and Guilt

Besides being "deep regret" about wrongdoing, remorse can also be guilt about wrongdoing. It is an easy mistake to conflate being guilty (being culpable, and so often one's juridical *status*) with having a sense of guilt, that is, *feeling* pain that one has done wrong and so being what Roberts calls "morally spoiled."[44] Herbert Morris expresses the sense of guilt this way: "Feeling guilt is feeling more than sorrow or regret that what one cares for has been hurt or damaged; it is pain mediated by the judgment, 'I am responsible for the damage.' In feeling guilt, we turn on ourselves like a scorpion biting its own tail."[45] If guilty people feel a sense of guilt, they are also sometimes remorseful because they construe themselves as "having committed an offense."[46]

Of course, people may have a pathological sense of guilt, and feel guilt when they have not done anything wrong. Equally, despite what people may claim or even believe, they may not in fact feel guilt when they say they do: for example, those with antisocial personality disorders "may learn to refer to 'guilt' when they experience negative affect after committing an antisocial act, and receiving punishment for it, even though they are actually experiencing regret (displeasure from being caught) rather than remorse."[47]

The feelings of guilt that people have are said to be the result of an internal "voice" that metaphorically does the equivalent of wagging a finger in accusation and condemnation. (The authoritative voice may be external or one's conscience or super-ego.)[48] Williams suggests that painful feelings of guilt are brought about by an "enforcer," an internal psychological agent, who promotes fear—fear at the anger of the internalized judge and fear of punishment meted out by an external judge.[49] Some will want to say that the "enforcer" comes from the conscience, and some will want to say that the conscience is a God-given faculty (e.g., Rom 2:12–16).[50]

44. Roberts, *Essay*, 223. Guilt can also refer to *knowing* that one has done wrong but without the sense of sorrow or guilt.

45. Morris, *On Guilt*, 312.

46. Roberts, *Essay*, 223. See also Thalberg, "Remorse," 545–46. Cf. Taylor, *Pride, Shame, and Guilt*, 100, 107. On guilt, see Greenspan, *Practical Guilt*.

47. Lilienfeld and Fowler, "Self-Report," 110.

48. We will refer in chapter 7 to Freud's view that emotions come from the unconscious, are expressed in the consciousness, and informed by the Superego.

49. In Williams, *Shame and Necessity*, endnote 1. See also Tudor, *Compassion and Remorse*, 132 who distinguishes between remorse as feelings that sometimes arise after wronging another and guilt feelings, which he defines as transgression against an authority figure. The distinction is artificial, and he himself concedes that the distinction is "somewhat stipulative."

50. The word "conscience" refers to the "senses involving consciousness of morality

There will be times that people will know that, whatever they do (and even if it is according to their values), their actions will bring about a degree of harm. Such a predicament is sometimes called "the dilemma of dirty hands." We might use the words of a popular expression to a person facing such a dilemma, "You are damned if you do, and damned if you don't."[51] Kai Nielsen suggests people should seek to do the lesser evil in such situations and accept that if they do the lesser evil, they do not do wrong, even if "whatever we do or fail to do leads to the occurrence of evil or sustains it."[52] This approach to the dilemmas people face may still affect the way they think about what sort of people they are and does not stop them from feeling guilt and remorse. Humber van Straalen suggests people are remorseful in these situations because, in doing what they believe to be wrong (even though it may be the lesser evil and the best that could be done in that situation), they still feel compromised and corrupted.[53]

Remorse and Apologies

Remorse can sometimes lead people to apologize for the wrong they have done.[54] Apologies may be evidence of what Jeffrie Murphy calls "moral character"[55] and of one of the morally virtuous responses that may result after a person realizes that he or she has done wrong.

People usually make apologies with explicit words of apology. However, it is possible to be remorseful but not to offer an apology; it is also possible to dissemble and apparently to show remorse when apologizing. If people are remorseful and apologize, it is usually because they believe they have done something wrong, unless of course they apologize out of a misplaced and even pathological sense of guilt or to appease at any cost. Sometimes, when people are remorseful and apologize, they demonstrate their remorse by acts of reparation or by offering some form of compensation.

Twenty-first-century western culture recognizes that to apologize is an appropriate way for all people, whether they are in the Judeo-Christian faith tradition or not, to mark that they have failed to keep to the standards they

---

or what is considered right" (*OED, s.v.* "conscience"). The nature of consciousness is outside the scope of this book, though we consider "conscience" in chapter 8. We also consider at length the "senses involving . . . what is considered right" in chapter 7.

51. See Walzer, "Political Action."
52. Nielsen, "There is No Dilemma," 22.
53. Van Straalen, "Remorse," 291–92.
54. We also discuss apologies in chapter 6.
55. Murphy, *Punishment,* 129.

hold, however and from wherever they may derive those standards.[56] Apologies, whether expressed in a face-to-face encounter, through repentance, by restitution, or penitential acts, for example, are intended to put right the past, and so to assuage the guilt of one's conscience, rebuild one's identity, and put right the wrong one has done. They are commonly regarded as a necessary (but not sufficient) condition of forgiveness,[57] and as beginning a process that addresses guilt about the past and ameliorates both unease in the present and possible disquiet in the future.

It is important to observe that people who receive apologies and then forgive wrongdoers often themselves experience incidental benefits, such as diminution of anger and resentment. Models of psychological therapy for unforgiveness often stress the psycho-social benefits that accrue to a person who forgives.[58] Sometimes overlooked are the benefits of forgiveness that accrue to *wrongdoers* whose consciences have become awakened to and troubled by the effects of their wrongdoing and who are in consequence remorseful. When forgiven, wrongdoers may have to learn to undo the effects of the harm that the wrongdoing has done to *themselves,* the wrongdoers, and to see themselves as no longer defined by the wrong they have done.[59]

Nick Smith makes the point that apologies are not "binary," i.e., we do not need to stipulate whether something is or is not an apology. Rather, we should think in terms of "how well [the apology] serves certain purposes and to what extent it conveys certain kinds of subtle social meanings." He also says that "apologies achieve varying degrees of diverse forms of meanings in contextually specific fields of significance." In other words, in the case of remorse, apologies are situational, and in part depend on how they are both intended and received.[60]

56. On apologies, see Tavuchis, *Mea Culpa*; Davis, "On Apologies"; Lazare, *On Apology*; Smith, "The Categorial Apology"; Gibney et al., *The Age of Apology*; Smith, *I Was Wrong* (especially p. 259, n. 1 for a bibliography of sources on apology); Bovens, "Apologies"; Radzik, *Making Amends*, 2–7; Martin, "Owning Up"; Smith, *Justice through Apologies*; Battistella, *Sorry About That*; and Helmreich, "Apologetic Stance." Much academic consideration has also been given to apologies for governmental wrongdoing, corporate and institutional apologies, apologies for criminal behavior, and apologies as a prelude to forgiveness. See, for example, Nobles, *Politics*.

57. In my view, forgiveness is *voluntarily* offered in response to another person's repentance: there is no duty to forgive (Bash, *Forgiveness and Christian Ethics*, 101–5, 176–77).

58. Bash, *Forgiveness and Christian Ethics*, 36–39.

59. See Gusdorf, *Mémoire*, 373, who describes this as a form of self-forgiveness. I think this is an intra-psychic process, not self-forgiveness (cf. Bash, *Forgiveness and Christian Ethics*, 13).

60. Smith, *I Was Wrong*, 12, 23. On the components of a genuine apology, see also Radzik, *Making Amends*, 92–97 and Battistella, *Sorry About That*.

An important aspect of a remorseful apology is that in its most richly textured form it needs not only to be expressed or delivered but also to be received. One therefore cannot apologize to an animal for having wronged it, because the animal does not have the cognitive framework to receive an apology in the way it is intended be received (though of course one may be able to put right the effects of one's wrongdoing to an animal). This is an example of being remorseful but not being able to apologize. One also cannot apologize to the dead, even if one is remorseful. (After I had started writing this book, I well remember feeling bewildered at my late father's funeral, because the officiating minister asked my father's immediate family, of which obviously I am a member, to stand before the open grave and to apologize to my late father for any matters about which we had not apologized to him in his lifetime.) To be clear: one may be remorseful, even though one cannot apologize or have one's apology accepted. This is a different situation from apparently being remorseful and being able to apologize but choosing not to do so: acting in this latter way brings into question the integrity of one's remorse.

Of course, when one is remorseful, feeling sorry about what one has done will not put right the relational rupture that doing wrong may have caused. Even if one acts to put right a wrong about which one is sorry to help repair the relational rupture, an apology does not undo the fact that a wrong act took place. In the words of the popular expression, "What's done is done." Michel de Montaigne (1533–92) made this point in his essay *On Repentance* when he wrote, "your fancy cannot, by wish and imagination, move one tittle, but that the great current of things will not reverse both the past and the future."[61] We can go further: the fact that a person has done wrong cannot be erased or negated. Remorse is like a form of lament that recognizes that the wrongs of the past are part of one's identity in the present, as well as in the future. In Hannah Arendt's words in *The Human Condition*, we now live with "the predicament of [the] irreversibility" of what we have done.

However, an apology that involves wrongdoers both admitting that they have mistreated their victims and putting right the effects of the wrong (such as repaying stolen money, correcting a misapprehension, and so on) will usually go a long way towards undoing or putting right the damage of wrongdoing.[62] Mere passivity (that is, knowing one has done wrong but doing nothing apart from acknowledging one has done wrong) is not enough: "moral repair" is needed and this involves treating "the victim as someone it was unacceptable to wrong."[63] From this, it will be apparent that if wrong-

61. This point is also made especially cogently in Jankélévitch, *Le Paradoxe*.
62. On making amends, see Radzik, *Making Amends*.
63. Helmreich, "Apologetic Stance," 75.

doers recognize that they have done wrong and are truly sorry, they will necessarily acknowledge that they are guilty. We explore these observations further at several points later in this book.

To live with the knowledge of one's wrongdoing and its irreversibility can be deeply painful, and we may seek to shield ourselves from facing such knowledge. We construct psychological defenses,[64] or we develop social or religious mechanisms that persuade us that we can expiate the wrongs we have done. Nevertheless, repentance and penitence that lead to penance and restitution do not restore the *status quo ante*; and no amount of remorse or regret can undo the past. Even to be forgiven by another is no more than to resolve the relational rupture that wrongdoing brings about.[65] Paul the Apostle never forgot that he had persecuted Christians (1 Cor 15:9); the stain of what he had done shaped both how he saw himself (1 Tim 1:13) and how others saw him (Acts 9:26–27).

Remorse and Language

As we have seen, regret and remorse comprise a medley of feelings and behaviors that can be described by a variety of (sometimes overlapping) words. Feelings and behaviors rarely exist in "pure" form except in the writings of theoreticians. As we have seen, "regret" can be described as a feeling on its own, though it will often be alloyed with other emotions, such as guilt and shame. Conversely, regret is also a feeling comprising parts of other emotions and actions, such as remorse, penitence, and repentance. It can also sometimes be a constituent part of a variety of behaviors, such as apologizing, doing penance, and so on.

There may be a variety of ways of feeling, expressing, and demonstrating regret or remorse in some cultures that other cultures conflate into fewer discrete ways. Words or their lack can be one of the indicators of this. An example (but not of remorse or regret) comes from a recent BBC online report indicated that there are 421 snow-related words and expressions in Scots, a minority language spoken in parts of Scotland, whereas there is no such subtlety in modern English.[66] As we shall see in many of

64. See Freud, *The Ego*.

65. Kelley, "Jankélévitch and Gusdorf," discussing the work of Gusdorf, *Mémoire*, and Jankélévitch, *L'Imprescritible*, who explore this question.

66. The information was uncovered by the compilers of the *Historical Thesaurus of Scots* (2015) by researchers at the University of Glasgow. See https://www.bbc.com/ideas/videos/which-language-has-400-words-for-snow/p063vmwx and https://scotsthesaurus.org. From the language of ethnopsychology, we can say that the idea of snow is "hypercognated," that is, it carries a wide variety of assumptions and understanding

the following chapters, words for emotions do not carry the same meaning in all cultures. In addition, words do not always have fixed meanings; we *give* them meanings that can vary with culture, context, or time. On apologies generally, Alison Dundes Renteln concludes that the "presumption of universality" in the meaning of the word "apology" is "unwarranted" and that the "dearth of empirical data on [the] cross-cultural status of apologies leaves us in a very sorry state."[67] Thus, in the English-speaking West in modern times, people usually regard an apology for past wrongdoing to be an indicator of moral caliber; in other cultures, an apology is a sign of moral weakness. For example, in her study on remorse and regret in ancient Greece, Laurel Fulkerson writes:

> In general, the modern western viewpoint esteems the feelings of regret and particularly remorse as a part of a beneficial rethinking and learning process. . . . The ancients have a different intuition, believing that one should refrain from doing in the first place things that one will later need to regret. . . . The remorseful individual in antiquity is, first and foremost, a person who has failed to act well rather than one who has learned a lesson.[68]

David Lambert has illustrated this point too when it comes to the word "repentance." In a carefully constructed diachronic study, he demonstrates that the Hebrew words commonly translated as "repentance" in the Old Testament have a variety of meanings even in the Old Testament, and the variety of meanings becomes more evident in later writings, especially in the period after the close of the Old Testament. What he is rightly concerned to identify is the meaning of the word "repentance" for particular groups at particular times, and he does not assume that the meaning is the same at all times, in all places, and for all peoples and cultures. He says that "we import certain categories . . . appropriate to contemporary, dominant notions of the self . . . when we use the concept, 'repentance,' to interpret various ancient Israelite practices." He concludes that it is not until the early formations of Judaism and Christianity in the first century AD that we see a view of repentance as being the initiative of individual human beings.[69]

(Levy, *Tahitians*, 284), though this is not to say that every use of a word for snow carries every assumption and understanding about snow.

67. Renteln, "Apologies," 78.

68. Fulkerson, *No Regrets*, 6.

69. Lambert, *How Repentance Became Biblical*, 150–51. See also Etzioni and Carney, *Repentance*, on repentance in an inter-faith setting. Etzioni concludes in an introductory essay that there is an "absence of concepts and processes of repentance . . . in Western civic culture," that is, an absence of a "set of shared values, mores, and rules that guide our life, especially but not only in our public life" (*Repentance*, 1).

One can go further and say that it is a mistake to think that "repentance" and "remorse" (or any other such word) have fixed meanings that
refer to something that exists: rather, words are hybrid terms that label,
classify, and identify what will almost certainly be thought of in different
ways according to time, place, culture, or context. Words for emotions are
cultural constructs describing psychic and physical states, without phenomenological identity outside their societal interpretation. So, when it comes
to remorse, for example, we might say that we make exist what we mean by
"remorse" when we ascribe meaning to the word, though of course if we are
to communicate well with one another, we need to understand the words
that we say and hear. The point I am seeking to make is that we have to be
sensitive to what people mean by the words they use, and we must be alert to
the varieties of cultural and semantic settings in which they may use those
words. James Barr warned of what he called "illegitimate totality transfer,"
the mistake of taking all of a word's possible associations and assuming that
the associations can all be read into each use of the word.[70]

This discussion takes us to the heart of a difficulty about words and
their meanings: language is embedded in cultural traditions, and words
do not *have* meanings in the absence of human intentions; rather, and as I
said earlier, we *give* words meanings, and even then, their meanings are not
fixed, absolute, or definite. We may not even agree about the meanings of the
words we use or hear. Ludwig Wittgenstein made this point about words in
Philosophical Investigations, saying that words do not have "sharp boundaries" but rather they have "blurred edges" and are "uncircumscribed," thereby
rendering them without definitive boundaries.

As for words for emotions such as remorse or regret, what is important
is the social environment and situation in which the words have developed
and are expressed. Paul Griffiths and Andrea Scarantino emphasize "the role
of social context in the production and management of emotions [*sc.* such as
remorse]" and argue that a "situated perspective on emotion recognizes that
the environment plays an active role in structuring and enabling emotional
engagements."[71] This goes some way to explain why some languages have no
word for remorse, even though, as we shall see later in this book, what might
otherwise be recognized as remorse is seen to exist, and why other languages,
such as English, have a well-developed repertoire of meanings for the word
"remorse." It also explains why discrete emotions in some cultures are not
known or recognized as discrete emotions in other cultures.

70. Barr, *Semantics*, 218.
71. Griffiths and Scarantino, "Emotions," 438, 443.

The following discussion of a modern example or remorse (or its lack) illustrates the cultural and semantic difficulties we may face when it comes to the word "remorse," particularly when those outside a western tradition of thought do not respond to wrongdoing with expressions of remorse in a situation that people from within a western tradition most likely would.

Various Japanese governments have been persistently criticized in the west (and even by some East Asian countries)[72] for what people take to be no more than Japanese expressions of regret for Japanese actions as a colonial power and in the Second World War.[73] Japanese governments have understood their statements to be expressions of remorse; others have seen them as little more than weasel words. What has been expected, but apparently never explicitly understood to have been freely given, is remorse, not only in words but also in actions—such as generous reparations for people affected. In contrast, Japanese politicians sometimes appear bewildered that what they apparently intend to be Japanese expressions of remorse about former wrongdoing do not appear to be accepted as expressions or remorse or to be enough.

The differences between what Japanese governments believe they have communicated and what others appear to have received arise for two principal reasons. First, the cultural framework in Japanese culture for giving and receiving apologies is different from the frameworks that many hold to whom Japanese apologies are addressed. Expressed simply, apologies are ubiquitous in Japanese culture to avoid *meiwaku* (trouble, inconvenience) and are delivered sometimes proactively, and certainly retroactively if not previously made. Because of the strong cultural drive to apologize, apologies sometimes have the appearance of being insincere. The person apologizing may be a proxy for the person truly at fault. Even if an apology appears to be insincere, the fact the apology has been made, even if palpably not a sincere

---

72. This suggests that the different responses to the wrongdoing are not wholly explained by diverse traditions of apology and remorse.

73. On Japanese apologies, see Tavuchis, *Mea Culpa*, 37–44; Renteln, "Apologies," 64–65, 66–68; Dahl, "Is Japan Facing Up to Its Past?" 241–55; and Battistella, *Sorry About That*, 138–39. Typically, Japanese people apologize far more than westerners, but the cultural framework of understanding of apology is different, for the need for atoning actions in consequence of an apology seems much less expected or practiced. The Japanese words for apology (in descending order of formality and strength) are *moshiwake arimaen* (or *moshiwake nai*), *suminasen, shitsurei shimashita, gomenasai,* and *shitsurei*. In private correspondence, Prof Toru Shinoda of Waseda University, Tokyo, told me that *moshiwake arimaen* and *moshiwake nai* mean "no excuse" (*moshiwake* and *moshiwake* both mean "excuse" and *arimaen* and *nai* both mean "no"). *Mhitsurei shimashita, gomenasai,* and *shitsurei* are often used to express a polite request for something to be overlooked (like "Excuse me" in English) rather than as an apology. *Suminasen* is rarely used.

apology, is culturally what matters, because the apology maintains the outward face of social and communal relations. In addition, the need for atoning actions in consequence of an apology is not widely expected in Japanese
culture whereas, in contrast, some who hear Japanese apologies also expect
atonement to demonstrate the integrity of the apologies.

It is also evident that not all Japanese people agree with or support the
apologies for Japanese actions as a colonial power and in the Second World
War. Apologies *are* offered, but not in the sense that some western people (for
example) might call an apology. It is also clear that not all wish to renounce
the cultural framework that celebrated the militarism that led to infamous
cruelty. In this case, we are dealing with more than a cultural difference to
do with apologies. Some also go further and even deny that claims about
the wrongs of the past are true. Visits by politicians to the Yasukuni Shrine,
which commemorates all who died in the service of the empire of Japan and
where 1,068 Japanese war criminals are buried and venerated, help to rein-
force the idea that the Japanese government's renunciation of its militaristic
past is at best ambivalent and at worst hypocritical.

The traditional form of Japanese apology has led to widespread dissatisfaction with and suspicion of the integrity of Japanese apologies for former
abuses for two reasons. First, because some Japanese people seem to regard
the apologies that are offered without correlative acts of reparation and atonement as sufficient by themselves. Second, because not all people renounce
the militarism and colonialism of the past. What is lacking, so people think,
is evidence of genuine repentance for and repudiation of former actions and
ways of thinking. In other words, the apologies have masked the need robustly to face the past. The commonly held view is that only when the past
has been faced and repudiated will there be a framework of confidence and
trust for future relations. Japanese governments, however, appear to disagree.

The issues I have outlined were clearly highlighted on the 75th anniversary of the Japanese bombing of the US Pacific Fleet at the naval base
at Pearl Harbor in Hawaii on 7 December 1941.[74] Some 2,400 American
service personnel died; many others were injured. On 27 December 2016,
the Japanese Prime Minister, Shinzo Abe, visited the US naval base and laid
a wreath of the National Memorial of the Pacific. In the presence of the US
President, Barak Obama, Shinzo Abe said this:

> As the Prime Minister of Japan, I offer my sincere and everlast-
> ing condolences to the souls of those who lost their lives here, as
> well as to the spirits of all the brave men and women whose lives

74. Compare the apology given on the 50th anniversary of the end of World War 2
(Battistella, *Sorry About That*, 130–32).

were taken by a war that commenced in this very place, and also
to the souls of the countless innocent people who became victims of the war. We must never repeat the horrors of war again.[75]

The word "condolences," which in English is taken to be an expression of
sympathy, does not imply responsibility or remorse. And apologizing to the
dead is not without its difficulties, too, as we have seen.

Exploring Remorse

This introduction to remorse has shown that remorse can be thought of as a
species of regret, and often an important reason why people apologize. We
have also shown that the language describing the emotions and resulting
behaviors associated with remorse will very likely be shaped according to
time, place, culture, or context, and sometimes conflated with other patterns of emotions and behavior.

From here on we trace the development of the emotion that today we
call "remorse" and that in former times was variously either not given a name,
or not distinguished from related emotions, or differently understood and
nuanced from today. We also look at some of the behaviors that result from
remorse. We begin with the Old Testament and go through to the twenty-first
century. By taking a historical approach, we uncover some of the influences
on and background to the contemporary approach to remorse. When we
reach the contemporary period, we explore present-day approaches to remorse (chapter 6); we then set remorse in the framework of current thinking
about emotions (chapter 7), morality (chapter 8), and the criminal law (chapter 9). Finally, in chapter 10 we offer some further reflections on the ethics
of remorse. Our aim is to produce a Christian ethic of remorse that makes a
significant contribution to modern debates and that is, as Roberts suggests of
moral frameworks generally, an "ordered [set] of concepts that bear on ethics
and morality" and so on "acting, thinking, and feeling."[76]

75. http://www.bbc.co.uk/news/world-us-canada-38447542.
76. Roberts, *Moral Life*, 14.

Chapter 2

Remorse and the
Ancient Israelites[1]

IN THIS CHAPTER, WE explore the way the ancient Israelites were remorseful. We look at the evidence we have about the nature and forms of their remorse and whether (and in which ways) the remorse of the ancient Israelites is different from remorse as it is understood and expressed in the contemporary period. Our source material is the Old Testament, though we do make occasional reference to Akkadian literature. Our approach will be inductive, and our starting point will be the way remorse is defined in the *OED* that is, as deep regret or guilt for moral wrongdoing. It is also necessary carefully to analyze the texts we consider so we avoid anachronistic readings of the texts.

With the modern definition of remorse in mind, we first explore what the ancient Israelites understood by what today we call "moral wrongdoing" and "emotions." We will find that the cultural and intellectual approaches of the ancient Israelites to these two concepts are markedly different from the ways they are now understood in the modern Judeo-Christian tradition of western thought. We then look at the ancient Israelite approach to remorse in detail.

1. I am grateful to Prof R. Walter L. Moberly for advice in connection with parts of this chapter.

Moral Wrongdoing in the Old Testament

In Greek thought and then later in western thought, abstract words such as "ethics," "morality," and "morals" are important philosophical tropes about the right way to live. There is no vocabulary in biblical Hebrew for such ideas, and we need to be careful not to read into the Old Testament anachronistic patterns of thought.[2]

Of course, the absence of words for ethics, morality, and morals does not mean that the ancient Israelites were not concerned about right and wrong, about moral emotions, or about the complexity of moral ambivalence. In the Pentateuch especially, there are codes of behavior: well-known are the Decalogue (Exod 20:1–17 and Deut 5:4–21) and the Holiness Code (Lev 17–26), for example. Some suggest that passages such as Lev 19:2 imply that God is a pattern for ethical behavior.[3] Ecclesiastes, Job, and even the Psalms clearly bring out that questions about how to live well in an ethical sense were important concerns to ancient Israelites. Almost the entire book of Proverbs (like much of the genre of "instructional literature" from the ancient Near East) is concerned with discerning the difference between right and wrong behavior, how such discernment takes place, and on what basis the discernment is founded. In Proverbs, words such as *mûsār* and *derek*, refer to disciplined instruction for right living and the right way to live respectively. There are also warnings about anger in Prov 22:24–25 and 29:22, for example; it is said that the foolish can be dominated by their emotions whereas the wise display a range of (what we today would call) virtues that include self-control (Prov 16:32; 29:11), patience (Prov 14:29; 19:11), and humility (Prov 11:2; 22:4). Even so, as recently as 2000, John Rogerson described the ethics of ancient Israelites as "often the Cinderella of Old Testament study."[4]

Rogerson's conclusion probably now no longer holds good, following new interest in the ethics of the ancient Israelites and especially following the publication of John Barton's *Ethics in Ancient Israel* in 2014. Barton's approach is to identify "evidence for the thinking [about ethics] of ancient

2. See Wilson, "Sources"; Davies, *Ethics of the Hebrew Bible*; and Haas, "Quest" on the methodological difficulties. On the difficulties of identifying emotions in the Old Testament, see Olson, "Emotion," 170–75. On the dangers of anachronistic readings, see Shweder, *Thinking*, 66–69 and Lambert, *How Repentance Became Biblical*. For obviously confessional approaches to ethics in the Old Testament, see Kaiser, *Towards*, (especially p. 37); Birch, *Let Justice Roll Down*; and Wright, *Old Testament Ethics*, for example.

3. Barton, *Understanding Old Testament Ethics*, and Davies, "Walking in God's Ways."

4. Rogerson, "Old Testament Ethics," 135.

Israelites and Jews" rather than to produce an ethics of the Old Testament.[5] He has written what he regards as a "missing chapter in the history of ideas" and "a missing chapter in the history of ethics" to provide "evidence for what various people in ancient Israel thought about ethical matters."[6] Barton observes that the Old Testament contains "evidence for thinking which, even if it does not constitute moral philosophy in the accepted sense, moves well beyond the assertion that certain moral norms are to be observed."[7] One reviewer of Barton's book summarizes his point as being that the "Israelites . . . were thinking about ethics, were in the habit of moral reasoning, before Socrates was born."[8] Even so, the question *why* certain types of behavior are right, and why others are not, is not as fully explored in the Old Testament as it is in philosophical ethics of the Greek period, for example.

One obvious answer is that right behavior results from heeding the commands (*miṣwōt*) of God, whether the commands are given directly by God (such as in the giving of the Ten Commandments at Sinai) or through prophets—and even also priests, kings, and parents—who were sometimes God's human mouthpieces. Some have suggested that Israel's moral norms arose out of its relationship to God[9] or as a response to God's election of and covenant with the people. Rogerson, who rightly says that there is more to ethics in the Old Testament than "apodictic, categorical laws as in the Ten Commandments,"[10] suggests that following Jürgen Habermas's method of "discourse ethics" can help to disclose "another dimension to Old Testament ethics."[11] Philip R. Davies's polemical conclusion about some of the Old

---

5. Barton, *Ethics*, 3–4. The difference is that the former (the ethics of the ancient Israelites and Jews) is part of a history of ethical thought (one of the purposes of this book) and the latter (the ethics of the Old Testament) is the way believers both then and even today might appropriate Old Testament ethical principles as part of their own practices. As best we can, I am assuming in this chapter an author-hermeneutic of "original meaning" and not discussing ways of reading the texts in ways either as not originally intended or as developed in later rabbinic or church traditions. I am also assuming that the Old Testament includes examples of the ethics of the ancient Israelites; from time to time, I also observe that there are points of similarity of approach with what we know of ethics from other ancient Near Eastern communities.

6. Barton, *Ethics*, 276.

7. Barton, *Ethics*, 2.

8. Van De Wiele, "Book Review," 105.

9. Birch, "Divine Character," 134, citing Brevard Childs and John Barton as exemplars of this approach.

10. So also, Barton, *Ethics in Ancient Israel*, 12.

11. Rogerson, "Old Testament Ethics," 131 and Rogerson, "Discourse Ethics," 17–26. His *Theory and Practice* is a collection of his published articles on Old Testament ethics.

Testament and other ancient Near Eastern literature (which takes an approach to ethics that has some similarities with the Old Testament) is that:

> so long as any ethical system presents its members with a set of rules of conduct which it claims to have divine origin and which must simply be obeyed on pain of punishment, I cannot see that we are dealing with ethics at all; rather, with a totalitarian system in which individual will and freedom only exist to be sacrificed to the supreme authority of . . . [a] deity.[12]

The apodictic approach to ethics is true of only parts of the Old Testament: there are other approaches to moral conduct in, for example, the instructional literature of the Old Testament. We should also note that the apodictic approach to ethics that Davies describes is set in the context of God's election of Israel, God's covenant with Israel, and God's love. The Israelites' obedience is predicated to be their response of love and gratitude to the grace of God (Deut 7:6–11) and is not the abject response of a subject people.

Looking at the Old Testament as a whole, what today we might call "moral dispositions" or "virtuous character" come from obeying God's commandments (*miṣwōt*). For example, those who obeyed would be *ṣaddîqîm* (righteous) and they would know the fear of the LORD (*yir' at YHWH*). They would also be *qĕdōšîm*, holy, that is, as being like God, as God is *qādôš*, holy.

Qādôš is a difficult word to explain and has a range of meanings. In English translations of the Old Testament, the word is usually translated as "holy," as we saw above. At the root of the word is the idea of being separate or set apart. God is *qādôš* because God is not like other gods; the people are to be *qĕdōšîm* because, by keeping God's commandments, they would be distinct from other nations who were not *qĕdōšîm*, since those nations did not have the law. *Qādôš* is not usually a word to do with ethics or morality but has a cultural and ritual context and refers to the identity that arises from being different from the surrounding nations. In some contexts, however (e.g., Lev 19:2; 20:7), *qādôš* probably has an ethical meaning. Jackie A. Nandé expresses what the word means in these places in this way: "The experience of God revealing himself as ethically holy calls for the human response to a holiness resembling his own."[13]

People fall short of obeying God's *miṣwōt* (commands) at one point or another, whether in relation to God or to other human beings. The verbs and nouns used in the Old Testament to describe the action of people who disobey

12. Davies, "Ethics and the Old Testament," 172.
13. *NIDOTTE*, 3:883.

God's *miṣwōt* are usually translated "to sin" and "sin" respectively or express these ideas with other words or phrases. The most common Hebrew verb that describes the action of sinning is *ḥāṭa*.[14] Etymologically, this verb suggests "to miss a goal or a way." The central idea of the verb is to miss "the goal or path of right and duty."[15] The point to notice is that *ḥāṭa* does not usually refer to an ethical or moral failure (though it clearly does in Gen 4:7, where the word is the cognate noun, *ḥaṭṭāʾ*) but to the failure—whether intentional or unintentional—to do a right action. It can also refer to sin as cultic trespass or ritual impurity. An example of another verb that describes the action of sinning is in Isa 53:6: in this verse, people are said to go astray (*tāʿāh*) [from God's path] and to turn (*pānāh*) to their own way [away from God's path]. (*Tāʿāh* can also mean to wander about like a drunkard!)

Penitential acts and remorse are appropriate responses after sinning. Deliberate and willful sins could not be expiated by sacrifices. In 2 Sam 12:1–14, for example, Nathan confronted David for deliberately sinning. Although Nathan assured David he would not die for the sin and that the LORD had "put away" his sin,[16] there is no evidence that David offered a sacrifice for his sin (and there would not have been need to do this, in view of Nathan's assurance).[17] Only unintentional sins could be expiated by the sacrificial system.

Outside the sacrificial system, death is the penalty for some sins, whether the sins were committed intentionally or unintentionally. The rituals of the Day of Atonement (Lev 16:21–26) were also outside the sacrificial system. In the ritual, the scapegoat bore *all* the sins of the people into the wilderness (Lev 16:22). Surprisingly, in this context, one of the words used for the sins of the people that the scapegoat bore is *pěšāʿîm*. This word is

14. On sinning and sin, see Cover, "Sin, Sinners"; Pieper, *Concept*; Anderson, *Sin*; Rawls, *Brief Enquiry*; and Nelson, *Sin*. For a traditional understanding of sin, see Berkouwer, *Sin*. For two useful histories of the doctrine of sin, see Jenson, *Gravity*, and Fredriksen, *Sin*.

15. BDB *s.v. ḥāṭʾa*, 2.

16. The verb is from *ʿābar*, and usually means pass over or (as in Mic 7:18) to overlook or forgive.

17. Professor R. W. L. Moberly has pointed out to me that between two of the words in verse 13 in the MT there is a larger than usual gap, signaled by the Hebrew letter *sāmekh* (short for "setumah," a paragraph divider), suggesting to the reader that something occurred after David had said, "I have sinned against the LORD." In Jewish tradition, what happened is that David expressed remorse and penitence, such as we see in Ps 51, and it was only after this expression of remorse that what we read in the second half of the verse took place, namely, that Nathan pronounced that God had "put away" David's sin and that he would not die. In other words, in traditional thought, verse 13 is a compressed version of what took place, with David's remorse and penitence left to the reader to interpolate from knowledge of David in other parts of the Old Testament.

usually found referring to willful, knowledgeable transgressions that are not in other contexts usually pardoned or cleared (e.g., Exod 23:21; 34:7). Thus, the sacrificial system is for unintentional sins only. As for deliberate sins, in some contexts God might choose to "pass over" the sins (as we saw with David's sins against Bathsheba) but in others there is no expiation, even if the penalty is death. On other occasions, *all* the sins of the people, even deliberate, willful sins, are borne by the scapegoat into the wilderness.

Emotions in the Old Testament

Contemporary studies have shown that emotions have an important place in ethics, morality, and morals, for emotions are involved in making moral judgments and in motivating people to behave in moral ways. (We discuss further in chapters 7 and 8 the relationship of emotions and moral conduct.) Studies about the ethics of the ancient Israelites have not usually explored what part emotions had in shaping the Israelites' moral judgments, in motivating them to behave morally, and in informing responses to violations of moral norms. We can try and work out from textual evidence how the ancient Israelites interpreted, explained, and categorized what they felt, and how what they felt shaped their behavior, but we cannot be sure about our conclusions, as will always be the case outside the contemporary period, in the absence of being able to test our hypotheses.

To complicate the way we might approach the study of the emotions of the ancient Israelites, it is important to observe that, not only are words for "ethics," "morality," and "morals" absent in the Old Testament (as we saw earlier), but also there is not a word denoting "emotion" or "emotions" as discrete, heuristic categories in Old Testament thought.[18] In the same vein, Françoise Mirguet suggests that there is doubt about "the existence of an isolated emotional realm in Biblical Hebrew's organization of human experience." She says that words that include what in the twenty-first century we might call "emotions" also "include actions, movements, ritual gestures, and physical sensations, without strict dissociation among these different dimensions."[19] Mirguet concludes from the words and concepts she does explore (remorse is not one of them) that for future studies:

> [s]tarting with our modern categories and lexemes may
> be inevitable, but we need to be prepared not to find strict
> equivalents. Not only may Biblical Hebrew lack a comparable

18. Lambert, "Mourning," 140. See also Russell, "Culture" and Wierzbicka, "Everyday Conceptions," 20–22.

19. Mirguet, "What Is an 'Emotion'?" 442.

vocabulary, but it may also configure the experience on an entirely different basis.[20]

She also observes that in the Old Testament "the fact that 'emotions' are socially rather than individually experienced . . . makes it expectable that discourses on such experiences in the Hebrew Bible are more about how to live together than about private and internal feelings."[21]

Even if "emotion" does not exist as a discrete category in ancient Israelite thought, there clearly is vocabulary[22] that points to the seat of what we now call "emotions." The following are important examples:

1. *Lēb* (heart): the ancient Israelites saw the heart as both the seat of affect and of intellectual thinking. Alex Luc says that the word has "a dominant metaphorical use in reference to the center of human psychical spiritual life, to the entire inner life of a person."[23] In the Psalms particularly, the word refers to intense emotions (e.g., Ps 16:9; 33:21; 34:18; 51:17; 84:2; and 105:3) and significantly, in Deuteronomy, faithfulness to the covenant begins with the heart and not with outward actions or rituals.

2. *Nepheš*: this is a difficult word to translate. It can variously mean "life," "person," "self," and "desire"; it can also refer to the inner person and the motivations of the inner person, "with all the emotions, desires, and personal characteristics that make each person unique," as in Deut 6:6.[24]

3. *Rûaḥ* (spirit): this word refers to "a person's or group's disposition, attitude, mood, inclination" and can refer to "character, nature, or condition." It is also "the seat of cognition and volition."[25] The word is used to indicate grief (Gen 26:25), discouragement (Exod 6:9), depression (1 Kgs 21:5), pride or humility (Prov 16:18–19 and Isa 66:2), and anger (Ezek 3:4), for example. It is also a synonym on occasions for *lēb* (heart).

20. Mirguet, "What Is an 'Emotion'?" 464.

21. Mirguet, "What Is an 'Emotion'?" 465. Much of the recent discussion is anticipated in Rodd, *Glimpses*. See also Spencer, *Mixed Feelings*, an edited book of essays on emotion in biblical literature.

22. There may be more than vocabulary: narratives may offer ethical instruction by highlighting virtues for hearers and readers to practice (Barton, "Understanding Old Testament Ethics," 65–74); see also Schlimm, *From Fratricide*, 135–84 on narratives in Genesis.

23. In *NIDOTTE*, 2:749–54.

24. Wright, *Deuteronomy*, 99.

25. Pelt et al., *NIDOTTE*, 3:1074, 1075.

At this point, we need briefly to anticipate our discussion of emotions in chapter 7. The ancient Israelites may have experienced what Paul Ekman calls "basic emotions," that is, emotions that are the result of evolutionary adaptations and so (in Ekman's view) common to all people at all times and in all places. Ekman lists happiness, disgust, fear, surprise, anger, and sadness as the basic emotions.

From the language used in translations, there is *prima facie* reason for thinking that the ancient Israelites experienced basic emotions. Happiness, disgust, fear, surprise, anger, and sadness are all in evidence in the Old Testament.[26] However, we cannot assume that the ancient Israelites understood these emotions in the same way as contemporary people do; neither can we assume that in Israelite thought the words that correspond to Ekman's six basic emotions necessarily have the same meaning *in Hebrew* as they do in contemporary, western thought.[27] For these reasons, Peter Paris warns that we must be careful not to "render ourselves vulnerable to anachronistic judgments" and so fail to develop "explanatory categories of a people's moral life . . . from within their own worldview."[28] We can see an obvious point of difference between a contemporary approach to the word "love" and the approach of the ancient Israelites. In Hebrew thought, the word is broad enough to include the sort of misaligned love that leads to willful, pre-meditated rape (2 Sam 13:1–19).[29]

The issues I have outlined are not just faced by historians of the ancient Near East. In "Unveiling Emotions in the Greek World," Angelos Chaniotis warns that ancient historians generally face complex methodological problems when trying to classify and interpret emotions in antiquity because the ancient historian "cannot study what people really felt." (The same is true of the study of emotions until the modern period.) At best, historians can make informed guesses, drawing on "external stimuli that generated emotions as well as cultural and social parameters that determined when and how emotions were represented in texts and images."[30] The intended audience as well as the date of texts or images should also be taken into account.

26. Spencer lists the emotions explored in the book on biblical emotions he edited (*Mixed Feelings*, 35–37): they include all the emotions in Ekman's list.

27. Pleins, *Social Visions*; Rodd, *Glimpses*; Barton, *Understanding Old Testament Ethics*.

28. Paris, "An Ethicist's Concerns," 173–74. Barton used the anachronistic heuristic category "natural law," for example (e.g., in "Understanding Old Testament Ethics" and in some later publications, but not in *Ethics in Ancient Israel*).

29. These points are made cogently in Schlimm, *From Fratricide*.

30. Chaniotis, "Moving Stones," 945; and see Chaniotis and Ducrey, "Approaching Emotions," 10–11.

In the remainder of this chapter, and with the caveats we have set out, we consider whether there is an emotion in ancient Israelite life that corresponds with the modern idea of interpersonal remorse, and if there is, we further consider to what extent the emotion shares similarities with and is different from interpersonal remorse in its contemporary setting.

Godward Remorse in the Old Testament

It is clear that Israel as a nation and individuals within it were (what we might describe today as being) remorseful about sins against God. In Ps 51, for example, David prayed a prayer of lament and entreaty for "deliverance from bloodguiltiness"[31] (verse 14) after deliberately sinning, even though he had already been told that the LORD had "passed over his sin" (2 Sam 12:13).[32] Remorse could be evidenced by fasting, by tearing one's clothes (2 Chr 34:19; Job 1:20) and by putting on sackcloth (2 Kgs 19:1), but the remorse may not necessarily have been the first step to repentance; rather it may have been a sign of distress about having done wrong[33] and distress that wrongdoing would still be punished.

The ancient Israelites did not have a word for remorse, although they did use words or phrases that today we can interpret as being remorse. The penitential psalms (Pss 6; 38; 51; 102; 130; and 143) give an especially clear view that at times what is now called "remorse about sins" was sharply felt and described by the ancient Israelites. Generally speaking, people described what they felt in specific ways with words such as "sad," "bitter," "ashamed," and "guilt," rather than by the word "remorse."

Certainly, the idea of contrition seems to be evident in the Old Testament. It is most obviously seen in some of the forms of the Hebrew root *dk*, which (as a verb, *dākāh*) can mean "to crush, break, or bruise" (for example, Ps 51:17)[34] and (as an adjective, *dakkā'*) "crushed" in Ps 34:18 (where it is in parallel with the phrase "broken in heart"), and in Isa 57:15 "contrite" (where it is in parallel with the phrase "lowly of spirit"). We might say of these words that they are like the modern word "pulverized"

31. See below, in the discussion about Joseph and his Joseph's brothers, as to what "bloodguilt" means.

32. Note, too, that the headings of the psalms are now regarded as not part of the psalms in their earliest forms. They were added for proposed imaginative, contextual readings of the psalms.

33. Lambert, "Mourning."

34. The verb is used in parallel with the word "broken." The sense here, as the *niphal* plural participle is being used, may be that these "crushed ones" are oppressed. The verbal root is often used of those afflicted or crushed by others (e.g., Isa 3:15; Psalm 94:5).

when used as slang, that is, feeling as crushed as if reduced to fine parti-
cles.[35] Not surprisingly, perhaps, there is even one form of the stem *dakhāʾ*,
which means "dust" (Ps 4:3).

Divine Remorse in the Old Testament

Before we consider passages where we might expect to find explicit examples
of interpersonal remorse (but, as we shall see, do not), it is worth asking
whether, since God is said sometimes to "change mind," "relent," or "repent"
(the verb used is *niḥam*), God's (anthropomorphically understood) regret and
even remorse could, and perhaps should, have become the pattern for remorse
for human beings? Such an approach might be an extension of Eryl Davies's
suggestion in an article that God can be a pattern of ethical behavior.[36]

Whether or not God did in fact relent and change mind seems to
have been the subject of internal debate within the Old Testament.[37] *Niḥam*
sometimes refers to a change of mind or repentance on the part of God.[38]
In other places, such as in Num 23:19[39] and 1 Sam 15:29, God is said *not*
to repent. In some passages, the implication seems to be that God could
change mind but either has not or will not.[40]

Whether or not God can change mind, it is forcing the meaning of
the word *niḥam* to suggest that the word can mean "remorse." The root of
the verb *niḥam* seems to be related to the Arabic verb that means "to sigh."
In Hebrew, the verb means "to be sorry" in three discrete senses: either to
console or comfort, or to have compassion, or to regret, repent, and change
one's mind. *Niḥam* suggests that one might sympathetically or compassion-
ately respond when one appreciates the difficult or distressing situation that
another faces.[41] One might also "sigh" at their predicament, and feel sorry,

35. According to the *OED*, the obsolete meaning of "pulverize" is "the action of
rubbing things together, or against each other; grinding, pounding or bruising (so as
to comminute or pulverize)." The etymology of the English word "contrition" is from
Latin, *contritio*, which means "the breaking of something hardened."

36. Davies, "Walking in God's Ways."

37. See Moberly, *Old Testament Theology*, 107–43.

38. We see this in Gen 6:6–7; Exod 32:14 (in response to Moses's prayer in verse 12);
1 Sam 15:11, 35; 2 Sam 24:16 (// 1 Chr 24:15); Jer 18:8, 10; 26:3, 13, 19; 31:19; 42:10; Joel
2:13–14; Amos 7:3 (in synthetic parallelism with *sālaḥ* [forgive]) 7:6; Jonah 3:10; 4:2.
Jer 15:6 implies that God had relented but would no longer do so.

39. Unusually, the verb here is *hithpael*, not *niphal*.

40. Ps 110:4; Isa 57:6; Jer 4:28; Zech 8:14. Perhaps also Ezek 24:14, where *niḥam* is
used in synthetic parallelism with *pāraʿ* (go slack) and *ḥûs* (spare).

41. Frequently *niḥam* relates to the *rāʿāh* (evil) that God intends to bring on people.

intending to comfort them, or one might, in view of another's state or condition, change one's mind about something one was intending to do or not
do. *Niham* can be deep regret for others, but *not because one has wronged
them*. In two places (Joel 2:13 and Jonah 4:2), *niham* is set in the context of
God's love, mercy, and graciousness. What we can say is that the word does
not reflect the modern sense of remorse, namely, deep regret or guilt for
moral wrongdoing. This is not surprising, since the Old Testament does not
attribute moral wrongdoing to God.

A common Hebrew word that expresses the idea of repentance is a
verb of motion, *šûḇ*, which usually means "to turn back, to return" and so
comes to mean "to repent."[42] *Šûḇ* does not mean "to be remorseful," for its
focus is usually on turning (either physically and directionally or in the religious sense of turning towards or away from God), and only rarely on the
inner disposition of the person who turns or on the reasons why the person
turns.[43] *Šûḇ* is also used of God turning (or not turning) from anger (e.g.,
2 Kgs 23:26), but not because God has done wrong. God may "turn" (*šûḇ*)
before God "relents" (*niham*).[44]

In answer to the question we posed above, the fact that God relents,
changes mind, repents, and turns from a previously decided purpose is not
a model for remorse for human beings, because God's changes are not because God has done wrong.

Interpersonal Remorse in the Old Testament

It would be naïve to suggest that people in ancient Israel did not feel remorse
about wronging other people. In the context of the social, cultural, and religious framework of ancient Israelite life, when we consider the absence of
written evidence that the ancient Israelites often or typically articulated feelings or expressed remorse about wronging other people, it is reasonable to
suggest that interpersonal remorse is not a psychological response that the
ancient Israelites took much notice of. The surviving evidence certainly suggests that they did not identify interpersonal remorse as a discrete category
of feelings; neither did they celebrate interpersonal remorse as evidence of
covenantal obedience. The following examples illustrate these observations.

42. *Šûḇ* and *niham* are used synonymously in Jer 4:28.
43. For an example of this much less common occurrence, see Jer 3:22—4:2.
44. Exod 32:12; Jer 31:19; Joel 2:14.

Saul

The clearest example of what may be interpersonal remorse in the Old Testament is 1 Sam 26:21. For the second time (the earlier occasion is in 1 Sam 24), David spares Saul's life, even though Saul had been trying to kill David. Saul recognizes that in attempting to kill David, he had "sinned," "acted foolishly," and "made a great mistake." It seems clear that Saul is acknowledging that he intends "no more [to] do [David] harm." From such a brief description in the verse it is not possible to be certain exactly what Saul meant and understood. However, what we can say is that his response acknowledges his wrongdoing and is coupled with an unequivocal statement addressed to David that he (Saul) would not repeat the wrongdoing.

Whatever precisely Saul may have meant, it is important to note that Saul first says that he had "sinned," and so sees his wrong as a wrong against God that had interpersonal consequences. It remains an open question whether, if he had not regarded his actions as sin, he would have felt the way he did towards David. In other words, the sequence of thought is that he had wronged David because he had sinned (here, probably God is at the forefront of Saul's thought), not that in wronging David he had sinned (here, David is at the forefront of Saul's thought).

Jephthah

Other examples of remorse in the Old Testament are difficult to find. Perhaps one example of interpersonal remorse is where Jephthah made an extravagant vow, the consequence of which is that he considered himself obliged to sacrifice his daughter (who is not named) (Judg 11:29–40)[45] and so brings his line to an end.[46]

Jephthah's self-imposed obligation to honor his vow may have been misplaced, for in other places in the Old Testament, ransoms or substitutions could redeem a vow.[47] Robert O'Connell explains why God did not intervene to prevent the sacrifice as being "the nemesis of Jephthah's arrogance, in attempting to mold YHWH's victory to conform to his own ambition."[48]

45. The Old Testament strongly condemns human sacrifice: Lev 18:21 and 20:2–5; Deut 12:31 and 18:10; and Mic 6:7.

46. For a detailed exploration of the story of the sacrifice and its place in early Israelite religion and practices, see Soggin, *Judges*, 215–18.

47. See 1 Sam 14:24–46, where a ransom is paid to redeem a rash vow and Gen 22 where God spares Abraham from having to sacrifice Isaac.

48. O'Connell, *Rhetoric*, 192.

Jephthah described himself as "brought very low" by the consequences of his rash vow,[49] but even here a careful reading of the text indicates Jephthah blamed his daughter for being the cause of trouble to him, rather than acknowledging that he and his vow were the cause of great trouble to his daughter (Judg 11:35).

David

We have already discussed the account of David's adultery with Bathsheba. It is commonly thought that David was remorseful after committing adultery with Bathsheba. This is clearly so in relation to God. However, a careful reading of 2 Sam 12:7–25 does not suggest that David was also remorseful towards Bathsheba, with whom he had committed adultery, or about engineering the death of her husband, Uriah, so that he (David) would be free to marry Bathsheba. David's only comment when Nathan confronted him about his adultery is that he had "sinned against the LORD" (v. 13), with no mention of Bathsheba or Uriah. Similarly, Ps 51, described in the superscription to the psalm as "A Psalm of David, when the prophet Nathan came to him, after he had gone in to [had sexual intercourse with] Bathsheba," indicates on the part of David a deep sense of guilt towards God, but not towards Bathsheba or her former husband.

Joseph's Brothers

Aspects of the Joseph cycle (Gen 37–50)[50] are also said to indicate remorse towards Joseph on the part of at least one of Joseph's brothers. The texts do not bear this out. In exploring the texts, as we do shortly, we need to understand that to shed blood is regarded as grievous sin and as a sin against God that brought "bloodguilt" on the murderers (Deut 19:10) with "reckoning for the blood" (Gen 42:22). Blood is regarded as embodying life (Deut 12:23),[51] and so to shed another's blood by murder is to deprive that other of the essential constituent of life.[52] Not unexpectedly, therefore, the words

49. The verb is *kāraʿ* and usually means "to bow down." Here, the verb probably means "to bow down in grief." The verb is *hiphil*, and so has the idea that Jephthah has been caused to bow down, as a result of the consequences of his vow.

50. For commentaries on the cycle, see Westermann, *Genesis 37–50*, and especially pp. 15–18 on relevant secondary literature, and Levenson, *Joseph*.

51. Animal blood also had "life" and because of this property was efficacious to make atonement for human sins (Deut 17:11).

52. See Hamilton, *Book of Genesis*, 527.

"blood" and "life" are sometimes attested as "lexical pairs."[53] We see evidence of such pairing in Gen 37:20–22, 26 where the idea of shedding blood is synonymous with taking life. In addition, shed blood is seen as violating the image of God that all people bear because to shed blood takes away life that God possessed and had imparted to human beings: see, for example, Gen 9:5–6. We also see that to shed blood and leave it on the ground is the marker to God that someone had been killed: such blood is the life of the deceased person. It is the blood, and not the sight of the corpse, that "cries out" to God (Gen 4:10).[54] Lastly, it is also important to appreciate that in later Jewish thinking, and apparently anticipated (or evident) in this early period, there are no sacrifices for sins deliberately committed. Thus, deliberately to shed blood and thereby to cause another's death is a sin for which there is no atonement through sacrifice.

With these observations in mind, we see that Reuben ensured that Joseph's brothers did not immediately kill Joseph,[55] but instead threw him into a pit. The suggestion appealed to Reuben's brothers because they probably thought that by leaving Joseph to die, perhaps from dehydration (Gen 37:24), they would escape responsibility for his death.[56] Reuben's intention had been to rescue Joseph at a later time (Gen 37:22), because, as Joseph's brothers later recognized, their actions would still have amounted to killing Joseph (Gen 37:26), albeit obliquely. While Reuben was absent, and to avoid being complicit in Joseph's death and at the instigation of Judah (Gen 37:26–27), Joseph's brothers decided to sell Joseph to Ishmaelite traders. When Reuben discovered this, he laments that he had not first been able to free Joseph and so stop the brothers from selling Joseph to the Ishmaelites (elsewhere called "Midianites").[57]

What does Reuben's lament mean? Is Reuben's reaction characterized (at least in part) by remorse?

Reuben's words of lament are, "and I, where can I turn?" (Gen 37:30). His remorse, if it is remorse, is a cry of self-pity;[58] there also appears to

53. Sperling, "Blood," 761.

54. This explains why Joseph's brothers say in Gen 37:26 that they would have had to conceal Joseph's blood if they had killed him.

55. Commentators suggest that this is not out of mercy but self-interest, for as the oldest of the sons, he knew Jacob was likely to hold him responsible for Joseph's safety (e.g., Ginzberg, *Legends*, 332).

56. On this see Levine, *Nahmanides*, 146–47 and Ginzberg *Legends*, 468 and 334, n. 36.

57. See Levenson, *Joseph*, 16–18 on the reasons for the textual differences.

58. Westermann's view is that Reuben is lamenting because he does not know where to turn "from his father's face," i.e., "he [Reuben] knows that he is the one who must

be no lament about what has happened to Joseph. There is no other obvious way to interpret Reuben's response except as being self-seeking and
self-serving, directed at himself and his situation, and apparently without
empathy for Joseph.

One might want to read Reuben's words as despairing because he is
so deeply grieved about what has happened to Joseph. However, I am unpersuaded that this can be so because Reuben colludes with a "cover-up"
(Gen 37:31) and with a lie to Jacob that Joseph had been mauled by a wild
animal (Gen 37:35). In other words, his actions suggest lack of empathy,
or at best a person so conflicted—whether to stand up to his brothers,
whether to free Joseph when he was in the pit, or whether to tell the truth
about what happened—as to render his supposed remorse compromised
by self-seeking and subterfuge.

Later, when for the first time Reuben and his brothers go to buy grain
in Egypt and do not recognize Joseph, now a very senior Egyptian official,
Reuben acknowledges that he and his brothers had "wronged" Joseph by
being complicit in what they believed to be his death (the use of the word
"blood" in Hebrew suggests this, and see Gen 44:20) for which the "reckoning" (Gen 42:22)[59] of bloodguilt, that is, penalties arising from the guilt of
unlawfully taking life, was required. The word "reckoning," when used in
this sense, always refers to what God demands or requires: in other words,
Reuben acknowledges he is facing divine reckoning for his former actions.
If he were remorseful at this point, it is Godward remorse, perhaps pointing
to shame for and guilt about being brought to account by God.[60] There may
also be a degree of self-pity because he is now suffering for the consequences
of his former sins. (Even here, Reuben attempts to excuse himself, by not
facing the fact that he had earlier failed to protect Joseph from his brothers' plan, and saying in 42:22, "Did I not tell you not to wrong the lad? But
you would not listen.")[61] This is a form of remorse that is not explored or
expressed in relation to the wrong done to Joseph, even though Reuben
knows (Gen 42:22) that wrong has been done to Joseph.[62]

---

answer when his father asks after Joseph" (*Genesis 37–50*, 42).

59. The verb used is *dāraš*. This is the only example of the use of this verb in this
sense in the *niphal*, though the verb occurs in the *qal*, where it means ask for, require,
or demand.

60. The word in verse 21 is the noun *ṣārāh*, which means "distress." It does not elsewhere refer to the distress of remorse.

61. Note that Reuben misquotes his earlier words (see Gen 37:21–22) and now
makes his former view seem rather more morally robust than it then appeared to be.

62. Even in 4:2–4 of "The Testament of Reuben" in *The Testament of the Twelve Patriarchs*, probably originally second century BC, Jewish tradition emphasized the pangs

Following the second visit to Egypt to buy grain, Judah's response to Joseph before discovering Joseph's true identity is more straightforward. Benjamin faced captivity as Joseph's servant because he had apparently stolen Joseph's silver cup. (In fact, Joseph had ordered it to be deliberately planted in Benjamin's sack.) In pleading for Benjamin's release, Judah understands the circumstances he and his brothers face as arising because "God has found out [our] guilt" (Gen 44:16). He implies that God is punishing them because of their guilt. Presumably, the "guilt" to which Judah refers includes guilt for selling Joseph to the Ishmaelites, and as far as he and his brothers know, for Joseph's likely death in servitude.

What is the punishment they were facing? I suggest that Joseph's actions are a ploy to make the brothers face the awfulness of losing a brother to forced servitude. The point is that the last time a brother of theirs had faced forced servitude—when Joseph was sold to the Ishmaelites—the brothers had shown no remorse or pity; this time, with the imminent likelihood of Benjamin being taken into servitude, the brothers could and did engage with what formerly they had chosen to ignore. They are now facing the horror of Jacob's incipient loss, as well as their own, in the way they should have done when they had sold Joseph to the Ishmaelites.

Judah acknowledges the guilt that he and his brothers bear for their former actions to Joseph: from Judah at least, Joseph's threatened actions against Benjamin bring a clear acknowledgment that he and his brothers have done wrong, and that they are facing God's judgment for their actions. They are now being made to experience the wretchedness of knowing that a brother is in captive servitude.

While Judah's words do not suggest remorse towards Joseph, they do suggest remorse before God about what he and his brothers had done to Joseph. His words unambiguously acknowledge guilt, seem to express acceptance of just punishment, and, although the text does not say this, probably indicate the opportunity on this occasion to experience the guilt and shame that he should have experienced when Joseph was sold to the Ishmaelites.

Other Possible Examples: Cain, Jacob, Moses, and David

Other parts of the Old Testament also have little interest in exploring whether wrongdoers are remorseful towards those they have wronged. From elsewhere in the book of Genesis, for example, after Cain had murdered his

---

of Reuben's conscience about his sin in relation to God, but not in relation to Joseph (Kugel, "Testaments").

brother Abel, Cain shows no remorse even though God attributes to him "personal moral responsibility" for his actions,[63] and when God asked him where Abel was, his response is to prevaricate (Gen 4:8–10).

When Jacob lies to his father, Isaac, and tricks Esau out of his birthright,[64] Jacob appears to show no remorse but flees for his life because he is afraid Esau will kill him (Gen 27:1–45). When Jacob meets Esau again, his behavior, which probably follows a ritual for peace and reconciliation, is designed to find favor with Esau (Gen 33:8–11) and neither explicitly nor implicitly suggests remorse on Jacob's part.

This interpretation is in contrast to Bill Arnold's view that Jacob stands before Esau in "complete submission, as a guilty servant stands before an overlord awaiting punishment."[65] Walter Brueggemann also regards the encounter to be evidence of "reconciliation" between the brothers.[66] Certainly, it is true that Esau no longer wants to kill Jacob (cf. Gen 27:41) and the ritual of peace and reconciliation is significant in this regard.

I remain unconvinced from anything explicit in the text that Jacob is remorseful; at the most, he follows what are probably Semitic rituals and ceremonial practices for reconciliation (rituals and practices that depended on outward actions and not necessarily on evidence of inner disposition) to ensure that Esau would not harm him, his family, or his possessions. Esau also follows such rituals, to demonstrate to Jacob that he no longer intends to kill him.[67] Claus Westermann rightly observes that "[t]he natural consequence of the reconciliation would be that Jacob and Esau go back to the same place."[68] That they do not go back to the same place suggests neither true reconciliation nor (on the part of Jacob) remorse, for even after Jacob and Esau are apparently reconciled, Jacob remains afraid Esau will kill him, and so chooses not to be in Seir with Esau but to separate permanently and live at Shechem (Gen 33:12–20).

For the sake of completeness, mention may be made of some other examples outside the book of Genesis. For example, Moses appears to show only fear of being found out, not remorse, after killing an Egyptian (Exod

63. Arnold, *Genesis*, 80.

64. The word denotes the privileges and advantages belonging to first-born sons. Birthright entitled the first-born at least to a double inheritance (Deut 21:17; 21:3). Birthrights could be lost (e.g., Reuben: 1 Chr 5:1) or apparently sold (as here, by deception: Gen 25:33).

65. *Genesis*, 288. See also Schlimm, *From Fratricide*, 166–69.

66. Brueggemann, *Genesis*, 272–73.

67. Cf. Kazen, *Emotions*, 155.

68. Westermann, *Genesis 37–50*, 526. See Arnold, *Genesis*, 290–91 for a different interpretation of why Jacob decides to live away from Esau.

22:11–15); though David recognized that his lie to Ahimelech in 1 Sam 21:2 had led to a slaughter of eighty-five priests and all who lived in their city, he apparently showed no remorse (1 Sam 22:19, 22).

Remorse and the "CAD Model of Ethics"

Why are there so few examples of interpersonal remorse in the Old Testament? The likely reason is because the primary focus of moral obligations is set in the context of human obligations not towards other people but towards God and towards Israel, the community of the people of God.

In a book on emotions and biblical law, Thomas Kazan draws on the work of social anthropologists and observes that "human morality can be classified into three basic clusters or categories," namely, "ethics of autonomy, community, and divinity."[69] This approach to ethics is typically known as "the CAD [Community, Autonomy, Divinity] Model" of ethics. We come back to this model at several different points in this book.

Expressed simply, with the ethics of divinity, people follow God-given moral standards; with the ethics of community, people have moral responsibility to engage in the communal processes of their communities and to hold to the ethics of their communities; and with the ethics of autonomy, people make meaningful, self-directed choices about how to live, free from the controlling interferences of others.[70] It has been shown that most cultures will emphasize one or two of these categories and that where there are well-formed ethics of community, the ethics of autonomy will be correspondingly weak, and *vice versa*.

As for individuals' ethics and emotions, their "character and meaning . . . are systematically related to the kind of ethic (autonomy, community, or divinity) prevalent in a cultural community."[71] In saying that

69. Shweder et al. "The 'Big Three,'" developed in Rozin et al., "CAD Triad," and Jensen, "Cultural Development."

70. From Shweder et al. "The 'Big Three,'" 134., Fig. 2.2. See chapter 5 on what Giddens calls "the ethics of modernity," which correspond in many ways with the "ethics of autonomy."

71. Shweder et al. "The 'Big Three,'" 134. Haidt and Joseph suggest that in each culture there are "moral domains," by which they mean universal modules (the four commonest are suffering, hierarchies, reciprocity, and purity), with each culture determining specific moral rules for each domain ("Intuitive Ethics"; and see Haidt, "The Emotional Dog," 827). The moral domains do not prescribe a universal morality, but they provide what Prinz (referring to Haidt and Joseph, "Intuitive Ethics") describes as "a universal menu of categories for moral construal" ("Is Morality Innate?" 381). Remorse is most likely to be situated in the domain of reciprocity and found in cultures that evidence the ethics of autonomy.

the ethics of autonomy are not much in evidence in ancient Israel is not to say that people did not have and practice interpersonal ethics. What is meant is that the subject-matter and content of inter-personal ethics are not derived from personal choice or speculative encounter. Rather, the subject-matter and content are God-given and to be practiced, whether or not they were thought to be appealing or appropriate. The ethics of ancient Israel are based on divine commands and their expression is in the community, Israel, with which it was believed that God had made a covenant. Not surprisingly, therefore, we see a strong emphasis on wrongdoing in relation to God (the ethics of divinity) and on wrongdoing in relation to the community (the ethics of community).[72] As interpersonal wrongdoing (of which remorse is an example) is associated with the violation of autonomy norms, that is, norms "that regulate how we treat individual persons" with the focus on the harms or rights of other individuals,[73] there is, as we would expect, next to no emphasis on wrongdoing in relation to individuals (the ethics of autonomy), especially because there is no recorded God-given command for people to express to other people their remorse about wrongs they have done to those people.

We see some of these principles illustrated in the story of Achan and the theft of spoils of war in Josh 7. Achan stole and kept an item of clothing, as well as silver and gold, following the destruction of Jericho, in contravention of Joshua's earlier injunction and of a divine command that all the spoils of war were to be destroyed (Josh 6:18–19; 7:11, 20–21). Though it is an individual who sinned, the sin is regarded as affecting the community (Josh 7:11)[74] and both the community as a whole (Josh 7:4–5), Achan himself (Josh 7:25), and Achan's family (Josh 7:24) are punished for the sin.

It is particularly difficult for a modern reader to understand why Achan's "sons and daughters, his oxen, donkeys, and sheep" were stoned to death and, along with "[Achan's] tent, and all that he had," then burned and buried under a pile of stones (Josh 7:24–26). The reason becomes clearer (but, to modern readers, perhaps still difficult) if we appreciate that the effect of the actions and omissions of an individual are understood not only as being on the individual but also on the community of which

---

72. On the way communities develop and sustain their patterns of ethics, see Haidt "The Emotional Dog"; Prinz and Nichols, "Moral Emotions"; and Chaniotis, "Social Construction." Todd observes parallels with Protestantism in early modern Scotland (*Culture*, 173–81).

73. Prinz and Nichols, "Moral Emotions," 123.

74. Hawk, *Joshua*, 111.

the individual is part, and so extending to those with whom he or she is connected by familial (or similar) ties.[75]

Despite these apparently persuasive approaches that suggest reasons for the apparent absence of interpersonal remorse in ancient Israel, an important note of caution needs to be introduced at this point. An analysis that identifies the clusters of types of human norms is an indicative task: it does not follow that the analysis necessarily explains the existence (or non-existence) of particular norms. We may observe a correlation, but not causation. The same argument applies to the way moral intuitions emerge. The models in use are based on fieldwork in and analysis of modern cultures. It has yet to be shown that the findings necessarily apply diachronically. What we can say is that when it comes to what modern people mean by "remorse," the models I have described above correlate with what we observe in the Old Testament.

As for the ethics of autonomy, we also need a further word of caution. Not all sociologists and anthropologists hold to a view of people as autonomous individuals. Émile Durkheim saw society as having an identity independent of individuals and as shaping the life of the individuals within it. In other words, people are shaped by the social categories and institutions of which they part. Even Adam Smith recognized that people are to some extent shaped by their individual social experience. It is now regarded as a "fallacy" to think that "human behavior patterns exist independently of their social relationships."[76]

Concluding Thoughts

I have set out some examples from the Old Testament of what may perhaps be remorse. In almost all the examples, the remorse (if it is properly to be called "remorse") is Godward-facing and arose when people realized that they had transgressed a divine injunction. In the Old Testament, their reaction is not called "remorse"; even so, their reaction is an easily identifiable emotion in the context of a recognized pattern of behavior that in later times is called "remorse." We use language from a later period to describe this emotion in the Old Testament, though we must be careful not to interpret the emotion outside its Old Testament context.

75. See Exod 20:5, for example, but compare Deut 24:16. On the need for destruction of what had become "holy things" because devoted to YHWH (*ḥerem*), see Soggin, *Joshua*, 97; Hawk *Joshua*, 117–18; and Moberly, *Old Testament Theology*, 53–74.

76. Campbell, *Seven Theories*, 87.

The same pattern of behavior and of response seems to be true generally in the ancient Near East. For example, Akkadian sources point to people with a deep sense of wrong against a god or gods[77] as well as people with a well-developed sense of guilt for wrongdoing[78] though with no record of a sense of guilt or remorse about interpersonal wrongs.[79] The same seems to be true of the Babylonians: in the Old Testament record of the reaction of king Darius (sixth century BC) to Daniel, Darius who sent Daniel to the lions was "much distressed and set his mind to deliver Daniel" (Dan 6:14). The Aramaic for "distressed" is a circumlocution, "it was bad to him," and although we might read these words as meaning personal regret and sadness, the text makes it clear that Darius did not think that he had also done wrong in relation to Daniel, as he was constrained to uphold the irrevocable "law of the Medes and Persians" (verse 12).

We have seen that ancient Israelite thought lacked "scaffolding" for developing an ethic of interpersonal remorse. This is not to say that people may not have felt what in a later period is called "remorse." However, the language, religion, and culture of the ancient Israelites militated against the expression of such an emotion, against reflection about it, and so against a substantive record of it in Israelite literature.

Ancient Israelites experienced regret, when they wronged other people. We probably see this in the example of Saul and David in 1 Sam 26:21. How much more specific we can be is difficult to say. Of far more significance to people were wrongs against God, because such wrongs are "sin" and so regarded as terrible and even terrifying in the sight of God.[80] It seems that interpersonal wrongs tend to be interpreted as sins against God and that this interpretation renders further reflection about the interpersonal dimensions of their wrongdoing unnecessary or even frivolous. Hence, David said in *prayer* to God in Ps 51:4, "Against you, you *only*, have I sinned, and done what is evil in your sight" when lamenting his adultery with Bathsheba and the engineered death of her husband.

We must be careful not to ascribe emotions in general as well as specific emotions in particular (such as remorse, shame, and guilt) to ancient people without good evidence that it is not anachronistic to do so. Our understanding of and approach to these categories of emotions have been developed

77. See Foster, *Before the Muses*, 724–25 (c. 1500–1000 BC).

78. See Foster, *Before the Muses*, 645.

79. There are no such records in Parker, *Ugaritic Narrative Poetry*; Foster, *Before the Muses*; Greenstein, "Wisdom"; and Halton and Svärd, *Women's Writing*, for example.

80. In the Babylonian *Epic of Gilgamesh*, Gilgamesh and Enkidu appear to have been remorseful for destroying a cedar forest and for murdering a friend because they knew they had angered the god Enlil (Al-Rawi and George "Cedar Forest," 74).

in the context of contemporary western culture. We shall see in chapter 7 that there is considerable debate about the extent to which whether even some emotions are diachronically and transculturally universal. We cannot assume that a modern framework of thought about emotions is appropriate to adopt when interpreting the Old Testament. What we can say is that in response to sin people made confession, offered sacrifices, and said they were contrite and repentant. On occasions they also acknowledged to other people that they had not acted as they should, as we saw in 1 Sam 26:21. We cannot now say with certainty that in these examples it is right to refer to people as having "remorse" towards those they had wronged. We can, however, make one observation with certainty: the Old Testament lacks language that indicates an interpersonal emotion that corresponds with the modern idea of remorse.[81] Beyond this, there is little we can say about the nature and form of interpersonal remorse in the Old Testament.

---

81. The emotion is "hypocognated," that is, because ancient Hebrew describes and refers to interpersonal remorse in few ways (if at all), the ancient Israelites would have at best only an elementary understanding of interpersonal remorse and correspondingly limited ways of expressing it (Levy, *Tahitians*, 324).

Chapter 3

Remorse in Greek Thought and Language[1]

Background

WHAT WE DISCUSSED IN the last chapter on the Old Testament are some of Israel's former oral traditions, almost certainly edited and adapted over many centuries. The oral traditions were put into written form probably from about the sixth century BC, although perhaps some parts were already in written form before then. (Other parts of the Old Testament, almost none of which we discussed, may not have been written until as late as the mid-second century BC.)

As far as we know, Greek literature has a comparable chronological history and pattern of development. Homer's epics are possibly as early as ninth century BC; they probably existed in oral form at first; and they were probably not put into writing until the seventh century. As far as we can tell from the fragments that survive, the early pre-Socratic period of Greek philosophy concerned mainly cosmological and physical speculations and come from the sixth century BC. Greek philosophy continued to flourish and develop in the late fifth to the fourth centuries BC. The best known of the philosophers are Plato's teacher, Socrates (d. 399 BC),[2] Plato (b. 427 BC), and Aristotle (384–322 BC). In the later third century BC, the philosophical schools of the Stoics and Epicureans were also important; the Stoics may

1. I am grateful to Professor Peter J. Rhodes for advice on matters relating to Greek thought and culture.

2. His work is known though the writings of Plato (b. 427 BC) and Xenophon (d. 354 BC).

well have influenced some of the underlying assumptions and values of the New Testament, particularly the writings of Paul.

In the fifth and fourth centuries, Phoenicia and Judaea were part of the Persian empire. There was a little Athenian involvement with Phoenicia but, as far as we know, no intellectual engagement. Despite this modest amount of contact, the oral and literary histories of Israel and of Greece, though comparable in their pattern of development, remained detached, and follow different intellectual routes, uninfluenced by each other until the Hellenistic period, which is regarded as beginning in 323 BC, the date of the death of Alexander the Great.

As we said in the last chapter, the ancient Israelites did not engage in an obvious way with the study of human emotions. In contrast, Greek philosophers were interested in the study of emotions. So, too, were ancient Greek physicians. For example, the physician Galen (Aelius Galenus or Claudius Galenus, AD c.130–c.200) in *de Temperamentis* developed a theory that temperament and emotional types were related to one of four fluids in the human body. The interest of the Greeks in emotions has had a significant influence on western thought to this day.

In the Hellenistic period, Jewish thought was influenced by Greek philosophy, and Jewish writers became more interested in the place of emotions in human identity and self-expression. Early Christian writings in the New Testament (which come out of a Jewish framework of thought) are also influenced by Hellenistic culture, as we shall see in chapter 4. In chapter 5, we see that Christian patterns of thought were further developed, most notably by Augustine (AD 354–430) and Aquinas (AD 1225–74). Augustine knew and engaged with some of the Greek writings on emotions, and in the case of Aquinas, the rediscovery of and reflection on Greek learning and philosophy especially influenced his writings.[3]

For the sake of completeness, it is worth adding that the Greeks were not alone in thinking about emotions in the first century BC: what is regarded as the classic period of Chinese philosophy ("The Hundred Schools of Thought") began in about 500 BC, though there had been a tradition of Chinese philosophy for at least three hundred years before then. Buddhism,

3. For a list of publications reflecting the "explosion of interest in the emotions that has affected both classics and biblical studies," see Fitzgerald, "Passions," 1–2. On the emotions of the ancient Greeks, see Konstan, *The Emotions*; Chaniotis, "Unveiling Emotions in the Greek World"; Irwin "Mental Health"; and Harcourt, "Aristotle." On ancient works on emotions, see Fitzgerald, "Passions," 6–12. On Paul's view of the emotions, see Aune, *Passions*, 221–37. For a general survey see Meyer and Martin, "Emotion." An important research project on emotions in ancient Greece is a current University of Oxford project entitled "The Social and Cultural Construction of Emotions: The Greek Paradigm" headed by Angelos Chaniotis.

which also has a tradition of reflection on emotions, began in what is now Nepal in the sixth century BC.

Emotions in Greek Thought

One of the questions that was debated among the ancient Greeks is whether there is a relationship between emotions and cognition. Within this debate, Plato regarded emotions as tainting and even perverting reason, though he recognized a place for cognition in emotion. In Aristotelean and Stoic thought, emotions are regarded as cognitions; unhelpful and painful emotions can be regulated, and even remedied, by re-appraising the cognitions that cause them.[4] In Book 2 of *Art of Rhetoric*, Aristotle discussed the relationship of cognition and emotional responses and, in many ways, he anticipated some of the modern discussion (and conclusions) on this question. He showed that emotional responses are intelligent behavior "open to reasoned persuasion in a way that bodily drives are not" and that they are "cognitive phenomena open to reason."[5] Aristotle's thinking creates a framework whereby remorseful feelings could be thought of as reasonable and intelligent, the result of thoughtful judgment and open to change through reason. So, too, in Stoic thought as Chrysippus (279–206 BC) and Seneca (4 BC–65 AD) explain it: in their view, painful emotions can be addressed by correcting false normative judgments.[6]

The most commonly used word for emotions among the ancient Greeks, *pathos* (singular, and *pathē* in its plural form), is sometimes translated "passion." *Pathē* can refer to the idea of emotions as we today understand them; they can also refer to anguish and to what one suffers, experiences, or is done to one.[7]

The word *pathē* is usually used pejoratively. In general, the Greeks thought reason and emotions are opposed to one another; reasonable people would therefore generally seek to control *pathē*.[8] It was recognized that some emotions (the *eupatheia*) are helpful, because they result from good judgment, but others are to be avoided because they arise from incorrect

---

4. Psychagogy (see below and in chapter 4) is based on this way of thought.

5. Fortenbaugh, *Aristotle*, 23 and 26.

6. In "Emotions and the Psychotherapy," Sorabji shows how the way the Stoics treated emotions anticipated many of the principles of modern cognitive behavior therapy. See also Sorabji, "Is Stoic Philosophy Helpful?"

7. Annas, *Hellenistic Philosophy of Mind*, 103, n.1.

8. Compare this view with Konstan's in "Emotions and Morality," who shows that especially in the work of Aristotle and Seneca there is a close relationship between morality and the emotions.

judgment. This does not mean having no emotions is the aim; rather, the aim is that emotions should be under control, with the result that one would be *apatheia*, free of suffering, with peace of mind and having clear judgment and equanimity.[9]

In approaching the study of emotions in ancient Greece, we need to bear in mind the same cautions we set out in chapter 2.[10] David Konstan puts it this way in relation to ancient Greek culture:

> there is not always a perfect overlap between the Greek and English emotional vocabularies. The tendency to use basic English emotion words as the regular counterparts for Greek terms may lead us . . . to overlook or discount significant differences in the way the respective sentiments are conceived and experienced in the two cultures.[11]

Unlike with the ancient Israelites, we are not dealing with religious documents but with written records, usually only of the elite in public, philosophical, or didactic discourse, and not the everyday thought and language of most people, who include women, children, and slaves. For this reason, a written setting may give us an unrepresentative sample of the way a word about an emotion is used or thought about. Even so, since written records are all that we have, it is often thought best, if we are to understand and identify emotions, to look at what we have from the written records in their context, and additionally to explore implicit assumptions and concerns in those records.

There is not one Greek word that has the same meaning and lexical range as the English word "remorse." This makes exploring the Greek approach to remorse difficult. There are some examples in ancient sources about shame for failure that leads to moral development and improvement.[12] However, these examples are rare, and generally, especially among those of high social status who are our source of written material,[13] the idea of feeling shame, and even remorse, for moral failure is rarely mentioned, and even when shame and remorse appear to be evident, they are not highlighted as

9. In "Early Roman Empire Stoics," 123, Krentz gives some common descriptions of *pathos* in Stoic thought: "'an irrational and contrary-to-nature motion of the soul,'" "'desire run rampant,'" (both from Diogenes Laertius, AD 180–240), and "'decision-making'" (Chrysippus, 279–206 BC).

10. See also Kloos, "Constructionism," 474 in relation to ancient Greece.

11. Konstan, *Emotions*, 4.

12. For example, Aristotle, *NE* 1128b10–12, 15–21.

13. See Sanders, "Beyond the Usual."

moral virtues.[14] For example, Laurel Fulkerson identified "something close to" remorse in Helen of Troy in the *Iliad*. She observes that the emotion is set "in a context that divorces her act [about which she feels remorse] from the responsibility for it; she uses the performance of remorse in order to demonstrate her own moral stature and to blame Paris."[15]

The absence of a significant measure of philosophical thought and language about remorse has mistakenly led some people to think that remorse and related emotions are not much in evidence among the ancient Greeks. Such a view is an oversimplification. It is correct to say that remorse is not an emotion much written about. For example, Angelos Chaniotis and Pierre Ducrey edited a book on emotions in texts, images, and other material culture in Greece and Rome;[16] the contributors to the book do not identify any emotions that we could recognize as remorse, regret, or repentance. However, there is a variety of words that in ancient Greek literature can sometimes mean "remorse," though the words can also mean something else (according to context) such as regret or repentance, for example. We have to understand the words in their context to interpret what they mean and to establish whether they refer to remorse as contemporary people now understand the word.

We next examine in detail Greek language about remorse, repentance, and regret. We highlight examples of the words both in secular literature and in the New Testament, though we have a bias towards the use of the language in the New Testament. Even though it is usual to consider separately the Greek of secular literature from the Greek of the Septuagint and of the New Testament, I can see no necessary reason why this should be so in a lexical study, especially as the principal lexica of the Greek language reflect on the meanings of Greek words from whichever sources they come. After our study of the language used, we consider the interpretation of our lexical findings in secular Greek literature; the next chapter considers the interpretation of our lexical findings in the literature of the New Testament.

---

14. In Aristotelean ethics, "the signature pleasure of virtue is pleasure in the fine (*kalon*) and . . . the correlative pain has the opposite, the shameful (*aischron*), as its object" (Meyer and Martin, "Emotion," 644). The four cardinal virtues of Stoic ethics are derived from Plato. They are wisdom, courage, justice, and temperance (*Republic*, iv.436–35).

15. Fulkerson, "Helen," 126.

16. Chaniotis and Ducrey, *Unveiling Emotions II*.

The Language of Regret

The verb *melō* (or sometimes *melomai*) from which compound forms of the root derive means "to care for" or "to be an object of care."[17] The root with the prepositional prefix *meta*[18] points to having care or concern about how one's actions have affected others or oneself. The antonym *ameleō* ("to have no care for," and so "to neglect, to be unconcerned") also exists.[19] *Metamelomai* usually means "to change one's mind, regret."[20] The *metamel-* word-group can vary from weak regret about "an act worthy of reconsideration on moral grounds" to "internal pain" about a misdeed.[21] For example, in Matt 21:29 it is used of a son who at first refused to do what his father wanted, and then "changed his mind," but in verse 32, where the word recurs, it seems to mean "repent," for it describes those who heard John the Baptist preach, who saw the effect John's preaching had on some of those who heard John, and who yet did not repent (*metamelomai*) and believe. In Heb 7:21, which is a quotation from Ps 110:4 LXX, *metamelomai* is usually translated "change one's mind," and refers to God's settled intention that Melchizedek and his descendants would be priests forever. In chapter 4, we discuss what *metamelomai* may mean in the interpretive contexts of Matt 27:3 and on the two occasions when it occurs in 2 Cor 7:8.

Another group of words that sometimes is connected with the idea of "remorse" is from the *metano-* word-group, examples of which appear in the New Testament. The root *metano-* means literally "thinking afterwards."[22] *Metanoia* means "repentance," and *metanoeō* means "to repent." These two words occur relatively frequently. *Ametanoētos*, meaning "unrepentant," occurs in Rom 2:5. With the *metano-* word-group in the New Testament, there is a perceptible change of emphasis of the word-group's semantic domain, for the word-group refers not only to a change of mind or to regret,

17. Examples in the New Testament of *melō* include Matt 22:16; Mark 4:38; 12:14; Luke 10:40; John 10:13; 12:6; Acts 18:17; 1 Cor 7:21; 9:9; 1 Pet 5:7. *Melomai* (to be an object of care, to be a cause of concern) also exists, but not in the New Testament. *Epimeleomai* (to take care for, to take care of) occurs in Luke 10:34–35 and 1 Tim 3:5.

18. The preposition *meta*, which is prefixed to many verb stems, expresses the idea of change (Moulton, *Grammar*, 317–18).

19. In the New Testament, see Matt 22:5; 1 Tim 4:14; Heb 2:3; 8:9; 2 Pet 1:12. The adjective *ametameletos* occurs in Rom 11:29, where it means "irrevocable," and in 2 Cor 7:10, where it means "without regret."

20. See from the New Testament Matt 21:29, 32; 27:3; 2 Cor 7:8 (twice); and Heb 7:21.

21. Fulkerson, *No Regrets*, 28, 32.

22. In the LXX, this Greek verb is used to translate the Hebrew verb *niham*, as to which, see chapter 2.

as in secular Greek literature, but also to a change of moral orientation in response to a sense of having done wrong.[23]

In *No Regrets*, Fulkerson lists additional words that can occasionally mean or be related to "remorse." She suggests *syneidēsis, synoida, aischynē,* and *analambanō.* These words occur in the New Testament, but in their context do not mean or suggest "remorse." Fulkerson identifies two other words, *synesis* and *aiodos,* that can mean remorse; *synesis* is a cognate noun of a verb that in the New Testament does not mean remorse. Fulkerson also lists a variety of other words; they are cognates of words that are in the New Testament. They are *metamelētos* ("repented of,") *metamelos* (a noun or adjective, referring to repentance or regret and in Prov 11:3 LXX), *metameleia* ("repentance, regret" and in Hos 11:8 LXX),[24] *metamelētikos* (an adjective), and *metamelei* (an impersonal verb). None of these words always means remorse, though they each can, according to context.

Remorse in Greek Culture and Politics

Despite the linguistic difficulties of identifying one word or one group of words that obviously means remorse, it is important to say at the outset that the Greeks did know of an emotion that today we would call "remorse." It is famously and obviously evident in the play *Oedipus the King,* by Sophocles, probably first performed in 429 BC. In the play, Oedipus, king of Thebes, discovered that in spite of his efforts to avoid doing so, he had killed his father, Laius (not knowing that the man he had killed was his father), and married his mother, Jocasta (not knowing that the woman he had married was his mother). The result is that Jocasta hangs herself, and Oedipus, having gouged out his eyes in grief and remorse, is banished to end his days wandering on the slopes of Cithaeron. His response and suffering have become a byword for tragic remorse and guilt, where ignorance and unwitting wrong lead to acts that have unintended outcomes.[25] The example of Oedipus notwithstanding, examples of remorse seen as a virtue are relatively rare in surviving evidence of Greek thought and practice.

The *metano-* and *metamel-* word-groups might be thought to be connected with the idea of remorse because remorse sometimes precedes or is part of repentance and regret: it is a short step for a word from these word-groups to be used as shorthand to mean repentance and regret respectively

23. Often overlooked, even among New Testament scholars, is the verb *metaballō,* which means "to change one's way of thinking" (LSJ II.2): the word occurs in Acts 28:6.

24. See also Aristotle *EE* 1240b22–4 and *NE* 1150b29, 1105a31–35, and 1166b24.

25. For a different interpretation, see Vellacott, "Guilt of Oedipus."

together with remorse. Certainly, Greek political history shows that the Greeks did know of "repentance" and "regret" in the sense of a change of mind and distress about decisions that had been made by previous public votes. We consider two examples where, in a modern setting, a community's change of mind might have been the result of remorse.

The first example is from Thucydides's *History of the Peloponnesian War* and concerns people who had been led by *pathē*, not reason, to make an unwise decision. In 427 BC, the Athenians suppressed the revolt of Mytilene and "under the impulse of anger"[26] decided to put to death all adult Mytilenean men and to enslave the remaining women and children. The following day a change a mind, that is, "repentance" (*metanoia*), came over them, as they realized "that the design they had formed was cruel and monstrous, to destroy a whole city instead of merely those who were guilty."[27] After public debate, the Athenians narrowly decided to kill only those they regarded as guilty (about a thousand men). It is evident from what Thucydides writes of the discussion that the basis of the revised decision was driven by the *realpolitik* of what would be in the Athenians' best interests and not, as formerly, the emotions of warfare and of the desire for revenge in victory.

The second example is from Xenophon's *Hellenica*, and is about a change of mind when people have been duped into doing what was "unreasonable."[28] Xenophon writes of the Athenian defeat of the Spartans in the naval battle of Arginusae in 406 BC. The Athenians voted to put to death their eight generals who had been involved in the battle because the generals, as a result of bad weather, had not retrieved Athenian survivors and corpses from the wrecked ships after the battle. The decision was reached improperly. Shortly after, the Athenians "repented" (the verb is *metamelō*) when they realized they had been "deceived" and had made an "unreasonable" decision because they had been misinformed.[29] The result of a vote was that they revoked their earlier decision: but the vote was too late, as six of the generals had already been executed. However, the people decided that "complaints should be received against those who had deceived" them.[30]

If these examples of repentance and regret imply remorse, the remorse is corporate, for the remorse, such as it is, is in a political setting, with no individuals personally acknowledging guilt for wrongdoing. The basis of the decisions in both examples is that the assembly (*ekklēsia*, in the case of the

26. Thucydides, *History of the Peloponnesian War*, III.xxxvi.2.
27. Thucydides, *History of the Peloponnesian War*, III.xxxvi.3–4.
28. Thucydides, *History of the Peloponnesian War*, I.vii.33.
29. Thucydides, *History of the Peloponnesian War*, I.vii.33.
30. Thucydides, *History of the Peloponnesian War*, I.vii.35.

Mytileneans) and the Senate (*boulē*, in the case of the conflict with Sparta) had not acted reasonably, with the implication that they had acted from *pathē* in a pejorative sense.

On close readings of these accounts, there is little to suggest that remorse is the cause of the repentance, regret, or change of decision. Thucydides writes of repentance on the basis of self-interest and Xenophon of regret on the basis of misinformation. In both cases, former lack of reason and rationality is the basis of the decisions, not remorse that indicates (in the definition in the OED) "deep regret or guilt for doing something morally wrong." These examples illustrate the general point that on the whole remorse is not a virtue that was heralded or celebrated by the Greeks.

Remorse in Greek Philosophy and Practice

In the Greek tradition of ethics, there is nothing corresponding to the Jewish codes of conduct and the apodictic laws in the Pentateuch. Rather, ethics were a matter of philosophical discourse, with a focus on virtues rather than a taxonomy of norms from which virtuous responses or specific lapses could be identified.

One of the aims of Greek philosophy was to identify *eudaimonia*, human flourishing or prosperity, and to clarify by reasoning what *eudaimonia* is and how it can be achieved. It is regarded as the highest human good.[31] Aristotle, for example, identifies *eudaimonia* with:

> the active exercise of [a person's] soul's faculties in conformity with excellence or virtue, or if there be several human excellences or virtues, in conformity with the best and most perfect among them. Moreover, this activity must occupy a complete lifetime.[32]

He describes virtue as:

> a settled disposition of the mind, determining the choice of actions and emotions, consisting essentially in the observance of the mean relative to us, this being determined by principle, that is, as the prudent man would determine[33]

31. See Rabbås et al., *Quest*.
32. *NE* 1098a15–16.
33. *NE* 1106b36–1107a2.

with the "mean" (sometimes called "the Golden Mean") being a moderate position between excess and deficiency in both actions and emotions that constitute virtue.[34]

The virtues (*aretai*) are regarded at least as essential constituents of *eudaimonia*, though virtues include more than qualities associated with ethics. Thus, one of the principal focuses of Greek philosophy was to understand the virtues, virtuous living, and emotions.

Good management of one's passions (by bringing them under control) is regarded as integral to moral advancement *(prokopē)* and to virtue and virtuous living.[35] To put this in modern terms, emotions are, in Aristotle's view, essential to the moral life, but they need to be well-managed and trained. The result of bringing one's passions under control is that one would have *metriopatheia*, restraint over the passions, as evidenced by freedom from excess or deficiency of the passions.

Despite their interests in emotions and in the public aspect of virtues (and so in emotions as contributing to the formation of what we have called "the ethics of community"), Greek philosophers had little interest in regret and remorse and did not regard them as examples of virtues. For example, the first-century BC Stoic philosopher Arius Didymus (d. 10 BC) does not list remorse in his discussion of *pathē*. He identifies the four typical, Stoic basic, primary *pathē*: pain (*lypē*), pleasure (*hedonē*), fear (*phobos*), and desire (*epithymia*). Under "fear," he includes as subclasses anguish, terror, dread, and shame; under "pain" he includes mental distress, grief, and sorrow. Though today we would regard some of these subclasses of *pathē* as sometimes being constituents of remorse, Arius Didymus does not make this connection.[36] In the Stoic view, such *pathē* arise from false judgments. One of the aims of the ethical project of the Stoics is to control such *pathē*, and especially *lypē*, pain or distress,[37] and so, along with control of the other *pathē* listed above, to achieve *apatheia*, freedom from emotion. This was the way to achieve happiness for it would result in a life of virtue, free from emotional disturbance.

The philosophers' lack of interest in regret and remorse is, as we would expect, reflected in the general lack of interest in regret and remorse more generally among the educated elite, whose interests are principally reflected in the records we now have. People were, of course, sometimes remorseful

34. On the mean, see *NE* 1106b15–29.

35. See, for example, Epictetus's discourse, *On Progress (Peri Prokopēs)*.

36. On this, see Krentz, "Early Roman Empire Stoics," 124–26.

37. See Singer, "New Distress," 180–98. Galen regarded *lypē* as a dangerous emotion if left unchecked and saw one of the aims of philosophy and medicine as seeking to achieve *alypia*, freedom from *lypē*.

and regretful, though, as I have said, remorse and regret are not obviously important components of Greek public discourse. The absence of remorse or regret for wrongdoing is apparent, for example, in "confession inscriptions" (which contain confessions of various offences and the propitiatory acts that people were to perform as a result) and typifies the way that regret and remorse are not regarded as evidence of virtues.[38]

The Greeks' relative lack of interest in interpersonal remorse is because the ethics of community have a preponderant place in Greek thought, with personal ethics being understood as for the good of the community. In particular, the public aspects of honor and shame (as well as their implications for ethics) have already been well explored.[39] It is well-established, for example, that to show regret resulted in lowered or diminished public status for wrongdoers. In addition, referring to Aristotle, what matters in Greek philosophy is not so much a sincere statement of remorse or regret on the part of wrongdoers but that wrongdoers recognize the superiority of their victims in the context of hierarchic patterns of relationships. Aristotle's approach to apologies and remorse focuses "entirely on relations of status and power . . . [and] has little to do with forgiving an admitted wrong."[40] When people were insulted, the prime concern was that the damage to their status and reputation was repaired, rather than that (as in modern thinking) they (sometimes also) receive an apology and so perhaps forgive the wrongdoer.[41]

There is another important reason why interpersonal remorse does not have a significant place in Greek thought and culture. Greek philosophers regard acting consistently with virtue as itself virtuous. Such a way of acting is a state of being or of mind consistent with virtue.[42] Those who show regret or remorse are seen unfavorably. This is because they have acted inconsistently with virtue and so lack consistency and virtuous character. It is also because they have failed to show a settled disposition of mind that determined the choice of virtuous actions and emotions. Such people are flawed in character, blameworthy, and even weak.[43] For these reasons, it was not necessary for Greek philosophers to develop a social

38. Chaniotis, "Constructing the Fear of Gods," 216–23. There is also no evidence of repentance.

39. See Peristiany, "Honor and Shame," Wallace-Hadrill *Patronage*, and summary essays by Moxnes, "Honor," and by Malina, "Understanding."

40. Konstan, "Assuaging Rage," 18–19; see Aristotle, *Rhet.* 1380a10–19.

41. Aristotle, *Rhet.* 1378a31–33.

42. Fulkerson calls such a state of mind "characterological" (*No Regrets*, 10, 45, 218–19). See also Konstan, "Assuaging Rage," 22–23 for examples from Plato, the Stoics, and Seneca.

43. See Fulkerson, *No Regrets*, 7–8, 45, 218–19.

and intellectual framework for identifying the components of remorse and regret or of other emotions related to specific moral lapses, because only people lacking in virtue do wrong. It is not so much identifying the nature of the lapse that matters as the fact that *any* lapse is evidence of inconsistency of character. Regret and repentance are therefore not celebrated in Greek philosophy as evidence of a virtuous disposition or of moral re-formation. Instead, according to Aristotle, a "good person is without remorse"[44] because (as we have said) a good person would not have acted in such a way as to need to be remorseful and to repent.

To avoid showing evidence of inconsistency when one could, mistakes were ignored or explained away and faults not admitted. Surprisingly to the modern reader, one might have regret for not acting consistently, rather than for the moral lapse itself.[45] Also surprisingly to the modern reader, regret (when it is evident) does not need to evidence inward sincerity and integrity, or change of character, because what matters is being consistent.[46]

In summary, we cannot speak of a well-developed ethic of regret or remorse. Since the Greeks believed that the character of adults was fixed, they valued consistency of character rather than developing one's character. The result is that if a person is virtuous, that person will be good, and so have nothing to be remorseful about. One could, of course, be remorseful if one acted in ignorance, as in the case of Oedipus; civic communities could regret decisions that had been made when misinformed, as we saw in the examples of the Athenians and the Mytileneans. But on the whole, good people act virtuously, and so do not do wrongs about which they need to repent and about which they should be remorseful. It is these reasons, which are an expression of the ethics of community, that principally explain why the ancient Greeks did not develop the idea of remorse and regret as virtues.

There may also be other reasons why Greek philosophers did not value an ethic of regret or remorse.

The first is general. It is that an emotion, such as remorse, might have been regarded with suspicion because it was a risk to reason and reasoning. Plato refers to "passions both fearful and unavoidable that pollute the divine." He lists passions such as:

> pleasure, a most mighty lure to evil; next, pains, which put good
> to rout; and besides these, rashness and fear, foolish counsellors

---

44. *NE* 1166a29.

45. Aristotle, *EE* 1240b22–4 as interpreted in Fulkerson, *No Regrets*, 9–10.

46. Cf. Aristotle, *Rhet.* 1380a14–15.

both; and anger, hard to dissuade; and hope, ready to seduce irrational sensation and . . . all-daring lust.[47]

Aristotle's approach to emotions is that moral education should help to shape emotions towards ends that were "choice-worthy" and "align" emotions with reason.[48] In the context of this way of viewing emotions, it is not likely that one would think that to be remorseful is to be virtuous or that remorse is an honorable response to wrongdoing; rather one would want to redirect or reshape one's remorseful feelings to thoughts and behaviors that lead to *eudaimonia* and the Golden Mean.

Second, among the followers of Epicurean philosophy, *ataraxia*, freedom from disturbance,[49] was, above all, to be prized as a pleasure. Epicurus's goal of life was pleasure through freedom from pain and from distress of the soul (or mental distress). His aim was to cure the soul of *pathos*, which in this context is not emotion but the suffering that comes from pain and distress. False empirical beliefs are to be confronted and corrected to effect the cure.[50] In Stoic thinking, emotions (*pathē*) were typically regarded as causing perturbation and imbalance, and so one aim of philosophy was to resist being controlled by the *pathē* and to expunge the inner disturbance that *pathē* sometimes brought. Acting in these ways would help to achieve *eudaimonia*. The goal of life was *apatheia*, the absence of unhealthy passions, with *ataraxia* as a by-product.[51] In thinking of ethics in these ways, remorse is to be avoided because it is a disturbing emotion and causes mental pain and distress.

Next, as we see in Plato's thinking for example, the human soul (pre-existing, immortal, and belonging to a world of permanent forms) and the body (mortal and temporal) are two separate entities that are temporarily joined during earthly life. Emotions are associated with the body, and (as is evident in some later patterns of thought, such as in Manichaeism) to some extent regarded with suspicion, because the soul is treated with favor, and the body (and so what is physical) disparaged. To put it in straightforward terms: in the modern period, we might wish to say that remorse can be

47. *Timaeus* 69D.

48. Bagnoli, *Morality and the Emotions*, 5. See also Aristotle, *NE* 1149a.

49. On *ataraxia*, see Striker, "Ataraxia," and O'Keefe, *Epicureanism*, 117–21. See also Epicurus (341–270 BC) in the *Letter to Herodotus* in Diogenes Laertius (AD 180–240), and *Lives* X.77 ("for troubles and anxieties and feelings of anger and partiality do not accord with bliss, but always imply weakness and fear and dependence upon one's neighbors"), and Lucretius (c.99–55 BC) in *Nature* II.7–15, on the mental stability that comes from being "fortified by the teachings of the wise."

50. Meyer and Martin, "Emotion," 646.

51. Sorabji, *Emotions as Peace of Mind*, 181–93.

an emotion that can lead to maturity and personal growth; in contrast, the Greek philosophers would say that virtuous people should train themselves not to be remorseful because remorse is an emotion, associated with the body, not the soul, and so to engage with and explore remorse is a distraction from personal growth and development.

Finally, the framework of Greek ethics is probably constructed around a model of perfectionist ethics that we see to varying extents until the period shortly before Christianity. As we observed above, the philosophers' view is that one of the keys to maturity is consistency of character; to show remorse is to indicate that one lacked consistency, having failed to practice moral virtue. The ancients thought that "one should refrain from doing in the first place things that one will later need to regret" and "the remorseful person in antiquity is . . . a person who has failed to act well rather than one who has learned a lesson." Changes of mind indicate weakness and failure to be consistent: they are not a sign of having learned from one's mistakes and so an improvement. Fulkerson adds that "the most common ancient reaction to a mistake . . . is to ignore it or argue it away."[52] Aristotle says, for example, "we are not pronounced good or bad according to our emotions but according to our virtues and vices."[53]

Put another way and seen more clearly in Plato and less so in Aristotle, Charles Griswold says that the ancients' view is that "*no* harm can come to a good person," presumably because of "the armature that virtue furnishes." More specifically, "[t]he perfected person is nearly or totally immune from mistakes in judgment; there is nothing of the past for him or her to undo, reframe or accommodate, at least so far as the past is connected with perfected agency."[54] In ancient philosophical traditions, a good person is "invulnerable to harm" and "will not himself harm others voluntarily."[55] As we have said, what this means is that a virtuous person should have nothing to be remorseful about, because such a person would not do wrong.[56] Paradoxically according to this way of thought, those who do wrong are the ones harmed, rather than those who are harmed, because the wrongdoers are damaging themselves by the wrongs they do.

David Winston concludes from a survey of Greek thought, "Greek philosophy had little interest in the feelings of regret and remorse that may

---

52. Fulkerson, *No Regrets*, 6, 9.

53. Taken from *NE* 1105a31 in an important section in 1105a31–1106a5; see also *NE* 1240b22–29. Konstan gives exceptions from the Life of Aesop, Version G, and from a Fragment attributed to Democritus (*Before Forgiveness*, 78, 79).

54. Griswold, *Forgiveness*, 10, 14.

55. Konstan, "Assuaging Rage," 20.

56. Plato, *Gorgias*, 527b4–5. See also Konstan, *Before Forgiveness*, x, 59.

at times lead an individual to a complete reassessment of his former life path and his conversion to a fresh course of existence."[57] Konstan writes much the same. He says that the "classical philosophers—and indeed, classical writers generally—seem to have had little interest in the themes of remorse or repentance."[58] Elsewhere he says that "remorse and repentance played little or no role in the process of reconciliation between wrongdoer and victim."[59] This lack of interest in remorse and repentance both reflects the ancient Greek culture of emotional expression, as well as shaping and reinforcing it. It also reflects the view that people act consistently according to their character.

Remorse and Shame

As we shall see in chapter 7, in some strands of contemporary thought, remorse and shame are related, as remorse is thought to be one kind of emotion that is sometimes related to feelings of shame. Shame is an individual's inner response to having done wrong and is typically a socially constructed emotion. As the ethics of shame (and, in contrast, honor) pervade much of ancient Greek culture, we might find a way of identifying what modern people call "remorse" from Greek traditions about shame.[60]

This is not the case. In Greek culture, shame is thought about primarily as a response to a person's wrongdoing being known about in a public or civic context. What was known about a person by others counted more than one's own conscience. The story of the ring of Gyges, the Lydian, in Plato's Republic illustrates the issues. Plato's brother, Glaucon, tells a story about a mythological ring that, if worn and twisted a certain way, makes the wearer of the ring invisible. Glaucon asks Socrates whether people, when invisible, could be so virtuous as to resist the temptation to do whatever they please, knowing that they would remain undetected. Glaucon says that if there were two such rings, with one worn by a just person and the other worn by an unjust person:

57. Winston, "Philo's Doctrine," 29; see also Winston, "Judaism and Hellenism," 4.

58. Konstan, "Assuaging Rage," 22. See also Kaster, Emotion, 80, 81. See the description of remorse in Stoic ethics in Graver, Stoicism, 193–94, though the work of Joannes Stobaeus (fifth century AD) on which it is based seems influenced by Christian understanding.

59. Konstan, Before Forgiveness, 59.

60. On shame and honor, see Cairns, "Representations"; Cairns and Fulkerson, Emotions, 11–20; and Sanders, "Beyond the Usual," 166–68.

nobody, it could be supposed, could have such an iron will as to stick to justice and have the strength to resist taking other people's property, while at the same time being capable even of taking from the marketplace whatever he wanted with impunity. He could go into houses and seduce anyone he pleased, kill and release from prison whomever he liked, and in all other matters behave like a god among humans. In acting thus, the behavior of neither would differ in any way from the other. Both would take the same course.[61]

From this, Glaucon suggests that "no one is voluntarily just, but [a person is just] only under compulsion" and that "in any circumstances where an individual thinks he will be able to get away with being unjust, he is so" (II.360d). The point Glaucon is making is that an individual will act justly only if the individual knows that others will see and know, and that there is no shame if one's misdeeds are private and known to the doer alone. The public face of what one does is what matters.[62] Later in *Republic*, Socrates says to Glaucon that people who abuse the power of the ring have enslaved themselves to their appetites, whereas those who decide not to abuse the ring's power remain in control of themselves and are happy. Justice is better for a person than injustice, and people should do what is just, whether or not they have the ring. Socrates says that "justice is the best thing for the soul itself and . . . it ought to perform just deeds, whether it has Gyges's ring or not."[63]

Remorse and the Training of Emotions

As we saw earlier, remorse is not a virtue to strive for; rather, it is an emotion that needs to be trained and brought under control to bring about *eudaimonia*.

It is not possible to talk about a unified Greek view about the right way to train human emotions: there are various schools of thought that had different approaches to and attitudes about this question.[64] The approaches could vary from promoting moral excellence through the training and disciplining

---

61. Plato, *Republic*, II.360b–c.

62. We see similar thinking reflected in Aristotle's writings, though of course Aristotle would not agree with Glaucon's conclusions. Aristotle says that shame influences people to refrain from wrongdoing (*Rhet.* 1383b12–14). He also observes that children are prevented from doing wrong and making errors by shame (*NE* 1128b16–18).

63. Plato, *Republic*, X.612b.

64. See Malherbe, "Hellenistic Moralists," 301–4; Nussbaum, *Therapy*; Sihvola and Engberg-Pedersen, *The Emotions*; and the essays in Fitzgerald, *Passions*, 29–150.

of human emotions to "strict control of emotions that allows very little scope for the modern ideal of spontaneity and self-expression."[65]

Rhetoric is one way that people could be persuaded of what is right and just, or be aroused and manipulated and so distort the way they respond to facts.[66] Aristotle condemns the misuse of rhetoric when it is to manipulate because it involves "arousing . . . prejudice, compassion, anger, and similar emotions" in an unscrupulous way.[67] The sophist Gorgias of Leontini (c.485–c.380 BC) wrote in *Encomium of Helen* 14 that the effect of rhetoric can be comparable to the effect of drugs (medication), bringing distress, fear, delight, and boldness; it can sometimes, he says, even "drug and bewitch the soul with a kind of evil persuasion."

It is undeniable that some rhetoricians achieved their goal in part through arousing emotions in ways that were inappropriately manipulative, and we see evidence of this in examples of ancient literature (e.g., Aristophanes's *Wasps*, first performed in c. 422 BC) where the ploys of manipulative rhetoricians are satirized and mocked.[68] Nevertheless, members of philosophical schools used rhetoric as a way to persuade people to live virtuous lives, and sometimes this involved not only an appeal to the intellect of the hearers but also an appeal to the emotions.

Aristotle understood judgment, opinions, and beliefs to be distinctive focusses of emotions.[69] Since "emotions are all those affections which cause people to change their opinion in regard to judgments,"[70] rhetoric, when addressed to emotions, could change beliefs. In similar vein, Plato, through the mouth of Socrates, describes rhetoric as "an art that leads the soul by means of words."[71]

Rhetoric had an important place in a well-lived life. Though the principal true aim of rhetoric is, according to Aristotle, to expound an argument persuasively[72] to bring about *eudaimonia*, another purpose of

65. Thom, "Passions," 74.

66. Aristotle, *Rhet.* 1354a16–18, 24–6.

67. Aristotle, *Rhet.* 1365a4. Dow argues in a "A Supposed Contradiction," 382 that Aristotle is here condemning "set-piece rhetorical devices aimed at manipulating emotions, which do not depend upon the facts of the case in which they are deployed" (and see Dow, *Passions*).

68. On arousing, displaying, and performing emotions as part of persuasion, see Sanders and Johncock, *Emotion*.

69. This is an early example of the important modern view that emotions are both cognitions and affect.

70. *Rhet.* 1378a.

71. *Phaedrus* 261A, and see 271C.

72. *Rhet.* 1354a11–26.

rhetoric is to appeal to and to shape emotions. This explains what seems to be the puzzling feature of the way Aristotle deals with emotions. His more extensive treatment of emotions is not in his treatise on psychology, *On the Soul*, but in his *Rhetoric*. Hence, one purpose of rhetoric was as a form of therapy for moral development. In a later period particularly, it was emphasized that one of the ways that emotions could be checked, guided, and re-shaped was by *psychagōgia*.

Psychagōgia is the rhetorical art of "winning men's [*sic*] souls" or "persuasion" (LSJ).[73] Clarence Gladd describes psychagogy as "a means of moral instruction . . . a pedagogical activity where the formation of a certain *paideia* is in view," with *paideia* meaning "the endeavor to make a person fit for life, including the formation of a person's moral and religious attitudes."[74] Ivar Vegge describes psychagogy as "the pedagogic method of moral philosophers in counselling and correction."[75] In some contexts, the word *psychagōgia* sometimes has "a negative undercurrent and characterizes the practice of flatterers"; at other times, it refers to "truthful guidance."[76] In other words, the meaning of the word is broad, and the word can be used pejoratively or in a complimentary sense.[77] Outside the New Testament, I have not been able to identify psychagogic activity aimed at *promoting* remorse.

Concluding Thoughts

Remorse is an emotion that was known to the Greeks but not described or referred to by a discrete word. In much the same way that in modern English the word "regret" is a hypernym for the many ways that people can be sorry (and sometimes remorseful), so in Greek the *metamel-* and *metano-* word-groups are hypernyms for a range of (sometimes overlapping) ways of being sorry and showing regret that also can include what today we call "remorse." Even so, remorse is little thought about or explored by Greek philosophers.

In Greek thought, virtuous people are guided by and follow a "settled disposition of the mind" (in Aristotle's words, quoted above) that determines

---

73. See the related verb *psychagōgeō* which in this context means "to win over, persuade" (LSJ).

74. Gladd, "Paul and Philodemus," 58.

75. Vegge, *2 Corinthians*, 380.

76. Gladd, "Paul and Philodemus," 17.

77. For an exploration of the use of the word in Greek literature, see the seminal article of Asmis, "Psychagogia"; see also Gladd, "Paul and Philodemus," 17–23 and Vegge, *2 Corinthians*, 49–50, 63–66, 254–57.

both their behavior and their emotions. To show remorse is evidence of lack of virtue because one will not have practiced the behavior to which one has a "settled disposition of the mind" to practice.

There may be exceptions. In a community setting, communities that had been duped and so not guided by reason, could show regret and change of mind, thereby showing that when properly informed they were guided by reason. We have not established that they were also remorseful. We have identified an exception in an interpersonal setting: Oedipus showed virtu-ous remorse. However, his remorse was not because of his personal *incon-sistency* with reason and virtue, but because unwittingly he had done wrong and so acted in a way that had led to unintended outcomes. In this context, his remorse is a sign of the *consistency* of his virtuous character, which is in evidence throughout, even though he had unwittingly done wrong.

We turn next to the New Testament to discuss to what extent in that body of literature remorse is identified and explored, and whether the con-temporary approach to remorse has its roots in the Christian thought of the New Testament.

Chapter 4

Remorse and the New Testament

In CHAPTER 3, WE saw that in some strands of Greek philosophy *pathē* were typically regarded as causing perturbation and imbalance and so regarded with suspicion. The same approach towards *pathē* is seen in some parts of the New Testament. For example, where the word *pathos* occurs, it has a negative meaning or is set in a negative context. At these points, secular Greek categories of thought are used to express traditional Jewish theology—and hostility—mainly about sexual impurity. In Rom 1:26, *pathos* means "degrading passions" (literally "passions of unworthiness"); in Col 3:5 it means "passion" and is included in a list of vices; and in 1 Thess 4:5 it is translated "lustful passion" (in a phrase that could be literally translated "passion of lust"). Those who "put to death" *pathē* (Col 3:5) would live the equivalent of a life of wellbeing and flourishing that is the aim of Greek philosophy, that is, (in Christian terms) a life pleasing to God.[1]

Though emotions associated with remorse and regret sometimes cause perturbation and even distress, they are not called "*pathē*" in the New Testament. Godward remorse about sin was already well-established in Jewish thought and spirituality and was regarded as an appropriate response to having done wrong. In this chapter, we trace the development of what in this book we call "interpersonal remorse," that is, a response to having done wrong to another person. It is not, of course, a new response, but in the New Testament it appears to be given some theological

---

1. This approach reflects the Stoic view that *eudaimonia* was characterized not by extinguishing emotions but being free from *pathē* by following reason. The sort of sexual passions referred to in the New Testament as *pathē* undermined the Stoic goal of clear judgment, temperance, and inner calm that are exemplified by self-discipline and self-control.

grounding and legitimacy as an expression of Christian faith and discipleship. In contrast with Greek thought, this kind of response is not regarded
as *pathos*, to be treated with suspicion and caution.

The Gospels

Several passages in the Gospels show people with emotions that in a modern-day setting might be interpreted as showing remorse.

Judas Iscariot[2]

In Matthew's Gospel, no motive is given for Judas's offer to the chief priests
to surrender Jesus into their hands (26:14–16).[3] Luke and John in their Gospels suggest that Judas acted the way he did because "Satan entered into
Judas Iscariot" (Luke 22:3) or "the devil . . . put it into the heart of Judas
Iscariot . . . to betray Jesus" (John 13:2; see also John 6:70–71; 13:27). (John's
explanation may be no more than a pre-psychological way of explaining
why Judas acted so foolishly.) In John's Gospel, there is emphasis on the fact
that what happened to Jesus is by God's foreknowledge and design, and not
because of human purpose or initiative. This might explain why there is no
reference in the Gospel to the Jewish political leaders paying Judas money
in exchange for information to betray Jesus.

The verb that Matthew uses for what Judas intended to do (*paradidōmi*)
is variously translated by words or phrases such as "hand over," "deliver," or
"betray," and any of these translations might be right: it is a case of context
and interpretation as to which is right. Raymond Brown, for example, argues that Judas did not "betray" Jesus but "gave [him] over."[4] Clearly Judas
did betray Jesus, for he was in cahoots with the Jewish religious and political
leaders and had accepted money in exchange for finding an opportune time
when Jesus could be arrested. He added to his deception by taking the arresting party to Jesus at night when Jesus was outdoors, away from crowds,
and in the presence of only the other eleven disciples. Because it was dark,
the Jewish leaders would not have been able to recognize Jesus among the
shadowy figures he was with. So, the leaders hid nearby, and Judas agreed

---

2. On Judas Iscariot in modern scholarship, see Maccoby, *Judas Iscariot*; Brown,
Death of the Messiah, 638–44, 652–60, 1394–1418; Paffenroth, *Judas*; Cane, *The Place
of Judas Iscariot*; Ehrman, *Lost Gospel*; and Gundry, *Peter*. Cane's monograph contains
an important chapter on the history of scholarship of Judas's repentance, pp. 127–45.

3. See also // Mark 14:10–11 and Luke 22:3–6; and see John 13:2.

4. Brown, *Death of the Messiah*, 211–13.

to point out which of the figures in the darkness was Jesus. Judas did this by greeting Jesus very obviously.[5] The leaders then came out of hiding and arrested Jesus.

According to Matthew (but not the other Gospel writers), when Judas "saw that Jesus was condemned to death" Judas had a profound change of heart about what he had done and recognized that he had "sinned by betraying innocent blood" (27:3–4). Deuteronomy 28:25 pronounces a curse on someone who "takes a bribe to slay an innocent person." In an attempt to undo the effects of what he had done and the curse he would be under, Judas attempted to return the money. The chief priests and the elders refused to accept the money, so Judas threw it into the temple, and in despair (presumably because of the curse he was under) he hanged himself.

In contrast, in Acts 1:18 Luke says that Judas kept the money he was paid by the Jewish leaders and bought a field (called "*Akeldama*" or "Field of Blood") with the proceeds. In Acts 1:18, Luke records Judas's grisly death from what appears to be an accident in the field or, according to some interpretations, an illness,[6] rather than from suicide. Luke writes that Judas died from "falling headlong" with the result that "he burst open in the middle and all his bowels gushed out."[7] The tradition about a field in connection with Judas's death is also in Matthew's Gospel but in a different way: in Matt 27:7, Matthew states that after Judas's death the chief priests used the money that Judas returned to buy "The Potter's Field" as a place to bury *xenoi*, that is, foreigners (non-Jews) or strangers (visitors to Jerusalem).

Reasons for the disparate accounts of Judas's death do not concern us here:[8] the point to note is that only Matthew refers to Judas's profound change of heart (Matt 27:3). What I have described as "Judas's profound change of heart" is a paraphrase of the verb *metamelomai*, which we met in chapter 3. Translators have variously translated the verb in this place as "seized with remorse" (NIV), "changed his mind" (ESV), and "repented" (NRSV). The different translations properly reflect the possible range of meanings of the word. Which translation is likely to be right in this context?

Matthew gives four reasons for Judas's response: it is because he saw that Jesus had been condemned (v. 3), because he had "betrayed innocent blood" (verse 4), because he had sinned and was now under the curse

5. Compare John 18:3–12.

6. In "Note," 279, Chase suggests that, according to Luke in the Acts account, Judas died of a medical condition.

7. Papias of Hierapolis (AD 60–130) gives an even more lurid account of Judas's death.

8. In *The Place of Judas Iscariot*, 54, Cane says that "no harmonization between Acts and Matthew is possible."

of God (verse 4), and because he had accepted money in circumstances when he should not have done (verse 3). "Repent" (NRSV) is therefore an unlikely translation, as Matthew regularly uses another verb, *metanoeō*, to indicate repentance. The NRSV translators may have chosen "repent" as a translation for this word for theological reasons, to indicate that in their view Judas was not beyond the redemptive, saving grace of God.[9] The translation is also unlikely because repentance usually indicates a forward-looking intention to do better in the future: given Judas's suicide shortly afterwards, Matthew does not indicate that Judas was thinking he had a future. "Changed his mind" (ESV) is also an unpersuasive translation, because Judas is horrified about the implications of his betrayal of Jesus. Such a translation seems too bland in the circumstances. In contrast, "seized with remorse" (NIV) seems to be the best translation in the context of Matt 27:3–5, especially given that people do not generally hang themselves when they no more than "change their mind."[10]

Does Judas's intention to return the money also point to the way *metamelomai* should be translated?[11] It is obviously a "change of mind" (he now no longer wishes to keep money he had formerly decided to keep) but it is also much more than only a change of mind: the intention to return the money is one aspect of a sense of dereliction about the folly of what he had done. It is also evidence of a form of repentance before God for sinning against God, because, by seeking to return the money, Judas is seeking to put right what he had done. He also admitted his sin publicly (27:4) and threw away the money to distance himself from the chief priests and the elders. (This is in contrast to the account in Acts 1:16–20 where Judas shows no repentance or remorse, for he chose to retain the money and to buy a field with it.)[12]

However, Judas cannot undo all the results of his betrayal, as Jesus had been condemned to death. One commentator puts it like this: "Matthew gives us a depiction of Judas in which he repents completely but does not believe in the possibility that Jesus or God could forgive him."[13] In fact, he cannot *repent* of his actions in their entirety, if by repentance we include the

9. Compare Cane, *The Place of Judas Iscariot*, 48.

10. On Judas's remorse, see Gundry, *Peter*, 58.

11. See Maccoby, *Judas Iscariot*, 57; Paffenroth, *Judas*, 111–18, especially 114–15; Gundry *Peter*, 59–62.

12. One wonders whether this is to suggest or even emphasize the supposed election of Judas to condemnation. The second-century account of Papias also makes no mention of remorse on the part of Judas: on the contrary, Papias describes Judas as "an example of godlessness" (Papias, frag. 4:2:3 in Ehrman, *Apostolic Fathers*).

13. Paffenroth, *Judas*, 115.

idea of something reparative or restorative, because there is nothing reparative or restorative that he could do to bring about the reversal both of the Jewish leaders' decision to hand over Jesus to Pilate and of Pilate's decision to execute Jesus. It is this realization that leads Judas to feel crushing remorse about the irreversibility of what he has done and to despair about his hopeless predicament. In his anguish, he seeks to rid himself of such of his actual and felt guilt as he can by throwing the money into the temple. It is much like Lady Macbeth who, in Shakespeare's *Macbeth,* sought to wash her hands to rid herself of her guilt (Act v, scene i). Just as Lady Macbeth's act was ineffective, so too is Judas's: neither act can reverse the effects of or expiate what has been done. Matthew also points us to an additional reason for Judas's despair, for Jesus had said, perhaps echoing Deut 28:25 (see above), "Woe to that man by whom the son of man is betrayed" (Matt 26:24). In other words, Judas had come to realize that Jesus had already affirmed there would be catastrophe and calamity for his betrayer.

What Matthew means by the word *metamelomai* is that Judas came to realize how appallingly foolish and mistaken he had been. In addition, Judas knew he was under God's curse for betraying innocent blood. As a result, he became profoundly despairing and remorseful. In a different context, Andrew Horne describes what is likely to go through the mind of a serious offender who is remorseful. Most likely the same would be true of Judas. Horne says:

> Apologies, forgiveness and reparation are . . . inadequate. . . .
> [T]he offender is left full of regret and guilt which he is unable
> to deal with, ruminating painfully on what he has done, wishing
> he could put the clock back, being pricked by his conscience,
> wishing he could make everything all right again . . . .[14]

Judas bitterly regretted what he had done and saw no way to peace or to atonement. He had no hope for the future and so he took his life.

Jewish thought had deep distaste for suicide.[15] Of the 960 whom Josephus said voluntarily died at Masada, only the last person who was left alive committed suicide: the others chose to die by one another's hands rather than commit suicide. The Greeks distinguished honorable and heroic suicides from cowardly suicides: the former were acceptable, the latter

---

14. Horne, "Reflections," 24.

15. See Judg 16:28–30; 1 Sam 31:4–5; 2 Sam 17:23; and 1 Kgs 16:18. For a survey on suicide in Jewish thought from biblical times, see Rosner, "Suicide."

condemned.[16] The Apocrypha, influenced by Hellenism, reflect the Greek approach to honorable deaths.[17]

In summary, the most appropriate way to describe Judas's emotional state is "despairingly remorseful," and I suggest that this is the correct way to translate the verb *metamelomai* in Matt 27:3. In chapter 6 I describe this sort of remorse as "lachrymal." Judas knew he had "betrayed innocent blood" and had also sinned against God.

Peter

Peter, like Judas, is remorseful after he had denied Jesus though, surprisingly, modern commentators have shown little interest in exploring Peter's remorse.[18]

In Mark 14:27–31,[19] Jesus forewarns the twelve disciples that they would desert him following his arrest. Peter affirms his loyalty and says that, even if the other eleven flee in fear, he would not. In response, Jesus warns Peter that he too would desert Jesus that night and that Peter would deny knowing him not just once, but three times.

Shortly after the conversation and following Jesus's arrest, Jesus is taken for what amounts to a show-trial held before the members of the Jewish Council at what is probably the house of the high priest. Peter, obviously fearful for his own life, watches proceedings from the courtyard. When questioned by a servant girl and some bystanders, and as Jesus had anticipated, Peter denies that he knows Jesus (Mark 14:66–72).[20] Peter recalls Jesus's forewarning, and "breaks down and weeps" (Mark 14:72). His denial of Jesus, made in order to protect himself, is at this point a wrong that he knows he did not have the courage to put right. He is overcome with shame and remorse about his naïve bravado earlier that day.

The words in Mark 14:72 that I have I have translated as "breaks down" above are unclear and one commentator has described them as "probably unintelligible."[21] They translate the verb *epiballō,* a difficult verb

---

16. Garrison, "Attitudes," 33.

17. 2 Macc 14:41–46 (Ragesh) and 2 Macc 10:12 (Ptolemy, a gentile).

18. See, for example, Perkins, *Peter;* Cassidy *Four Times Peter;* Hengel, *Saint Peter;* and Bockmuehl, *Simon Peter.* Cf. Gundry, *Peter,* who denies Peter is remorseful.

19. // Matt 26:31–5; Luke 22:31–34; John 13:36–8.

20. // Matt 26:69–75; Luke 22:56–62; John 18:15–28.

21. Evans, *Saint Luke,* 828. Evans thinks this is why Matthew and Luke rewrite what Mark says (Matt 26:75 and Luke 22:62).

with a wide range of meanings.[22] Most simply, the verb means to "throw upon" something (reflecting the common meaning of the two Greek words that make up this compound verb), in the way that waves, for example, break over the hull of a boat (see Mark 4:37) or how one might describe one's manual actions when arresting someone (Matt 26:50). Some suggest that the verb here means "begin" (thus, Peter "begins to weep"), and LSJ suggests that the word here means to "think on" or "give attention to" (thus, Peter "thought on what he had done and wept"). Both these suggestions seem tame and fail to capture that Peter had realized he had wretchedly failed a friend to whom he had promised loyalty to the point of death. The more likely meaning, and one that better fits both the usual meaning of the components of the verb *epiballō* (to "throw upon") and the context of the verb in this passage, is that Peter left the courtyard, perhaps flung himself down on the ground outside, and (as Matthew and Luke, as well as Mark, say) broke down in tears.[23]

One of the characteristics of the sort of remorse that Peter experienced is that the remorseful person is deeply troubled (perhaps to the point of despair) by self-recrimination and guilt, often because there is no way to put right the wrong that has been done. Peter would have recalled his brave words of loyalty to Jesus, his boast that he would be more resolute than the other eleven, and then remembered that, when challenged, he cowered in fear, and lied to save himself, denying that he even knew Jesus. Such remorse can seem like merciless, unending torment for the wrongdoer's conscience. In time, the sharpness of the torment may remit, and the frequency of its occurrence may diminish, but the feeling of guilt may never fully go away, usually because there is no victim to forgive the wrong. This is what I will describe in chapter 6 as "stronger remorse."

It did not, of course, stay like that, because Peter, unlike Judas, had a subsequent encounter with Jesus. Even before the encounter, one senses that Jesus knew of Peter's deep remorse and shame. Early on, there are hints of forgiveness and restoration for Peter. For example, we can re-punctuate and rephrase in the following way the words spoken on the morning of the resurrection to the women at the tomb. A young man, probably an angel,

---

22. For a detailed discussion of the possible range of meanings of *epiballō*, see Marcus, *Mark 8–16*, 1020–21 and Brown, *Death of the Messiah*, 609–10.

23. John writes of three denials and of the cock crowing only once. He omits any mention of Peter weeping (John 18:15–18, 25–27). Gundry argues that Matthew presents Peter as a false disciple and apostate "destined for damnation" and that Luke and John, who wrote after Matthew, "portray him instead as rehabilitated after his denials" (*Peter*, 100, 103). Gundry makes too much of Matthew not including a post-resurrection encounter between Jesus and Peter.

sitting by the empty tomb where Jesus had been buried, said "Go and tell his disciples—and [even] Peter [too]—that Jesus is going ahead of you to Galilee . . ." (Mark 16:7).[24]

John's Gospel describes how Jesus addresses Peter's remorse (John 21:15–19). Peter is by the Sea of Tiberias with Jesus in his resurrected form. Jesus has obviously already forgiven Peter, despite later church traditions that those who denied Jesus would themselves be denied by him. Jesus asks Peter whether *Peter* loves him. Implicit in the question is a statement that *Jesus* loves Peter and has forgiven him, notwithstanding Peter's previous denial of Jesus. In other words, Jesus (probably again) confronts Peter's remorsefulness with love and forgiveness, and invites Peter to set aside his remorse and to re-engage with his former love for Jesus, in order to experience a restored relationship.[25] I suspect that if one remains remorseful towards someone, it is possible to love that person in only a diminished way; I also suspect that being offered love and forgiveness in such a situation heals the torment of remorse and turns it into life-giving repentance. However, the *status quo ante* cannot be restored. Peter was a chastened, wiser man for the experience of boastful bravado, egregious failure, and later restoration. He is thereby better equipped, through failure and then forgiveness, to take up the commission to pastor early churches.[26] In my view, Peter's behavior is an unambiguous example of interpersonal remorse that leads to repentance and restoration.

The Parable of the Prodigal Son

In the parable (Luke 15:11–32), some think that the younger son showed remorse "when he came to himself" (v. 17). Certainly, he recognizes that he had "sinned against heaven" (verses 18, 21) and seems to be remorseful about his wrongdoing before God. However, the younger son does not say he is remorseful about wronging his father for, though he recognizes that he has sinned *before* his father (verses 18, 21), he does not say he has sinned *against* his father. His sin against God is evident *to* his father, as it is to other people, but the younger son does not say he has deep regret about the way he has wronged his father. His intention in returning is not to put

24. It is possible to trace what are sometimes called "the steps to post-traumatic growth" (McGrath, "Post-Traumatic Growth," 291) in Peter's experience.

25. Benson omits this important factor in the way he traces Peter's psychological growth ("Death and Dying," 81–83).

26. For a study of this story, see Aus, *Simon Peter's Denial*. This study uses early Jewish sources to explore the imagery of the account.

right what he could by reparative acts; rather, it is to be treated as a hired servant (verse 19) so that he could be fed because he was hungry (verse 16). He may also have felt remorse, but this emotion is not articulated in Luke's account of the son's return.

Paul and the Pauline Corpus

Paul's Persecution of Christians

It is commonly said that Paul was remorseful about having supported and participated in the execution of Stephen[27] and about having persecuted Christians[28] before his call on the road to Damascus.[29]

Paul himself refers to his former persecution of Christians in Gal 1:13 and Phil 3:6. In 1 Cor 15:9 he says he is "the least of the apostles" and "unworthy to be called an apostle" because he had persecuted Christians. In Eph 3:8, a later passage, which is probably a post-Pauline edited version of Paul's former writings, he says he is the "least" of all people, presumably because he had formerly persecuted Christians. Paul certainly lived with the shameful recollection of what he had done; he also regarded himself as having diminished status as an apostle and human being because of his former actions. These passages do not explicitly refer to or describe remorse, though remorse, as well as guilt and shame, seem implicit. Though presumably Paul knew he had been forgiven for those actions, the stain of the guilt remained with him.

In another post-Pauline passage (1 Tim 1:13–15), which (like Eph 3:8) is probably based on an edited version of Paul's own earlier writings, there is even a hint of self-excuse when he says that he had formerly acted "in ignorance and unbelief" (verse 13). The passage understates any former sense of remorse he may have had. Nevertheless, the sense of having done wrong remains clear, for he also says that God had shown him grace as "the foremost of sinners" (verse 15).

Since Paul was almost certainly remorseful, what kind of remorse is his remorse? It is lucid remorse,[30] since Paul does not dwell on his former sins and errors pathologically. He remained deeply ashamed of his sins and errors and did not ignore the fact of what he had done, though he recognized his later faith and understanding explained and contextualized his mistakes. We know

27. Acts 7:58—8:1 and 22:20 for Paul's role.
28. Acts 8:3; 9:1–2, 13, 26; and 22:19.
29. Acts 9:1–18, with 22:6–16 and 26:12–18.
30. I explain this phrase further in chapter 6.

from elsewhere that he believed that God's justification made him righteous, notwithstanding his sins; we see in the passages we have considered that he knew that God's justification did not unpick the fact of the past or reverse it. The persistent nagging of Paul's conscience, reminding him of what he had done, means he could not forget those actions of the past, and his integrity, as he was reminded of the past, means he would not.

The Corinthian Church

Rather less dramatic and very much more complicated is Paul's exploration of what may be remorse in 2 Cor 2:5–11 and 7:5–16. The verses we are to consider are not straightforward, and their interpretation will depend on a number of choices that we make about the context and background of what Paul writes.

According to some of the interpretive choices that we make, Paul might well be describing some of the characteristics of what today we would call "remorse." L. L. Welborn clearly sees the place of remorse in these passages and writes of "Paul's vivid description of the Corinthians' emotional journey from 'remorse' to 'repentance.'"[31] If Paul is writing about remorse on the part of the Corinthians, it is noteworthy that he adapts existing language to explain what he means. He has to do this because, as I have already said in chapter 3, Greek lacks a discrete word or word-group the only or principal meaning of which is "remorse."

An Offender

Paul writes of an offender who experienced deep regret (*lypē*), probably remorse, about his wrongdoing (2 Cor 2:7). The word *lypē* usually means "grief," though in this context it seems to mean "deep regret" or "remorse."[32] The offender was in need of the restorative comfort and support of the Corinthians, in part because the offender had been punished for the wrong he had done (2 Cor 2:6 and 7:11). From Paul's description, the offender seems to have been overwhelmed with guilt and shame, and these emotions are characteristic of people with remorse. The way Paul refers to the offender may subtly allude to the way that Judas Iscariot had himself been overwhelmed with guilt and shame; it may also be a covert warning to the

---

31. Welborn, "Paul and Pain," 548.

32. In 2 Cor 2:5, *lypeō* clearly does not mean "remorse"; it is confusing how, in the space of three verses, Paul uses the same word-group with disparate meanings.

Corinthians that if they did not reintegrate the offender into the church community, the offender was at risk of falling into the same irredeemable despair as Judas. The important point to note is that Paul uses the word *lypē* to suggest the idea of remorse.

The Corinthians

Paul writes in 2 Cor 7:8–16 as though the Corinthians had been remorseful. However, we cannot be certain that the Corinthians had been remorseful, as the words Paul uses can mean "distress" or "grief" and as we have only Paul's account of what Titus had said of them and Paul's (perhaps tendentious) interpretation of Titus's report.[33] We also do not know what the Corinthians had been remorseful about.

For rhetorical purposes, Paul may also have chosen to interpret the Corinthians' fear of dishonor and shame as remorse.[34] Somewhat confusingly, too, though Paul refers to the Corinthians' supposed remorse, he also says in 2 Cor 7:11, "At every point you have proved yourselves innocent in the matter." If the Corinthians were innocent from the start, Paul's statement raises the question whether they had, and could have, been remorseful at all.

Ivar Vegge regards Paul's expressions of confidence in the Corinthians' response as "idealized," that is, they are:

> rhetorical devices of persuasion which undergird an implicit or explicit command, appeal or request . . . for mutuality, solidarity, fellowship, friendship and reconciliation between the Corinthians and Paul, or [for] an appeal to give Paul space and recognition as an apostle.

In the case of 2 Corinthians, he concludes that implicitly "Paul praises and idealizes the reconciliation of the Corinthians with himself in a minor, separate conflict . . . in order to exhort the Corinthians to a full and perfect reconciliation with himself . . . ."[35]

Paul uses a noun, *lypē*, and a verb, *lypeō*, to describe the response of the Corinthians to his letter (2 Cor 7:8–11).[36] He also refers to their

33. See Thrall in *Critical and Exegetical Commentary* who insightfully explores Paul's language in 2 Cor 7:5–16.

34. For examples of such fear, see Patera, "Reflections," 115–16.

35. Vegge, *2 Corinthians*, 35, 381.

36. Readers of Greek may in some places (e.g., 2 Cor 7:8–9) want to read *lypeō* as meaning (in the active voice) "to cause remorse" and (in the passive voice) "to be remorsed," that is, "to become remorseful." However, the form of *lypeō* when meaning "to cause remorse" is not factitive (i.e., as indicating that the action of *lypeō* causes a result,

"repentance" (vv. 9, 10). He distinguishes between "worldly grief [*lypē*, which here is probably remorse] that leads to death" and "godly grief [*lypē*, which here, again, is probably remorse] that produces repentance leading to salvation and that is without regret" (2 Cor 7:10). What Paul means by the Corinthians' "godly grief" is remorse that led not to "death" but to life and inner health because they had repented. The outcome is that the Corinthians were *ametamelētoi* (2 Cor 7:10).

Ametamelētoi is a noun derived from the verb *metamelomai* prefixed with *a* to indicate a negative form of meaning. We have seen that *metamelomai* means "remorseful" when describing Judas; we shall see below that in 2 Cor 7:8 *metamelomai* almost certainly means "to regret." From the context of 2 Cor 7:10, it is likely that the noun means "without remorse," that is, the Corinthians were no longer remorseful because matters had been put right, or that they were without regret because they had been remorseful and put matters right, or that they were not regretful about having been remorseful and repented.[37]

Second Corinthians 7:10–11 read in these ways anticipates what we say in chapter 6 about lucid remorse: it is remorse that leads to repentance and acts of repair and restoration, with the result that wrongdoers move on, forgiven and in a renewed relationship with the person formerly wronged. In contrast, remorse that "leads to death" is remorse that does not lead to repentance, acts of repair, forgiveness, and renewed relationships. This could be a description of Judas's remorse in Matt 27:3–4.

As we have seen, *lypē* is a technical term in Stoic philosophy for pain, one of the four generic (negative) emotions (*pathē*). Paul is not following a Stoic approach to *lypē* in this letter to the Corinthians in at least two ways. First, Paul is self-evidently not demonstrating the Stoic ideal of "self-mastery" (*engkrateia*), for the letter is florid and emotional, demonstrating "a clean reversal" of the Stoic approach to emotions;[38] second, Paul's use of *lypē* is, in comparison with Stoic use, "anomalous, even shocking,"[39] for Paul seems to regard *lypē* as one of the "good emotions," *eupatheiai*. If this is right, we have an example of remorse being regarded as a godly, virtuous emotion. We come back to this question later in the chapter. However, there

---

remorse). This perhaps no more than illustrates that Paul is using current language to express a thought or idea, remorse, in new ways for which there is no obvious existing language.

37. It is possible that "without regret" could refer to "salvation" rather than to repentance, as in ESV, thereby avoiding what Welborn has called an "elegant oxymoron" ("Paul and Pain," 552).

38. Welborn, "Paul and Pain," 568.

39. Welborn, "Paul and Pain," 565.

are considerable doubts about the accuracy of Paul's views of the Corinthians' response and, as commentators have suggested, Paul's views may be part of a series of rhetorical devices to achieve intentions that do not have anything to do with remorse or regret.

Paul

In 2 Cor 7:8, Paul writes of his own regret (or possibly remorse) about an earlier letter. C. K. Barrett regards the verse as a "quite impossible sentence [to analyze and interpret]" and thinks it to be "a compound of a number of sentences, each of which represents part of what Paul wished to say."[40]

Paul acknowledges that his earlier letter had distressed and grieved (*lypeō*) the Corinthians (2 Cor 7:8b). Presumably, Titus had passed on this fact to Paul. In the first half of verse 8, Paul says he does *not* regret (*metamelomai*) having distressed them.

Why were the Corinthians distressed and grieved, and was their response a form of remorse? One reason for the Corinthians' response is probably because Paul's letter may have contained correction (but compare verse 11b) that at first the Corinthians did not welcome. Given that the Corinthians had heeded Paul's corrective advice and apparently sent by Titus a favorable reply to Paul's letter, their "grief" might here mean "remorse."

Was Paul himself remorseful or regretful about writing the letter? He says he both did not and did regret (or both was not and was remorseful about) writing the letter (verse 8). He uses the verb *metamelomai* to describe his feelings, the same verb that Matthew uses of Judas's remorse in Matt 27:3.

It is hard to see how Paul could have been remorseful if he had no more than written a letter of correction; it was necessary and right to do at the time. The Corinthians' distress had only been short-lived, and the period of Paul's knowledge of their distress was even more short-lived, presumably lasting no longer than it took to read (or hear) the single report from Titus that the Corinthians had been, and were no longer, distressed.

If this interpretation is correct, Paul would have had no reason to feel anything but what Amélie Rorty calls "passing light regret"[41] for the distress he had caused. Paul seems to mean no more than that he had understood and empathized with the initial distress the Corinthians had felt, in much the same way that a person might say, "I am sorry you hurt your arm in an accident."

40. Barrett, *Second Epistle to the Corinthians*, 209.
41. Rorty, "Agent Regret," 493.

We can take another view about what Paul means when he writes of his feelings. He may have regretted sending the letter because of the tone of the letter. In other words, Paul may have (rightly) written giving correction and instruction but have done so in a manner that was not appropriate.

I suspect it is likely that Paul had written intemperately to the Corinthians. Second Corinthians 10:10 supports the view that the Corinthians had taken exception to the tone of some of Paul's earlier letters and perhaps also to the one Paul is referring to in 2 Cor 7. Second Corinthians 10–13 illustrate that Paul *did* write letters that were confrontational, combative, scathing, and critical. Paul's relief in 2 Cor 7:8 could be because (certainly at this point) the Corinthians had overlooked the tone of his earlier letter but heeded its contents.

If Paul had written intemperately, how do we explain Paul's earlier statement in verse 8 that he did not regret having written the letter? It seems that at this point Paul celebrates that his letter had produced the desired outcome. It is as if he thinks "the end" (the desired outcome) justified "the means" (in part, an intemperate letter), and in any event, as he says later in verse 8, the Corinthians had only been distressed for a short period. In other words, at this point, he appears to say that he neither regrets nor is remorseful about using wrong methods to achieve an overall goal that is good. This is consequentialism at its least attractive and defensible.

Psychagogy

Scholars have come increasingly to recognize points of similarity between Paul's writings and some of the popular philosophical understanding about "the passions" (i.e., what today we would call "the emotions"). David Aune, for example, writes that "Paul's conception of the passions cannot be properly understood apart from the philosophically informed cultural codes that permeated Greco-Roman society."[42]

Some have said that Paul's use of emotional language in 2 Cor 2:3–11 and 7:8–13 shows Paul's debt to popular philosophical understanding particularly sharply. It has been argued, for example, that Paul uses emotional appeal (*pathos*) to ensure that the Corinthians responded favorably to him and to ensure they would feel shame and even enmity towards the visitors with whom Paul so strong disagreed.[43] Welborn argues that Paul draws on well-known rhetorical ploys to elicit pity, anger, and zeal.[44]

42. Aune, *Passions*, 232.

43. Sumney, "Paul's Use."

44. Welborn, "Paul's Appeal."

In addition, Clarence Gladd suggests that Paul is taking a psychagogic approach (see chapter 3 on psychagogy) in the way he corrects the Corinthians' faults in order to bring about their spiritual development and maturity.[45] He says that Paul's "moral exhortation and letter writing [are evidence of] . . . methods of psychagogic guidance similar to those of other contemporary moralists."[46] It is right, according to this approach, to inflict *lypē* (harsh rebuke to bring about repentance) but not so as to bring about destruction and ruin. This would in part explain why Paul refers to the excessive censure of the Corinthians that nearly brought about the destruction of the wrongdoer, and also refers to his own censure of the Corinthians that brought about their supposed repentance for their former behavior. However, the "use of criticism, threats and punishment, and the use of (idealized) praise as a device for promoting development and further growth," which Vegge identifies as typical of a psychagogic approach to moral development (and which Vegge sees exemplified in Paul's approach in 2 Corinthians), can hardly be said to be unique to or the discovery of practitioners of psychagogy.[47]

In an article, Welborn develops Gladd's approach and conclusions. He observes that Paul's treatment of "remorse" and "repentance" demonstrates that Paul was generally aware of the way philosophers treated the place of emotions in moral development. He also observes that although Paul usually follows a Stoic model of emotions, his treatment of "pain" (*lypē*), (one of the Stoic four cardinal passions the presence of which amounted to a flaw in the character of a sage), is "anomalous." One result is that Paul ends up "as the harbinger of an upheaval in the ancient therapy of the emotions" and "as the architect of the 'self as sufferer', which, by the end of the second century, had achieved significant cultural currency."[48]

Another reason for suggesting that Paul is using the word *lypē* anomalously is that, according to Arius Didymus, *lypē* is felt "whenever we fail to get that for which we had an appetite or encounter that which

---

45. Gladd, "Paul and Philodemus," 316–19. Other writers on psychagogy in the New Testament include Meeks, *Moral World*, 40–64; Fitzgerald, "Passions"; Kloppenborg, "James 1:2–15"; and Sturdevant, "Incarnation." In the field of pastoral psychology, see Collins, "Psychological Hermeneutics."

46. "Paul and Philodemus," 186. The justification for a psychagogic approach is based on Aristotle's thought. Fortenbaugh says that "[o]nce Aristotle focused on the cognitive side of emotional response and made clear that an emotion can be altered by argument because beliefs can be altered in this way, it was possible to adopt a positive attitude towards emotional appeal" (*Aristotle*, 18).

47. Vegge, *2 Corinthians*, 50.

48. Welborn, "Paul and Pain," 548, 565.

we feared."[49] Paul is not suggesting to the Corinthians that they should master the *lypē* that they felt. If Paul is using the word *lypē* in knowledge of Stoic understanding, he sharply and, perhaps even provocatively, distinguishes himself from mainstream Stoic philosophers, for he suggests that moral virtue can result from "godly *lypē* that produces repentance leading to salvation and that is without regret" (2 Cor 7:10). In other words, *lypē* is not necessarily an emotion to be mastered, but to be welcome as an agent for change. The Corinthians had experienced grief (by which Paul probably means "remorse") *eis metanoian*, that is, that had produced repentance. The effect of what Paul may be doing is to re-work commonly-held contemporary views about *lypē* and to introduce into Christian thought a place for interpersonal remorse that leads to repentance.

Welborn's suggestion is supported by the way that Luke, who is writing for a more obviously Hellenistic readership, presents Jesus in a way understandable to a Hellenized readership. In his account of the Garden of Gethsemane, Luke does not mention that Jesus was "grieved" though both Mark and Matthew do.[50] Luke probably wrote with an eye to his Greek readers, who would have regarded grief as one of four cardinal passions and so not a sign of Jesus's sage-like role.[51]

It is also worth also bearing in mind three further observations that suggest we should be cautious about the conclusions of those who overly rely on the writings of first-century philosophers and popular rhetoricians to interpret the New Testament. First, Paul explicitly eschews the approach and perhaps even the wiles of the popular philosophers in 1 Cor 1:18–31. This may, of course, be no more than "special pleading" and itself a rhetorical ploy, much like Mark Antony denying that he wanted to "praise Caesar" and insisting that he intended no more than to "bury Caesar," when the opposite (and what he had denied) was clearly the case.[52] However, the views of the rhetorical critics evidently contradict Paul's statements in the same passage in 1 Cor 1 that the gospel does not need human reinforcement through rhetoric but has its own persuasive power. Second, though in Paul's writings there are points of correlation with the style and approach of popular philosophers, there are also some important points of difference: for example, and unlike in the popular philosophers, Paul does "not provide a well-designed plan for mastering the passions similar to those developed in the philosophical

49. Krentz, "Early Roman Empire Stoics," 125.

50. Mark 14:34 (*perilypos*) and Matthew 26:37 (*lypeō*).

51. The idea of Jesus becoming overcome with grief, a profoundly human emotion, has raised questions about the passible aspects of Jesus's human nature (Madigan, *Passions*).

52. Shakespeare, *Julius Caesar*, iii.2.

schools of his day."[53] At the very least, then, Paul's use of the rhetorical style and conventions of the popular philosophers is significantly moderated as a result of Paul's understanding of the gospel and the Christ-event. It is certainly the case that Paul does not slavishly follow them. Last, it may be methodologically unsound to read Paul's writings as if he were fully aware of and trained in, and were acting according to, contemporary Greek philosophical thought. Paul was a Hellenistic Jew, educated (at least in part) in a Jewish, not a Greek, context (Phil 3:5), and, according to Acts 22:3, trained by Gamaliel, an esteemed "teacher of the law" (Acts 5:34) in Jerusalem. While many of the ways of thinking and values that arose from Greek philosophy had permeated Hellenistic culture in a general way and so would have been known to Paul, we should remember that Paul was a Pharisee and a leather-worker, not a trained philosopher. It is therefore not surprising that he shows no more than some familiarity with Greek philosophical tropes and no evidence of expertise or consistent understanding.

In closing, we should bear in mind the criticisms that were made of the psychagogic approach in other contexts by philosophers: psychagogues were sometimes accused of being beguilers, flatterers, duplicitous, fickle, deceitful, and cunning, for example.[54] These are the very objections that the Corinthians seem to have had about Paul (to which Paul alludes in 2 Cor 10–13) and that Paul, as a result of the return of Titus, seems to think had been satisfactorily addressed. As I suggest above, Paul's approach in the passages we are considering may disclose lack of integrity on Paul's part, and this perhaps explains the subsequent, and more severe, disruption of the Corinthians' relationship with Paul in 2 Cor 10–13. If the Corinthians thought that Paul's approach was psychagogic, it appears they also thought he shared some of the same flaws as psychagogues.

Concluding Thoughts

In this chapter we have discussed several examples of remorse. Sometimes, words intending to denote remorse are used; at other times, the idea of remorse is implicit from the context. In these contexts, the semantic domains of three words (*metamelomai*, *lypē*, and *lypeō*) unusually include what in later a period clearly means "to be remorseful" and "remorse."

In the case of Judas, Matthew describes Judas as having remorse because Judas had "betrayed innocent blood," a sin for which he was under the curse of God. The verb Matthew uses to describe Judas's remorse is

53. Aune, *Passions*, 231.
54. Gladd, "Paul and Philodemus," 18–19.

metamelomai, an untypical, but not impossible, meaning of this verb. Peter's remorse, in contrast, arose because he had failed to be the loyal friend and supporter that he promised Jesus he would be. He was restored by Jesus's post-resurrection love and forgiveness. Paul's remorse about the way he formerly persecuted Christians is Godward-facing remorse, not inter-personal remorse. The prodigal's remorse is also Godward-facing.

We have also referred to other possible examples of interpersonal remorse in 2 Corinthians. The first is an offender who seems to have been almost overwhelmed with remorse (*lypē*) for what he had done. The second is the response of the Corinthians to whom Paul had written to correct. Their response is, according to Paul's description of it, remorseful, arising from "godly *lypē*," with repentance followed by acts that sought to put right what was wrong. If Paul's description is correct, this is an example of lucid, interpersonal remorse. In contrast, Paul refers to *lypē* that leads to "death": the sort of remorse that Judas had may be what Paul has in mind. Thus, we see in Paul's hands, the semantic domain of the word *lypē* extend to what, to modern readers, is remorse. There are some persuasive reasons for thinking that Paul's description of the Corinthians' response to his letter, whether or not the response is remorse or something else, is an idealized interpretation, verging on "spin" (that is, deliberate misrepresentation to achieve a desired outcome or impression) to bring about his own purposes. Whether or not the Corinthians' remorse is real or a tendentious assertion of Paul, Paul clearly recognizes interpersonal remorse as virtuous.

Last, Paul uses language that could mean "remorse," when describing his own emotions. The verb he uses, *metamelomai*, is the same verb that Matthew uses to describe Judas Iscariot's despair and remorse. Most likely in its context in 2 Cor 7:8, the verb means "regret," as there is no evidence of repentance, apology, or restitution. Additionally, in the space of one verse, Paul says he both did, and did not, experience the emotion described by the verb, suggesting that the emotion could hardly have been deeply experienced.

In closing, two observations remain to be made. First, as we have seen, some emotions are treated differently in the New Testament from the way they are treated in many of the surviving examples of secular Greek texts. Greek philosophy had almost no place for celebrating an ethic of remorse or an ethic of repentance. Certainly, we can say that early Christians valued (in Aristotle's words) "a settled disposition of the mind"[55] and consistency of (godly) character; on occasions, and unlike the Greeks, they also recognized a place for remorse and repentance. The new approach

---

55. *NE* 1106b36–1107a2.

is reflected especially in Paul's writings in 2 Corinthians and in the New Testament traditions about Peter. It marks the start of a change in the way remorse came to be regarded. Paul in particular uses existing language, *lypē* and *lypeō*, in a new way and with a developed meaning to describe what is now called "remorse." *Metamelomai* is used with a wide spectrum of meaning from "remorse" to "regret."

Second, and as we shall see, interpersonal remorse has only slowly become accepted in the repertoire of Christian ethics, and even then, only in an understated, low-key way. Judas's remorse has been relatively little lauded because it led to such a despairing death; Peter's remorse has been relatively little explored because the example of his remorse and his subsequent experience of forgiveness for denying Jesus are probably regarded as atypical, given his unique place in the early church. The examples of interpersonal remorse in 2 Corinthians are relatively little considered and followed, because Paul uses a word that usually means "grief" or "sorrow" and because what he writes is confusing, opaque, and at times almost perverse. Paul also confusingly uses of himself the same word that Matthew uses to describe Judas's remorse. In Paul's own case, the word clearly means no more than "regret." Nevertheless, in the New Testament, the framework of an ethic of interpersonal remorse is set. This framework is modelled not on the tenets of Greek philosophy, for Greek philosophy militated against the development of an ethic of interpersonal remorse, but (as we shall see at various points in this book) on the gospel itself.

Chapter 5

Christian Remorse after the New Testament

WE COULD CALL MUCH of the period after the close of the New Testament and at least until the Reformation "the Age of Remorse," for it is a time with a well-developed and widely recognized theology of sin. It is also a time during which being deeply regretful about sin is an important characteristic of Christian spirituality.

In this period, Catholic theologians use the word *contritio* (contrition) to describe deep regret about sin. Less often they use the word *compunctio* (compunction or, in modern English, remorse). The two words are not synonyms, for, as we shall see at the Council of Trent (1543–63),[1] contrition is described as also including "a firm purpose of not sinning in the future," which is not a necessary part of what it means to be remorseful. This period is therefore more obviously the "Age of Contrition" than the "Age of Remorse," even though, in relation to deep regret or guilt about sin, the titles amount to much the same.[2]

---

1. The Council sought to restate and clarify traditional Catholic doctrines following the Reformation.

2. Roberts prefers to use the word "contrition" to describe what he calls the "central phenomenon of the Christian life" (*Spiritual Emotions*, 98). Contrition and remorse mean much the same in the book, though in Aquinas's thought they are categorically different.

Remorse and Penitential Acts

Many pre-Reformation Catholic theologians emphasize the detail of what it means to be deeply sorry about sin and set out how people with consciences troubled about sin could make satisfaction through the sacrament of penance.[3] Catholic teaching put an emphasis on temporal punishment through penitential acts that were aimed at reshaping and reforming sinners' behavior. These acts are sometimes also called "penance" or "mortification." Mortification involves "the subjection or bringing under control of one's appetites and passions by the practice of austere living, esp[ecially] by the self-infliction or voluntary toleration of bodily pain or discomfort" (*OED*). Penance could be "by fasts, alms, prayers, and the other pious exercises of a spiritual life"[4] or:

> not only by punishments voluntarily undertaken of ourselves
> . . . , or by those imposed at the discretion of the priest according
> to the measure of our delinquency, but also, which is a very great
> proof of love, by the temporal scourges inflicted of God, and
> borne patiently by us.[5]

Penance and penitential acts are part of the "sacrament of penance." The sacrament of penance also involves confession of sins to a priest, and the receiving of absolution for mortal sins (that is, sins that put one's salvation at grave risk).[6]

In the early period of the church, those who had committed grave sins sometimes confessed their sins to the bishop, and after completing penitential acts (such as fasting, pilgrimages, helping to build or repair churches) would receive absolution from the bishop or from the bishop's representative. Penitents were often required to wear discrete clothing to mark themselves out; they were also required to sit separately in churches.

By the Edict of Milan in AD 313, those who had committed grave sins could enter the Order of Penitents. Penitents were given public penance and they were required to worship separately from those outside the Order. Restrictions, called "interdicts," were placed on penitents. Interdicts could

3. Aquinas does occasionally use the phrase "remorse of conscience" (*remorsum conscientiae*), e.g., at various points in *ST* IIa.q.85–8.

4. Chapter XIV of Session VI of *On Justification* at the Council of Trent.

5. Chapter IX of the First Decree *On the Most Holy Sacraments of Penance and Extreme Unction* of Session XIV at the Council of Trent. Penance is also discussed in the First Decree of Session VI, *On Justification*, at the Council of Trent.

6. See chapter I of the First Decree *On the Most Holy Sacraments of Penance and Extreme Unction* at the Council of Trent; see also Kaster, *Emotion* and Sorabji, *Moral Conscience*, 73–96.

include the requirement to abstain from conjugal relations or (for the single) not to marry; sometimes interdicts were imposed for life. In the fifth and sixth centuries, entering a monastery could be a substitute for public penance.

Outside the Order, Irish missionaries introduced regular, individual confession of sins, followed by appropriate penance. The style and content of the penance were intended appropriately to match the gravity of the sins confessed. In the sixth to the eleventh centuries especially, *libri poenitentiales* were circulated: they were "some of the most ambitious encyclopedias of vice ever composed in any language . . . [with] a range of sins unflinchingly catalogued"[7] and with penalties prescribed. Some of the *libri* were even translated from Latin into the vernacular. Before the thirteenth century, penance was sometimes almost an adjunct of the secular law, as some of the *libri* are "scarcely distinguishable from contemporaneous works of secular law, imposing fines rather than penances for various acts of violence."[8] The practice of penance became more of a distinctive rite and less of an adjunct to secular law after the Fourth Lateran Council of 1215.

Especially before the Lateran Council, penance continued to be severe, and included fasting (sometimes for lengthy periods), increased church attendance, and even pilgrimages, with the pilgrims in some cases wearing or carrying indications of the sins for which they were paying penance. In Europe particularly, there was also the practice of public, ritual humiliation,[9] such as by corporal punishment or through requiring penitents to wear yellow crosses. This latter practice sometimes resulted in the sinner becoming "a community pariah with grave social and economic consequences, such as difficulty or impossibility in finding employment."[10]

By the eleventh century, the practice had grown up of penance sometimes being paid not by the sinner but by a surrogate, usually a monk. The effect was still to pay the satisfaction that was owed to God on account of sin. Kevin Madigan says that "[i]t did not matter who made . . . satisfaction; what mattered was that it was made and God's honor restored (just as a bank does not care who pays a debt to it so long as it is repaid with interest)."[11] In addition, a donor who endowed a monastery would have his or her penance "prayed down" by the intercessory prayers of the community the donor had founded; this was the case even if the donor's sins were egregious. No matter how much penance was said, it was believed by the thirteenth century that

7. Jurasinski, *Old English*, 22.

8. Jurasinski, *Old English*, 26.

9. Postles, "Penance," and Jurasinski, *Old English*, 28–29.

10. Madigan, *Medieval Christianity*, 207.

11. Madigan, *Medieval Christianity*, 53.

penance could only be consummated in *post mortem* purgatory. However, the purchase of indulgences resulted in the remission of some periods of time to be spent in purgatory. There were also occasional plenary indulgences, which remitted all sins and so the full period of purgatory.[12]

The Canterbury Tales written by Geoffrey Chaucer (d. 1400) satirizes and pillories some of the practices of the Catholic Church, including a lackadaisical or money-grabbing approach to penance and indulgences: *The Pardoner's Tale* and *The Friar's Tale* are examples. In contrast, some believe that *The Parson's Tale* is "a confessional manual designed for the priest to use" beginning with "a discourse on penitence and confession."[13] This is in keeping with the existence of *libri poenitentiales* that still existed at the time.

Contrition, Sin, and Emotions in the Medieval Period

Early Christian thinkers after the period of the New Testament were influenced by and in literary dialogue with Greek and Latin writers from the pre-Christian period. They sought to incorporate what they could from these writers, and to rework into the evolving patterns of Christian thought what they understood accorded with the Christian tradition. The Bible remained the framework for Christian thought. Gregory of Nyssa (c.335–c.394) observed that, though secular philosophers could reflect on the soul and the passions as they wished and according to whichever philosophical presuppositions on which they wanted to build, Christian thinkers were constrained by the framework of the Bible, which was "the rule and measure of every teaching."[14]

An obvious point of conflict between pre-Christian writers and the evolving Christian traditions is about the right response to sin: in contrast with the traditions of Greek philosophy, wrongdoers in the Christian tradition were to acknowledge, deeply regret, and repent of their sins. These responses are a sign of virtue and grace, not moral weakness.

Early Christian thinkers also appreciate that true penitence involves responses that include what we might today call "emotions," such as remorse.[15] They also recognize that some responses could lead people into sin,

12. Indulgences are still a practice of the Catholic Church: see 1471–79 of the Catechism of the Catholic Church 1992 (http://www.vatican.va/archive/ENG0015/_IN-DEX.HTM).

13. Delasanta, "Penance," 242.

14. Nyssen, *On the Soul and the Resurrection* (tr. Roth), 50, 58.

15. For a summary of historical research on emotions, see Tamiolaki, "Emotions,"

and (like Greek philosophers) they regard potentially disruptive responses as needing to be brought under control. Origen (184–253) and Didymus the Blind (313–398), for example, "distinguished between spontaneous, involuntary affective movements [on the one hand][16] and passions [*pathē*] . . . over which agents exercised at least some measure of authority [on the other hand]."[17] Of course, not all such responses that we might now call "emotions" (as we do sometimes hereafter) are seen as disruptive. Some, such as love and remorse, are evidence of Christian virtue and discipleship, and so are to be developed as well as celebrated.

The leading medieval theologians explored the place of emotions in ethics—including contrition ("sorrow of soul, and a hatred of sin committed, with a firm purpose of not sinning in the future"),[18] an emotion associated with penance—as part of a godly way to live. What they write can be seen as Christian responses to such of Plato, Aristotle, and the Stoics about the *pathē* that they knew. Augustine of Hippo (354–430) is the leading Christian thinker about emotions in the first millennium in the period of the church[19] and Thomas Aquinas (1225–74) in the first part of the second millennium.

Augustine uses a variety of words to describe what today are called "emotions." They include the words *passiones, animae, motus, affectus, libidines, affectiones, perturbationes*. Emotions (*affectiones animi*) are good and praiseworthy when they agree with reason and truth, and when they are rightly directed by the human will (*voluntas*). If need be, emotions are to be "moderated and restrained" by the mind so that "they are converted into instruments of justice." The result will be that "no one of sound judgment would find fault" with emotions such as anger, sadness, and even fear, if these emotions are directed to save sinners from perishing.[20] As a consequence, "a right life" will have emotions "in the right way" and "a perverse life will have [emotions] in a perverse way."[21]

15–16. Until about two centuries ago, "emotions" as a psychological category did not exist (King, "Emotions," 168 and Lombardo, *Logic*, 224–27; see Dryden, "Passions," on Aquinas and emotions). On occasions, we use the word "emotions" below as shorthand to refer to what medieval thinkers meant by passions, affections, and related words.

16. The Stoics called such emotions *propathē* (instinctive reactions).

17. Layton, *Propatheia*, 262.

18. As defined in chapter IV of the First Decree *On the Most Holy Sacraments of Penance and Extreme Unction* at the Council of Trent.

19. On Augustine and emotions, see Scrutton, "Emotion."

20. Augustine, *City*, 9.5; see also *City*, 14.6.

21. Augustine, *City*, 14.9.

Presumably, remorse (had Augustine referred to it) would be an emotion "in the right way" in Augustine's taxonomy, for he specifically praises "compassion" (which is related to empathy, a constituent element of remorse) as a laudable virtue. He describes compassion as "a kind of fellow-feeling in our hearts for the misery of another that compels us to come to his aid if we can."[22] He also praises the Corinthians[23] for "feeling the grief of repentance" because such grief, another element of remorse that we have identified, is a sign of an appropriate response to sin. Not surprisingly, Augustine disagrees with the Stoics for wanting to achieve *apatheia* (absence of emotion or "equanimity").[24] Elsewhere he argues that "there is no, or virtually no, difference between the position of the Stoics and that of the other philosophers [e.g., Plato, Aristotle] on the passions and the disturbances of the mind. Both sides defend the mind and reason of the wise man against the domination of the passions." He adds that despite what they appear to say, the Stoics "do not really consider . . . passions [such as compassion] to be vices when they occur in the mind of the wise man, just so long as they carry no force contrary to reason or to the virtue of the mind."[25] Augustine says that if all Christians were to eliminate all emotions from their minds, it would mean the elimination of love, an emotion that remains in the life to come.[26] By making a place for some emotions in this way, Augustine makes a place for remorse in Christian theology and spirituality.

Augustine does not write much about the damage that sin and wrongdoing could do to human relationships. Repentance, remorse, regret, and contrition were mainly, for Augustine, Godward-facing emotions or actions. There are hints that he saw that these emotions and actions are relevant for putting right and sustaining interpersonal relations after wrongdoing. However, Augustine does not develop this idea, probably because he saw interpersonal wrongdoing as principally an offence against God and so (in his mind) to be understood as needing to be addressed within the framework of confession to God, of absolution from God, and of penance to satisfy God.

In the later medieval period,[27] the leading thinker about emotions is Thomas Aquinas (1225–74), who was influenced by the recently rediscovered writings of Aristotle.[28] Though Aristotle, like Plato, was a dualist, he

22. Augustine, *City*, 9.5.

23. Augustine, *City*, 14.8, 9.

24. Augustine, *City*, 9.4, 5 and 14.9.

25. Augustine, *City*, 9.4.

26. Augustine, *City*, 14.9.

27. For a general survey, see King, "Emotions," 167–88.

28. For important studies on Aquinas and emotions, see Pasnau, *Thomas Aquinas*; Lombardo, *Logic*; and Dryden, "Passions."

held not to the idea that human beings were two substances, body and soul, but to the idea of two principles that together constituted one substance or being. Aquinas builds on Aristotle's ideas. Aquinas thinks that the soul is two-part, comprising an "animal" part that had to do with the body, and a "higher" part that concerns the intellect and will.

The passions (*passiones*) are situated in the animal part of the soul. Aquinas lists eleven passions in his treatment of the passions in *Summa Theologiae*.[29] Six belong to the concupiscible appetite: love, hatred, desire, aversion, joy, and sadness (or "sorrow"); five belong to the irascible appetite: fear, courage, hope, despair, and anger. The taxonomy of the passions is not exhaustive,[30] as we see below in Aquinas's discussion of the relationship between sadness (identified as one the passions) and pain. Aquinas believes that the passions are reactions with somatic manifestations.[31] An example of this might be a person's emotional responses when attacked.

Aquinas distinguishes "passions" from "affections" (*affectiones*). Affections are responses to what can be understood but not perceived, and without physiological expression necessarily.[32] Examples of affections are truth, justice, and honesty or (to continue with the example of a passion that I suggested above) how one might feel if one *thought* about being attacked. Like the passions, the affections are also situated in the animal part of the soul.

In many ways, Aquinas anticipates some of the modern discussion about emotions. He says that, when passions are governed by reason, they contribute to the moral goodness of actions.[33] This approach to the place of reason seems to correspond to what Magda Arnold means by intuitive appraisal and reflective appraisal. Arnold was influenced by Thomist theology in her approach to the study of emotions. (We discuss Arnold's work further in chapter 7.) Though passions are not acts of the will, Aquinas thinks that people are ultimately responsible for their passions, even if it is beyond their power to control their passions in particular instances.[34]

Aquinas explores the passion "sadness" (or "sorrow") (*tristia*) and considers its relation to "pain" (or "grief") (*dolor*).[35] "Internal" penance is

29. Aquinas, *ST*, 1a2ae.22–48.

30. Dryden, "Passions," 346.

31. Aquinas, *ST*, 1a.2ae.24, 2.

32. Aquinas, *ST*, 1a.2ae.2, 3.

33. Compare Pasnau, *Thomas Aquinas*, 237 and King, "Aquinas," 209 on Aquinas's view on the place of cognition in emotions.

34. Miner, *Thomas Aquinas*, 100–108.

35. Aquinas, *ST*, 1a2ae.35–39, and in Articles 8 and 9 of *ST*, 3a.84, part of the discussion on penance.

sorrow and grief for the sins one has committed,[36] and he says it lasts a lifetime. He agrees, from 2 Cor 2:7, that comfort can moderate grief for sins committed. He also warns that excessive sorrow is sinful because it leads to despair, and so should be tempered.

Aquinas says contrition (*contritio*)[37] is part of the sacrament of penance.[38] The sacrament consists of contrition of heart (*contritio cordis*), verbal confession of sins (*confessio oris*), and satisfaction in works (*satisfactio operis*). "Perfect" contrition is repentance for sin and is motivated by faith and the love of God. *Contritio* is not one of the *passiones* involving sorrow or pain; rather, it is a virtue.[39] When contrition is part of penance and an act of the will (and not merely an expression of emotions), it is supernatural sorrow for sin, stirred up in the human heart by grace and it comes out of a person's reverential fear of God.[40]

Aquinas observes that, etymologically, *contritio* comes from the verb *terere*, "to grind." To be contrite is to "detest one's own will by which sin was committed" and is "sorrow regarding and, in some way, crushing the hardness of the will." Not following God's commands makes people "rigid and hard" and so they need to be "broken" to force them away from wanting to disobey God. Contrition is "breaking and crushing," a "grinding down" to bring people back to God's commands.

According to Aquinas, penitence is an integral part of the sacrament of penance. Thus, a penitent person grieves over sins committed, as they are an offence against God and because the penitent person seeks amendment of life. Penitence was regarded then, as it still is today (though now treated as integral to the Sacrament of Penance and Reconciliation), as having an essential part "[i]n the pursuit of eternal salvation" and "designed to discipline, forgive and console sinners, as well as to restore broken communities, discourage repeated bad behavior and cultivate virtue."[41] It is an act carried

36. "External" penance is confession to a priest, priestly absolution, and satisfaction. This does not last a lifetime.

37. See Aquinas's *Commentary on the Sentences of Peter Lombard,* Book IV, Distinction 17, Question 2 (Mortensen, *Saint Thomas Aquinas*).

38. On penance, see Book IV, Distinctions 14–22 of the *Commentary*.

39. The same is true of *compunctio*.

40. In contrast, sorrow for sin that arises from baser reasons, such as fear of deserved punishment, is not "contrition" but "attrition." Attrition may give place to contrition if the motive for repentance changes to repentance, faith, and the love of God. However, attrition cannot become contrition because the reason for attrition does not include repentance, faith, and the love of God. See Letter, "Two Concepts."

41. Thayer, *Penitence*, 4. On penitence until the thirteenth century, see Sorabji, *Moral Conscience*, 73–96. On late medieval penitence, see Luardi and Thayer, *Penitence*.

out by those who seek priestly absolution for the sins they have committed after they have been baptized.

At this point, what is important to note about Aquinas's approach to contrition—and this is where his approach differs from some modern approaches to remorse—is that he understands contrition to be a Godward-facing virtue, gifted by God through grace, and is not the result of human *passiones*. In contrast, sadness and pain about sin are *passiones*. For these reasons, according to Aquinas's way of thought, modern-day remorse is like one of the *passiones* but not like *contritio*, which is an outward working of a gift of grace. In other words, we cannot equate contrition with interpersonal remorse in Aquinas's thought. We should also note that the approach of Aquinas to interpersonal wrongs is *theo*centric: wrongs against other human beings are wrongs against God. Aquinas does not refer to wrongdoers feeling remorse (or emotions like remorse) towards those whom wrongdoers have wronged.

Two popular medieval works take much the same approach to remorse. The first is the *Ayenbite of Inwyt* (the "again-biting of inward knowledge") or the *Remorse of Conscience,* a treatise on Christian morality, written in Middle English in the Kentish dialect. The book is regarded as a poor translation of the French work, *Le Somme des Vices et de Vertues* by Laurentius Gallus (1279). The English translation is dated 1340. It is an extensive and grim exploration of sin in its many forms; an 1866 edition[42] extends to 271 pages of almost unremitting bleakness. The work is not so much about remorse, as about repentance of sin against God and about the awakening of the inner conscience to the extent of human sinfulness. The treatment of the Seven Deadly Sins is particularly forbidding. The second is a more popular work, a poem, probably wrongly attributed to Richard Rolle (1305–49), called *The Pricke of Conscience*. It was written at about the same time as *Ayenbite of Inwyt*. The poem is thought to have been the most popular poem in Middle English. The poem highlights "the sting of remorse that can lead to repentance."[43] Again, the focus is on repentance towards God, without any thought to putting right or being sorry about offences against other people. James Morey's Introduction to the book describes the range of expressions for remorse in Middle English. They include "prick of conscience," "stimulus carnis" (sting of the flesh), "stimulus conscientiae" (sting

---

42. The version is edited from an autograph in the British Museum by Richard Morris and was published in London by N. Trübner & Co.

43. From the Introduction by James H. Morey (http://d.lib.rochester.edu/teams/text/morey-prik-of-conscience-introduction). On remorse, see also Chaucer, *Troilus and Criseyde* 1.554–57.

of the conscience), and "ayenbite of inwyt" (which Morey here translates as "the again-biting of inner-intelligence").

In summary, despite its emphasis on contrition, the focus of Catholic theology and practices throughout this period were Godward with next to nothing about remorse in the context of interpersonal relations. We can also say that remorse was seen as in the context of what now we call "the ethics of divinity" (with people following God-given moral standards as taught by the Church) and "the ethics of community" (with moral responsibility to engage in the community of the Church and to live under its magisterial authority and teachings).

Remorse, the Reformation and Beyond

The Reformation in England was initiated by Henry VIII's marital problems and led to Henry VIII successfully challenging the power and authority of the Catholic Church in England. The reforms he introduced were influenced by the Continental Reformers, though with an "idiosyncratic" course and outcome[44] that, in the longer term, resulted in the retention of the episcopate, clerical vestments, and choral worship, all set in the context of a state church with royal supremacy and buttressed by the Thirty-Nine Articles and the *Book of Common Prayer*.

Various dissenting movements[45] objected to what its adherents regarded as the incompletely reformed character of the Church of England in its more-or-less final form of the Elizabethan settlement of the late sixteenth century. The objectors included a wide-ranging group called "Puritans"; denominations known as Presbyterians, Baptists, Quakers, and Congregationalists also came into existence and were legally recognized by the Act of Toleration of 1689. In the eighteenth century, a breakaway group of dissenting Anglicans became known as "Methodists."

As to dissenting Protestantism generally, though not a unified movement, its demand was for "faith and holiness."[46] Among Methodists, for example, the focus was on communal life and piety with an emphasis on "a new life, characterized by peace, joy, and confidence." Even though "personal and social change" and "family, industry, and sobriety" were regarded

44. Larsen and Noll, *Oxford History*, xv.

45. In the nineteenth century, dissenters were generally called "nonconformists."

46. Elliott, "The Bible in Protestantism," 584. Remorse and contrition are not referred to in a survey of holiness in nineteenth-century England (Bebbington, *Holiness*).

as important, we can infer that remorse about wrongs against other people was not emphasized.[47]

Generally, the focus and the areas of debate among dissenters included (to varying extents) questions about repentance (principally in relation to sin against God),[48] the primacy of Scripture for faith and conduct, the sacraments, the implications of John Calvin's theological writings, and the importance of mission. Sin was seen as wrongdoing against God, and interpersonal wrongs were relatively little stressed.[49] Alec Ryrie puts it like this: "If repentance allowed sinners to see themselves clearly, it also, crucially, allowed them to see God clearly,"[50] but not, apparently, to put right their relationships with their neighbors. Nevertheless, some saw the benefit of seeking to "aspire to reconciliation and pacification" with sinners, though this seems usually to have been promoted by clergy and not individual wrongdoers.[51] In short, remorse about *interpersonal* sin is not an obvious trope, despite the apparent individualism of some dissenting theologies.[52] In the later period of the twentieth century, dissenters developed new theological emphases that addressed systemic wrongdoing, such as in relation to the oppression of women or the poor, but again generally without asking how individuals best engage with and put right specific, interpersonal wrongs with those they have wronged.[53]

Why is it that Protestantism generally failed to develop a theology of contrition and remorse? Perhaps one reason arises from the Protestant view that faith alone is sufficient for salvation. Medieval Christianity saw moral effort as a necessary part of a person's journey of faith towards salvation, with "moral effort" including remorse and contrition.[54] Martin Luther (1483–1546), for example, had anguished over whether his contrition for sin was sufficient for proper repentance and so priestly absolution. By 31

47. For example, from Holmes, "Methodists," 134–35, 138.

48. Ryrie, *Being Protestant,* 49–62.

49. This is obvious from what is *not* in the series of four volumes of Protestant nonconformist texts edited by Sell, *Texts.*

50. Ryrie, *Being Protestant,* 61.

51. Ryrie, *Being Protestant,* 400–401.

52. We can see this about the Puritans (Packer, *Quest*) and about the early Protestants (Collinson, *The Religion of Protestants,* but see pp. 251–52 on whether such spirituality was individualistic). On nonconformists, see Bebbington, *The Nonconformist Conscience* and Bebbington, *Victorian Nonconformity.*

53. In "Emergent," Lord traces the forms of emergent and adaptive spiritualities of dissenting movements in the twentieth century; none he identifies gives a significant place to resolving interpersonal wrongs by remorse, repentance, and restitution.

54. A better understanding of Aquinas on *contritio* (such as we saw above) would have meant a different approach to contrition.

October 1517 when, according to tradition, he posted the *Disputation on the Power of Indulgences* (also known popularly as the "Ninety-Five Theses") to the door of Wittenberg Church, Luther had come to the view that the grace of God for salvation was not through moral effort, but through faith alone in response to God's call. The ensuing widely held emphasis in much Christian theology that remorse and contrition are the *result* of faith moved the focus of attention to faith as the all-surpassing source of grace in Christian spirituality. Luther's attack on what he regarded as "dead works" and "works of the flesh"[55] for salvation (these include remorse and contrition as prerequisites of salvation) have led later Christian theologians to be cautious about emphasizing the importance of interpersonal remorse and contrition, even though remorse and contrition may properly be regarded as the result of salvation, not its reason.

Of course, there remained a place for Godward remorse in Protestant spirituality. For example, in "Tears That Make the Heart Shine?" Peter Damrau traces what is meant by "godly sadness" in German pietism of the seventeenth century. The emphasis was on self-examination, with the result that believers grieved before God about their sins and about their sinful nature. Among the German pietists, there appear to be no records about reflection on godly sadness for wrongs done to other people, except insofar as they were evidence of human sinfulness before God.

Another example is the Presbyterian kirk in Scotland, where penance and repentance became "arguably the central ritual act of protestant worship in Scotland."[56] However, from the evidence Margo Todd surveys, penance was typically for sins such as apostasy, fornication, adultery, slander, or (less seriously) for absence from the kirk, drunkenness, and quarrelsomeness.[57] Other sins for which people were repentant included "offering hospitality to gypsies, playing the trumpet on the sabbath," uttering "infamous libels and slanderous tickets" and being violent.[58] Even in these latter cases of interpersonal wrong, the kirk did not mandate that remorse and repentance should be directly expressed to the victims of wrongdoing; instead, wrongdoers prayed in the kirk, expressing their repentance and entreating *God* for forgiveness by all offended by the wrongdoing, with the kirk, and not the victims of the wrongdoing, agreeing to the re-admission of the wrongdoer, though sometimes "the role of taking the penitent by the hand to receive him or her again was assigned to a member of the congregation who had

---

55. These are New Testament phrases.
56. Todd, *Culture*, 129.
57. Todd, *Culture*, 138, 135, 157.
58. Todd, *Culture*, 135, 152–54.

been wronged by the offender."[59] A minister could examine a penitent to ensure that repentance was genuine; the victim does not appear to have taken part as well.[60] In other words, victims were sometimes bystanders to and no more than observers of the ritual of penance and repentance in the kirk, although one can imagine that wrongdoers may have sought to right the wrongs their victims had suffered before the wrongdoers were accepted back into the kirk. Nevertheless, the actions of wrongdoers are understood in the surviving records to be offences against God and the kirk, and not primarily against victims *qua* individuals within it.[61]

In the twentieth and early twenty-first century, new churches grew up, often as a result of the Pentecostal and charismatic movements. In these churches, the emphasis is on spirituality, God's intervention through prophecy and miracles (sometimes referred to as "signs and wonders"), the illumination and guidance of the Holy Spirit, and existential encounter with God through the Bible for personal devotion and mission. The focus tends to be on evangelism and preaching, church fellowship, and worship,[62] rather than on a developed theology about interpersonal relationships. There has also been a revival of fundamentalism that, according to James Barr, is characterized by the doctrine of biblical inerrancy, hostility to modern theology and the modern critical study of the Bible, and "an assurance that those who do not share in [the fundamentalists'] views are not really 'true Christians' at all."[63] Those with such spirituality appear little interested in interpersonal remorse but on what they see as doctrinal and theological distinctiveness, unalloyed by what they regard as liberal and Catholic errors.[64] Another important twentieth-century movement is "liberation theology," a movement that aims "to proclaim God as Father in a world that is inhumane,"[65] aiming actively to address contemporary, systemic political issues that are relevant to suffering communities.[66]

---

59. Todd, *Culture*, 167.

60. Todd, *Culture*, 156.

61. See Todd, *Culture*, 170–73 for a summary, emphasizing "the subordination of the individual to the larger community" (p. 173).

62. Rybarczyk, "New Churches," 597.

63. Barr, *Fundamentalism*, 1. Those who identify themselves as evangelical Christians but not fundamentalists often share many of the same views as fundamentalists: see Chapman, "Evangelical or Fundamentalist?"

64. See the conclusions in Bebbington and Jones, *Evangelicalism and Fundamentalism*, 366–76.

65. Gutiérrez, *Power*, 57.

66. Rowland, "Liberationist Readings."

In the post-Reformation period, the exception to the trend of over-looking the place of remorse is evident in the practice of some Anabaptists, such as in parts of the Mennonite tradition, where (especially in the twentieth century) there is a tradition of emphasizing interpersonal remorse as part of promoting peace-building, reconciliation, and conflict resolution, and in developing the principles of restorative justice.[67] John Howard Yoder (1927–97) is an influential Mennonite who brought Mennonite theological thought to a wide audience outside Anabaptist traditions.[68] Another Mennonite, Howard Zehr (b. 1944), is sometimes called "the father of restorative justice"—a system of justice in which interpersonal remorse about wrongdoing has a key role.[69]

In short, Christian spirituality after the Reformation has given relatively little thought to ways to address and put right interpersonal wrongs and has tended to regard them principally as sins against God. There are signs of modest change in some expressions of Christian spirituality in the late twentieth century, such as we see with the Mennonites.

Remorse and the Ethics of Autonomy

Despite the lack of a significant place for remorse and contrition in post-Reformation Christianity, a significant change occurred in the period following the Reformation—a change that took place outside the framework of the Catholic Church and of the Reformation churches generally. In this period, and increasingly following the Enlightenment, the ethics of autonomy (meaningful, self-directed choices about how to live, free from the controlling interferences of others) became important, and the ethics of community gradually lost their dominant place. Western culture became more individualistic, less collectivistic, and this led to a recognition of the place and rights of individuals in schemes of ethics. Ethical values that were more focused on individuals and their needs—and so focused on self-actualization, personal choice, and self-expression—developed as a result. These values prized intellectual autonomy that freed people to pursue their own ideas and interests.

---

67. See, for example, Jeschke, *Discipling*, and an address at the Mennonite World Conference in 2015: https://mwc-cmm.org/content/walking-conflict-and-reconciliation. The Mennonite Central Committee promotes peacemaking, conciliation, conflict resolution, and restorative justice, sometimes with rituals designed to express remorse (e.g., https://uwaterloo.ca/grebel/publications/conrad-grebel-review/issues/winter-2016/complication-mennonite-peace-tradition-wilhelm-mannhardts).

68. See, for example, Yoder, *The Politics of Jesus*.

69. Zehr, *Changing Lenses*. Ron Claassen, another Mennonite, has also been influential in the development of restorative justice.

They also prized affective autonomy and so opened the way for people to pursue positive experiences that benefited themselves.[70]

Various explanations have been put forward to explain how and why these changes came about.[71] The most obvious one is the loosening of medieval Christianity on western thought, leading people to think autonomously, that is, outside the structures of thought delivered by the church.[72] Other suggestions include freedom from threats to survival, coupled with the benefits of economic development that enabled people to pursue "self-actualization."[73] In the more recent past, Max Weber (1864–1920) suggested that the rise of Protestantism also contributed to the changes.[74]

Undoubtedly the lessening of the power and influence of the Catholic Church as a result of the Reformation weakened the strongly collectivist societal structures that had been shaped, and even controlled, by the Catholic Church. Among non-Catholics, there was a move from seeing identity and purpose as coming from participating in church life, from sharing in striving for the goals of churches, and even from identifying with churches and their social structures. Instead, identity and purpose came to be understood as the result of the expressed needs of individuals as individuals understood them outside the common goals of churches and the churches' narratives of self-understanding. Personal autonomy, self-fulfillment, and the importance of individuals and their rights, rather than duties and obligations set by churches had a new place. Room was thereby made for interpersonal remorse to develop in the repertoire of interpersonal human emotions that were thought about, understood, and analyzed.

In an important book, *Modernity and Self-Identity* (1991), Anthony Giddens has described the characteristics of "modernity," a way of thinking and being in post-feudal Europe and other nation states that are industrialized and capitalist. Modernity has come about as a result of "the breakaway from fixed practices of the past" and from "increasing social control over . . . life's circumstances."[75] He says modernity is "emancipated . . . from

70. For a brief history of the changes, see McGrath, "Transition," and Kent, "Transition."

71. See Sorabji, *Moral Conscience*, 127–200 who traces the history of the movement for freedom of conscience from the seventeenth century to the mid-twentieth century.

72. Carroll, *The Wreck of Christian Culture*. In *Origins*, Macfarlane argues that individualism in English society extends back as far as the thirteenth century.

73. Maslow, *Motivation*.

74. But compare Todd, *Culture*, 173–74.

75. Giddens, *Modernity*, 211.

conditions of hierarchical domination"[76] and from "the dogmatic imperatives of tradition and religion."[77] Thus, modernity is:

> a post-traditional order, in which the question, "How shall I
> live?" has to be answered in day-to-day decisions about how
> to behave, what to wear, and what to eat—and many other
> things—as well as interpreted within the temporal unfolding
> of self-identity.[78]

The result is that individuals have "achieved a certain level of autonomy of
action"[79] and so have "lifestyle options . . . guided only by the morality of
'authenticity.'"[80] As for "authenticity," it is "a pre-eminent value and a framework for self-actualization."[81]

What this means in practice is "the reflexive project of the self [has
come] to the fore."[82] This is "a process whereby self-identity is constituted
by the reflexive ordering of self-narrative"[83] and is the result of the "modern
self" longing for "a sense of wellbeing."[84] In this new pattern of thought,
justice and equality have become important values of self-identity, and it is
easy to see why interpersonal remorse has come to the fore, for remorse is
a way for people to acknowledge that they have treated others unjustly and
without regard for their status as equal human beings. Relationships and
trust (which Giddens calls "intimacy") are also important in the ethics of
modernity; remorse is an emotion that acknowledges one has defiled such
a relationship and trust.[85]

Giddens's purpose is mainly to reflect on the characteristics and consequences of modernity in a global and political setting. He also reflects
on how existential questions about self-identity and personhood have an
influence on questions affecting moral issues concerning the self and body.[86]
His book points to the way that the ethics of "modernity" and the "late modern age" could lead to a new interest in remorse, repentance, and regret.

76. Giddens, *Modernity*, 14.

77. Giddens, *Modernity*, 210.

78. Giddens, *Modernity*, 14.

79. Giddens, *Modernity*, 214.

80. Giddens, *Modernity*, 226.

81. Giddens, *Modernity*, 9.

82. Giddens, *Modernity*, 155.

83. Giddens, *Modernity*, 224.

84. Giddens, *Modernity*, 171.

85. In many ways, Giddens's concept of the "ethics of modernity" corresponds with
how we have been describing "the ethics of autonomy."

86. See Giddens, *Modernity*, 221, for example.

To restate Giddens's case in the context of the language of this book, there were new opportunities for individuals to act autonomously and to make lifestyle choices that are guided not by the ethics of divinity or by the ethics of community but by the morality of authenticity and self-actualization. In other words, the ethics of autonomy are now embedded in structures of what Giddens calls "the late modern age."

Of course, as we saw in chapter 2, not all sociologists and anthropologists hold to a view of people as autonomous individuals. We can go further: we can no more than correlate the rise of individualism and the ethics of autonomy with social, political, and economic changes. Modern Catholic social teaching, beginning with Pope Leo XIII's encyclical *Rerum novarum* (1891) and continued by successor Popes since then and in the Second Vatican Council (1962–65), has also attempted to restrict the hegemony of the ethics of autonomy in modern thinking, and to reintroduce a place for social justice and the idea of the common good in ethical decision-making.[87]

Surprisingly, despite the changes in secular thinking and practice, Christian theology has failed to develop a theology of interpersonal remorse in the period after the Reformation, as we have seen. In later chapters, we show that it has been secular thinkers and writers, beginning most obviously in the twentieth century, who have "discovered" interpersonal remorse (along with the longer- and better-known emotions of regret, shame, compunction, guilt, and so on), given it a discrete label, and explored its ambit in interpersonal relations. One result has been that the offence of wrongs against other people has come to be seen more clearly for what it is, namely an affront to their integrity and personhood. The subject of the wrongdoing is now not God but other human beings.

Remorse and Interpersonal Forgiveness

The latter half of the twentieth century has seen a new interest in the study of interpersonal forgiveness among philosophers, psychologists, and, more recently, theologians. The result has been a newly discovered appreciation of and place in theology for interpersonal forgiveness; one might have expected a newly revived (if not newly discovered) theology of interpersonal remorse alongside the renewed interest in forgiveness, for regret, remorse, and repentance usually precede interpersonal forgiveness. So far, in Christian theology, perhaps surprisingly, this has not been so.

87. See, for example, DeBerri and Hug, *Catholic Social Teaching*; Himes, *Modern Catholic Social Teaching*; and Kim, *Introduction*.

An example of an omission to reflect on remorse is in the work of Archbishop Desmond Tutu in the Truth and Reconciliation Commission in South Africa. The Promotion of National Unity and Reconciliation Act (1995), which set up the Commission, provided that those who acknowledged and made to the Commission "full disclosure of all relevant facts" (Section 20(1) (c)) relating to acts committed under the former *apartheid* regime that were associated with a political objective and that amount to gross violations of human rights could obtain amnesty from prosecution for their crimes. The aim of this approach was to bring about (in the words of the Act) outcomes such as "reconciliation" and "restoration" through truth-telling.

Archbishop Tutu believed that it was important that those who appeared before the Commission and who acknowledged their crimes should be forgiven by those they had wronged. Victims were to forgive, whether or not the wrongdoers showed evidence of remorse or regret: all that was required of wrongdoers was that they should do what the Promotion of National Unity and Reconciliation Act required, namely, fully to disclose their crimes to the Commission. Tutu believed and repeatedly said that, so long as there was *acknowledgment* of wrongdoing, forgiveness would be beneficial for the well-being of the victims, as well as beneficial for South African society generally. (Tutu went further at other times. He believed that it was right for victims to forgive unconditionally, even when the wrongdoing was perpetrated by unknown individuals on behalf of state institutions.)[88] It is important to observe at this point that the introduction of the idea of forgiveness into the South African Truth and Reconciliation Commission was at the initiative of its Chair, Archbishop Tutu, for promoting forgiveness was not one of purposes of the Commission or even mentioned in the 1995 Act.

Tutu's approach strongly reflects the ethics of community. He fused the individualistic Christian notion of forgiveness with the African view of forgiveness, which is captured by the corporate idea of *ubuntu*, a concept that assumes that corporate and social needs take priority over what is personal or individualistic.[89] However, Tutu's approach to interpersonal forgiveness does not take into account that interpersonal forgiveness usually best takes place in the context not only of acknowledgment of wrongdoing by wrongdoers but also of evidence of regret, remorse, and appropriate acts of reparation. It is true that the 1995 Act made provision for financial reparations for victims of wrongdoing under the *apartheid* regime. The reparations came from the national government of South Africa. The

88. Tutu's views on forgiveness are set out in Tutu 1999 and in Wiesenthal, *The Sunflower*, 268.

89. Battle, *Reconciliation*.

amount of the reparations was regarded as too little, and as coming too late. Even more importantly in my view, the reparations did not come from the wrongdoer. In other words, those who did the wrong did not need to show remorse or repentance, whether by words, attitudes, or actions: they only had to acknowledge that they had done wrong and make full disclosure. Many victims felt that they were being pressured to forgive without receiving justice for what they had suffered. To put it bluntly, an ethic that regards unconditional forgiveness (that is, forgiveness that takes place outside remorse, repentance, and reparations or appropriate acts of restitution) as a moral good is an enfeebled ethic that produces short-term "fixes" but not long-term good for victim and wrongdoer alike.[90]

Remorse and Contemporary Christian Spirituality

Modern Christian spirituality recognizes the disabling power of a conscience affected by remorse and guilt; it has also retained long-held practices and rituals that symbolically or (in the minds of some) actually purge guilt before God and wash the conscience clean.[91] Remorse is an important, but significantly under-regarded, emotion in the repertoire of Christian ethics that is integral to Christian spirituality. As we saw in chapter 1, Robert C. Roberts regards contrition (which is another name for remorse) as one of the "especially fitting ways to grasp the central Christian truths."[92] To neglect remorse in both its Godward-facing forms and its interpersonal forms is to neglect an important component of Christian spirituality.

The Catholic Church

In the modern Catholic sacrament of penance, a priest, on behalf of God, hears confession of sins and pronounces God's absolution, just as in the medieval period. Still integral to the sacrament are contrition and penitence: they result from self-examination and are evidenced by determination not to do wrong again.

90. See Cose, *Bone to Pick* for anecdotal examples. For more on the Commission and Tutu's role, see Bash, *Forgiveness and Christian Ethics*, 107–10, 124–27.

91. In part, this development is due to the "rediscovery" of emotions in Christian thought and spirituality: see Pattison, *Challenge*, 185–92.

92. Roberts, "Emotions as Access," 83.

Contrition and penitence are still, as formerly, outward expressions of feelings of sorrow or regret for having done wrong, that is, for having sinned. They can be a form of remorse, expressing deep regret or guilt. In the sacrament they are Godward-facing responses, though they can be about wrongs that people do to one another and regarded as sins against God. The wrongdoing (or sin) may be venial (at the less severe end of the spectrum of severity) or mortal (regarded as a grave threat to salvation).

Besides pronouncing absolution, the priest can determine penance, that is, penitential actions the wrongdoer is to do. The actions are intended to be ways for the wrongdoer to demonstrate feelings of sorrow or regret about the wrongs. In carrying out the penance, the wrongdoer demonstrates evidence of repentance, that is, amends for the wrong, and satisfaction and expiation for the wrong.[93] In modern Catholic theology, "penance" is now also regarded as a moral virtue, like penitence.[94] Sin and remorse about sin are primarily set in the framework of the ethics of divinity, and it is fair to say that the Catholic Church still does not have a well-developed theology of interpersonal remorse as part of the sacrament of confession. Significantly, the *Catechism of the Catholic Church* (1992)[95] describes "The Sacrament of Penance and Reconciliation" as being for "pardon from God's mercy for the offense committed against him"[96] without reference to offences against individuals, though part of what it means to offend against God could include offences against individuals. The word "remorse" does not occur in the English index of the *Catechism*.

The Church of England

The Church of England has developed three services in *Common Worship: Christian Initiation* that seek to address how penitents may be restored after "separation through sin." The first and third services are for corporate settings and need not concern us further. The second is called "The

---

93. The sacrament of penance fits comfortably with a Freudian interpretation of remorse. For Freud, remorse is the sense of guilt that arises after having committed a misdeed and "is itself a punishment and can include the need for punishment" (*Civilization*, 131, 136). What the sacrament adds is a promise of expiation and forgiveness after remorse and punishment.

94. See, for example, "The Virtue of Penance" in http://www.newadvent.org/cathen/11618b.htm.

95. http://www.vatican.va/archive/ENG0015/_INDEX.HTM.

96. *Catechism of the Catholic Church*, 1422. See also 1440. The sacrament is considered in 1422–98.

Reconciliation of a Penitent" and is in two forms.[97] They both include confession of sin to a priest, an act of contrition, and absolution.

In the services, confession is made to God and to the priest, and not to the victim. Wrongdoers will then hear pronounced of themselves that they are the recipients of divine forgiveness (and so, according to the liturgy, that they are recipients of reconciliation to the community of the church) even if they have neither sought nor received the forgiveness of or reconciliation with their victims. This approach addresses guilt and remorse about sin from a Godward perspective and from a community's perspective; however, it does not make a place for the voice of victims or ensure that those who have wronged others have sought to be restored to those others.

The nearest the services come to encouraging engagement between wrongdoers and victims is in the Exploratory Guidelines,[98] which state:

> The priest should give whatever help may be required to enable the penitent to articulate those sins for which absolution is desired. Such help will often be given before the liturgical rite is celebrated as part of an extended pastoral conversation. . . . Sometimes, in the light of such counsel, particular issues may be clarified and motives examined: the role of the priest is to enable the penitent to make confession with integrity.

The prefatory material to the Act of Contrition also encourages "the penitent to make restitution and may recommend some prayer or action as a sign of repentance."[99] Nevertheless, it seems surprising that the church should have developed a liturgy that omits to make a place for recognizing the pain, suffering, and emotional violation of the victims of a penitent's wrongdoing; it is also surprising that absolution can be pronounced without making it mandatory for wrongdoers first to be forgiven by and reconciled with those they have wronged. The pattern in Matthew's Gospel is that wrongdoers should *first* seek reconciliation with those whom they have wronged and *then* attend to worshipping God (Matt 5:24). One might have expected this to be the pattern for the service called "The Reconciliation of a Penitent." It is hard to avoid the impression that the approach of the services to restoring people and communities affected by sin fails to do justice to the complex ethical, social, psychological, and *theological* issues that usually also need to be addressed.[100]

97. *CW-CI*, 266–89.

98. *CW-CI*, 267.

99. *CW-CI*, 276, 283.

100. A report (entitled "Report of the Seal of the Confessional Working Party") from the Church of England in 2019 offers a more nuanced approach: https://www.

As for regular services in the Church of England, remorse continues to be thought of as a theocentric emotion in response to sin against God. We see this clearly in some of the forms of public, corporate confession of sin that have been an integral part of many Christian liturgies throughout the period of the history of the church. In "Morning Prayer" and "Evening Prayer" according to the *Book of Common Prayer* (1662), for example, the words of the confession are:

> Almighty and most merciful Father; we have erred, and strayed from thy ways like lost sheep. We have followed too much the devices and desires of our own hearts. We have offended against thy holy laws. We have left undone those things that we ought to have done; and we have not done those things we ought to have done; and there is no health in us. But thou, O Lord, have mercy upon us, miserable offenders. Spare thou them, O God, which confess their faults. Restore thou them that are penitent . . . .[101]

A modest change took place in the late-twentieth century as the idea of remorse and remorsefulness in relation to interpersonal wrongs came to be explored. The change is reflected in the form of confession for Holy Communion in the revised liturgy of the Church of England in the Prayers of Penitence in the *Alternative Service Book* (1980); the change was also carried into the liturgy in *Common Worship*.[102] The confession includes the phrase (which I have italicized in the following quotation) "we have sinned against you *and against our neighbour.*" The confession seeks God's forgiveness for the sin against God of wronging one's neighbor.[103] It seems to assume that worshippers have already sought and obtained the forgiveness of their neighbors.[104] Significantly, there is no place in the service that emphasizes that unforgiven interpersonal wrongdoing needs to be addressed

---

churchofengland.org/more/media-centre/news/working-party-report-ministry-confession. The Report says that "[r]econciliation through Christ always concerns both reconciliation of the other with God and of those who have done wrong with those against whom it has been done. It cannot be reduced to a private 'transaction' between God and the penitent, insulated from human relationships and from the need for justice" (paragraph 1.10).

101. A similar style of confession is used in the service of Holy Communion.

102. See *CW-SP*.

103. The confession could also imply that to wrong one's neighbor is to sin against one's neighbor. Generally, "sin" is the word to describe wrongdoing against God, not other human beings. The words are also ambiguous because they could suggest to some that to confess to God one's sin against a "neighbor" is an effective way of addressing (and even resolving) the sin against one's neighbor.

104. In the same, way, the "exchange" of "the peace" also assumes that worshippers are in good standing with one another.

interpersonally before one comes to worship or as a result of conviction in the service. In other words, person-to-person wrongdoing is triangulated with sin against God and is seen from a Godward perspective.

The Language of Christian Remorse and Secular Contemporary Thought

Outside modern church traditions, penitence tends to be an unfashionable idea in today's world. There are exceptions. Linda Radzik, for example, in *Making Amends*, has sought to understand atonement, which of course presupposes penitence, in a secular framework. R. A. Duff suggests that punishment for crime should be understood to be a form of penance, a self-imposed suffering, which expresses contrition and is socially restorative.[105] His view has been criticized on the grounds that the essence of penance is voluntary choice to make amends[106] as well as reformation and restoration,[107] whereas the objectives of legally imposed sentences for crime are usually punishment and retribution.[108]

Despite these modern attempts to link modern secular practices with some of the language and practices of the church, the narrative underlying the symbolism of confession, penitence, penance, and contrition is now largely lost on many people in an age that is increasingly post-Christian. Even so, the need for mechanisms and rituals remains if the "ayenbite of inwyt" (the bite of the inner conscience) is to be assuaged. Psychological therapy now often takes the place of religious practices.

Concluding Thoughts

In the period after the New Testament, Christianity developed a rigorous theology of remorse towards God for sins against God. There was—and remains—little thought about remorse towards people for wrongdoing that affects people. Despite the saying of confession in many churches, which usually contains an acknowledgment of sin "against God and our neighbor," as in the service of Holy Communion in *Common Worship*,[109] little

105. Duff, *Trials*. On retributive self-punishment, see Radzik, *Making Amends*, 30–44.

106. Sandis, "Public Expression."

107. Baker, "Penance."

108. On the differences between retribution and penance, see Duff, "Intrusion"; Murphy, *Punishment*, 115; and Weisman, *Showing Remorse*.

109. *CW-SP*, 169, for example.

thought has been given to what it means to "sin" against one's neighbor or how people can put right such "sin." The emphasis has been on love for God, and not on love for God *and* neighbor, as pointed out powerfully by Lisa Sowle Cahill in a different context.[110] The services called "The Reconciliation of a Penitent" in *Common Worship: Christian Initiation* in the Church of England missed an important opportunity to address the omission. As we see in the next chapter, it has been largely secular philosophers and thinkers who have explored the nature, form, and framework of interpersonal remorse. As a result, Christian theology now has the opportunity to develop a coherent theology of interpersonal remorse, reflecting and where necessary adapting modern reflection about interpersonal remorse.

110. Cahill, *Global Justice*, 1.

Chapter 6

Remorse in Contemporary Understanding

REMORSE, BEING REMORSEFUL, AND remorsefulness are important modern cultural markers. Apart from a new object (people, rather than God), the words have not gone "out of fashion" in popular thinking in the way that, for example, the words "compunction" and (to some extent) "penance" and "penitence" are not now in widespread use.

In contemporary thinking, the noun "remorse" refers to an emotion, typically deep regret or guilt, which describes one of the ways wrongdoers may respond if they have done something wrong.[1] "Remorseful" is an adjective that describes a response of remorse (literally, to be "full" of remorse); "to be remorseful" is the state of being or the condition of being remorseful; and "remorsefulness" is a noun that describes the continuing condition of a person who has remorse about either one or many wrongs. It can also describe a disposition or character trait.

---

1. On modern studies of remorse, see Thalberg "Remorse"; Rosthal, "Moral Weakness"; Thalberg, "Rosthal's Notion"; Teichman, "Punishment and Remorse," 344–46; Cox, *Remorse and Reparation*; Tudor, *Compassion and Remorse*; Fulkerson, "Metameleia"; Kierkegaard, *Purity*, 10–12; Proeve and Tudor, *Remorse* (from a legal and psychological point of view); Fulkerson, *No Regrets*, 15–18; Smith, *Justice through Apologies*. On remorse and psychotherapy, see the double issue of volume 5 of *The Psychotherapy Patient* (1988). On remorse and self-forgiveness, see Kelley, "Jankélévitch and Gusdorf." On remorse and its relation to *paenitentia* ("regret" in Latin), see Kaster, *Emotion*, 80–83. See also the comments on remorse in Taylor, *Pride, Shame, and Guilt*, 97–107, and Taylor, "Guilt and Remorse"; Roberts, *Essay*, 222–27; Konstan, *Before Forgiveness*, x and 59; and Roberts, *Moral Life*, 169–71 and 174–76. See Switzer, "Remorseful Patient," 275–90 (remorse as sorrow) and Willis, "Prisoner," 301–15 (remorse as grief). On the difference between remorse and regret, see Taylor, "Guilt and Remorse," 66–77.

Laurel Fulkerson summarizes the place of remorse in contemporary, secular thinking. She writes that "remorse is central to a conception of the individual as a moral actor in the western world. It is how we distinguish the morally repugnant (so-called sociopaths) from the morally sound."[2] She also rightly observes that remorse is "undertheorized . . . in the modern world"[3] and says that studies are confined mainly to the fields of jurisprudence and clinical psychology. We might add that in the contemporary, as well as in the pre-modern, world, theologians have thought relatively little about interpersonal remorse.

Describing Remorse

We explore contemporary remorse in this chapter drawing on three models at various points.

Adapting one way to classify the properties of emotion-states,[4] we can say that, like all emotions, remorse may be described by its properties in at least six ways: its scalability (the degree of its intensity), its valence (the degree of its unpleasantness), its persistence (the extent to which it outlasts its initial cause), its bodily effects (how remorse affects the whole organism, such as by a raised heartbeat as well as by neurological pointers), its automaticity (the fact that the emotions that comprise remorse are not deliberate, voluntary, or a matter of choice), and its importance as a socially communicative signal (a way of showing how we appraise what we have done).

Being remorseful also usually touches three discrete relationships. Most obviously, it can touch the wrongdoer's relationship with the victim. It also touches the wrongdoer's relationship with himself or herself with feelings that may be variously called remorseful, contrite, or regretful. Being remorseful can sometimes (but not always) extend to the victim's relationship with third parties, people whom Piers Benn, writing in a different context, calls "secondary" or "tertiary" victims, that is, people indirectly affected by the wrongdoing in varying degrees.[5]

Thirdly, Robert C. Roberts suggests that emotions such as remorse are "concern-based construals." He says that "to construe a situation in certain terms is for the situation to strike one, or impress one, or appear to one, as having that character." For the construal to become an emotion, the construal must impact itself and have a causal explanation. In other words,

2. Fulkerson, *No Regrets*, 16.
3. Fulkerson, "Metameleia," 242.
4. From Adolphs and Anderson, *The Neuroscience of Emotion*, 66–96.
5. Benn, "Forgiveness and Loyalty."

there must be the "active concern of the subject [who is] impinged upon by the other dimensions of the construal."[6] This also is a useful starting point for recognizing what may be remorse.

It is important to add that there is a range of ways that people may experience remorse. Remorse may be in stronger or weaker form and may be what Raimond Gaita has called "lucid"[7] or it may be pathological, corrupt, or egocentric. We explore the varieties of remorse below; at this point, we no more than anticipate our later discussion with the brief summary I have given.

Remorse as a Communicative Emotion

Contemporary people recognize more clearly than many in the past that remorse can be communicative, that is, it expresses social and personal awareness that interpersonal behavior has been shameful and fallen short not only of one's own standards but also of the standards that other people hold. To this extent, remorse is an ethic of community. In its stronger form and in its outward effects, such remorse is one way to acknowledge that former behavior deviated from social norms and caused distress to others. It expresses a renewed commitment to societal values and the common good, and repudiation of former wrongdoing. Remorse is also "a form of the recognition of the reality of others—those whom we have wronged."[8] It is "the pained recognition of the meaning of the wrong one has done" and "the recognition of what it means to be *guilty* of having wronged someone."[9]

Because remorse is a communicative emotion, it is also an emotion that concerns relationships. Joanna North refers to the "other-orientation" of regret,[10] which is also true of remorse, a more intense form of regret. Ervin Staub refers to the "connected self"[11] (or what some call "self-in-community") that has positive connections with others: remorse can rupture those connections and even a victim's sense of personhood.[12] Taking up the same thought, Jacqueline Taylor says that remorseful people are likely to act in recognition of their connectedness with other people and so "[be]

---

6. Roberts, *Essay*, 101.

7. Gaita, "Ethical Individuality," 126–27.

8. Gaita, *Good and Evil*, 48–49; see also 51–52.

9. Gaita, *A Common Humanity*, 4.

10. North, "'Ideal,'" 31.

11. Staub, *Psychology of Good and Evil*, 52–68, and 61–64 especially.

12. In Christian theology, some hold the view that not only is "self-in-community" the basis of personhood but so also is "self-in-communion" with God (Rudman, *Concepts*; Gascoigne, *Public Forum*; and Thatcher, *Living Together*).

well-positioned to value others, to be sensitive to their needs, and to help them."[13] If people acknowledge that they have done wrong, their acknowledgment can be a way to re-affirm their respect for the people they have wronged. Remorse does not undo what people have done; rather, remorseful people create a new narrative that enables those who have been damaged by the wrongdoing to experience a measure of social and inner healing.[14] Remorse therefore can have not only interpersonal benefits but also benefits for the wellbeing of the social networks of which people are part.[15]

Remorse is "based on a fundamental ethical identification" with other people and their value.[16] This important characteristic of remorse arises from the human capacity to enter into ethical and social relations. For example, Edward Shafranske suggests that "in remorse . . . the disturbing affliction of estrangement is acknowledged and unburdened" and that the absence of remorse may indicate impairments of the capacity "for empathy and human rapport."[17] In other words, remorse is also in part having empathy for the victim(s) of one's wrongdoing.[18] It is important to add that regarding God as the victim of human sin is to make the mistake of treating God anthropomorphically.

Remorse and Apologies

We have already discussed apologies in chapter 1. We now make some further comments.

The components of apologies are cognitive, affective, conative, and attitudinal.[19] Edwin Battistella identifies what he calls "the social and linguistic diagnostics" of a public apology: they include demonstrating moral awareness of having done wrong, being specific about the wrong and owning to having done it, and not making excuses. The same applies to an apology that is not in a public context.[20]

13. Taylor, "Moral Sentiment," 272–73.

14. About half of volume 63(3) of the *Journal of the American Psychoanalytic Association* explores a psychoanalytic psychology of repair (which includes remorse) after gross human rights abuses (2015).

15. On this dual focus of remorse, see Tudor, *Compassion and Remorse*, 127.

16. Thomas, "Remorse and Reparation," 132.

17. Shafranske, "Significance," 19, 31.

18. I discuss empathy and remorse more fully below.

19. Bovens, "Apologies."

20. Battistella, *Sorry About That*, 86.

Sometimes, public expressions of remorse set in the context of an apology may be no more than carefully crafted words in an attempt at damage-limitation, to win back favor or a lost reputation.[21] Richard Jones has described some forms of remorse in public apologies as "damage limitation worthy of a corporate PR team."[22] Such apologies may be the result of deep regret not for wrongdoing but for the unwelcome consequences of having been found out. Jeffrie Murphy refers to this sort of behavior as "a public linguistic performance";[23] Jean Bethke Elshtain calls it "contrition chic," meaning "a bargain-basement way to gain publicity, sympathy, and even absolution by trafficking in one's status as victim or victimizer."[24]

Seen this way, such public expressions of remorse are "weasel words," that is, statements aimed at suggesting that something meaningful is being said but which, on closer analysis, contain little of value or meaning, or which are not sustained in the longer term by evidence of a change of practice or behavior. The words are little more than cynical manipulation, image-making, evasion, or obfuscation.

One way to test apparently remorseful words is to see whether they lead to the desire for better things or a change of behavior. (Some readers may know that young children may be quick to say "sorry" to avoid adult displeasure but rather less quick to behave differently in the future!) Reparation, restitution, and other actions designed to put right the effects of former wrongdoing can demonstrate that remorse is genuine and has integrity. Roberts regards "deep" remorse as including a sense of indebtedness to make reparation for one's blameworthy acts about which one feels remorseful.[25]

Of course, it cannot be proved whether people are remorseful or whether their stated desire for better things and their change of behavior are only pretense; at best, the genuineness of a profession of remorse can no more than be tested for plausibility, coherence, consistency, and long-term change. Context also needs to be looked at: for example, is the remorse instrumental, to avoid punishment, or is it valued for itself, as a moral good? But even if we are persuaded that someone's remorse is genuine, we can never be sure, and people can be manipulative or devious in order to impress. In short, remorse is easy to fake because no one can know what a

---

21. On falsity in remorse, see also Joyce, "What Neuroscience," 375, 386–87; Murphy, *Punishment*, 144–48; Proeve and Tudor, *Remorse*, 7–28, and chapter 9.

22. Jones, "Anatomy."

23. Murphy, *Punishment*, 165.

24. Elshtain, "Politics and Forgiveness," 11. The phrase seems to have been coined by Shapiro in 1997 in an article in *Time Magazine*: see Jeffrey, "When Is an Apology?" 607.

25. Roberts, *Moral Life*, 170.

person truly thinks and feels, and, despite our best endeavors, we ourselves may not even know what we truly think and feel.[26]

The following appears to be an example of genuine remorse. On the face of it, it appears to illustrate what we shall later see are the principal elements that are typical of remorse, namely, being appalled, bewildered, and sometimes even shocked at what one has done. The example concerns Steve Rannazzisi, a comedian. This is what Rannazzisi posted on his Facebook page and Twitter feed:[27]

> As a young man, I made a mistake that I deeply regret and for which apologies may still not be enough. . . . I told people that I was in one of the World Trade Center towers on 9/11. It wasn't true. I was in Manhattan but working in a building in midtown and I was not at the Trade Center on that day. I don't know why I said this. This was inexcusable. I am truly, truly sorry. For many years, more than anything, I have wished that, with silence, I could somehow erase a story told by an immature young man. It only made me more ashamed. It is to the victims of 9/11 and to the people that love them—and the people that love me—that I ask for forgiveness.[28]

Is Rannazzisi's remorse an example of genuine remorse, or is it an attempt at damage limitation? Of course, we do not know for sure. It certainly reads as a "textbook" example of profound remorse. However, it is worth noting that Rannazzisi only responded with a public statement of remorse after a reporter from *The New York Times* contacted him in September 2015 to confront him with the lie, a lie that he had repeated for fourteen years.[29] Rannazzisi may have been remorseful before he was "outed"; however, the integrity and credibility of his remorse would be more compelling, and perhaps more plausible, if he had initiated his statements on Facebook and Twitter before he knew he was to be exposed.

---

26. We discuss remorse (and ways of testing its supposed genuineness) in relation to the criminal law in chapter 9.

27. As reported in http://6abc.com/news/comedian-says-he-lied-about-being-in-wtc-on-9-11-issues-apology/987235/ on 16 September 2015.

28. On apology with and without a request for forgiveness, see Szablowinski, "Apology." Almost certainly, one cannot ask the forgiveness of the dead: see Bash, *Forgiveness and Christian Ethics*, 171.

29. https://www.nytimes.com/2015/09/17/arts/television/steve-rannazzisi-comedian-who-told-of-9-11-escape-admits-he-lied.html.

Remorse, Self-Pity, and Resentment

Sometimes what is loosely called "remorse" can be the result of people being no more than self-pitying, crushed, or feeling self-loathing. Such people often end up "stuck" in this condition, trapped in pathological self-pity and bitterness, and facing what Rowan Williams calls "a real restriction on what [they are] able to think and feel about [themselves] . . . ."[30] It points to a form of psychological self-punishment for being what they see as bad in themselves.[31] To borrow and adapt Gaita's language, and to create a neologism, we might say this kind or remorse is "illucid." This is the sort of remorse, I suggest, that Paul is describing in 2 Cor 7:10 as "worldly grief [remorse] that leads to death."

There is also a kind of so-called remorse that is more like resentment—resentment that arises because wrongdoers know that they have been "found out," seen for what they truly are: dishonest, deceitful, and even perverted. What we see is self-pity, and evidence of an emotional sore in people who know that their folly has been discovered and that what they wanted people to think they were like has been exposed as sham and veneer. They are angry that they have been caught; they do not acknowledge their guilt and personal responsibility; they are not committed to changing for the better in the future. This is the emotion of the hypocrite, resentful about not being successful at tricking others into believing a lie, and without the integrity to change for the better. This is not true remorse, as it is self-seeking, self-serving, and inwardly dishonest. I suggest this is an example of what Michael Proeve and Steven Tudor mean when they describe some kinds of remorse as "distorted."[32] It is also another kind of "illucid" remorse.

Remorse and Empathy

A truly remorseful person understands, engages with, and shares the feelings about the wrongdoing that those they have harmed have experienced. In other words, such people have empathy for their victims, as we said above.[33] They will feel more than sympathy, that is, pity and sorrow, for

30. Williams, *Lost Icons*, 122.

31. If one were to express these thoughts in categories of Freudian psychoanalysis (Freud, *New Introductory Lectures*), we might say that the remorse is one of the expressions of the Superego, a part of the mind that internalizes rules and learned from one's parents and figures of authority.

32. Proeve, *Remorse*, 2.

33. On empathy, see Eisenberg, "Empathy"; Haidt, "Moral Emotions," 861–62 (who thinks "compassion" would be a better word); Tangney et al., "Moral Emotions," 362–63

their victims. The empathy of a remorseful person will have three aspects: a *cognitive* aspect (the ability to identify and understand another's emotions), an *affective* aspect (the capacity to respond with an appropriate emotion to another's mental state), and a *somatic* aspect (a physical reaction to another's emotion state).

Empathy can point to a realization that wronging others is to use and abuse them, and irresponsibly to use power.[34] Wrongdoing can degrade and humiliate another person, and fuse both disdain and one's misplaced conviction of superiority with deviant patterns of behavior. If empathic people become remorseful, it is their consciences' way of acknowledging that their failure, about which they are rightly guilty, has impacted on others, who have suffered as a result. This aspect of remorse is anticipated in the Hebrew verb *niḥam*, which ranges in meaning from "to be sorry" and so to regret or to change one's mind,[35] to "to be moved to pity, have compassion."[36]

There is debate about whether empathy is an emotion. Jesse Prinz thinks not. He says that "[e]mpathy is a vicarious emotional response. Empathy is not itself an emotion but is rather a way that some emotions come about."[37] June Price Tangney et al. describe empathy as "an emotional process with substantial implications for moral behavior" and describe empathy as "a moral emotional process" that is "other-oriented."[38] Tudor also does not see empathy as an emotion, for he describes empathy as "the projection into the situation of the Other so as to feel what he feels."[39] When all three aspects of empathy (cognitive, affective, and somatic) are in evidence, Prinz is right in his description of empathy as an "emotional response," and Tangney et al. are right to call empathy an "emotional process." One of the outcomes of the response or process can be remorse.

(for a useful outline of research); Prinz, "Moral Emotions," 531–34; Zahavi and Overgaard, "Empathy"; and Prinz "Against Empathy."

34. Schweiker points to the importance of using power responsibly and justly, to "serve a value beyond itself, the good of existence" and not for "the valorization of [one's own] power" (*Responsibility*, 226).

35. This is the interpretation usually selected in the LXX. See, for example, Hos 11:8 (noun) and Zech 11:5 (verb). In these places, the LXX translates the Hebrew with the Greek word *metameleia* (change of purpose, regret, repentance) and *metamelomai* (to regret, to be remorseful) respectively.

36. This interpretation is sometimes reflected in modern translations but apparently ignored by the LXX translators.

37. Prinz, "Moral Emotions," 521.

38. Prinz, "Moral Emotions," 362.

39. Tudor, *Compassion and Remorse*, 87; see also 79, 87–92. See also Duffy and Chartrand, "From Mimicry," 456.

Feeling empathy or compassion for another person because of the harm one has caused them can lead not only to remorse but also to "depression, self-hate, and feelings of inferiority."[40] To move from remaining trapped in destructive emotions, one should seek to put right what one can, to learn from mistakes, and to commit to being different in the future. As I have already suggested, repentance, restitution, and acts of penance can be practical ways to put right (as best one can) one's former failures and not to remain trapped in guilt about the past.

As for those lacking in remorse, one reason might be because such people lack empathy and show signs of being indifferent to and callous about having hurt, mistreated, or otherwise wronged another person. Rather than showing empathy, such people might justify and rationalize the hurt they have caused. In effect, they disregard or violate the rights and integrity of their victims, without appreciating or caring about the moral and social degradation they are inflicting. In Gaita's language in *Good and Evil*, they fail to recognize the "reality" of the person they have wronged. We might also say that they lack conscience because they lack "the readiness to feel guilty."[41]

Remorse as Affect

The word "remorse" points to troubling and vexing memories, and to the bite or sting of the conscience when people realize that they have not lived up to their own or others' expectations. We still speak, for example, of "the pangs" of remorse and conscience. Charles Darwin describes "the soul-shaking feeling" that is remorse and distinguishes it from "slight regret or repentance."[42]

The contemporary approach to remorse recognizes that remorse is deep regret or guilt about wrongdoing. It also recognizes that remorse is deep regret or hurt about the pain, hurt, and suffering that one's wrongdoing has caused to those who have been wronged. This is an important change of emphasis and approach in the way remorse is understood. We can trace a development in the way people have thought about the object of remorse: in former times, the object was God and God's moral order; in the Enlightenment period, the object became the moral order (whether or not seen as laid down by God); in contemporary times, the object of remorse includes those affected by one's wrongdoing. In the following exploration of contemporary remorse, we see something of all these approaches in the ways people explain what they mean by "remorse."

40. Hauck, "Remorseful Patient," 14.

41. Freud, *Civilization*, 131.

42. Darwin, *The Descent of Man*, 138.

Remorse, in its most richly textured form, is an expression of one's sense of fault,[43] and one's own judgment about one's acts or omissions in relation to a person or community, or about an event or circumstance of which one is the cause. It is an expression of self-blame,[44] an acknowledgement of personal responsibility for having done wrong. Remorse tends to point to a conscience alerted to and sensitive about one's failures or reprehensible actions. Roberts describes remorse as "a construal of oneself for having blameworthily violated some standard one is concerned to honor, and as being indebted for reparation for it."[45] (This can be the sort of remorse described by Paul in 2 Cor 7:10 as "godly grief . . . that leads to salvation without regret.") We can include remorse among what Peter Strawson has called the "reactive attitudes," that is, responses to good or ill in ourselves that also include attitudes related to blame, such as resentment, indignation, and guilt.[46] It is best to think of remorse not so much as "an emotion" but as "emotions," that is (as we see further below), a compendium of evaluative responses that may include feelings of guilt, shame, disgust, self-blame, and embarrassment, for example.

Remorse reflects the values one regards as important, and amounts to a statement about the status, worth, and integrity of the people who have been wronged. Remorse can arise when people realize they have violated and degraded another person. This is one of the reasons why Gaita says that remorse may be a form of shock, in the same way that grief can arise through "the shock" of losing another person.[47] He says that it can leave the wrongdoer with "bewildered grief,"[48] just as Paul in 2 Cor 7:10, 11 uses the word "grief" almost certainly to mean what in a later period is called "remorse."

In some examples of remorse, the deep regret that one feels may include feelings of shame or embarrassment. Embarrassment is a response to not being seen in the way one wanted or thought oneself to be.[49] Shame

43. Roberts, *Essay*, 222.

44. This aspect of remorse has been little explored. Sher's monograph, *In Praise of Blame*, explores the attribution of blame by one person to another, and not self-attribution of blame; see Coates and Tognazzini in *Blame*, who also explore self-blame.

45. Roberts, *Moral Life*, 170.

46. Strawson, *Freedom and Resentment*. In *Responsibility*, Wallace offers a narrower definition of reactive attitudes which nevertheless is broad enough to include remorse, since he includes guilt among the reactive attitudes.

47. Gaita, "Ethical Individuality," 127.

48. Gaita, *A Common Humanity*, 31, and see 33–34, 93.

49. Roberts rightly points out that remorse is more than embarrassment because embarrassment does not have an object to do with personal failure, namely, one's

is a painful feeling of humiliation or distress caused by believing one has done wrong or is blameworthy. They are subjective responses to one's actions.[50] Bernard Williams thinks that shame, rather than guilt, is more likely to help wrongdoers understand their conduct and to "rebuild" the self.[51] Like remorse, embarrassment and shame are egodystonic, that is, they are thoughts that are in conflict with the needs and goals of the ego or with one's self-image.[52] Acts that repair the causes of the embarrassment can help resolve the psychological pain.

On the whole, remorse is an autonomic response when one becomes aware of one's wrongdoing and its effects, and so not a matter of choice, although one can imagine people who choose to disregard the promptings of their consciences if the feelings of remorse are unacceptable to their conscious minds. Such people dampen and bury their responses. According to psychoanalytic theory, even if they "repress" remorseful feelings, the feelings are likely to continue to influence their unconsciously driven behaviors and affects.[53]

Usually, remorse is not initially obvious publicly or in a widespread way; it is in the first place typically a private emotion, especially because what people mean by "remorse" and "remorsefulness" are feelings and attitudes describing an emotion and an inner condition about one's own sense of guilt. Indeed, many people regard what they have done and the resulting feelings of guilt and shame as not being something they want others to know about; at the most, they want only those affected by the wrongdoing to know about the wrongdoing and their remorse.

Unlike repentance, remorse does not carry with it an assumption that the wrongdoer will necessarily put right the wrong,[54] though, of course, the wrongdoer may intend to put right the wrong, at which point remorse

---

wrongdoing (*Spiritual Emotions*, 101).

50. For a useful exploration of shame, see Prinz and Nichols, "Moral Emotions," 135–36, and Taylor, *Pride, Shame, and Guilt*, 53–84. On the place of shame in remorse, see Tudor, *Compassion and Remorse*, 166–88 and Proeve and Tudor, *Remorse*, 63–70.

51. Williams, *Moral Luck*, 92–94.

52. The term "egosyntonic" was introduced by Freud in his 1914 paper, *On Narcissism*, 67–104. Such a response is evidence that one's response to wrongdoing correlates with one's personality and beliefs, namely, that one believes that one's actions were wrong. The idea has been developed to include its opposite, "egodystonic."

53. Freud, *Five Lectures*.

54. Cf. Thalberg, "Remorse," 554 ("genuine remorse must include a disposition to mend one's ways"); Tangney, "Shame and Guilt," 135; Greenspan, *Practical Guilt*, 135; Proeve and Tudor, *Remorse*, 45; Fulkerson, "Metameleia," 244; and Fulkerson *No Regrets*, 15. Rosthal criticized Thalberg, in "Remorse" on this point (in Rosthal, "Moral Weakness") which Thalberg conceded in "Rosthal's Notion."

will combine with repentance. Such a combination is what Tudor calls "moral acknowledgement" and "remorseful responsiveness" that lead to communicative actions, (which Tudor describes as "the work of redemption" and "atoning acts"), such as confession, apology, repentance, reparation, and even "receiving just reproach and punishment."[55] Remorseful people who do not seek to put right the effects of their wrongdoing have a "weaker" form of remorse, either because they do not experience remorse as a communicative emotion or because they choose not to perform the communicative actions that can follow from true remorse. In other words, true remorse will result in wrongdoers seeking to repair the relational and material consequences of their wrongdoing.

Some actions cannot be put right, no matter how remorseful the wrongdoer, even if the wrongdoer repents. For example, remorse and repentance will not bring back to life a victim of murder. This was the issue Judas Iscariot faced after the death of Jesus. It is also possible that wrongdoers may sometimes not be able to put right the effects of their wrongdoing even if they want to, as their wrongdoing has affected secondary and tertiary victims: these victims may be too remote from the wrongdoer for the wrongdoer to make amends.

A repentant wrongdoer who is remorseful about an act or omission that cannot be put right is in a cleft stick: if the wrongdoer wishes to repent and to put right the wrong to demonstrate his or her moral re-formation, the wrongdoer cannot; if the wrongdoer does not seek to put right the wrong, the integrity of the wrongdoer's repentance (and so remorse) may be brought into question. What typically happens in this sort of situation is that remorseful, repentant wrongdoers undertake self-imposed charitable, punitive, or morally worthwhile acts to demonstrate the wrongdoer's renewed character and moral compass. Such actions were formerly called "penance." A clear example is Nagase Takashi, who became deeply remorseful about his part in the torture of prisoners who helped build the Burma-Siam railway to link Bangkok and Rangoon. To express his remorse in the absence of being able to communicate remorse face-to-face with those whom he had wronged, Nagase built a Buddhist temple at the site of the bridge by the river Kwai, promoted reconciliation

55. Tudor, *Compassion and Remorse*, 45, 189–90. This point was crisply summarized in an article in *The Sunday Times* entitled "Sorry, Cardinal, but Forgiveness Requires a Touch of Remorse" by Brenda Power (19 September 2010), who wrote, "You can't expect mercy while minimizing your responsibility, qualifying your apologies and seeking to dodge the penalties attached." She was referring to a statement made by Cardinal Sean Brady about child sexual abuse.

(especially between Thailand and Japan), was active in pacifist causes, and set up charitable foundations for war survivors.[56]

Herbert Morris summarizes some of these observations clearly but in different language, referring to guilt, which is one of the constituents of remorse: people feel guilt, he suggests, when they are distressed because they have failed to keep to the "internalized norms" they are committed to keeping, with the result that they feel "obliged to confess, to make amends, to repair, and to restore" because they have relational attachments resulting in "a desire to restore bonds."[57] In other words, the distress and guilt that Morris describes correspond with what we are calling "remorse" in its more lucid form. The wrongdoer's response is to initiate acts of restitution.

In summary and for clarification, I suggest that besides *empathy* (see above), remorse in its most richly textured form has four principal characteristics. These characteristics are thoughts and feelings that result in:

1. An acknowledgment that the union of one's moral or personal values was previously misaligned and led to wrongdoing in relation to other people;

2. An inner lament for one's failure to hold to one's values;

3. Disappointment and a sense of shame, embarrassment, and even grief about one's own failure; and

4. Behavior that seeks to put right the effects of one's wrongdoing.

In these four respects, remorse is *interpersonal, retrospective,*[58] and *ethical.* It is also *cognitive, experiential,* and in its more lucid forms directed at *restoration and repair.*

We can also say that remorse is an emotion; that remorseful people direct blame, disappointment, and perhaps even disgust at themselves for being morally at fault; that remorseful people sometimes think that they deserve punishment for what they have done; that they may also feel guilt, and be embarrassed and ashamed; and that remorse is prosocial in its outcome because it can motivate them to behave better in the future and lead them into doing reparative acts.

56. Lomax, *Railway Man,* 251–53. See Nagase's own account in *Crosses and Tigers.*

57. Morris, "Decline," 66–67.

58. Shabad, "Remorse," 113.

Different Kinds of Remorse?

When people are remorseful, the degree of intensity (scalability) of emotion and the degree of unpleasantness (valence) that they feel will vary. So too will the persistence of the feelings of remorse, that is, the extent to which the remorse outlasts its initial cause.[59]

Murphy suggests that remorse involves "more than guilt." Also, in his view, the word "remorse" properly applies only to "those extremely powerful guilt feelings that are appropriately attached only to gravest wrongs and harms" and when "one has inflicted such a moral horror on one's victim that he or she may never again have a secure grasp of their place in the world or the meaning of their lives."[60] In his view, remorse is a "kind of *hopelessness* [that] is essential to the inconsolable bite of conscience" and ". . .seems to involve the idea that the wrong one has done is so deep, has involved such a wanton assault on the very meaning of a person's human life, that one can in no sense ever make it right again—such a possibility being permanently lost."[61] There is no remedy for the harm because the harm is irreparable. In contrast, where a person has guilt feelings about other types of wrongdoing, Murphy seems to suggest that "remorse" is not an appropriate way to describe feelings about the wrongdoing.

Murphy's distinction is helpful for drawing attention ("for conceptual clarity")[62] to the scalability and valence of remorse. It is also helpful for distinguishing between, on the one hand, wrongs in respect of which nothing at all can be done to ameliorate their effects and, on the other, wrongs the effects of which can be mitigated. The way language is used still treats guilt for serious wrongs as "remorse" even when the wrongs can be put right. With different emphases but with the scalability and valence of types of remorse in mind, I suggest that remorse is best thought of as either "stronger" or "weaker" in character.[63] In both cases, we are describing remorse by the "prototype" of what we understand remorse to be.[64]

---

59. The scalability and valence of affect is another way of regarding the word "remorse" as having "fuzzy boundaries" (see Russell, "Circumplex," 1165–66).

60. Roberts seems to limit remorse (which he calls "contrition") to this sort of profound regret because its focus is not so much on a particular thought or deed but on the wretchedness of the "condition or state of the self" that led to the wrongful action as a result of which the "self" is "spoiled" (*Spiritual Emotions*, 100, 108).

61. Murphy, *Punishment*, 140, 141.

62. Murphy, *Punishment*, 142.

63. Bassett et al., "Feeling Bad," refer to different "colors" of remorse.

64. Shaver et al., "Emotion Knowledge," 1062.

To feel remorse in its stronger form is, to adopt (and adapt) what Murphy suggests, to suffer, to feel inner anguish "akin to a kind of *horror*,"[65] and to feel "haunted" by guilt and regret about the past[66] because of having done wrong that cannot be put right, as well as a sense of loss about "an aborted future":[67] no amends, no atonement, and no reparation can ever restore the victim to how he or she was before the wrong occurred.[68] This sort of remorse points to a self-critical moral conscience and carries painful, biting, and even cutting memories about moral failure that taint the future. It is gnawing self-accusation that leads to a fissure at the core of a person's consciousness.[69] Those who experience it have "inner agitation of the heart."[70] From the language of literary criticism, we might say that such remorse is "lachrymal," that is, it has to do with weeping and tears.[71]

James Gilligan is probably also describing this kind of remorse when he describes wrongdoers who are in such "a most uncomfortable, distressing, 'disequilibrating' mental and emotional state that [they] simply cannot tolerate or leave alone, any more than they can avoid wanting to scratch an itch. . . . [It is an] uncomfortable, undesirable and intolerable feeling."[72] John Deigh puts it like this:

> Where the evil one did is irredeemable, where one is responsible for irreparable injury, say, or death, remorse may move one to no course of conduct that resolves it. In these cases, remorse is like grief. Where a person is overcome or stricken with remorse, we may expect, as with the grief-stricken, paralysis of the will to set in. So, too, like grief, remorse tends to an exclusive focus on the past.[73]

I suggest the following if we talk of remorse in its more intense forms: remorse is the "lash" of one's conscience, in response to the folly of behavior that one deeply regrets or to the sort of person one recognizes

65. Proeve and Tudor, *Remorse*, 32.

66. Stern, *Psychotherapy*, xiii.

67. The phrase is in Cerney, "If Only," 235, referring not to grief but to guilt and resentment.

68. Cf. Thalberg, "Remorse," 552 and Fulkerson, *No Regrets*, 15–16.

69. Lévinas, *Otherwise*, 125.

70. Kierkegaard, *Purity*, 11.

71. *Lacrimosa* means "weeping" in Latin.

72. Gilligan, "Agenbite," 4, note 1.

73. Deigh, *Sources*, 50.

one is or has become.[74] It leads to what Tudor in a different context calls "significant suffering."[75]

The feelings associated with these types of stronger remorse never truly dissipate because the offender is trapped in a cycle of despair and failure about irreparable harm that has been caused; at best, in course of time, the "lash" of such forms of remorse is less often felt and its lacerations less obviously deep.[76] This is suffering that, in Aristotle's words (referring to a different sort of suffering), tends to "destroy and annihilate" the wrongdoer's *eudaimonia* because wrongdoing ("evil") has come "from a source from which good ought to have come."[77] These sorts of remorseful people may, in their waking hours, put behind them the memories, but in the night hours, the footfall of remorse will still from time to time trouble consciences that have no more than a veneer of peace. In this sense, remorse can be a deeply merciless emotion.[78]

One implication of these observations is that there is a class of wrongs that are so reprehensible as to be outside the ambit of restoration and reparations or that, because of the nature of the acts, are beyond the possibility of repair. One may be remorseful about such wrongs, but nothing that a human being can do can sufficiently atone for them. The wrong is "inexpiable," to use the term popularized by Vladimir Jankélévitch in *L'Imprescritible*.

The way I have described this type of the stronger form of remorse fits with traditional Judeo-Christian categories of thought, for, apart from by the atoning act of God, the wrongdoer in such cases often believes that the wrong cannot be "expiated" (that is, cleansed or purified from the continuing moral stain of the wrong, with the guilt removed), resulting in reconciliation with the victim and a cleansed conscience for the wrongdoer. The wrongdoer may also feel there is no hope of "redemption," that is, being rescued from the consequences of having done wrong and so of being restored and regaining the integrity, self-esteem, and good repute he or she has lost through having done wrong. Judas Iscariot had this sort of remorse. It is the condition that Paul observed about himself in Rom 7:13–20, and so lamented, "Wretched man that I am! Who will deliver me from this body of death?" (Rom 7:24), before celebrating the fact that the redemption for which he longed came through faith in Jesus Christ.

74. In "Eternal Remorse" 141, Meyer describes remorse as "retributive pain." See also Jankélévich, "La Mauvaise."

75. Tudor, *Compassion and Remorse*, 13, and 42–45.

76. This is what Kierkegaard appears to be referring to in *Upbuilding*, 17.

77. Aristotle, *Rhet.* 1386a.

78. For a clear description of this sort of remorse drawn from literature, see Meyer, "Eternal Remorse," 145–48.

In my view, there are other forms of stronger remorse that relate to wrongs that are grievous but *can* be put right, such as by lies corrected, injuries healed, kidnapped children returned, for example. They can also be corrected through confession, apologies, reparations, and even punishment.[79] Sometimes, remorse of this kind can lead to "rehumanization" so that "the offender proves to himself that he is not a monster but a moral being"[80] and so able to mature as someone who can show "emotional growth" and "authentic concern and compassion" for others.[81] This is the emphasis in Gaita's understanding of what he calls "lucid" remorse. For such growth to happen, the offender will need to move to repentance and (where possible) to apology to experience a renewed inner moral disposition. This sort of remorse is "a needed creative response to guilt and regret" and so "foundational for all psychotherapy" that can lead to "an enlarged moral landscape."[82] Of Christians whose consciences sting with remorse, Søren Kierkegaard says that because remorse "awakens concern" and is an expression of "true inwardness of spirit," remorseful people will hasten to confess their sins and put right what they can, because—not deceived by the likelihood of a long life but having death and judgment in view—they will regard themselves as with "not much time at their disposal."[83] In other words, the sort of remorse Kierkegaard describes impels a person swiftly to respond in contrition and with confession.

Can "rehumanization" happen with the passing of time and no more? Gaita rightly thinks not. In his view what heals guilt and remorse are "repentance, atonement, forgiveness, [and] punishment."[84] Even after these acts, the wrongdoer does not forget the wrong: rather, the wrongdoer learns to remember the wrong in a new and appropriate way. The wrong is not denied, but "re-framed" and "re-configured," seen in a new context after psychological and interpersonal work that heals and restores. It seems this is the way the Apostle Paul regarded his former persecution of Christians (e.g., 1 Tim 1:12–14).

---

79. Nevertheless, the nature of the wrong, its impact on the victim *and* on the wrongdoer may, from a psychological viewpoint, still leave the victim irreversibly scarred and the wrongdoer with a deep sense of unease and shame. This approach to remorse accords with Freud's suggestion that remorse is an expression of guilt (*Civilization*, 131). See Deigh, *Sources*, 81–83 and 86–90 on Freud's explorations of the relationship between remorse, guilt, and conscience.

80. Proeve and Tudor, *Remorse*, 171.

81. Stern, "Psychotherapy," 9, 1.

82. Stern, "Remorse," xiii, xiv, and "Psychotherapy," 10.

83. Kierkegaard, *Purity*, 12.

84. Gaita, "Ethical Individuality," 126.

Of course, this form of stronger remorse sometimes includes the response of people caught in a cycle of despair and melancholy that could be healed but whose psychopathologies leave them trapped in the guilt and shame of their wrongdoing. Such responses are destructive to what Gaita calls "the severity of lucid remorse": they are pathological responses to having done wrong, namely, responses such as self-hatred, being mawkish or maudlin, or wallowing in a sense of worthlessness. He warns that self-obsession and self-indulgence are among the "many and infinitely subtle corruptions of remorse."[85] Such responses are misplaced expressions of shame and corruptions of a sense of guilt, and they distract remorseful people from straightforwardly acknowledging that they are guilty of having done wrong and from seeking to put right what they have done where they can. Tudor elegantly puts it this way:

> There is, of course, a kind of *chronically* remorseful person . . . who "wallows" in her remorseful suffering and does not try to work towards her redemption. For whatever reasons, she has become "stuck" at the stage of suffering remorseful feelings and lacks a desire for "moving on" in such a way as to redeem herself.[86]

In contrast, a cogent example of a person with "the severity of lucid remorse" (which in this case though "lucid" was also inexpiable) is Nagase Takashi, whom I refer to above.

Weaker remorse has some of the elements of stronger remorse, but not necessarily all, and not so intensely. Weaker remorse is more akin to some forms of deep regret, and in its weakest forms is sometimes difficult to distinguish from regret. Roberts calls some forms of such remorse "shallow."[87] Time sometimes heals the frequency and intensity of such remorse.

As with all emotions, remorse, especially weaker remorse, can be understood as being on a spectrum of intensity and clarity, and (to a greater or lesser extent) as sometimes being mixed with, or coalescing into, other emotions. For example, Irene may from time to time recall leaving a friend with a mistaken impression twenty years ago, and still squirm when she remembers what she did. The passage of time, the new circumstances that she and the person she wronged are now in, and the lessons learned from having done wrong now render the remorse no more than an occasional, painful memory. Likewise, if James, who has drunk too much alcohol, makes sexually inappropriate advances to Katherine, his best

85. Gaita, *A Common Humanity*, 33–34. See Pouncey, "Inappropriate Regret," on inappropriate regret.

86. Tudor, *Compassion and Remorse*, 191.

87. Roberts, *Moral Life*, 170.

friend's wife—advances that Katherine resists—James may both apologize to Katherine and her husband and promise to moderate his drinking. He thereby demonstrates that he is repentant. His apology is accepted and the friendship between the three of them is restored. James may recall long afterwards, with embarrassment and shame, the folly of his behavior, thereby showing evidence that he is remorseful. But for most of the time, his former misbehavior is not at the forefront of his mind and he continues to enjoy a social relationship with Katherine and her husband.

There are also some people whose remorse is at the weaker end of the spectrum of remorse but who, if they were to examine their consciences a little more carefully, would find that their remorse should be sharper and more focused. Such people construct psychological defenses to stop themselves from engaging with and feeling the full force of what they have done.[88]

People Who Do Not Show Remorse

There are some people who do not feel remorse but who know that they have done wrong. Lack of feelings of remorse do not preclude such people from repenting, seeking reconciliation, and putting right what they can. Anecdotally, the effect of such actions can be to engender feelings of remorse, but even if the actions do not engender remorse, the actions in themselves are right.

There are other types of people who are so well defended about their wrongdoing that they do not wish to engage with the viewpoint and feelings of their victims, and they do not wish to repent. Such people cut themselves off from the grace of being able to learn and change. They have, in the words of 1 Tim 4:2, consciences that are "seared."

Does Remorse Produce Moral Change?

If remorse produces moral change, we might say that remorse can be the trigger for deep-seated moral re-formation, the fruit of recognizing that one has shamefully failed as a responsible moral agent. Seen this way, remorse is a catalyst for renewal, or a teacher that drives a person to live and act differently in the future. The end-point of this sort of remorse is inner renewal.

I do not think that remorse on its own brings about change. Paul suggests that it does in 2 Cor 7:10, when he writes that "godly grief [remorse]

---

88. On psychological defenses and remorse, see Moore "Re-Morse," and Vaillant, "Where Do We Go from Here?"

produces repentance that leads to salvation [i.e., wellbeing] without regret." Emotions do not produce actions but may result in cognitions that lead to actions, such as repentance or restitution. The outcome may then be moral re-formation, which may be one aspect of what Paul means by "salvation" in 2 Cor 7:10. There is an important difference between being remorseful ("I feel deeply ashamed of and guilty about what I have done") and choosing to put right the wrong and to live differently in the future, which is being repentant. This is probably what Proeve and Tudor mean by "lucid and rational" remorse.[89] Remorse can therefore be an important component of deep-seated moral and behavioral reform, but not the direct cause of it. What we are speaking about is not *remorse* that leads to moral change, but *remorse-with-repentance* that leads to moral change.[90] The fact that remorseful people are also sometimes repentant people has led to the outcomes of remorse and repentance being often spuriously correlated and the two wrongly conflated. It is significant, in my view, that there is no verb derived from the noun "remorse."[91] This lends support to the view that remorse, being remorseful, and remorsefulness are, as I said at the start of this chapter, respectively an emotion, a state, and a disposition, but *not* an action, "to remorse."

It has been argued that remorse that leads to feelings of guilt and to an acknowledgement of personal wrongdoing motivates people "to choose the moral paths in life" and "appears to motivate reparative action, foster other-oriented empathy, and promote constructive strategies for coping with anger." In contrast, remorse that leads to shame is "linked with the tendency to focus egocentrically on one's own distress" and leads to people "turn[ing] tightly inward" and even to anger and hostility.[92] We can restate the research as looking to what I have called "remorse-with-repentance" (corresponding to remorse that "leads to guilt" above) and remorse-without-repentance (corresponding to remorse that "leads to shame" above). In the case of "remorse-with-repentance," people will be remorseful and repentant about something they have done. They may seek to make reparation and ask for (and receive) forgiveness. If so, they are

89. Proeve and Tudor, *Remorse,* 2. In a legal context Weisman argues that genuine remorse involves admission of responsibility, appropriate and evidenced displays of feeling, and indications of personal transformation (*Showing Remorse,* 23–46).

90. Roberts suggests that the intention to amend one's life through repentance is, for the Christian, a response to experiencing oneself "as forgiven or having the prospect of forgiveness" (*Spiritual Emotions,* 107).

91. Contrast, for example, "being repentant," which is a condition and state of mind, and "to repent" which is the act of a repentant person.

92. Tangney et al., "Moral Emotions," 350–55 and Tangney and Dearing, *Shame and Guilt,* 24. See also Tudor, *Compassion and Remorse,* 185–88 on "moral shame" and its relation to remorse.

likely to be able to put the matter behind them because they have engaged in a communitarian, participative process that is usually restorative in its outcome. In contrast, in the case of "remorse-without-repentance," people are likely to face isolation and loneliness, because they have not sought restored relationships or put right former wrongs.

Is Remorse Pathological?

Is remorse "positively damaging, a shackle to be thrown off" and "a morbid condition in need of therapy" because it is "morbid, self-indulgent, or cognitively empty"?[93]

Paul Hauck suggests that the view of "modern psychology" is that remorse is "a product of old-time religion."[94] He argues that remorse is "always a neurotic emotion" because remorseful people, who rightly conclude that they have behaved badly, feel guilt, because their bad behavior makes them "worthless, bad, or evil human beings who deserve to be excoriated."[95] This mistake, he says, arises because they "fail to separate behavior from person"[96] and "rate [themselves] by [their] actions." He adds that we "recognize some folly in our actions and we crucify ourselves for being imperfect to the degree that we would commit such folly."[97]

Certainly, remorse, and the guilt feelings associated with it, can be pathologically perverse, obsessively ruminative, and a sign of failure to have the courage to put another's wellbeing first and so to apologize and to seek to put right the wrong one has done. In this latter respect, it is a self-indulgent emotion (the phrase is Bernard Williams's),[98] and like any emotion, remorse can be corrupted and abused as a result of the psychopathology of the holder of the emotion. It is true, too, that people sometimes feel remorseful about what are not in fact moral wrongs or feel remorse in the "wrong" way, by which I mean, respond disproportionately severely to a wrong, or direct their remorse into emotional masochism or self-pity, for example.

---

93. This view was rejected in Tudor, *Compassion and Remorse*, 129, 133. The discussion in this section is in part based on this book, pp. 128–33.

94. Hauck, "Remorseful Patient," 18.

95. See also Dublin, "Remorse," 161–74; Parsons, "Forgiving-Not-Forgetting"; and Willis, "Prisoner," 301–15; but cf. Eidelman, "Sorry," 175–89.

96. I regard this approach as flawed because dualistic: see Bash, *Forgiveness and Christian Ethics*, 61–62. A much more plausible view than Hauck's is "by their deeds [literally, 'fruits'] shall you know them" (Matt 7:20).

97. Hauck, "Remorseful Patient," 14.

98. Bernard Williams, *Moral Luck*, 44–5.

It is important to say that not all guilt is pathological, leading to psychological morbidity. There is rightly a difference between saying, "I am guilty of having done wrong, and I accept responsibility for having done that wrong" (on the one hand) and "I am guilty of having done wrong, and so I am a worthless person" (on the other). People who have a sense of guilt because they know they are responsible for having done wrong may choose to put right the wrongs they have done and grow in maturity in the future without a self-blame that is a masochistic pre-occupation or self-destructive. Hauck conflates what I describe above as two types of guilt, and appears to deny the former as guilt, regarding it only as "errant behavior" and "undesirable shortcomings."[99]

Richard Parsons advocates that remorseful people should self-forgive so as to "stop wasting time and energy punishing [themselves] for an event which is past."[100] I doubt that self-forgiveness is possible without the prior forgiveness of the victim;[101] I also doubt that a wrongdoer's sense of horror about having acted immorally can be alleviated by a response that is self-interested and self-centered, and neither moral nor owning and remedying the wrong. Parsons seems to confuse self-forgiveness with self-acceptance; the latter is of course possible, even after having done great wrong.[102]

When remorse is a form of psychological self-flagellation, it brings about no more than intra-psychic pain. In such a case, it is likely to be a moral and psychological cul-de-sac, which can lead to despair, bitterness, and destructive self-mortification. In contrast, shame and guilt, and the emotions associated with shame and guilt, are important for regulating "the individual's transactions with the environment and the individual's development of the self."[103] Remorse, of which guilt is a constituent, can be a transformative emotion that leads to healing for both victim and wrongdoer.

To decry remorse because of those who pervert it is to make the mistake of denying and rejecting what is good because of the less-than-good that sometimes corrupts it. There is a place for guilt, and to reject its place and value is, in Gaita's words, to threaten "a proper understanding of good and evil, and [a] proper sense of our humanity and of the independent reality of others."[104] Coherent and principled remorse is an expression of probity and

99. Hauck, "Remorseful Patient," 18.

100. Parsons, "Forgiving-Not-Forgetting," 272.

101. Bash, Forgiveness and Christian Ethics, 13–18.

102. On self-forgiveness, see also Cerney, "If Only," 235–48 and Cherry, "Uses and Abuses," 69–81.

103. Barrett, How Emotions Are Made, 25. See also Baumeister et al., "Interpersonal Aspects of Guilt."

104. Gaita, Good and Evil, 50.

right-mindedness, a reasonable and reasoned response to moral cognizance, that can heal "guilty suffering" in both wrongdoer and victim.[105]

As I have said, when remorse is partnered with repentance, it can lead to change. Victims sometimes acknowledge that knowing that a wrongdoer is remorseful can help the process of healing and recovery, for they come to realize that the wrongdoer is genuinely sorry, has apparently "turned over a new leaf," and may even be seeking to put things right. At this point, the wrongdoer's perceived remorse merges into healing from the viewpoint of the victim, and sometimes also for the offender.

Remorse in Contemporary Understanding and Christian Ethics

We have seen in this chapter that interpersonal remorse has "come of age." After being neglected by philosophers, ethicists, and theologians for nearly three millennia, remorse, as an interpersonal emotion, has now been carefully analyzed and its significance properly recognized. Remorse has also been explored in some works of fiction.[106] The roots of contemporary remorse are in the ethics of divinity, and much of the way we describe remorse, as well as its conceptual framework, come from Judeo-Christian traditions of spirituality. However, interpersonal remorse is now most commonly explored and referred to in secular settings reflecting an autonomous approach to the ethic of remorse, and is relatively neglected in Christian spirituality and theology.

The important point to note about contemporary remorse is that the ambit of the object of remorse (that is, what the *OED* calls "moral wrongdoing") has been expanded and now includes the effects of wrongdoing on individuals. To cause another person to suffer when one does wrong is part of what it means to behave unethically and compounds the initial wrong itself. Of course, philosophers have always had in mind human good and wellbeing as aims of moral philosophy, but philosophers have often approached human good and wellbeing through deontological or consequentialist ethics, with the focus on the ethics themselves, and not on what people suffer when the

105. Gaita, "Ethical Individuality," 126.

106. See Dostoevsky's *Crime and Punishment*. In *Moral Life*, Roberts explores remorse in Dostoevsky's *Anna Karenina* (1877) and Dickens's *Great Expectations* (1861). For the interested reader, the *Harry Potter* books by J. K. Rowling contain some astute reflections about the place of remorse in interpersonal relations. For comments about remorse in the *Harry Potter* books, see especially the essays by Deavel and Deavel (pp. 62–63), Taliaferro (pp. 230–33, 236–39, and 242–45) and Walls and Walls (pp. 253–55, 261) in Bassham, *Ultimate Harry Potter*.

ethics are ignored, overridden, or disregarded. The significance of the horrors of human suffering after wrongdoing have sometimes been understated in the pursuit of rightly formulated ethical principles.[107]

It is particularly surprising that the Christian church has not more robustly recognized that causing others to suffer through wrongdoing is more than to wrong God. The focus has principally been on deontological ethics—with God as the object of interpersonal wrongdoing—and not on the victims of wrongdoing or the anguish that human beings suffer through wrongdoing at others' hands. To love others as oneself and treating others in the way one wants to be treated oneself are the basis of the ethics Jesus taught. It seems to me to be lamentable that the focus of the Christian church has sometimes not primarily been on these two straightforward principles but on rules, regulations, rubrics, directions, and procedures. I wonder if it is a case of "straining out a gnat and swallowing a camel" (Matt 23:24). The misaligned approach to theological ethics that I have described probably explains why some mainstream churches have not developed a contemporary theology of interpersonal remorse; we discussed the omission in the last chapter and saw it most obviously in the continuing traditions of the Catholic Church and in recent liturgical developments in the Church of England.

Christian theology and spirituality need to make a new place for the Christian virtue of interpersonal remorse as one of the ways to acknowledge and lament wrongdoing, to recognize and take account of the relational damage that wrongdoing can cause, to grieve with those who have suffered the effects of wrongdoing, and to encourage wrongdoers to repair wrongdoing and its consequences. A well-drawn theology of remorse will balance deep regret for and guilt about one's wrongdoing *and* the effects on others of that wrongdoing. Such a theology will better describe interpersonal remorse if well-informed from contemporary critical reflection about remorse, though as we shall see, Christian theology also has an important contribution to make to an enhanced understanding of and a renewed approach to interpersonal remorse.

---

107. Of course, there are exceptions among philosophers: Lévinas (1906–95) and Jankélévitch (1903–85) are notable examples. Perhaps this is not surprising as they were Jewish writers deeply affected by the horrors of the Holocaust.

Chapter 7

Remorse and Emotions

Introduction

ETHICAL BEHAVIOR IS USUALLY best described as a type of action or process. For example, "to forgive" is described in the *OED* as an action, "to give up resentment against, pardon," though to forgive can also be a process.[1] In contrast, ethical dispositions and conditions are emotions or feelings but not actions. To continue with the example of forgiveness, Robert C. Roberts uses a neologism, "forgivingness," to describe the disposition to forgive and to explore the emotions associated with forgiving others.[2] Remorse and remorsefulness are emotions, describing deep regret or guilt.[3] As we said in an earlier chapter, one cannot "to remorse," that is, to act when one is remorseful; rather, if one is remorseful, one may (for example) repent or make restitution—but not necessarily.

We have said that remorse indicates a feeling of deep regret or guilt. With some notable exceptions (such as in the writings of Roberts), relatively little modern theological study of emotions in general has been undertaken. In this chapter, we offer a critical appraisal of current understandings of emotions and the ways people understand both emotions and cognitions to be related in order to develop an enlarged (theological) understanding of remorse.[4]

1. Bash, *Forgiveness and Christian Ethics*, 38 and 166–68 but compare Scarre, "On Taking Back."

2. Roberts, "Forgivingness."

3. Roberts lists 160 separate nouns in English for emotions (*Essay*, 181). Remorse is one of the emotions he lists.

4. I am not separately considering conscience, which I take to mean our

In a provocatively titled book review ("What the Devil Are Emotions?"), James M. Jasper asks, "Are [emotions] one or many things? Are
they part of our culture, part of our social structure, part of our biology?"[5]
His questions point to what is, in contemporary thought, an almost be-
wildering variety of approaches to, and lack of consensus regarding, the
analysis and understanding of emotions and of emotional experience.[6]
For example, in the contemporary period, functionalists approach emotions such as remorse by reference to what a person is trying to do and the
outcomes the person is seeking to bring about.[7] In contrast, Paul Griffiths
says that psychological categories of emotion should be described homolo-
gously (i.e., by similarities due to commonalities), rather than in terms of
shared function.[8] Behaviorists focus on behavior: they argue that behavioral
evidence is needed to establish a psychological hypothesis. This means, for
example, that only remorseful behavior, and not the inner mental process-
ing that leads to remorse, can be the proper object of study.[9] Experimental
psychologists explore brain mechanisms and many regard emotions as
produced by "reinforcing stimuli, that is[,] rewards and punishers" and as
"evolutionarily adaptive as they provide an efficient way for genes to influence our behavior to increase their fitness," with emotions experienced
through "the brain mechanisms of emotion."[10] Lastly, structuralists identify
basic emotions by searching for and classifying autonomic responses, facial
responses, or responses from the central nervous system that are related to
internal emotional states. This model does not give a place to the role of
intentionality in the formation and expression of emotions.

In the western tradition of thought, remorse is sometimes named as an
emotion on its own, a "stand-alone" emotion, in the same way that, for example, anger or fear or guilt are often regarded as "stand-alone" emotions. Remorse is also sometimes called a "complex emotion"[11] (as we shall see below)

---

self-awareness of the moral principles to which we hold, our self-evaluation of our
conduct, and our self-motivation to act in response to our principles. Conscience understood in these ways corresponds to the description of emotions in this chapter and
of wrongdoing in the next chapter.

5. The review is of *What Emotions Really Are* by Griffiths.

6. On the history of emotions see Plamper, *History*, and Frevert, "History."

7. See, for example, Campos et al., "Functional Perspective," 285, 287 and Adolphs
and Andler, "Investigating Emotions."

8. Griffiths, *What Emotions Really Are*. See Clark on Griffiths in "Relations."

9. The work of early behaviorists, such as B. F. Skinner, is now not followed as a
result of Chomsky's review ("Review") of Skinner's *Verbal Behavior*.

10. E.g., Rolls, "Emotion Explained," vi.

11. This is a term used by Griffiths (see below).

by which it is meant that "remorse" is a portmanteau term for a collection of emotions (comprising all or some of guilt, shame, regret, fear, anger, self-pity, for example) which, when taken together, can also be regarded as a discrete emotion called "remorse." Obviously, we are here limited, as well as guided, by the language we have and the taxonomical categories we use. As I say below, words for emotions such as remorse are no more than labels for what we, in our culture and traditions, regard as important to identify and describe. In short, in these senses, "emotions are made, not triggered."[12]

In the last chapter, we set out six of the ways by which emotions can be measured, evaluated, and described: they are scalability, valence, persistence, their bodily effects, automaticity, and their roles as socially communicative signals. In this chapter we use the same criteria at various points where relevant. We should note that approaching emotions in these ways no more than answers *what* is an emotion, such as remorse, from an empirical viewpoint and ties emotions to both bodily and environmental processes.[13] The approach does not answer *how* we know what emotions are, and *why* we have particular emotions on particular occasions. In straightforward terms, an empirical approach to emotions in this way points to the fact that the words we use for emotions are no more than labels that we choose for particular "bundles" of responses; we interpret what we think the "bundle" to be; and as a result we give the "bundle" a name, such as "remorse." Constituents of the "bundle" may be interpreted in different ways (and so given different names) according to a variety of variables, such as context, culture, psychology, environment, traditions, and so on. It is not always clear from a psycho-social viewpoint whether remorse is different from certain other emotions, such as regret or guilt, for example.[14] Sometimes the differences between emotions that we label as distinct from one another cannot be empirically demonstrated, even though we may give the emotions different labels.[15] To put these observations in simple terms, a raised heartbeat may indicate something other than that we are falling in

---

12. Barrett, *How Emotions Are Made*, 34.

13. Scarantino, "Philosophy of Emotions," 32–33. The questions can also be expressed as asking whether emotions are feelings, motivations, or evaluations (Scarantino, "Philosophy of Emotions"), and whether they should be described physiologically or (as in Elpidorou and Freeman, "Phenomenology," 507) phenomenologically.

14. See the different ways Roberts classifies (i) remorse, guilt, and contrition; (ii) regret; (iii) embarrassment and shame (*Essay*, 240). Scarantino seeks to explain how emotions are different from one another by her motivational theory of emotions ("Motivational Theory," 178–80).

15. Schachter and Singer, "Cognitive, Social, Physiological." See also Gaita, *A Common Humanity*, 4, 34.

love. As C. S. Lewis succinctly observed in *A Grief Observed*, "No one ever told me that grief felt so like fear."[16]

One of the underlying reasons for the lack of clarity about what we mean by "emotions" and the varieties of emotions is that the language we use for emotions is pre-scientific and may be referring to only some aspects of emotions. We tend to try to fit the interpretation of our emotional experiences into the language and scientific categories that we have about those emotional experiences. For these reasons, we do not regard emotions for which we do not have words as discrete emotions, and we conflate such emotions with other emotions for which we do have words. (To my chagrin, I can give a light-hearted example from my own experience. I did not know the meaning of the word "schadenfreude" until adulthood, although I had experienced what I now understand to be schadenfreude and the emotions associated with schadenfreude. Once I knew the word and its meaning, I recognized that the pleasure I had felt at others' misfortune could be described as a discrete emotion by one word.) To avoid such difficulties, some suggest that theories about emotions should rely only on empirical data alone and exclude subjective states that depend on pre-existing labels for their articulation as discrete emotions.[17]

Another reason for the lack of clarity is because the labels we give emotions are not universally congruent: it is a mistake to think that "the emotional repertoire represented by everyday English is necessarily universal."[18] What people in one culture call "remorse" might not be named at all in another culture, or might be identified by several words, or even words that overlap in meaning.[19] Emotions may be expressed in a variety of ways with different emphases cross-culturally. In other words, remorse in one culture may not correspond to remorse in another, as we saw especially clearly in chapter 1 (in relation to the Japanese approach to remorse) and in chapter 3 (in relation to the ancient Greek approach to remorse).

These observations are increasingly widely recognized. Anna Wierzbicka, in her seminal study on the linguistic and intercultural study of emotions, writes that "the concept of 'emotion' is culture-bound."[20] Vivek Dhareshwar writes of modern Indian traditions of thought about guilt that:

16. Lewis, *A Grief Observed*, 3.

17. Adolphs and Andler, "Investigating Emotions."

18. Konstan, *Emotions*, 7. See also Sabini and Silver, "Why Emotional Names," 1.

19. See Fischer and Tangney, "Shame and Guilt," on different understandings of shame, guilt, and embarrassment in the USA, China, and Italy.

20. Wierzbicka, *Emotions*, 6. We saw in chapter 2 that even the word "emotion" does not exist as an obvious category in Old Testament thought.

in most cases, we have neither the words nor, more importantly, the concepts to capture [the] domain of morality [i.e., guilt]. It would be hard to find in any of the Indian languages a word to translate "guilt." Of course, the absence of a word itself does not show that the concept does not obtain, but it is an important clue, nonetheless. What we have is a much more complex experience which can only be described by using a combination of honor, pride, shame and humiliation.[21]

Jan Plamper surveyed anthropological studies of emotions and concluded that, when taken together, "they destabilize any idea of pancultural emotions" and concluded "no discipline has done so much to shatter the idea that feelings are timeless and everywhere the same as has anthropology."[22] To this we may add Françoise Mirguet's conclusion that "individual emotions are diversely constructed in different historical, cultural, and social contexts."[23]

In approaching the study of remorse, we also need to be aware that a person's sense of remorse may not be what it seems, for emotions such as remorse can delude and mislead people, and people may be mistaken in the way they describe what they believe to be their emotions. We may think we are remorseful or regretful, but our remorse or regret may be a psychological defense to avoid the painful consequences of what we have done, or the remorse or regret may be driven by neurotic guilt and shame. In such situations, remorse or regret may serve a social function or be evidence of psychopathological disorder.

In addition, sometimes a person may feel remorseful, not in response to a specific situation of wrongdoing, but as a general state or feeling, such as we might say of someone who feels good or bad, happy or sad, energized, or weary. These states are called "core affects" and sometimes they are called "moods."[24] Emotions are different from moods, for moods are "objectless states, lacking the intentionality of fully-fledged emotions."[25]

---

21. Dhareshwar, "Valorizing," 226. Earlier observers mistakenly concluded that some strands of Hindu thought do not have an ethic that corresponds with the western idea of remorse (Cave, *Redemption*, 17, 73–74, 90, 97, 189).

22. Plamper, *History*, 77, 146.

23. Mirguet, "What Is an 'Emotion'?" 445.

24. Achino-Loeb observes that "it is hard to find an evidentiary basis for affective phenomena" ("Agency in Emotions," 560).

25. Nussbaum, *Anger*, 254. See also Goldie, *Emotions*, 144–45 and Burton, *Heaven and Hell*, 16, 30.

Remorse and the Contemporary
Approach to Emotions

Emotions have been explored in modern disciplines such as evolution-ary biology, psychology, and (more recently) in neurology, anthropology, neurobiology, and developmental psychopathology, for example. A young discipline, anticipated by Charles Darwin but developed only in the twen-ty-first century, is evolutionary psychology, which builds on the work of evolutionary biologists.[26]

Analyzing remorse through the scientific study of emotions can give enhanced understanding about remorse, but this approach may be at the risk of reductionism or over-simplification, for none of the scientific disciplines seems to offer a satisfying explanation of what emotions *are*.[27] They also do not reflect the understanding of and approaches to emotions of other, non-western, intellectual traditions. As has been said, "Not everything that can be counted counts, and not everything that counts can be counted."[28]

The scientific approach to the study of emotions has challenged an un-derlying, implicitly dualistic view of much traditional thought, namely, that human beings are in part physical beings, subject to physical processes, and in part "souls" or consciousness that think, have feelings, and freely make choices other than according to physical processes. To express simply the dualistic way of thinking, physical, bodily processes conform to scientific "laws," whereas thinking, feeling, and choosing take place in the "soul" or consciousness, which are not the subject of such laws. Hence people both live in a universe that is deterministic and have, and can exercise, free will. On the basis that people have souls, theologians have argued that people are responsible for their choices, such as to do wrong or to repent, for example, and so subject to the judgment of God for their choices. It was thought that the capacity to be remorseful resides in the soul or consciousness and that people freely choose whether or not to be remorseful.

In consequence of work in the sciences (as to which, see below), emo-tions are now thought to be part of embodied human existence. To put it straightforwardly, the generally held modern view is that bodies can exist without emotions (and some people, who suffer from certain illnesses, do

---

26. Darwin, *Origin*, 488. On evolutionary biology, see Cosmides and Tooby, "General Deontic Logic," 91; Dunbar and Barrett, *Oxford Handbook*; Silk, "Empathy," 115–25; Buss, *Evolutionary Psychology*; and Kurzban and deScioli "Morality," 770–87.

27. On reductionism, see Nagel, "What Is It Like to Be a Bat?" and Pope, *Human Evolution*, 56–75.

28. Cameron, *Informal Sociology*, 13. The quotation is sometimes wrongly attrib-uted to Albert Einstein (1879–1955).

not have the full range of emotions generally recognized as typical of human beings), people have emotions because they have bodies, and people cannot have emotions without bodies. From this, some would suggest that remorse, like other emotions, is no more than a bodily response and experience.

Scientific evidence certainly points towards the view called "naturalism," namely, that everything that exists is part of the natural world of material and physical realties, and that what exists conforms to natural laws. In other words, there is no "exemption from causality."[29] The evidence also points to causal determinism, the hypothesis that all our actions are determined by causes and that "all mental processes have neural correlates governed by laws of nature."[30] A line of thought that began in Freudian psychoanalysis also suggests that human beings are subject to unconscious drives and so are the subjects of "psychic determinism." To put this in psychoanalytical terms, the ego is "not as free as we would all like it to be and . . . no one is responsible for [his or her] unconscious."[31] Some regard work by Benjamin Libet as establishing that conscious thoughts do not cause behavior (as his research showed that some brain activity started before the subjects in his experiment decided to act);[32] however, his work may no more than establish that decisions to act do not originate in consciousness. Some recent empirical research also suggests that "emotions drive us independently of cognitions and decisions."[33]

If emotions, such as remorse, are only, and no more than, the result of physical processes and independent of cognition and volitional decision-making, modern science presents a significant challenge not only to the sort of Christian thought I have been describing in this book but also to much of the thinking that underlies moral philosophy and moral psychology. It would be unreasonable, so some people think, to hold people to account for choices over which they appear to have no control. It would also be unreasonable to expect them to hold themselves responsible for those choices. (To parody the argument, one could say, "It is not I who do wrong but my unconscious!") By this scheme of thinking, remorse is redundant, for it is not a reasonable response for people to be remorseful about what they do not freely choose to do; neither is it reasonable to be remorseful at all, because they do not freely choose to be remorseful. As William Schweiker puts it succinctly, "In order to be held responsible an

29. Baumeister, "Constructing a Scientific Theory," 237.

30. Nahmias, "Is Free Will an Illusion?" 20.

31. Speziale-Bagliacca, *Guilt*, 3, summarizing Freud, *Obsessive Actions*.

32. Libet, "Unconscious Cerebral Initiative."

33. Bagnoli, *Morality and the Emotions*, 17.

agent must act voluntarily."[34] Valerie Tiberius sets the issue in the context
of what she says science "proves":

> [T]o take moral questions seriously we must assume that we are
> autonomous, rational beings living in a world that is infused
> with moral significance to which we can respond appropriately
> or not. But science proves that we are not like this, so moral
> questions cannot be taken seriously and moral philosophy has
> no point.[35]

Tiberius's summary reflects the view that if people are the subject of
causal determinism, they cannot also be autonomous and so morally responsible for their choices. We can put the issue this way: for some, emotions are no more than "neurobiological affect programs" that have "arisen
through biological and social evolution." If this is right, accountability and
responsibility for choice may be inappropriate, unless we can show that
emotions are "educable and malleable."[36]

Limitations on human autonomy have also been highlighted by philosophers. Some suggest that the choices people make may depend on "moral
luck," that is factors, which are not only psychological, that are outside their
control.[37] Thomas Nagel writes that moral luck is seen "[w]here a significant
aspect of what someone does depends on factors beyond his control, yet we
continue to treat him in that respect as an object of moral judgment."[38] In
his view, moral luck can arise from the way things turn out (resultant luck),
from the circumstances in which one finds oneself (circumstantial luck),
from who one is (constitutive luck), and from what one has become from
previous circumstances (causal luck).

But does science "prove" what Tiberius suggests science claims it does?
To differing extents, some take a "compatibilist" approach, and do not assume
that naturalism excludes all possible forms of free will. For example, Freud
appears not to have held strictly to the view that people cannot freely choose,
and the term "the Freudian ambiguity" is sometimes used to highlight the

34. Schweiker, *Responsibility*, 142. Schweiker explores the nature of moral freedom
and responsibility in pp. 142–48.

35. Tiberius, *Moral Psychology*, 16. See the important essays on the implications
of neurobiology for understanding free will and moral responsibility in volume 4 of
Sinnott-Armstrong, *Moral Psychology*. See also Pope, *Human Evolution*, 158–87 for an
extended exploration of the relationship of freedom and responsibility in the context
of determinism.

36. Bagnoli, *Morality and the Emotions*, 17.

37. Williams, *Moral Luck* (and in Statman, *Moral Luck*) and Nagel, *Mortal Questions*.

38. In Statman, *Moral Luck*, 59.

"contradiction in Freud's position," namely, that Freud also "subscribed to the opinion that there was an area of freedom in the human psyche, an area where choices and decisions were possible."[39] Others suggest that naturalism does not correlate with determinism, if by "naturalism" we mean no more than that people live in a natural world that is subject to scientific laws.[40] Eddy Nahmias observes that "research in neuroscience and psychology is not in a position to settle the long-standing debate about the compatibility [or non-compatibility] of free will and determinism. . . . Nor should [scientists] assume that science is establishing that determinism is true . . .—indeed, the dominant theory of quantum physics would suggest it is not."[41] Others suggest that the question "free will or determinism?" is expressed too starkly, and that a better way to frame the questions, still within the framework of evolution and natural selection, and with freedom understood in the context of a continuum, is to construct a theory of "causal freewill" and ask these questions, "To what extent and in what sense(s) do humans act freely" and ". . .what inner processes make those actions possible?"[42]

Three of the other answers of compatibilists to the view Tiberius describes are these. In the first place, people may have evolved freely to practice moral behavior[43] or to take personal responsibility for their actions.[44] In other words, choices can be freely made within the framework of natural processes, and not from within a "soul" outside the natural world. Nico Frijda argues in "Emotion Regulation and Free Will," for example, that free will is not a matter of action being undetermined. People may make choices and can elect to do what is important rather than what is urgent or expedient. Stephen J. Pope argues that "the ability to exercise moral responsibility was made possible by the evolution of the human brain and . . . [by the] higher cognitive and emotional capacities" that human beings have. He adds that "human freedom is best understood in terms of evolved human nature and not as a bizarre exception to everything else known scientifically about human beings."[45] Secondly, and this is related to the

39. Speziale-Bagliacca, *Guilt*, 189.

40. See also Baumeister, "Constructing a Scientific Theory," 237–40 for an exploration of some of the questionable scientific assumptions against free will.

41. Nahmias, "Is Free Will an Illusion?" 7.

42. Baumeister, "Constructing a Scientific Theory," 237, 235. Baumeister's suggestion is that free will is "a process of steering rather than starting behavior": "Constructing a Scientific Theory," 249.

43. See on Haidt below, and also Strawson, *Freedom and Resentment*, especially as explained in Deigh, "Reactive Attitudes," 199–208.

44. Gazzaniger, "Mental Life."

45. Pope, *Emotions*, 185, 187.

first point, people may be causally determined to make (free) choices and to think what to do. This means that not all their choices will be causally determined, though some may be. Determinists in this mold recognize that people still make evaluations and moral judgments about what to do and are responsible for their moral choices.[46] Thirdly, Nahmias observes that there is a distinction between conscious mental processes, which have neural correlates that scientists can measure, and other processes that precede the neural processes. It is reductionist to say, he suggests, that since neural processes are observed when people make moral choices, those neural processes explain the moral choices.[47]

In the view of some, especially philosophers, determinism "has always been conceptually questionable," with the result that, for all the difficulties about the idea of free will, we still need to "make some kind of sense of our status as beings who are, in some respects and in various degrees, in charge of our lives and accountable to others."[48] Determinism does not explain *what* people will do and *when* they will do it. Additionally, as Owen Jones observes, "a predisposition [toward certain behaviors] is not a predetermination," for emotions do influence behavior and "biology does not dictate behavior in any single individual."[49] Nevertheless, according to the current direction of scientific research, the case against free will in the sense that free will "entails actions originating with conscious thought"[50] is strong, though most scientists would agree that the case against any form of free will has not been proved. Our intuitive sense that in some way we have a degree of free will, and the basis of our societal social and moral structures—namely, that people usually have free will and so have capacity for self-determination and are responsible for what they do[51]—cannot often be reconciled with all the scientific evidence and with all the current hypotheses. But at least the evidence may make us more cautious towards those who do not have the capacity, always wisely, freely to make good choices. There will be some who constitutionally cannot show remorse, for example.

46. See Tiberius, *Moral Psychology*, on the place of moral psychology in the study of emotions and pp. 127–66 for a summary of the relationship of moral responsibility and determinism.

47. Nahmias, "Is Free Will an Illusion?" 20. Schweiker believes he resolves the conundrum by showing that a Christian acts through faith in God (*Responsibility*, 148, 179).

48. Watson, *Free Will*, 9, 25.

49. Jones, "Laws," 285, 289.

50. Baumeister, "Constructing a Scientific Theory," 249.

51. Nagel, "Freedom."

We now explore some ways of thinking about emotions that have contributed to reshaping the traditional, pre-modern patterns of thought about emotions and so about remorse in particular.

Remorse as Physiological Change

William James (1842–1910), a philosopher-psychologist, regarded emotions such as remorse as "epiphenomena," that is, the results of bodily changes, and not the causes of any action. Feeling and experiencing the physical changes that have bodily expression *are* the emotions. This is counter-intuitive, for we typically think that the perception of having done wrong can lead to an emotional response, such as remorse, and that certain physiological changes, such as weeping, may then result. According to this way of thinking, emotions are bodily responses; they are not cognitions.[52]

James's approach has been challenged on several counts. First, the experimental work of Walter Cannon (1871–1945) postulated what is now known as the "Cannon-Bard Theory," namely, that physiological changes in people and the experience of emotions are (*contra* James) not always separate and independent, and that arousal does not have to occur before the emotion is experienced.[53] Next, Cannon also argues that emotions are intentional states.[54] We can express his observation like this, inverting something that Jerome Shaffer wrote[55] (and which we quote correctly below) to make a different point from Shaffer's: getting emotionally worked up must involve more than just physiological/sensational effects, namely, beliefs and desires that lead to physiological/sensational effects. Third, it has now been shown, whereas it had previously only been suggested, that bodily processes are not of themselves sufficient for people to identify which particular emotions they are experiencing.[56] A cognitive process is also almost certainly needed to distinguish different emotions, especially when more than one emotion corresponds with the same physiological reaction. In other words, emotions

52. See James, *Principles*, and James, "What Is an Emotion?" James's theory is also sometimes called the "somatic feedback" theory. Carl Lange (1834–1900) developed similar ideas as James's at around the same time (referred to in Solomon, *What Is an Emotion?* 65). In *Emotions*, Goldie adapted James's work. James's approach is reaffirmed in Robinson, "Emotion." James's work has been developed as "the embodied appraisal theory" (Prinz, *Gut Reactions*, and *Emotional Construction*). Some neuroscientists are neo-Jamesians, e.g., Damasio, *Descartes's Error*; and Prinz, *Gut Reactions*. For a summary of the latest research, see Friedman, "Feelings and the Body."

53. Cannon, *Bodily Changes*.

54. See also Dewey, "Theory of Emotion."

55. Shaffer, "Mental Events," 163.

56. Schachter and Singer, "Cognitive, Social, Physiological."

need some basis of cognition and rationality if they are more than mere moods. Last, James's theory does not explain that emotions need an object, appraisal, and sometimes a subject. For example, if Arthur is remorseful because he lied to Bethany, Arthur will need to be remorseful *about something* (an object, his lie) because he realizes (appraises) that he has done wrong to Bethany (a subject); his remorse is not wholly explicable as being no more than a physiological reaction. One therefore has to be remorseful both *about something* and *towards someone.*

Remorse as Evolutionary Adaptation

Charles Darwin wrote about remorse in his research on the human species in *The Descent of Man, and Selection in Relation to Sex* (first published in 1871). The aim of the book (taken from his introduction) is to consider whether human beings have descended from pre-existing forms, the manner of human development, and the significance of differences between different human races. His observations led him to conclude that remorse is "an overwhelming sense of repentance"[57] often felt in relation to a "duty" or "rule" that people hold "sacred"[58] and that "remorse bears the same relation to repentance, as rage does to anger, or agony to pain."[59] This suggests that he saw remorse as a universally found emotion. In *The Expression of the Emotions in Man and Animals* (1872) Darwin went further and explored the biological nature of emotions through an empirical, inductive approach in order to understand the way emotions are expressed.

There has been considerable debate about the implications of *The Expressions of the Emotions*. In the 1955 edition, edited by Margaret Mead, Mead argues that Darwin's work pointed to emotions being culturally relative. Paul Ekman, who edited the 1973 and the 1998 editions, argues the opposite. He believes that Darwin's work shows that emotions are determined through evolutionary development, that they are universal (that is, innate, not learned), and that human beings share them in varying degrees with other mammals.[60] In other words, his view is that Darwin regarded human emotions as having developed from the emotions of more primitive species from which human beings evolved. Such emotions are

57. Darwin, *Descent*, 138.

58. Darwin, *Descent*, 128, 157.

59. Darwin, *Descent*, 138.

60. In *Primates*, De Waal shows that some higher primates appear to have moral emotions.

evolutionary adaptations and one of the ways that organisms developed solutions to challenges they faced.[61]

The biological basis of Darwinism runs the risk of reductionism. Stephen R. L. Clark rightly observes that human nature "demands that we inhabit other worlds of meaning than the merely biological."[62] If we did not, he asks, how could we have formulated modern biological theory? He also says that "a *strictly* Darwinian biology cannot sensibly be considered true. If it were, we could neither have the wit to find it out, not any duty to admit it if we did" because it is a theory that "entails that we could never have the intellect or moral virtue to discover or to recognize its truth."[63]

Darwin's work has, among others, been taken forward by Paul Ekman, an evolutionary biologist. Ekman thinks that Darwin's research shows that the six "basic" emotions that he (Ekman) has identified (happiness, disgust, fear, surprise, anger, and sadness) are the result of evolutionary development, and not the result of conscious or volitional moral choices.[64] In Ekman's words, the "expressions of our emotions are universal (that is innate, not learned) and the product of our evolution."[65]

In general terms, Ekman believes that emotions evolved for their adaptive value for life's tasks. He says that "basic" emotions are universally recognized from facial expressions.[66] Basic emotions are emotions that are "short-term, stereotypical responses involving facial expression, autonomic nervous system arousal . . . [with] [t]he same patterns of response occur[ring] in all cultures."[67] Such emotions are non-cognitive. Outside these basic emotions, he appears to regard what else is also popularly regarded as an emotion as not truly an emotion[68] (because they involve cognition), though he acknowledges that there are "families" of emotions that are similar but not identical in form to basic emotions.[69]

---

61. See also Keltner et al., "Social Functionalism," 117, 121 on emotions as adaptations. Nesse suggests that guilt developed in response to threats that early hominids experienced ("Evolutionary Explanations," 278).

62. Clark, *Biology*, 3.

63. Clark, *Biology*, 7.

64. See Ekman, "Basic Emotions." There is no agreed definition of basic emotions. See the description in Clark, "Relations," 77–78.

65. In Darwin, *Expression*, xxii. Not all people agree with Ekman's interpretation of Darwin: see Plamper, *History*, 164–72.

66. Ekman, "Biological and Cultural Contributions," and Darwin, *Expression*, in the "Afterword."

67. Griffiths, *What Emotions Really Are*, 8.

68. Ekman, "Basic Emotions," 57.

69. Ekman, "Argument."

There are some obvious drawbacks to Ekman's view that emotions can be recognized from facial expressions.[70] First, it is possible to mask facial expressions that express one's emotions; second, it is possible to mimic facial expressions (as actors often do) without also having the emotion that corresponds with the facial expression; and third, basic emotions can cause a variety of facial expressions besides the expressions that Ekman identifies as the ones that are (supposedly) uniquely and universally recognizable.

Ekman's categories also suffer from methodological problems.[71] The first is that some basic emotions are composite emotions and comprise emotions that are not only basic. If such emotions were not composite, we would have difficulty distinguishing (for example) surprise about unexpectedly inheriting a large sum of money, surprise about being punched in an unprovoked attack, and surprise that comes from unexpectedly meeting a long-lost friend. For these reasons, some suggest that emotions can be combinations of basic emotions and thoughts, together with learned emotional responses, with the most frequent combinations given names because identifiable. Such combinations of emotions are sometimes called "self-conscious emotions."[72] In a chapter on self-conscious emotions, Michael Lewis includes in this category embarrassment, empathy, shame, guilt, and regret, which (as we have seen) can all be constituents of remorse.[73] Kurt Fischer and June Price Tangney say self-conscious emotions are "founded in social relationships, in which people not only interact but evaluate and judge themselves and each other."[74]

Surprisingly, perhaps, given that such important consequences about the nature of emotions follow from Ekman's work, Ekman's list of six basic emotions does not seem to be fixed. He has suggested two additional emotions:

70. See, for example, the criticism in Fridlund, "Human Facial Expressions"; Gendron et al., "Perceptions"; Fernández-Dols and Russell, "The Science of Facial Expression"; and Barrett, How Emotions Are Made, 42–55.

71. Ekman has summarized the challenges to his view (Darwin, Expression, in the "Afterword").

72. On self-conscious emotions, see (besides the literature quoted below), Roberts, Essay, 20–36 (analyzed in contrast with "basic" emotions) and Haidt, "Moral Emotions," 859–62.

73. Lewis, "Self-Conscious Emotions."

74. Fischer and Tangney, "Self-Conscious Emotions," 3. We discuss self-conscious emotions further in chapter 8.

contempt, and a combination of shame and guilt.[75] He has also considered including embarrassment and awe.[76] He suggested others in 2011.[77]

Some think that basic emotions are (at least to some extent) culturally constructed.[78] Patricia Greenspan says, for example, that basic emotions have a degree of plasticity that allows for culturally-shaped changes to re-shape them.[79] Others say that the mistake that Ekman seems to have made is that he has used western cultural constructs as his starting point in seeking to understand and identify the way societies understand emotions and their expression.[80]

Even if the category of basic emotions as Ekman means them is correct, most people think that there *are* emotions that are not basic emotions. Some have suggested that these emotions (and here remorse could be included) are analogous to basic emotions but have some important differences.[81] For example, they cannot be scientifically measured in the same way people say that basic emotions can. It is not that such emotions are not emotions but that they are a different genus of emotion with cognition playing an important part. Baird describes the relationship of basic (she calls them "primary") emotions to self-conscious emotions in this way: she says that primary emotions are relatively few and have been "hard-wired or genetically determined" and are "consistent across cultures." They are like "primary colors in that by varying the combinations and intensities, the entire spectrum can be created." Self-conscious emotions are a pastiche of primary emotions and are "more complex and subtle" than primary emotions. What distinguishes self-conscious emotions from primary emotions is that self-conscious emotions "require a cognitive awareness of not only the existence of the thoughts of others, but also the ability to speculate regarding the contents of these thoughts."[82]

There is evidence that self-conscious emotions vary across cultures, as one might expect if cognition is involved. Part III of Rom Harré's edited

75. Ekman, "Basic Emotions," 55.

76. Ekman, "An Argument for Basic Emotions," 170. In *Emotion*, Plutchik has identified eight basic emotions. He suggests that some human emotions are combinations of some of the basic emotions. He identifies remorse as such a blend. Aspects of his book has been heavily criticized, e.g., by Camras, "Review."

77. Ekman and Cordaro, "What Is Meant?"

78. For example, Shweder and Levine, *Cultural Theory*; Harré, *Social Construction*; Lutz, *Unnatural Emotions*, 5; Heelas, "Emotion Talk"; Griffiths, "Modularity," 256–57.

79. Greenspan, "Learning Emotions."

80. Barrett, *How Emotions Are Made*, 53–55.

81. Griffiths, *What Emotions Really Are*.

82. Baird, "Adolescent Moral Reasoning," 332.

book is on the social construction of emotions and sets out the results of empirical work on the cultural relativity of emotions.[83] The taxonomy of ancient Greek emotions also does not match a modern taxonomy of emotions. David Konstan observes that "the set of emotions that Aristotle treats in his *Rhetoric* . . . exhibits important discrepancies with modern lists, sometimes cutting across categories by which we discriminate emotions."[84] Konstan gives a number of examples of emotions that appear to be cultural constructs,[85] and observes that, until recent years, there was not even a Tibetan word for "emotion."[86] (We saw in chapter 2 that the ancient Israelites also did not have a word for "emotion" and "emotions.") Konstan quotes the work of Roy Grinker,[87] who gives as an example the Korean emotion *han*, which has no parallel in the western emotional register. Grinker says that *han* "refers to a consciousness of ongoing trauma and a lack of resolution and reconciliation. Paradoxically, however, *han* also provides a means of resolution. . . . *Han* is a distinctive psychological concept . . . ."[88]

In chapter 2, I explored some of the difficulties in interpreting emotions both diachronically and synchronically. In view of these difficulties, it is unlikely that we can produce compelling evidence that emotions are universal. Some also deny that some emotions are "basic" as Ekman means the term because none of the meta-analyses of experimental data has "found consistent and specific emotion fingerprints in the body.[89] Additionally, the challenge for scientists is that, despite research, there remain "wild disagreements among the list of basic emotions proposed by experts."[90] In short, Ekman *assumes*, but does not prove, that his list of emotions is irreducible and that the basic emotions he identifies correspond to those for which we have names in English.[91]

There are other challenges to Ekman's work. First, when it comes to psychological traits and emotions, evolutionary adaptation is difficult to prove because (unlike in the case of fossil remains) there is no record to

83. Harré, *Social Construction.*

84. Konstan, *Emotions*, 15.

85. See also Harkness and Hitlin, "Morality and Emotions," 463–66.

86. Konstan, *Emotions*, 3.

87. Grinker, *Korea*, 78–79.

88. Konstan, *The Emotions*, 266, n. 17. See Evans, *Emotion*, 1–2 on the Japanese word *amae* for which there is no corresponding word in English. For more examples, see Schlimm, *From Fratricide*, 21–28.

89. Barrett, *How Emotions Are Made*, 18, 52.

90. Roberts, *Essay*, 130.

91. Griffiths and Scarantino rightly warn against theoretical approaches to emotions that rigidly categorize emotions ("Emotions," 449).

examine. Second, biological and neurological explanations of emotions as physiological mechanisms do not explain how, when, and why human beings feel particular emotions, and why they are significant. Although the neurosciences describe "the physical substructure of the emotions," they do "little, if anything, to clarify how, when, why, and by whom humans become angry, jealous, sad, or embarrassed"[92] and, we might add, "remorseful."[93] Last, Paul Griffiths suggests that as human beings and animals share common descent, they also share some common emotions. He calls these emotions "affect program emotions" and lists them as surprise, anger, fear, sadness, joy, and disgust. He regards such emotions as present in all human beings and related species. He also writes of "complex emotions" (he formerly called them "higher cognitive emotions") such as remorse to describe other types of emotions. Complex emotions are, he says, unique to human beings, socially constructed, and so not homologous (having similarity due to common descent) to basic emotions.[94] Griffiths's work is regarded as a significant challenge to Ekman's approach.[95]

After a careful summary of Ekman's work, Plamper starkly concludes that "[f]rom the standpoint of the natural sciences and according to the principles of scientific procedure and verity, Ekman's work is bankrupt. More exactly, empirical proof for his hypotheses could be said to be very weak" but he agrees that the possibility is still open that "someone, somewhere, could produce other evidence that would still confirm the hypotheses."[96] In short, Ekman's case, that the only emotions are "basic emotions" that are the result of evolutionary development (with remorse not being among them), has not been made out. It is a case, I suggest, of having to distinguish between claims that have been empirically established (which Ekman's have not) and those that are ideological (which Ekman's sometimes are).[97]

Remorse as a Cognition or Evaluation

We have seen in chapter 3 that Greek philosophers in the Aristotelean tradition thought that there is a relationship between emotion and cognition. There is evidence of the same view about emotions in the modern period from as early as the eighteenth century. According to Sabine Roeser, the

92. Miner, *Thomas Aquinas*, 2.
93. See also Tallon, "Christianity," 120–21.
94. Griffiths, *What Emotions Really Are*.
95. Clark, "Relations."
96. Plamper, *History*, 158.
97. The distinction is expressed this way by Clark, *Biology*, 309.

Scottish philosopher Thomas Reid (1710–96) "held to a cognitive theory of moral emotions." Reid wrote, for example, that "there are moral feelings that are the result of a moral judgment made by reason."[98] A cognitive approach to emotions (that is, the view that emotions are cognitions with intentional contents, and so are equivalent to judgments) is also partly in evidence in the work of Errol Bedford[99] and Anthony Kenny[100] and became more carefully articulated in the work of Robert Solomon,[101] who all understand emotions to be judgments. Among recent philosophers, Martha C. Nussbaum has formulated an important theory of emotions in her monograph, *Upheavals of Thought* (2001) that deliberately looks back to the Aristotelean and Attic approach.

Basing her approach on earlier work such as Solomon's, Nussbaum suggests that emotions are evaluative judgments, that is, "appraisals or value judgments," for they involve intentional thoughts or perceptions that have a focus in view.[102] There is also critical evaluation of the object of appraisal from the viewpoint of the subject. Emotions can be "background" (by which Nussbaum means emotions in their unarticulated or unconscious forms) or "situational," and "general" or "particular." Importantly, in her view, emotions make a valuable contribution to the moral life. Nussbaum regards desires, appetites, and other instinctual responses that can drive behavior as cognitively shaped in some ways, though there is a long philosophical tradition going back to Aristotle in *De Anima*[103] that this is not always so. Emotions are distinguishable from one another if they involve different evaluations or judgments: thus, remorse is distinguishable from regret if we can identify different types of evaluation in each emotion.

Applying Nussbaum's description of emotions, a person who feels remorse will have had remorseful thoughts ("intentional thoughts or perceptions") about something ("a focus in view") and is deeply ashamed ("critical evaluation") of his or her actions ("the object of appraisal.")[104] In

---

98. Roeser, "Reid," 178.

99. Bedford, "Emotions."

100. Kenny, *Action*.

101. E.g., Solomon, "On Emotions"; *Passions*; "Philosophy of Emotions"; and "What Is an Emotion?"

102. Nussbaum, *Upheavals*, 4. See also Kenny, *Action*; Arnold, *Emotions and Personality*; Lazarus, *Psychological Stress*; Solomon, *The Passions, What Is an Emotion?* 10 ("emotions are judgments"); and Lazarus, "Appraisal."

103. Aristotle, *De Anima* 432a15–433b30.

104. Viewed this way, emotions such as remorse require "a range of sophisticated conceptual abilities . . . [and] appear to be paradigmatically conceptual thoughts, which demand possession of concepts such as moral imperative, self, and ideal" (Griffiths and

other words, remorse involves thought, judgment, and evaluation, and is rooted in a cognitive response to one's actions. Obviously, too, the object of appraisal needs to matter to the subject from the subject's viewpoint. Such a response is also situational and particular. Seen this way, remorse is obviously an emotion that is rooted in antecedent cognition.

Nussbaum rightly notes that emotions and how we articulate them are socially constructed. We see this particularly clearly when it comes to remorse, for example: what is meant in the West in the twenty-first century by the emotion that we call "remorse" seems to be part of a widely recognized family of emotions. However, not all aspects of that family of emotions fully correlate with every instance of what people mean by "remorse," and some aspects of that family of emotions are called by other names, or apparently are not named at all, in some societies.

There is considerable debate about whether Nussbaum is right that emotions are only ever thoughts (or "cognitions") as she widely defines them.[105] (This is to be expected because of Ekman's claim that basic emotions are not a response to cognitions.) In the case of remorse, it is easy to see that the emotional response called "remorse" *is* the result of an evaluative, critical process of thought, for it is not easy to see how one cannot feel the emotion of remorse in a non-cognitive way, unless one talks of a "remorseful mood" or "remorseful disposition." Cognitions and emotions are, of course, not the only component of emotions. We now quote Jerome Shaffer accurately, who observes: "getting emotionally worked up must involve more than just beliefs and desires, namely, the physiological/sensational effects of those beliefs and desires."[106]

As regards Nussbaum's views generally, there are at least three other points of debate: first, the theory has no place for the emotional responses of animals and infants, which, though intentional, are widely thought not to be based on evaluative cognition. Second, the theory runs the risk of being circular because it excludes emotions that are not also based on cognitions. For example, someone whose cognition is that household spiders are harmless may nevertheless be afraid of them: it is implausible to say that their fear, because it is not based on cognition, is not an emotion. (This objection is sometimes labelled as the objection of "recalcitrance to reason.") Last, it is possible to have a belief or cognition that does not result in a corresponding emotion. For example, someone may be in a dangerous situation but not feel

---

Scarantino, "Emotions," 441–42).

105. The debate is anticipated in Deigh, "Cognitivism."

106. Shaffer, "Mental Events," 163.

fear. This leads to the obvious point that cognition, if it is to be regarded as an emotion, must also produce a physiological reaction.[107]

Psychological Theory and Emotions

Seminal work on psychotherapy and the psychology of emotions was conducted by Sigmund Freud (1856–1939), whose work challenges many of the conclusions of physical scientists. His work has important implications for the study of remorse, although his conclusions are not consistent or systematic.[108]

Sometimes Freud regards emotions, such as remorse, as affects, that is, autonomous bodily events that precede cognition and other psychological processes. Elsewhere, in Freud's view, emotions are intentional states that can give rise to, and so cause, actions.[109] At this point we see clearly the difference between an emotion, which is a response to a specific stimulus that results in something intentional, and an affect, such as a mood, which is not caused by a specific stimulus and is not necessarily about anything. Freud regards emotions as coming from the unconscious (the Id) with expression in the consciousness (the Ego) and informed by the Superego, which, according to Freud, internalizes parental authority, focusing on parental strictness and severity, rather than on parental nurture and love. In other places, Freud's regards emotions as no more than the Id's unconscious instincts and innate drives.

According to Freud's thinking, emotions can be both conscious and, if repressed, unconscious. Despite being repressed, unconscious thoughts can influence the behavior of people, sometimes leading them to behave in irrational ways. This may explain why otherwise blameless people sometimes behave in ways that are out of character and for which they become deeply remorseful. As is well known, psychoanalysis can help people to identify what is unconscious and influences conscious behavior.[110]

More specifically, according to Freud, remorse is "a *sense of guilt* after having committed a misdeed."[111] Some regard Freud as using different

---

107. This latter observation comes from the earlier work of Lyons, *Emotion*.

108. For a history of emotions' research in psychological literature, see Fischer and Tangney, "Self-Conscious Emotions," 4–6; Deigh, *On Emotions*, 1–12 and 215–32; Plamper, *History*.

109. Freud, "Concepts," 24.

110. I cannot find much psychoanalytic literature about remorse. The exception is the collection of essays edited by Stern in *The Psychotherapy Patient* (1988).

111. Freud, *Civilisation*, 131 and see Marks, "Remorse," 318–21.

terms (remorse and guilt) for the same feeling.[112] Freud adds that remorse
"relates only to a deed that *has been done*, and, of course, it presupposes that
conscience, the readiness to feel guilty, was already in existence before the
deed took place."[113] Since Freud suggests that anger is one of the constituents of guilt and since in his thought guilt is a constituent of remorse, anger
will be one of the constituents of remorse.

According to Freud, remorse in its most compelling and cogent form
can be a tutor, to train people not to yield to the temptation to do wrong in
the future. Other kinds of remorse, he suggests, are effete and do not bring
about the transformation of moral character. He says:

> A man who alternately sins and then in his remorse erects high
> moral standards lays himself open to the reproach that he has
> made things too easy for himself. He has not achieved the essence
> of morality, [that is,] renunciation [of immoral conduct] . . . .[114]

Magda Arnold (1903–2002) looked at how perception causes and
arouses emotion. In order to arouse an emotion, in her view there must be
perception and appraisal.[115] "Appraisal" is the process of thought that results
in the significance of a situation for an individual to be construed or evaluated. She defines emotion as:

> the felt tendency toward anything intuitively appraised as good
> (beneficial), or away from anything intuitively appraised as bad
> (harmful). This attraction or aversion is accompanied by a pat-
> tern of physiological changes organized toward approach or
> withdrawal. The patterns differ for different emotions.[116]

Arnold's work is regarded as seminal, and she has been called "the found-
ing mother of appraisal theory."[117] Her conclusions accord with Aristotle's
observations about the place of appraisal through cognition and reason in
the study of emotions.

---

112. Speziale-Bagliacca, *Guilt*. Empirical studies tend to confirm that regret, guilt,
and shame cluster together (Proeve and Tudor, *Remorse*, 53–54).

113. Freud, *Civilisation*, 131.

114. Freud, *Civilisation*, 177.

115. Arnold, *Emotions and Personality*, 171.

116. Arnold, *Emotions and Personality*, 182.

117. The phrase is quoted in Cornelius, "Magda Arnold's Thomistic Theory," 976,
998. Cornelius says that Arnold attributed Aquinas's thought on emotions to be the
inspiration of her work.

The appraisal process is "direct, immediate, nonreflective, non-intellectual, autonomic, 'instinctive', 'intuitive.'"[118] From the viewpoint of remorse ("the felt tendency," which is emotion), we can see that remorse can happen at the point of "intuitive" appraisal. Remorse can also occur as result of "reflective" appraisal, a deliberative and rational process that follows intuitive appraisal and that both modifies the original "intuitive appraisal" and influences the "felt tendency," that is, the emotion. "Cognitive Appraisal Theory," the name for Arnold's approach, analyses the different types of appraisals involved in the emotion process.[119]

Andrea Scarantino summarizes the place of the work of Arnold and her successors as establishing that "a subject's appraisal . . . is a major determinant of the differences among different emotions."[120] Appraisal stands alongside the importance of the place of bodily, physical changes that lead to feelings and emotions, observed (as we have seen) by James, for example. In other words, as a result of Arnold's work, it has been recognized that an emotion such as remorse is a combination of appraisal and feeling.

Lastly, Nico Frijda (1927–2015) understands emotions to be an individual's relationship to and so a response to his or her environment. He believes that emotions are "hardwired" and subject to biological laws and are not entirely under voluntary control.[121] They arise "in response to events that are important to the individual's goals, motives, or concerns."[122] In his seminal work on emotions, he described an emotion as:

> the readiness (or unreadiness) to enter into contact or inter-action with some object, and the mode of that contact or interaction . . . . Different motivational states or states of action readiness exist. . . . Emotions are tendencies to establish, maintain, or disrupt a relationship with the environment.[123]

Frijda identifies four of the different ways that the word "emotion" can be used.[124] Three of the four ways have to do with actions and reactions

---

118. Arnold, *Emotions and Personality*, 165.

119. Others have built on Arnold's work. For example, Solomon, *The Passions*; Marks, "Theory"; Roseman, "Cognitive Determinants"; Solomon, "Philosophy of Emotions"; Lazarus, "Cognition," and "Emotions"; Nussbaum, *Upheavals*; Scherer et al., *Appraisal Processes*; Scherer, "Appraisal Considered." See also Scarantino, "Philosophy of Emotions," 33–36 for a summary.

120. Scarantino, "Philosophy of Emotions," 36.

121. Frijda, "Laws" and see Frijda and Parrott, "Basic-Emotions."

122. Frijda, "Laws," 351.

123. Frijda, *Emotions*, 71.

124. Frijda, "Evolutionary Emergence," 609–10.

that are measurable as types of "behavior" or "bodily symptom" and so are the primary concern of scientists. The other way includes a more subjective element that he describes as follows:

> [A]n emotion is assumed to exist when an action or reaction appears to have come over a person. In such case, the action, reaction, or feeling takes control of the person, motivates him or her to do things against some of their other intentions and sometimes against better judgments. There are times at which people profess to being invaded by feelings, and when their faces betray that they do not know what has happened to them.[125]

Thus, remorse is the action tendency to communicate guilt about one's actions and (sometimes also) the intention to put right, as best one can, the outcome of one's wrongdoing. Frijda further suggests that some action states have "control precedence," meaning that some emotions "can interrupt other processes and block access to action control for other stimuli and other goals."[126] In other words, and as people know in their experience, some emotions, such as remorse, can become overwhelming and dominate one's thoughts, feelings, and actions.

Frijda also identified some of the actions and reactions that may come over people. One of them can result in a "null state," that is, a state of "explicit absence of relational activity." This might be sadness or self-pity, which is typical of illucid remorse. Another identifiable or measurable action or reaction that may come over a person is the intention to "execute a given kind of action."[127] In the case of remorse, this might be repentance or reparation or the intention to apologize.

Frijda discusses the place of appraisal in emotions. He wrote that:

> How events are appraised *during* emotions appears often to result from cognitive elaboration of the appraisal process *eliciting* the emotion. The products of such elaboration are often what provide the characteristic flavor of experience.[128]

Thus, besides appraisal eliciting an emotion, appraisal during the experience of an emotion provides "the characteristic flavor of the experience," which in the case of remorse may be guilt, shame, and embarrassment, typical interpretations of the experience.

125. Frijda, "Evolutionary Emergence," 610. See also Frijda, "Place," 371.
126. Frijda, *Emotions*, 460.
127. Frijda, *Emotions*, 22.
128. Frijda, "The Place of Appraisal," 371.

Remorse and Neuroscience

Many neuroscientists formerly suspected there were specific brain regions for particular emotions.[129] In other words, it was supposed that there could be a region of the brain that is the source of remorse. Some people, typically psychopaths, who show signs of lack of remorse, have suffered ventromedial or orbitofrontal damage to their brains.[130] This suggests a reason why these people do not (and even cannot) show remorse.

The first published study of brain imaging studies of moral judgments was published in 2001.[131] As a result of recent work, it is now regarded as generally a mistake to identify any one emotion with any one specific brain region, although it has been established through neuroimaging that guilt, an integral part of remorse, shares (along with other emotions) a variety of identifiable brain regions.[132] However, even if certain specific neural systems and paths are active, it does not necessarily mean that the subject is experiencing emotions typically associated with that pathway.

Concluding Thoughts

James Russell observes that "one of the mysteries of psychology is how it has been possible to define and construe emotion in such apparently incompatible ways, from biologically fixed modules similar to reflexes to cognitive structures to socially constructed roles.[133] It is clear that there is not a single modern category that adequately combines the empirical and theoretical approaches to emotions, or that adequately describes emotions.[134] There is also "a lack of consensus on many fundamental issues" to do with the study of emotions[135] and so of remorse. Perhaps that this is so should be obvious, for Thomas Nagel convincingly showed nearly half a century ago that the subjective nature of consciousness (and so of

129. Sander et al., "Appraisal-Driven," 219.

130. Baird, "Adolescent Moral Reasoning," 364 and Kennett and Fine, "Internalism," 186.

131. Sinnott-Armstrong, *Neuroscience*, xiii.

132. Moll et al., "Cognitive Neuroscience," 13.

133. Russell, "Core Affect," 167.

134. A significantly under-researched area of study is the relationship between gender and emotions and in particular how emotions, such as remorse, contribute to the construction of gender identity (Schrock and Knop, "Gender and Emotions").

135. Hamann, "Integrating Perspectives," 187. See Adolphs and Anderson, *The Neuroscience of Emotion*, 104. An entire edition of *Emotion Review* in 2018 explored a diverse range of approaches to understanding emotions in the neurosciences.

emotions) subverts attempts to explain mental processes (and so consciousness and emotions) only by objective means.[136]

In an attempt to avoid such difficulties, Griffiths suggests broad, over-
arching categories with some shared commonalities to explain and describe
emotions.[137] Klaus Scherer suggests there are five components to all emotions: neurological processes, subjective feeling, motor expression, cognition, and desire.[138] Others, such as Roberts, deny that such categories are
useful (there is no "neat categorical scheme") or that there is "one category,
albeit one that is fuzzy on the edges and held together in part by family
resemblances." Rather, he thinks that "the study of emotions can be legiti-
mately undertaken from a variety of disciplinary angles and with a variety
of methods . . . [with] each . . . especially fitted to answer its own kind of
questions."[139] Frijda goes further and writes:

> There is good reason for the failure of efforts to define emotions.
> The phenomena I classed as "emotional" do not have a core that is
> common to all behavior and feeling patterns that are called "emo-
> tions." . . . "Emotion" . . . refers to a loose collection of phenomena,
> and the boundaries of such collections are not clearly drawn.

Later he says:

> The phenomena that led to the use of the word emotion and
> the different emotion words are the outcomes of several sets
> of processes that are functionally independent, and each can
> occur in isolation.[140]

In an earlier article, he says that it is now widely accepted that emotions are
"'multicomponent phenomena'" such as feelings, or involuntary or impul-
sive behaviors, that can be understood in a variety of (sometimes incompatible) ways, and that when we refer to "emotions" we refer to "a collection of
processes and not to a single or a solidly integrated entity."[141]

Despite these difficulties, I now offer what I think are some unexcep-
tional, general comments as a framework for reflecting theologically on
remorse as a Christian ethic based on the observations in this chapter. The
approach is functional and situated, taking the view that most emotions

136. Nagal, "What Is It Like To Be a Bat?"

137. Griffiths, What Emotions Really Are and "Modularity," 71.

138. Scherer, "What Are Emotions?'

139. Roberts, Essay, 20, 36.

140. Frijda, "The Evolutionary Emergence," 610, 618.

141. Frijda, "Point of View," 60, 67, 69. So also, Sander et al., "Appraisal-Driven,"
219–20.

are cognitions and that culture plays a significant role in the way people understand and interpret their emotions. The approach I am suggesting leaves room for recognizing that emotions in some way may be the result of evolutionary adaptation but does not go as far as Ekman in saying that some emotions are universal and innate, and not the result of cognitive choices or socially conditioned.

There are compelling reasons to say that at least some emotions are culturally shaped and developed, and there is convincing evidence that even what may be "basic" emotions take different forms in different societies and can only be correctly interpreted within the cultural frameworks of those cultures.

It seems to me that the most persuasive and least problematic way to approach the study of remorse is to adopt Roberts's approach and regard remorse, like most emotions, as a concern-based construal with communicative functions. There is also strong empirical evidence to support the approaches of people like Arnold, Lazarus, Solomon, Nussbaum, and Frijda and recognize that (according to their sometimes differing approaches) emotions, such as remorse, have a significant cognitive component, and are shaped by intuitive and reflective appraisals that result in what Frijda calls "action readiness," that is, actions or reactions that motivate people to do something. Set within this framework of thought, we can "assume" that an emotion exists, as Frijda says. Not all emotions fit this analysis (the person irrationally afraid of harmless spiders illustrates an exception) but most do, and remorse obviously does.

This approach does not undermine a monist approach to human identity; it leaves unaddressed underlying questions of metaphysics; it acknowledges that emotions are recognizable as physiological changes that are set in a reciprocal relationship with cognitions; and it leaves room for human accountability for actions and reactions.

In this setting, "remorse" is the name given to a particular set or "bundle" of responses to what one has done. The responses are the result of critical evaluations and judgments about one's behavior. Part of the purpose of this book is to identify and explore not only some of the components of the responses, deep regret or guilt, but also the subject of the evaluations and judgments, namely, behavior that one regards as wrong.

Chapter 8

Remorse and Moral Knowledge

Moral Knowledge and Moral Awareness

As REMORSE IS DEEP regret or guilt about wrongdoing, we now explore some of the ways people understand what wrongdoing is by identifying the commonly accepted sources of moral knowledge. This chapter is not a statement or defense of Christian ethics; rather, it is an exploration of and critical reflection on how ethics are described and thought about, mainly in secular thought. We engage mainly in other parts of this book with the place of Christian ethics as components of interpersonal remorse.

Remorse, the Conscience, and Moral Emotions

In former times especially, the conscience was regarded as giving moral awareness of right and wrong.[1] In the New Testament, for example, the conscience is called *syneidēsis*. It is the faculty that alerts people to God and to divine ethics (e.g., Rom 2:14–15), gives access to moral knowledge that is already within human beings, and alerts people to what is right or wrong to do (e.g., Acts 23:1; 24:16; 1 Cor 10:25–29). In a later period, the Franciscans (such as Bonaventure [1217–74]) located conscience in the emotional side of human nature, and for Aquinas (and generally in the Dominican tradition) conscience is the mind making moral judgments. Aquinas distinguishes *synderesis*, the intuitive grasp of first principles

---

1. On conscience in the New Testament and generally, see Kirk, *Conscience*; Pierce, *Conscience*; Wall, "Conscience"; Gula, "Moral Conscience"; Grisez and Shaw, "Conscience"; Smit, *Social Evolution*, 82; and Sorabji, *Moral Conscience*.

or standards, and *conscientia*, the process of evaluating the rightness or wrongness of particular actions by applying first principles. The Catholic sacrament of penance makes the examination of one's conscience, in other words, the critical self-examination of what one has done or not done, an integral part of Christian spirituality, with a focus on sins and so the need for atonement and absolution.

The contemporary, secular term "moral emotions" corresponds, to some extent, with what was formerly called the "conscience."[2] "Moral emotions" are best understood in a setting of moral norms, with moral emotions being the emotions that people may have when (for example) they have done wrong and disregarded a moral norm. Remorse is obviously one of the moral emotions. If an emotion is to be regarded as a moral emotion, it will involve a judgment about or evaluation of one's own conduct.[3] One therefore cannot be remorseful without self-judgment and self-appraisal.[4]

Sometimes, when people use the phrase "moral emotions" they mean that some emotions are constitutively and distinctively moral. This view is mistaken, as there are "no distinctively moral emotions" and the term "moral emotions" is a "misnomer" if it refers to a "proprietary class" of emotions.[5] Jesse Prinz writes that moral emotions are not solely "dedicated to morality"; they can have "important functions outside the moral domain" and even occur in non-moral contexts.[6] For example, people may feel disgust[7] because of contamination, or disappointment because they are overlooked for promotion at work; they may have guilt as the survivor of a tragedy, or they may feel ashamed because they did not score well in an exam. These same emotions (disgust, disappointment, guilt, and shame) may also be directed towards a *moral* object and when they are, they may

2. Moral emotions are different from conscience as previously understood in at least three ways: first, there is a new emphasis on emotions; second, it is not assumed that the moral norms that are the subject of moral emotions are God-given; and third, the way moral norms are identified is not through a universal faculty that corresponds with the conscience.

3. Prinz, "Moral Emotions," 534. See also Cornelius, "Magda Arnold's Thomistic Theory," 987–94; Prinz, *Emotional Construction*, 68; Tangney et al., "Moral Emotions"; and see Solomon, "On Emotions." Darwin suggests that "lower animals," that is, those who are not human beings do not feel remorse (*Descent*, 135, 138) but later research suggests that some higher primates do have moral emotions (De Waal, *Primates*).

4. In *Emotions*, 201, Frijda describes what is obviously remorse or regret as "painful self-evaluation due to some action evaluated negatively and for which the person holds himself responsible."

5. Prinz, "Moral Emotions," 536.

6. Prinz, "Moral Emotions," 519, 535.

7. On moral disgust, see Rozin et al., "Disgust," 821–22.

be collectively called "remorse." In other words, the same emotions may sometimes be "moral" and at other times "non-moral" according to the object they appraise; additionally, if an emotion is to be regarded as moral in some way, it must "motivate morally praiseworthy behavior."[8] The most obvious example of non-moral remorse is when a person is apparently remorseful for having been found out or caught out. I discussed this type of "distorted" remorse in chapter 6.

Remorse is a moral emotion that results from intuitive or reflective appraisal that one has violated a moral norm to which one is committed. To put it another way, remorse will be a moral emotion if (in Roberts's words) one construes oneself as having blameworthily violated a standard one is concerned to honor and if there is an object in respect of which a moral judgment of wrongdoing has been made. We can amplify and clarify what we mean in the following three scenarios:

1. Sometimes, the deep regret or guilt is not about an object in respect of which a *moral* judgment of wrongdoing is made. For example, the judgment may be deep regret that one has failed to buy a lottery ticket on an occasion when the numbers one invariably uses for the lottery ticket win the jackpot. In these circumstances, the deep regret is not a *moral* emotion but an emotion about a non-moral object (one's failure to buy a lottery ticket).

2. If the deep regret or guilt is about a choice that at the time was morally justified but which later turns out to be mistaken, less good than another choice one could have made but did not, or had undesirable (and previously unforeseeable) consequences, can one be remorseful, even though the object of the remorse is a choice that at the time was morally justified? I think it is reasonable to feel remorse about morally justified behavior that in hindsight was mistaken or caused harm, on the basis that a morally virtuous person will seek to act wisely, do good, and promote the wellbeing of others. (We discuss this further in chapter 10.)

3. One may make a morally right choice but not out of virtuous character. For example, one may regret having to do the right thing. In these circumstances, one may be remorseful if one comes to regret deeply or feel guilt about one's former lack of virtue.

The point to note in the three scenarios is that it is not that the emotion itself is moral but that if the object is construed as morally wrong or bad,

8. Prinz, "Moral Emotions," 532, 534.

or as undesired and unintended, the result is an emotion based on an antecedent moral appraisal. In such situations, people loosely speak of "moral emotions."

Moral Knowledge and the Bible

In former times (and sometimes still today) ethics were taken from what were understood to be God's commands for human conduct. In other words, God's commands were the *a priori* moral principles from which normative ethics were derived. As a result of approaching the Bible as a (or "the") source of normative ethics, people were sometimes remorseful when they believed that they had not followed the commands of God.[9]

A view that is still held by some practicing Christians is that the meaning of biblical texts is self-evident. This view is mistakenly based on (and an extension of) what is sometimes called "the doctrine of perspicuity" (clarity). The doctrine in its authentic and more limited form is set out in the following way in the Westminster Confession of Faith (1646, Chapter 1.7), citing 2 Pet 3:16 and Pss 119:105, 130:

> All things in Scripture are not alike plain in themselves, nor alike
> clear unto all: yet, those things that are necessary to be known,
> believed, and observed for salvation are so clearly propounded,
> and opened in some place of Scripture or other, that not only
> the learned, but also the unlearned, in a due use of the ordinary
> means, may attain unto a sufficient understanding of them.

Approaching the Bible as a source of normative ethics raises an obvious difficulty. Modern approaches to biblical interpretation have shown that there is a multiplicity of ways of interpreting the biblical texts. The result is that even if we are confident that the biblical texts are the basis of normative ethics, we cannot be certain how to interpret the texts or that our interpretation of the texts is correct. We can put it sharply like this: God may have given an explicit, incontrovertible biblical text that is the basis of Christian ethics; however, God has not given an explicit, incontrovertible hermeneutic indicating how to interpret the text. This is not to say that the texts have no value or that we do not or cannot make proposals about what they may mean: it is that (as with *all* texts) our interpretations will always be provisional, and subject to re-appraisal.[10]

---

9. As will be evident throughout this book, I take a reflective approach to the Bible as a source of moral norms, basing my starting point on the ethical principles of Jesus.

10. Roberts suggests that "any moral framework that includes the notion of

David Hume (1711–76) observed that we cannot deduce what we ought or ought not to do from what is or is not the case. In other words, we cannot derive values from facts. Hence, to derive an imperative (such as an ethical mandate) from an indicative (that is, a statement of fact)—typical sometimes of the basis of ethics in the letters of Paul, for example—is irrational in the sense that an imperative derived from an indicative cannot be defended in logic.[11] Such a (mistaken) approach to moral reasoning is to fall into what is called "the naturalistic fallacy." Some are therefore critical of the Bible as a source of received knowledge about ethics, especially as the parenetic sections of the New Testament are explicitly derived from preceding doctrinal sections. Of course, the parenetic sections still have value as statements of ethical norms: what is disputed is the cogency of the bases of deriving the norms

Moral Knowledge and Sentimentalism

Some empiricists reject the Bible as having an authoritative place in thought and reason solely by virtue of the Bible's claimed status as being "the word of God," for they regard knowledge as information received through the senses by observation and by verification through experimentation. In addition, the early empirical philosophers approached the place of emotions in moral conduct in a way that is different from the traditional Christian approach, for they regard emotions as central to ethics and argue that moral action occurs when sentiment (emotion) is combined with reason. In other words, emotions are affective states of consciousness that, when combined with reason, are reasons for or causes of actions. Contrary to many previous traditions of thought, the empirical philosophers do not regard emotions and feelings to be inimical to reason; rather, they believed it to be "rational to be emotional."[12] For example, Hume wrote that "reason is, and ought only to be, the slave of the passions, and can never pretend to any other office than to serve and obey them."[13] In his view, emotions ("sentiments") have a place in making moral judgments[14] and that whether an action is right or wrong

---

unqualified moral obligation, and yet leaves out God as the Lawgiver, is inconsistent" (*Moral Life*, 22).

11. Hume, *Treatise*.

12. Evans, *Emotion*, from an unnumbered page of the Preface.

13. Hume, *Treatise*, 462.

14. Hume's views were developed by Smith (1723–90). For a critical view, see Kirk, *Conscience*, 13–26.

cannot be inferred by reasoning alone or otherwise than by perception.[15] Of course, reason still has a central place in Hume's scheme: reason contributes to the interpretation of the feelings of approval or disapproval that people have.[16] Notwithstanding the place of "sentiment" in moral conduct, I have been unable to find discussion about remorse in the writings of the empirical philosophers. The omission is surprising, though I suspect the reason may in part be because remorse is so obviously an emotion connected with Christian spirituality and because at the time remorse was typically understood to be the response of people who had sinned against God.

The part sentiment was regarded as holding in the moral life diminished for a period as a result of the influence of Immanuel Kant (1724–1804). He emphasized "pure reason" (reasoning without experience or sense data) as the basis of and motivation for moral judgments and moral knowledge. He did, however, recognize a role for emotions in ethics and placed respect, conscience, moral feeling, and love for humanity "at the ground of morality," regarding them as sensibilities that made people responsive to their moral duties.[17] Nevertheless, one of the (probably) unintended consequences of Kant's writings is a period of neglect of the place of emotions in moral philosophy. The neglect was later compounded as a result of the influence of logical positivism in English philosophy (developed in the work of Ludwig Wittgenstein [1889–1951]) and as a result of the influence of the Wiener Kreis, a group of philosophers and scientists who met in the University of Vienna from 1924–36.[18] One result has been that the "wrongdoing" aspect of remorse has been well analyzed, but the "deep regret" and "guilt" aspects relatively neglected. In other words, the cognitive component is usually emphasized, and the affective component under-explored.

---

15. Hume, *Treatise*, 468–69.

16. Examples of moral sentimentalists include Thomas Hobbes (1588–1679) (not in a discrete work but in various places); René Descartes (1596–1650) in *Meditations* (1641) and *Passions* (1649); Baruch de Spinoza (1632–77) in *Ethics* (1677); John Locke (1632–1704) in *Essay*, 229 (1689) (where he regarded emotions as "internal sensations," that is, recurring states of mind that were either "simple" or "complex," and if "complex," then a combination of "simple" states of mind); David Hume (1711–76) in Book 2 of *Treatise* (1739), *Enquiry* (1751), and *Dissertation* (1757); Jean-Jacques Rousseau (1712–78) in his principles of moral psychology in *Discourse* (1755) and *Emile* (1762); and Adam Smith (1723–90) in *Theory* (1759).

17. Kant, *Practical Philosophy*, 399, and *Anthropology*. For comment, see Sherman, "Place of Emotions," and Herman, *Practice*. See Williams, *Problems*, 207–29 for a critique of Kant's view and Prinz, "Moral Emotions," 520 for a nuanced summary of the place of emotions in Kant's thought. For a summary of modern re-appraisals of the place of Kant's approach to moral psychology, see Bagnoli, *Morality and the Emotions*, 9–11.

18. See, for example, Ben-Ze'ev, "Emotions and Morality," 195–200.

Nevertheless, moral sentimentalism has continued to hold a place in western thinking. A post-Enlightenment exponent of moral sentimentalism, for example, is Arthur Schopenhauer (1788–1860), who argued, in his 1840 book, *On the Basis of Morality*, that compassion is the motive for moral behavior. In Section 16 (headed "Statement and Proof of the Only Genuine Moral Incentive") he wrote that compassion is:

> the immediate *participation*, independent of all ulterior considerations, primarily in the *suffering* of another, and thus in the prevention and elimination of it. . . . Only insofar as an action has spring from compassion does it have moral value; and every action resulting from any other motives [*sic*] has none.[19]

In Section 18, Schopenhauer explores "the virtue of loving-kindness" and roots it not only in the ethic of love in the New Testament[20] but also in the ethics of eastern religions and in Latin authors. In his view, "the only true origin of loving-kindness" is by participation in another's "needs and distress." Such participation is "the sole source" of actions when they "*have moral worth*." Although Schopenhauer does not say this, remorse will have what we might call "moral value" since (to adopt his words from another context) it "spring[s] from compassion" and is "*participation* . . . in the *suffering* of another."[21]

Moral sentimentalism also has its contemporary defenders (sometimes called "neo-sentimentalists").[22] For example, Paul Rozin et al. refer to "self-conscious emotions."[23] They say that self-conscious emotions are emotions about "the moral worth and fit of the individual self within a community": when thought of this way, such emotions typically include regret, shame, embarrassment, and guilt. Secondly, self-conscious emotions also reflect "a similar concern for the integrity of the social order, but now turned outward to others": this class of self-emotions include "other-critical" emotions such as contempt, anger, and disgust. There is a

19. Schopenhauer, *On the Basis*, 144.

20. Jesus summarized the ethics of the Old Testament as the basis for Christian ethics, namely, love for God and love for one's neighbor (Matt 22:34–40; see Paul in Rom 13:9–10 and James in Jas 2:8).

21. Schopenhauer, *On the Basis*, 163. A modern example of this approach is Taylor, "Guilt and Remorse."

22. On neo-sentimentalists, see Tappolet, "Values and Emotions."

23. In Rozin et al., "Disgust." We first met the term "self-conscious emotions" in chapter 7 in connection with the work of Fischer and Tangney, "Self-Conscious Emotions," and Baird, "Adolescent Moral Reasoning."

REMORSE AND MORAL KNOWLEDGE

third class of self-conscious emotions that are "triggered by the suffering of others": they include pity and sympathy.[24]

If we follow this approach, remorse is an emotion that is inward-facing, in that remorse usually presupposes that an individual has a sense of failure, with resulting feelings of guilt, shame, and embarrassment; it is also outward-facing (because it is "triggered by the suffering of others"), in that remorseful individuals sometimes see their moral failure in the context of its impact on others and the communities of which they are part.

Prinz, another neo-sentimentalist, suggests that "the seeds of remorse and guilt" come from "emotional conditioning" that allows people to construct "behavioral norms from [their] innate stock of emotions."[25] Such conditioning gives people the disposition to respond to particular actions in particular ways, so that a person whose conditioning disposes them to be remorseful will respond remorsefully when a situation requires it. Specifically, in relation to remorse, he says that if "caregivers punish their children for misdeeds, by physical threat or withdrawal of love, children will feel badly about doing those things in the future" and remorse will be the longer-term behavioral norm that the children develop.[26] In other words, in Prinz's view, the deep regret and guilt about a moral wrong that we say typically constitutes remorse are the result of behavioral conditioning and emotional norms.[27]

Jonathan Haidt, also a neo-sentimentalist, has developed what he calls the "social intuitionist model" to describe how the ethics of right conduct come about.[28] Haidt says that "moral intuitions come first and directly cause moral judgments." They are "a kind of cognition, but . . . not a kind of reasoning." The intuitions are autonomic and immediate

24. Rozin et al., "CAD Triad," 575. Tangney et al., in "Moral Emotions," say that people with "dispositional tendencies" typically experience self-conscious emotions. This suggests the rather obvious statement that people are more likely to feel remorse and related emotions if they have a remorseful disposition.

25. Prinz, "Is Morality Innate?" 368. Prinz identifies three psychological mechanisms that contribute to the formation of emotional conditioning and so social rules: meta-emotions (emotions about emotions), perspective-taking (third-party concern and empathy), non-moral preferences and behavioral dispositions (by which he means social behaviors that lend themselves to moralization), such as reciprocity. He also identifies situational factors that contribute to the formation of moral rules. These include social pressures that lead to rules of conduct ("Is Morality Innate?" 404–5).

26. Prinz, "Is Morality Innate?" 404.

27. On the sociology of emotions, see Lively and Weed, "Sociology of Emotion."

28. Haidt, "The Emotional Dog." Haidt appears to be addressing one of the lacunae in Darwinism and Neo-Darwinism observed by Stephen R. L. Clark, namely, that it is not obvious that Darwinism "is compatible with moral and political virtue" (*Biology*, 88). Biggar also poses the problem sharply in "Evolutionary Biology," 152–53.

responses, without conscious or deliberate engagement; people are aware
of the effects of the responses but not the processes that bring them about.
Moral intuitions in his view are social norms and values that people hold
to without appraising them; they are also the result of behavioral conditioning and emotional norms. Moral judgments that come this way are
what he calls "gut reactions." The example of a moral judgment that Haidt
gives is that when questioned, people were not able to give reasons why
some examples of sibling incest are wrong. In contrast to moral intuitions,
"[m]oral reasoning is usually an ex post facto process," offering justification and explanation for what we intuitively think is wrong.[29]

Haidt is right if he means no more than that sometimes people follow
values derived from internalized natural or social norms without perhaps
much, or even any, antecedent cognition and appraisal.[30] He is also right that
one function of emotions can be to give "an initial indication of the proper
direction in which to respond," though as we shall see below, in the view of
Aaron Ben-Ze'ev, only limited weight should be given to the place of emotions
in shaping the response.[31] However, he overlooks the fact that sometimes people engage in moral reasoning without first engaging with moral intuitions
and that sometimes people disregard moral intuitions for moral reasons after
critical reflection of the moral intuitions.[32]

Clearly, some moral beliefs and practices are based on autonomic, intuitive responses and are not the subject of critical, reflective appraisal. The
subjects of these responses are aware only of their outcomes, and (in contrast with conscious, deliberate moral reasoning) not the process that leads
to the outcomes. As we saw in chapters 2 and 3, it is also clear that some
beliefs and emotional responses can be explained as the result of conditioning and socialization. However, a mature approach to moral knowledge
makes a place for moral reasoning with the result that intuitive responses
are sometimes modified or adapted, and new, more thought-out intuitive
responses formed. Moral knowledge arises from cognitions, or from intuitions, or from both in a reciprocal relationship.

29. Haidt, "The Emotional Dog," 814. This seems to me to be no more than a rep-
lication of Arnold's cognitive appraisal theory. See also Haidt and Björklund "Social
Intuitionists" and Haidt, *Righteous Mind*.

30. Thagard and Finn revert to the term "conscience" and regard it as "a kind of
moral intuition" that is "both cognitive and emotional" ("Conscience," 168, 156).

31. Ben-Ze'ev, "Emotions and Morality," 206, 209. See Sinnott-Armstrong, "Framing Moral Intuitions," 74.

32. Haidt's method and conclusions are also heavily criticized in an essay by Daniel
Jacobson, "Moral Dumbfounding."

Moral Knowledge and Evaluations

Another challenge to the idea of moral knowledge was articulated particularly clearly in the twentieth century. A. J. Ayer (1910–89) criticized the nature of normative ethics, and not just the way they might be derived. He argued that moral statements are no more than evaluations, expressing a desire, emotion, or preference and are not based on reason.[33] Ayer wrote that "In saying that a certain kind of action is right or wrong, I am not making any factual statement, not even a statement about my own statement of mind. I am merely expressing certain moral sentiments."[34] It is, of course, true that moral statements cannot be empirically tested and so fail the criterion of verifiability. However, most philosophers think that ethical statements are more than statements about feelings, even though it is not possible conclusively to show why.[35]

Moral Knowledge and Moral Realism

Many would say that attempts to find a verifiable core of normative ethics in moral codes in human societies, a core that exists independently of opinion and culture and that can be generalized to all people at all times, have, to date, been unsuccessful: the variation of moral codes in the world and the widespread variations even within codes have led many to conclude that there is not such a core of ethics common to all people. Not surprisingly, given the widespread scientific and philosophical challenges to the idea of moral knowledge and normative ethics as objective, John L. Mackie begins his monograph on ethics (the subtitle of which is "Inventing Right and Wrong") with these provocative but defensible words: "There are no objective values."[36]

Such conclusions have been challenged by moral realists, who argue that moral facts and moral knowledge exist and that their existence is independent of beliefs about or perceptions of them.[37] Related to this view is "moral non-naturalism," namely, the view that moral facts exist and have truth-value

33. Ayer was heavily influenced by his early training at Vienna, where he learned the positivist doctrine that ethics are not rational, but, if anything, a matter of subjective emotions.

34. Ayer, *Language, Truth, and Logic*, 107.

35. Joyce goes even further and suggests that moral statements are accompanied and caused by emotions ("What Neuroscience," 374–75).

36. Mackie, *Ethics*, 15. Compare Wreen, "Mackie," and Machan, "Why Moral Judgments" who attempt, unsuccessfully in my view, to rebut Mackie's conclusion.

37. Shafer-Landau, *Moral Realism*.

independently of, and are compatible with, the natural sciences.[38] Set against
these approaches to morality are approaches from the natural sciences that
view morality as derived (for example) from evolutionary adaptation, from
cultural conditioning, or from genetic makeup. In other words, this latter
view holds that morality is culturally constructed and can be wholly explained
by the natural sciences.[39] The cross-cultural universality of emotions and the
evolution of altruistic behavior in humans are also taken as support for the
naturalistic approach. However, the universality of emotions may be the result
of responses to moral facts; altruistic behavior is not a moral belief; and the
emotional response of disgust is also sometimes taken to be the source of
moral responses.[40] On balance, the case against moral realism certainly cannot be taken as having been incontrovertibly made.

Moral Behavior and Emotions

A focus on emotions alone can lead to an unstable ethic and to unpredict-
able behavior; a focus on behavior alone can lead to right behavior that does
not cohere with a person's inner disposition. The latter is the basis of Jesus's
criticism of the Pharisees in Matt 23 and his strictures about anger and lust
in Matt 5:21–30 and in other places in the Sermon on the Mount in Matt
5–7. Emotions and behavior need to be rightly balanced.[41]

In the modern period, the importance of emotions is increasingly recognized as having a significant part in *shaping* moral behavior.[42] The pace of

38. Cuneo and Shafer-Landau, "The Moral Fixed Points."

39. See, for example, Street, "Darwinian Dilemma," and Prinz, "Is Morality Innate?"

40. See Pizarro et al., "On Disgust," who cast doubt on a supposed causal link between disgust and morality.

41. An example of a one-sided approach to ethics is in Swinburne's monograph on
the atonement. He does not discuss contrition, or remorse, or compunction as components of what he sees as the four elements of atonement (repentance, apology, reparation, and penance). See Swinburne, *Responsibility*, 81–84.

42. The approach is called "conative" because its focus is on how one acts on feelings
(affect) and on thoughts (cognitions). The change of approach to the place of emotions in shaping moral behavior was stimulated by an important essay by Anscombe
in "Modern Moral Philosophy, Williams's essay "Morality and the Emotions" (in
Problems, chapter 13, from an article first published in 1963), and further taken up by
Murdoch (in *Sovereignty*, especially). At the time when Williams wrote, he noted that
moral philosophy had "push[ed] the emotions out of the picture" of analytical philosophy (*Problems*, 208). More generally, renewed interest in the study of emotions by
philosophers followed an article by Bedford in 1956–57 ("Emotions"), a book by Kenny
in 1963 (*Actions*), and a monograph on emotions by Solomon in 1976 (*Emotions*). For
a brief introduction to the different ways to approach ethics and ethical questions,
see Shafer-Landau, *Fundamentals*. On the history of study of emotions, see Solomon,

change is accelerating as the relationship of emotions and moral behavior is becoming better understood. It is also accelerating because of the growing significance of a new discipline called "moral psychology," a discipline that combines insights from psychology as well as moral philosophy. The result has been a new place for virtues, consciousness, and emotions in contemporary moral philosophy[43] and in related fields such as the cognitive science of morality[44] and moral psychology.[45]

Reflecting on the modern approach to emotions in philosophy, Ben-Ze'ev says that emotions are "an initial indication of the proper direction in which to respond"[46] and that:

> [i]f our moral decisions were reached only through intellectual deliberations, then our decisions would be morally distorted insofar as they would be one-sided, neglecting important aspects of our lives. The presence of conflict between the intellectual and emotional systems is frequently useful from a moral viewpoint, since it indicates a moral predicament to which we should pay attention.

As for cognitions and normative ethics, he says that:

> [n]eglecting the role of intellectual deliberations in morality is as dangerous as neglecting the role of emotions. Although emotions serve as our moral compass, the compass may in some cases provide inadequate directions.[47]

An important attempt that, in effect, gives a place to both emotions and reason is based on the work of John Rawls in *A Theory of Justice*. Rawls suggests that there needs to be "reflective equilibrium" between moral principles, intuitions, and the considered judgments that one holds. In the process, one weighs "various proposed conceptions" and either revises one's "judgments to accord with one of them or [holds] fast to [one's] initial convictions." The principles that we would choose will then "match our considered judgments"

"Philosophy of Emotions," 3–15; Stearns, "History," 16–29; Frevert "History"; Plamper, *History*, 40–74. For a summary of the main lines of thought and debate, see Cates, "Conceiving Emotions." Volume 3(3) of *Emotion Review* (2011) is devoted to emotions and morality.

43. Nussbaum and Rorty have been strong proponents of the new approach. Roberts has written important books on the place of emotions in the moral life (*Essay*, *Spiritual Emotions*, and *Moral Life*).

44. D'Arms and Jacobson "The Moralistic Fallacy."

45. Roberts, *Essay*; Thagard and Finn, "Conscience," 150, Bagnoli, *Morality and the Emotions*, 4; and see volume 1 of Sinnott-Armstrong, *Moral Psychology*, xiii–xvi.

46. Ben-Ze'ev, "Emotions and Morality," 206.

47. Ben-Ze-ev, "Emotions and Morality," 208.

and *vice versa*.[48] Rawls's approach opens the way for emotions and intuitions to play a part in the process of reflective equilibrium, for moral principles may need to be re-examined if the behavioral outcomes of their application seem repugnant intuitively or emotionally.[49]

Rawls's approach has critics. Peter Singer, for example, summarizes and critiques Rawls's position this way:

> [I]t follows from [Rawls's] views that the validity of a moral theory will vary according to whose considered moral judgments the theory is tested against. There is no sense in which we can speak of a theory being objectively valid, no matter what considered moral judgments people happen to hold. If I live in one society, and accept one set of moral judgments, while you live in another society and hold a quite different set, very different moral theories may be "valid" for each of us. There will be no sense in which one of us is wrong and the other right.[50]

Singer also points out that Rawls's approach leaves unresolved "whether a moral theory is supposed to match the considered moral judgments of an individual, or of some larger group, such as a society."[51] He also says that in effect Rawls is:

> systematizing the considered moral judgments of some unspecified moral consensus. This . . . task . . . is . . . a descriptive task from which, without supplementation from other sources, no normative or action-guiding consequences can be derived. We cannot test a normative theory by the extent to which it accords with the moral judgments people ordinarily make.[52]

I disagree. We *do* "test a normative theory by the extent to which it accords with the moral judgments people ordinarily make," because some normative theories sometimes suggest solutions to moral problems that are palpably absurd. For all the rhetoric, moral theories are reached in part inductively from what people ordinarily feel, do, and believe.

---

48. Rawls, *Theory*, 48.

49. This approach seems implicit in Roberts's view that evaluating emotions as true or false is by "consulting the best of our moral traditions and other relevant data, suitably processed by critical reflection" (*Moral Life*, 103).

50. Singer, "Sidgwick," 494.

51. Singer, "Sidgwick," 495.

52. Singer, "Sidgwick," 515.

The "somatic marker hypothesis" has also helped to clarify the role that emotions play in decision-making, and supports the view that reason alone is not a sufficient cause of moral behavior.[53] Rather, the markers:

> are the "gut reactions" which we experience when we are confronted with moral problems. They guide us when we encounter similar situations or problems. . . . [They] become the guides for making quick judgments and decisions, and tell someone how he or she should evaluate the situation ("good or bad").[54]

The implications of these observations for remorse are obvious. Moral behavior is determined by the reciprocal evaluation of both intuitive emotions and reason: the dominance of either emotion or reason to the neglect of the other can lead to imbalance and lack of self-reflective, critical engagement with thoughts, actions, and behaviors. Reflective equilibrium and the somatic marker hypothesis generally offer sensible, practical approaches to the place of emotions in remorse. Some people may have intuitive emotional responses that are congruent with the ethical norms they hold. In contrast, a person may be overcome with feelings of remorse about something as a result of their intuitions and emotions but the moral principles that they hold may lead them to realize that to feel remorse in such a situation is misplaced.[55] Careful reflection may rebalance the original intuitive and emotional responses. Conversely, people may do something wrong but ignore the promptings of their consciences or the moral principles that they hold. An interested onlooker may alert them to their lapse. An example of such an onlooker from the Old Testament is Nathan in 2 Sam 12:1–15, who confronted David some months after he had committed adultery with Bathsheba and had staged the death of Uriah, her husband. David's response in verse 13 is, "I have sinned against the LORD." In other words, as a result of what Nathan said, David more-or-less immediately re-appraised what he had done by a process of reflection with the result that his emotions, moral principles, intuitions, and considered judgments became realigned in equilibrium.

53. Damasio, *Descartes's Error*.
54. Smit, *Social Evolution*, 182.
55. Compare Bennett, "Huckleberry Finn," 125–27.

Remorse, Moral Foundations Theory, and Prosocial Emotions

Moral Foundations Theory ("MFT") developed out of Haidt's work on the social intuitionist approach to morality, with Haidt and others seeking to identify the sources of the intuitions that they believed underlay the moral judgments that were caused by autonomic moral intuitions. In the first iteration of the theory in 2004, Haidt and Craig Joseph propose that all people have "intuitive ethics" as a result of evolutionary adaptations to challenges.[56] These ethics are suffering, hierarchy, reciprocity, and purity. The ethics take local forms and so result in culturally variable virtues according to the "cognitive modules" of each of the four sets of ethics.

The 2004 iteration of the theory was developed in a 2013 article which sets out five modules (in the article, called "foundations") of ethics: care/harm, fairness/cheating, loyalty/betrayal, authority/subversion, and sanctity/degradation.[57] The first two are treated as person-focused and so "individualizing," to do with care and fairness, and the remainder as group-focused and so "binding," clustering around the notions of loyalty, authority, and sanctity. Table 1 of the article sets out the characteristic emotions and relevant virtues of each of the foundations. The most obvious links with remorse are with the individualizing foundations, i.e., the care/harm foundation (evidenced by emotions such as compassion for victims, caring, and kindness) and the fairness/cheating foundation (evidenced by emotions such as anger, guilt, fairness, justice, trustworthiness).

The MFT arose out of dissatisfaction with the prevailing view about the scope of the concerns of moral philosophy. According to the 2013 iteration, moral philosophy is limited "to concerns about individuals harming or unfairly treating other individuals," with the "autonomy and/or welfare of the individual as the starting point for ethical enquiry." Remorse obviously fits well in such a scheme of morality. Some think "group-level moral concerns" have lost their proper place in the concerns of moral philosophy, a place that they had held before the nineteenth century.[58] To address what is seen as too narrow a focus of the current approach of moral philosophy, the MFT is designed to define moral systems by their function with social systems in view.

---

56. Haidt and Joseph, "Intuitive Ethics." Shweder's work (to which we have referred in this book, e.g., Shweder, "The 'Big Three'") influenced Haidt and Joseph in the development of the MFT. De Waal argues that moral motivation is founded in emotional responses (in *Good Natured*, and see Clark, *Biology*, 89–92).

57. Graham et al., "Moral Foundations Theory." A sixth foundation, liberty/oppression was added in Haidt, *Righteous Mind*.

58. Graham, "Mapping the Moral Domain," 366, 367.

(To this extent, it is an attempt to reintroduce the ethics of community into mainstream thought.) Haidt and Selin Kesebir wrote that:

> Moral systems are interlocking sets of values, virtues, norms, practices, identities, institutions, technologies, and evolved psychological mechanisms that work together to suppress or regulate selfishness and make social life possible.[59]

With such an approach to ethics, there is a less obvious place for emotions, such as remorse, for such emotions concern disruptions to individual relationships. Nevertheless, there is room for an "individualizing" approach to ethics in the "harm" and "fairness" foundations, although it is perhaps significant in the literature I have referred to about the MFT that none of it explores (except in a passing way) "individualizing" emotions such as remorse, regret, and guilt. To put the change of emphasis in the language of this book, we can say that with a renewed emphasis on the ethics of the social life of the community, we can expect a diminished emphasis on the ethics of autonomy (of which remorse is an example). However, even if one gives a (re)new(ed) place in ethics to "group-level concerns," remorse still remains an important emotional response if one violates "group level concerns" because individual acts of wrongdoing can have an effect on "group-level concerns."

Some of Haidt's earlier work points to his interest in "group-level concerns." In a 2003 article, he wrote that moral emotions have "prosocial action tendencies." He clarifies that "[t]he more an emotion tends to be triggered by . . . disinterested elicitors, the more it can be considered a prototypical moral [prosocial] emotion." Haidt says there is "no neat division between moral emotions and nonmoral emotions" but so long as the emotion, in the context of its culture, shares features of being the response of a disinterested elicitor resulting in prosocial action tendencies, the emotion is a moral emotion.[60]

In the article, Haidt discusses "other-regarding"[61] emotions and describes them as "those emotions that are linked to the interests or welfare either of society as a whole or at least of persons other than the judge and the agent.[62]" For Haidt, emotions are moral if the motives of the person with the emotion is disinterested, rather than (presumably) self-seeking

---

59. Haidt and Kesebir, "Morality," 800. See also Haidt's 2003 definition of moral emotions as "any emotion that leads people to care about the world, and to support, enforce, or improve its integrity" ("Moral Emotions").

60. Haidt, "Moral Emotions," 854, 864–65.

61. The phrase is Taylor's in "Guilt and Remorse," 68.

62. Haidt, "Moral Emotions," 853, with the italics removed.

and self-advancing.[63] In taking this approach to emotions, Haidt is follow-ing Darwin's lead in regarding moral behavior as a form of social behavior. Korrina Duffy and Tanya Chartrand rightly make the obvious point that prosocial behavior "is related to moral behavior because moral actions are generally prosocial."[64]

Whereas thinkers in earlier generations might have attributed a mor-al sense to divine providence and human conscience, Haidt regards affec-tive responses as "panhuman products of evolution and cultural scripts that are shaped by local values and meanings . . . found in all cultures" with "differences in some of their components of emotional experience."[65] In other words, he sees prosocial emotions as set in cultural contexts that result in local expression and linked to the interests or welfare of others. Prosocial emotions are also the result of evolutionary developments; they are adaptations to deal with long-standing threats and opportunities in social life. What gives expression to the variations is whether the emotions are set in a culture that construes the self as independent (developing au-tonomous ethics) or inter-dependent (developing the ethics of commu-nity), and whether the social structure is hierarchic (perhaps suggesting the ethics of divinity) or egalitarian.[66]

If Haidt is right that emotions are "panhuman products of evolution," he will have identified an objective basis to moral emotions; moral emotions will then also be normative because they are universal.[67] However, this begs the question whether what he identifies does in fact exist independently of opinion and culture and whether it is as "panhuman" as he says. Haidt's con-clusions about universal moral emotions also run counter to the view that Jan Plamper summarizes (quoted in chapter 7) that anthropological studies of emotions indicate that the idea of pancultural emotions is an illusion.

The emotions Haidt labels as moral are, in his view, moral only on some occasions. This is because one needs a convergence of prosocial ac-tion tendencies and a high degree of disinterestedness on the part of the person Haidt calls "the elicitor."[68] In other words, a moral emotion is not

---

63. Haidt's approach also highlights that moral emotions will be more acutely felt when they cohere with a society's values and ideologies.

64. Duffy and Chartrand, "From Mimicry," 455.

65. Haidt, "Moral Emotions," 855.

66. Haidt, "Moral Emotions," 859.

67. David Sheard in personal correspondence points out to me that the evolution-arily endowed facility of the experience of emotions does not imply that any particular emotions are the result of evolution or that any particular emotion has an objective basis.

68. Haidt says as much in "Moral Emotions" in his commentary on Figure 45.1.

constitutively or distinctively moral or non-moral: its character is determined by the motives and actions of the subject.

Haidt does not specifically refer to remorse as one of the moral emotions because it is not an obviously prosocial emotion, unless remorse leads to acts of restitution. However, remorse clearly is a moral emotion according to Haidt's description of moral emotions: it is obviously linked to the interests or welfare of another individual in a society, and the more disinterested its form, the more lucid its nature. Haidt's description of guilt and compassion[69] is also broad enough to include the characteristics of what we have identified to be essential components of remorse. Remorse may also be related to an evolutionary process that in a later work Haidt calls "reciprocal altruism" that has to do with justice, fairness, and rights.[70] However, by "prosocial action tendencies" Haidt seems to have in mind more than prosocial action tendencies directed towards one person (the victim of wrongdoing in respect of whom the wrongdoer is remorseful). It is also a moot point to what extent action tendencies resulting from remorse can be said to be "disinterested." This is because actions that result from remorseful feelings can be intended as much to relieve the suffering of the remorseful person with a guilty conscience as they can be to put right the wrong that has been done.

Haidt's description of moral emotions helpfully clarifies why remorse can be such a variegated moral emotion. We can see from his work that remorse, in its more lucid forms, comprises aspects of the emotions that he identifies as moral, principally because we can say that remorse is "linked to the interests or welfare . . . of persons other than the judge and the agent," has what Haidt calls having "prosocial action tendencies," and often leads to repentance, reconciliation, and acts of restitution.[71] In contrast, what we have described as "illucid" remorse is more self-centered, lamenting what one's wrongdoing has done to one's own reputation and sense of self-esteem. Such remorse often cannot be said to be "linked to the interests or welfare . . . of persons other than the judge and the agent." We can see that remorse is a particularly clear example of an emotion that has fluctuating moral identity because, as a prosocial moral emotion, it is sometimes more inward-facing than other-person focused.

Despite what Haidt says, making prosocial action tendencies the criteria of moral emotions is problematic, despite the literature he and others have surveyed to develop the five ethical foundations, because what is

69. Haidt, "Moral Emotions," 860-2.

70. Haidt, "New Synthesis," 1001.

71. The term "prosocial" is now commonly part of certain types of economic theory (Blume and Durlauf, *The Economy*) and is a diagnostic category of certain types of psychological disorder in DSM-5.

prosocial is relative and culturally dependent. This can be illustrated from the changing way that homosexual behavior is viewed. In some societies, people say that homosexual behavior is wrong because it is believed to be a threat to social wellbeing and stability. In other words, in the view of people in such societies, it is not prosocial behavior. Increasingly commonly, the view of many is that homosexual behavior is *not* a threat to social wellbeing and stability. Understood Haidt's way, prosocial behavior is no more than the view of the majority, no matter how prejudiced, ill-informed, and ignorant that view may be. So long as people believe that their emotions lead them "to care about the world, and to support, enforce, or improve its integrity"[72] they have a basis to defend actions that others, in a different social setting, may regard as repugnant.

On the other hand, Haidt's approach rightly challenges some traditional approaches to normative ethics: to take the converse of the example above about homosexual behavior, many in some societies would say that prosocial norms about homosexual behavior have rightly challenged some schemes of normative ethics that regard homosexual behavior as morally wrong. The result has been that normative ethics have been critically reappraised and modified in view of a widely supported and endorsed new approach to some aspects of sexual ethics.

We make four final observations about Haidt's approach. First, Haidt's theory does not address what Geoffrey Goodwin observes, namely, that prosocial behavior "is not sufficient for morality because many prosocial behaviors are morally neutral, and some may actually be immoral if they bring about bad ends."[73] Second, even values that are thought to have come from evolutionary adaptations cannot be the basis of normative ethics. To think that they do is to fall into the naturalistic fallacy and move from what is descriptive (looking at questions such as whether evolutionary adaptations shape the content of moral behavior and moral judgments) to insist that the normative (concerning the justification of moral principles and how people ought to behave) follows. Next, at times what appear to be prosocial, moral emotions will be clouded by self-interest, subjectivity, and psychological defenses, and so in their expression may involve a degree of self-deception.[74] Last, the Golden Rule, as Jesus enunciated it, offers a

72. Haidt, "Moral Emotions," 855.

73. Goodwin, "Prosociality," 466. Compare an earlier view that even the "moral emotions" do not always and do not necessarily "presuppose moral values" (Lyons, *Emotion*, 91).

74. Sigmund Freud called such processes "defenses" and suggested that, in order to deal with life's conflicts and problems, the Ego may unconsciously adopt defense mechanisms to ward off unpleasant feelings, such as anxiety. Psychological defenses

radical inversion of prosocial ethics. Rather than starting with "those emotions that are linked to the interests or welfare either of society as a whole or at least of persons other than the judge and the agent,"[75] the Golden Rule starts with the interests or welfare of the *individual actor* and regards these as the way the individual actor should treat *others*.[76] Attitudes towards homosexual behavior make the point clearly: rather than an individual asking, "What does society think or regard as being in its interests and welfare?" as the basis for normative ethics about homosexual behavior, the approach that the Golden Rules requires an individual to take is to regard as the basis of the individual's attitudes and actions the way the individual would himself or herself wish to be treated.

Remorse and Evolutionary Biology

As we have seen, some have suggested that moral norms and human emotions are rooted in biological, bodily processes and shaped by natural selection. The suggestion was sharply brought to the forefront of discussion in *Sociobiology: The New Synthesis* by Edward O. Wilson.[77] The book has been criticized for overstating its case, namely, that *all* social behavior has a biological basis. Even so, later research has increasingly shown evidence that some "judgments of morality" (such as, for example, the basis of punishment for wrongdoing):

> have neural correlates in the nerve centers of the brain [and] that the behaviors produced by these areas are largely biological, automatic, and apt to have at one time played a key adaptive role in avoiding harm and improving cooperation.[78]

Evolutionary biologists and evolutionary psychologists believe that:

> humans bear species-wide (and in some cases sex-wide) physical, information-processing commonalities that have evolved to yield predispositions toward certain behaviors in the face of

include repression, denial, regression, and projection. Freud's daughter, Anna, developed her father's approach in Freud, *The Ego*.

75. Haidt "Moral Emotions," 853, with the original italics removed.

76. Gascoigne writes that "a truly interpersonal understanding of the self" requires for its full realization "an understanding that recognizes . . . the values of individual subjectivity" (such as we might see as a result of the application of the Golden Rule); he also balances this with criticism of individualism, and so says that individual subjectivity "depends on committed relationships to others" (*Public Forum*, 231).

77. See also Kazen, *Emotions*.

78. Koppel and Fondacaro, "Retribution," 199.

certain categories and confluences of stimuli and predisposi-
tions toward other behaviors in other contexts.[79]

There may be some truth in these views, but they run the risk of being
reductionist, that is, of making the mistake of reducing statements about
subjective mental states to statements about what is physical, without any
loss or change of meaning.[80]

Concluding Thoughts

Since remorse is an emotion about moral wrongdoing, it is important to
identify which actions or omissions are morally wrong and so are appropriately the subject of remorse. Former clarity and agreement about the Bible
and the conscience (understood as being a God-given faculty that discloses
divine standards for human beings to practice) as sources of moral knowledge no longer hold a significant place in much contemporary discourse. In
secular, contemporary thought, the new ways of identifying the sources of
moral knowledge are problematic, as we have seen. As a result, there is no
agreement about what necessarily constitutes moral wrongdoing.

An important modern re-awakening has been to the place of emotions
in the moral life. However, there is wisdom in taking a cautious approach
to the implications of this re-awakening, for emotions can cloud good judgment and drive an elicitor towards self-deception and self-justification. An
approach to the moral emotions that links emotions, such as remorse, with
the welfare and interests of the person wronged does not guarantee that the
quality and integrity of an elicitor's reflective appraisal will be free from possible corruption. It is easy to be too kind on oneself, and not kind enough to
one's victims, when it comes to the suffering one has caused to others.

Despite the proper caution about the place of emotions in the moral
life, emotions clearly do have a place in shaping moral behavior and in ethical decision-making.[81] What is also widely accepted is that moral judgments
"often occur with emotions."[82] At least three reasons have been given for
seeing and making a connection between emotions and behavior. First,
emotional responses[83] alert us to be what good behavior may be. They

79. Jones, "Laws," 284.

80. Nagel, "What Is It Like to Be a Bat?"

81. Nusbaum, *Upheavals,* 43. Debate is robust outside questions to do with remorse:
see, out of many examples, Haidt *Righteous Mind*; Greene, *Moral Tribes*; Damon and
Colby, *The Power of Ideals*; and Decety and Wheatley, *The Moral Brain.*

82. Prinz, "Moral Emotions," 522.

83. Strawson calls them "reactive attitudes" in *Freedom and Resentment.*

"promote or detect conduct that violates or conforms to a moral rule."[84] Such responses are "critical for moral systems as they give an indication of when a behavior either goes against a moral code or is exemplary of what a proper person in that society would do."[85] Emotions contribute to moral evaluation and *vice versa*: people regard something as good or bad according to the moral response that they have to it.[86] Second, without emotions such as shame, guilt, embarrassment, remorse, and even fear, one might well do nothing in response to a violation of a moral norm.[87] Emotions can alert a person to correct or mitigate their behavior. Thus, emotions are "functional sign-posts for evaluating . . . behavior and can provide instantaneous feedback as to how greatly that act either supports or breaks the strictures of moral systems."[88] Last, emotions can also complement and affirm moral norms. In other words, emotions do not necessarily subvert the integrity of a person's moral character (as some seem to fear) but can play a part in supporting and upholding a person's moral convictions or help lead to a person's moral development.[89] They can also help to "motivate morally praiseworthy behavior."[90] To put it pithily, moral behavior tends to make people feel good and so motivates them to continue to behave in a moral way.[91] Bad behavior can make them feel awful.

In short, we cannot get away from a link between emotions, moral knowledge, and the moral life, whether emotions are the cause, the effect, or constituents. Bernard Williams rightly observes that emotions have a place in authenticating a person's moral statements. He specifically considers the relevance of remorse as an indicator of a person's moral sincerity, and writes that the relevance of remorse is "obvious" where a wrongdoer demonstrates remorse not in "unproductive self-punishment," which is a "misdirected substitute for action," but where the wrongdoer "seek[s] to put things together again," such as by "reparative action." What is important is not so much a person's statements, in his view, but rather "reference to [a person's] emotional structure of . . . thought and action."[92]

---

84. Prinz, *Emotional Construction*, 68

85. Harkness and Hitlin, "Morality and Emotions," 452.

86. Prinz, "Moral Emotions," 520.

87. Carlsmith and Gross, "Some Effects of Guilt"; Katz et al., "Ambivalence"; Harris et al., "Effects of Confession"; Baumeister et al., "Guilt."

88. Harkness and Hitlin, "Morality and Emotions," 452.

89. Taylor, *Pride, Shame, and Guilt.*

90. Prinz, "Moral Emotions," 534.

91. Tiberius, "Does Virtue?"

92. Williams, *Problems*, 222, 223.

Chapter 9

Remorse and Punishment[1]

IN THIS CHAPTER, WE explore at various points three underlying questions that are sometimes raised in the context of the criminal law.[2] The first is whether expressions of remorse should be considered as a reason to mitigate punishment (that is, suffering or harm as an expression of disapproval) imposed on a wrongdoer. The second is whether punishments are an effective way to develop or enhance feelings of remorse in a wrongdoer. The third is how, or whether, we can tell that a person's remorse is genuine.[3]

Punishment

When it comes to the criminal law, which is concerned about legal guilt, people are treated as blameworthy for and liable to punishment for their past (or continuing) actions, even if many years have elapsed since the crime was committed, and whether or not they have repented and lived blameless lives in the years following. In Britain, for example, there is no Statute of Limitations for criminal acts, and people remain liable for "historic crimes" notwithstanding that the wrongdoers have long repented of their wrongdoing.[4]

1. I would like to thank His Honour Judge Christopher Prince, Resident Judge at Durham Crown Court and the Honorary Judicial Recorder of Durham, for reading and commenting on an earlier version of this chapter.

2. As we said in chapter 1, it is important to bear in mind the difference between "guilt" (a feeling that one has done something wrong or the fact of having done a wrong act) and being "guilty" (being culpable or one's juridical status). See also Buber, "Guilt," on the difference between neurotic guilt and "real" guilt.

3. On these questions, see Murphy's seminal essay in *Punishment*, 129–80.

4. On the morality of statutes of limitations for criminal wrongs, see Roberts,

It is no defense to say, "The wrong I committed happened in the past; I have repented and made reparation. I am now a different person."[5] The passing of time neither severs the fact of wrongdoers' agency, nor lessens legal culpability, nor entitles wrongdoers to a reduction in sentences of punishment.[6]

The basis of guilt in the criminal law is that people are capable of freely making choices, and so should be held to account for them.[7] We have seen in chapter 7 that some lines of modern thought challenge the idea of freedom of choice and personal responsibility for one's actions. The criminal law seems to take account of this with the idea of mitigation when it comes to sentencing, for people with a demonstrably reduced degree of personal responsibility may receive a sentence of diminished severity.

Punishment for legal wrongdoing is obviously a social necessity, regarded by many as needed to promote and sustain social cohesion, to express and communicate society's distaste for actions that threaten its stability and identity, and to ensure that victims do not alone bear the consequences of wrongdoing.[8] Linda Radzik disconcertingly observes, "although most people agree that crimes ought to be punished, there is no consensus as to why this is the case."[9] In the same vein, Joel Feinberg describes punishment as "theoretically puzzling and morally disquieting."[10]

The usefulness and value of punishment can be pragmatically demonstrated on at least two obvious grounds: first, no rational person wants to suffer the pain and humiliation of punishment (and so punishment has a deterrent effect); second, punishment expresses society's disapprobation of proscribed behavior. However, and as I have said, there is no agreement

---

"Justice," "Morality," and "Another Look." See also French, "Self-Blaming," 589.

5. In a civil context, this point is posed sharply by Michel de Montaigne (1533–92) who, in an essay on repentance, argues that people cannot be held responsible in the present for what they did in the past. At the end of a paragraph discussing the point, he concludes, "I do not blame myself, I accuse my fortune, and not my work" http://essays.quotidiana.org/montaigne/repentance/. See also Kolnai, "Forgiveness," 219–20.

6. See Tasioulas, "Punishment and Repentance," 305–21 (and the sources he cites): he critiques the view that repentance is a ground for mercy.

7. The futuristic 1971 film *A Clockwork Orange* (directed by Stanley Kubrick) explores the relationship between personal responsibility and the freedom to make moral choices. On the film, see Calhoun "At What Price Repentance?" On neuro-interventions as criminal rehabilitation, see Pugh and Douglas, "Neurointerventions," and Pugh and Maslen, "Drugs," both without reference to the film. See also Teichman, "Punishment and Remorse," 343.

8. See also Murphy, "Last Words," (especially p. 31) on the regrettable necessity of punishment.

9. Radzik, *Making Amends*, 5.

10. Feinberg, "Expressive," 397.

about the theoretical basis of punishment or about the justification of how
(and whether) punishment is morally right.[11]

We know that punishment may sometimes serve as a wake-up call and
focus a wrongdoer's attention on the urgent need fully to let remorse do its
regenerative and healing work. There is evidence that some people, even
those whose behavior has been well established as violent and murderous,
can and do change when they acknowledge responsibility for what they
have done and the need for change, though anecdotally it is not often the
case that the imposition and experience of punishment has been ascribed as
the principal reason for moral re-formation.

Remorse and the Desire to be Punished

Those guilty of criminal wrongdoing are sometimes remorseful.[12] We have
seen that remorse is one of the starting points that can lead to moral re-formation and a change of heart. Remorse is not itself that re-formation and change
of heart; rather, it can indicate that one's conscience is ready to engage with
what needs to change and with what one needs to become.

Remorseful feelings may include both a desire to be punished and
uncomplaining acceptance of punishment for having done wrong. It can be
a way to acknowledge guilt, the feeling of being "morally spoiled"[13] and to
express that one's own moral outlook about the wrong in question is now
aligned to the moral outlook of one's community. Michael Proeve and Steven
Tudor observe that a "genuinely remorseful person . . . will positively want to
receive his just punishment. To be closed to any thought of . . . punishment
will usually be taken as a sign that what is felt is not genuine remorse."[14]

Some wrongdoers say that if they can "pay the price" for their wrongdoing by being punished, they can thereby expiate their guilt. It may "feel"
right to wrongdoers, their victims, and even their communities that wrongdoers are punished for this reason. However, such a view of punishment is
problematic. First, there is no logical or moral connection between doing
wrong and being punished for doing wrong.[15] Punishment is a pragmatic

11. On the "good" of punishment, see Scarre, After Evil, 113–38.

12. The most thorough book on remorse and the criminal law is Proeve and Tudor, Remorse. The clearest brief introductions to the philosophical issues pertaining to
punishment for criminal wrongdoing are Hart, "Prologomenon," and Brooks, Punishment. For a description of punishment (and its relation to remorse) in the early modern
period, see McIlvenna, "Punishment," 195–98.

13. Roberts, Essay, 223.

14. Proeve and Tudor, Remorse, 133.

15. See Hanna, "Passions," for example, who argues that punishment, in the sense

way to deal with wrongdoers and wrongdoing, and for wrongdoers to deal with their consciences. Punishment can be justified on consequential and instrumental grounds but not otherwise. In addition, it is a fiction to say that punishment can expiate the fact and effect of having done wrong and any ensuing feelings of remorse, for an act, and its consequences, once done cannot be undone. Last, a view of punishment as paying one's debts to society may also, in the minds of some, have the unintended effect of obviating the need for remorse, because punished wrongdoers may think that, since they have paid the penalty for their wrongdoing, they are thereafter discharged from moral responsibility for what they have done and for seeking to make restitution or reparations.

Remorse and Self-Punishment

Sometimes a remorseful wrongdoer may not face a form of judicial punishment because, for example, the wrong is a moral (not a criminal) wrong or because the wrongdoer is no longer likely to be the subject of a prosecution if, for example, there is not enough evidence that is likely to bring a conviction. What, then, will happen if a remorseful wrongdoer believes he or she still deserves to be punished?

Of course, it will be important to establish whether the wrongdoer's desire to be punished is irrational or pathological, indicative of loss of perspective or perhaps even of masochism. As Linda Radzik succinctly puts it, "wrongdoers who express their sense of guilt through the single-minded pursuit of their own suffering appear short sighted and self-absorbed."[16]

It is appropriate to feel guilt for violating moral norms, and sometimes, in response to the guilt they feel, wrongdoers choose self-punishment, the self-imposition of a penalty, as a way to atone for having done wrong, to deal with the guilt they feel, and to indicate their remorse.[17] There are some forms of self-punishment that are akin to a penance and so are neither pathological, nor irrational, nor masochistic. Radzik gives as examples giving a sacrificial gift or performing acts of community service.[18]

---

of suffering or harm imposed on a wrongdoer to express disapproval, is unjustified.

16. Radzik, *Making Amends,* 38.

17. Teichman, "Punishment and Remorse," 344–46. Readers of J. K. Rowling's *Harry Potter* books, which at various points (through characters such as Dumbledore, Snape, Pettigrew, Voldemort) explore the forms that remorse can take, may like to know that Nelissen refers to "the guilt-induced tendency for self-punishment that arises if there are no possibilities to compensate the victim directly" as "the Dobby effect" (Nelissen, "Guilt-Induced Self-Punishment," 139).

18. Radzik, *Making Amends,* 32.

Self-punishment is, however, difficult to justify on pragmatic or theo-retical grounds. Self-punishment may take the form of deliberately brood-ing over having done wrong and choosing not to deal with the wrong and the memory of it in a constructive way. To my mind, this is a form of psy-chological self-harm. Neither can self-punishment be retributive, because retributive punishment is a painful, and usually unwelcome, action that a third party carries out and imposes on a wrongdoer. Self-punishment in this context involves an odd bifurcation of self on the part of wrongdoers, for they act as judge, jury, and "executioner" in their own causes.

When wrongdoers have reached the point of recognizing their errors but are not yet confident they are re-formed, there are more effective ways to achieve long-term, morally upright patterns of life than by self-imposed punishment. There is no point to additional self-punishment if the aim to promote therapeutic, restitutive, or restorative outcomes is already in place.

The underlying issue, it seems to me, is how one best deals with the guilt one feels because one has done wrong. One appropriate way to deal with guilt, I suggest, is not by self-punishment but by acts that result from repentance and remorse and to make amends. Such acts include apologies, restitution, and reparations, for example. Their intended outcomes are, as much as can be, the restoration and healing of relationships, and the rever-sal of the consequences of the wrongdoing. Such acts will demonstrate not only that wrongdoers acknowledge, condemn, and repudiate their former wrongdoing but also that the wrongdoers are committed to right living, acknowledge their accountability for the wrong, and want to right the con-sequences of what they have done. Acts like these seem to me to be a con-structive way to right wrongs; punishing oneself may be, if not masochistic, an act of self-hatred or a self-absorbed, narcissistic response that adds to the suffering caused by the wrong. It is also unlikely to satisfy victims.

Remorse and the Theoretical Bases of Punishment

Some regard punishment as instrumental, intended to produce remorse in the offender. John Tasioulas has argued that part of the purpose of punish-ment is "hard treatment . . . intended to communicate to the wrong-doer justified censure for their wrongdoing" and that the offender is "intended . . . to experience remorse and eventually come to repent of his wrong-doing by willingly undergoing the punishment meted out to him as a justified pen-ance." The result will be that the offender's "future behavior and attitudes" will change and the offender will "achieve some kind of reconciliation with both his victim and the wider community whose norms he has violated."[19]

There is, however, no compelling evidence that punishment *necessarily* leads to lucid remorse and thence to moral re-formation, though one can more easily see that punishment might lead to "illucid" forms of remorse, such as when a wrongdoer experiences deep regret bordering on self-pity for having to endure punishment after having done wrong. Nietzsche's view, for example, is that prison does not promote repentance and remorse, and that punishment hardened and alienated people, strengthening their determination to resist.[20] There is also evidence of high rates of recidivism among former prisoners. It was said in 2016 that in the UK, 46 percent of all prisoners will re-offend within one year of release and 60 percent of short-sentenced prisoners will re-offend within the same period.[21]

In Britain, Section 142 of the Criminal Justice Act 2003 sets out the purposes of sentencing. They are a combination of the main theoretical approaches to punishment. The purposes are:

1. The punishment of offenders,

2. The reduction of crime (including its reduction by deterrence),

3. The reform and rehabilitation[22] of offenders,

4. The protection of the public, and

5. The making of reparation by offenders to persons affected by their offences.

According to all the main theories of punishment and to Section 142 of the Criminal Justice Act, remorse appears to be irrelevant to sentencing,[23] even though remorse is sometimes considered in mitigation. The aims and purposes of most other reasons for punishment are usually explained by a mixture of theoretical approaches drawn from three bases, namely,

---

19. Tasioulas, "Punishment and Repentance," 283–84.

20. Nietzsche, *Genealogy.*

21. From a press release dated 8 February 2016 from the British Prime Minister's Office at 10 Downing Street (see https://www.gov.uk/government/news/prime-minister-outlines-plan-for-reform-of-prisons).

22. In Britain, sentencing guidelines for those aged under eighteen years state that the purpose of sentencing is to be rehabilitative (Section 1.2, Sentencing Council, *Sentencing*).

23. Bagaric and Amarasekara, "Feeling Sorry?" "Remorse" is not listed in the index of subjects in Brooks, *Punishment.*

punishment as retribution, rehabilitation, or deterrent and justified on the basis either of desert or of utilitarianism.[24]

Remorse and Retribution

Retributivists[25] argue that people who have done wrong deserve to be punished, both because they have done wrong and regardless of whether they are remorseful.[26] Retributive punishment is thought of as right in itself, and not because of its outcomes or consequences.

Kant argues that every crime needs to be cancelled by retaliation on the criminal in order that the moral order may be restored.[27] In such a scheme of justice, diminished punishment as a result of a criminal's remorse will not sufficiently restore the moral order, and the views of wrongdoers about their former wrongdoing (such as feelings of remorse or regret or shame)[28] are irrelevant. In practice, however, an offender's remorse is often taken into account when it comes to sentencing.

Some suggest that "retributive emotions that promote a punishment response" are the result of "a highly complex, biologically hard-wired network of regions in the brain, shaped by evolution . . . to increase fitness for survival by deterring future harm and fostering cooperation."[29] In other words, it may be that retributivist emotions are biologically determined in

24. Brooks favors a "unified" approach to punishment. This approach "defends the idea that punishment may address multiple penal goals within a coherent and unified framework" (*Punishment*, 211).

25. Leading modern writers on retribution include Morris, *On Guilt*; Fingarette, "Punishment"; Moore "Moral Worth," *Placing Blame*; Hampton "Correcting"; and Murphy, *Punishment*. Murphy sets out some of the approaches to and defenses of retribution in "Last Words." For a short critique of retribution, see Feinberg, "Expressive," 421–22 and Scarre, *After Evil*, 116–20. For a critical review of retributivism and for an alternative model that nurtures repentance and eschews shaming wrongdoers, see Braithwaite, "Repentance Rituals."

26. Teichman criticizes the notion of desert in "Punishment and Remorse," 337. On desert and punishment, see Sher, *Desert*, 69–90.

27. Kant, *Philosophy of Law*, 194–96. On Kant and retributivism, see Sorell, *Moral Theory*, 129–64. On the view that Kant is less than a "*thoroughgoing*" retributivist, that is, that he adopts "the justifying aim [of punishment as] the control or reduction of crime" and does not regard imposition of deserved punishment "as its own justification," see Scheid, "Kant's Retributivism," 263–64, 279–81 and Kant, *Groundwork*, 251–53.

28. Hampton in Murphy and Hampton, *Forgiveness and Mercy*, 133 sees this point very clearly.

29. Koppel and Fondacaro, Retribution," 194. See also Frijda, "The Evolutionary Emergence."

human beings and that the philosophical underpinning of retributivism is *post hoc* justification.

Others suggest that retributivism is derived from one of the traditions of thinking in the Judeo-Christian religious tradition. Expressed simply, the tradition, which was principally developed in the Middle Ages in Europe by Anselm and Aquinas, is that the model of sacrificial offerings in the Old Testament and the model of the atonement seen in the death of Jesus in the New Testament are retributivist and point to penal sacrifice as the basis of salvation.[30] However, treating salvation as based only on Jesus's penal sacrifice (which to many is doubtful as penal) does not take account of other, important traditions of thinking in the Judeo-Christian religious traditions that are integral to salvation, such as, regret, repentance, remorse, restitution, and reparation. Jesus said to the woman caught in an act of adultery, "Go and sin no more" (John 8:11), an injunction that is an important component of what it means to be not "condemned" (John 8:10, 11) but saved.

Another approach to retributive punishment is to say that in a retributive scheme of ethics, punishment is meted out on the basis of what Kant calls the wrongdoer's "inner viciousness." A remorseful and repentant wrongdoing should receive a lesser sentence on this basis, since the wrongdoer shows less evidence of "inner viciousness" than a wrongdoer who remains resolutely unmoved with having done wrong. But might we be duped by counterfeit remorse? Can we ever be sure that a wrongdoer's supposed remorse is anything more than a well-presented sham?[31]

Rather than arguing that there is a link between retributive punishment and remorse, anecdotal evidence and common sense suggest that oftentimes people deeply regret having been caught out; if they could offend again without being caught, perhaps they would. We reflected on the story of the ring of Gyges, the Lydian, in Plato's *Republic* in chapter 3, which explores this question. Such deep regret is not true of remorseful people who recognize that they have failed morally and who are deeply ashamed of their failure.

Despite its prevalence, retributive punishment has not been proved to achieve very much, except, in the case of imprisonment, to take malefactors out of society for a time. Surprisingly, what the most common form of punishment, imprisonment, has been shown to achieve is often further to criminalize offenders, because offenders in prison learn from other offenders. Prison, it is said, is a school for crime, not remorse or rehabilitation,

30. Anselm of Canterbury (c. 1033–1109) in *Cur Deus Homo*, developed by Aquinas. See Aquinas, *ST* II–I, Q. 12, 21 where retribution, justice, and human wrongdoing are linked.

31. See Murphy, *Punishment*, 16–61 for an excellent discussion of these points.

as statistics for recidivism show. In short, linking a theory of retributive punishment with aspirations for moral reform through remorse is indefensible logically and analytically, and lacks an adequate evidence base. I strongly suspect that most theoretical bases of retributive punishment are ideological, shaped by popular culture, by prejudice, and (in the West) by a misunderstanding and misreading of the Judeo-Christian tradition that is purportedly retributivist. (Even if retributivism is not founded on a misunderstanding and misreading of the Judeo-Christian tradition, it by no means follows that people should follow and practice the supposed retributivism of God.) Retributivism probably covertly reflects humanity's innate cruelty and humanity's desire to control and contain the moral ambivalence that honest people recognize exists in themselves.[32]

Remorse and Rehabilitation

Another theory of punishment is based on a utilitarian view. The theory rightly assumes there is something deeply distasteful about deliberately inflicting punishment and suffering on another person. It asks the question: what is the purpose of retributive punishment? If the purpose is to make the criminal suffer for having done wrong, retributive punishment is cruel, vindictive, and repulsive to the conscience. If it is to restore the moral equilibrium, there is no equilibrium to restore, as the idea of a moral equilibrium is a fiction used to justify the imposition of suffering for wrongdoing.

According to the utilitarian, the justification of punishment is if the good that can come out of punishment cannot be achieved by other means or if there is no alternative to punishment.[33] The argument is that "the ultimate purpose of punishment must be to promote happiness or lessen unhappiness. Since crime causes unhappiness, punishment is justified . . . insofar as it controls or reduces crime—through special and general deterrence, incapacitation, and so on."[34] This approach can be related to an obviously Christian approach to punishment because it meets the criteria of "those motivated by agape [love]" because (according to Jeffrie Murphy's view of such an approach) we can see that it "contribute[s] to, or at least do[es] not retard, the moral and spiritual rebirth of criminals."[35]

32. Nietzsche, *Genealogy*.

33. In "The Three Rs," Sommers suggests a model of punishment that combines retributivism with rehabilitation and that victims should be involved in the determination of the appropriate and just punishment.

34. Scheid, "Kant's Retributivism," 262.

35. Murphy, "Christian Love," 156. Murphy does not link love with rehabilitation in his essay.

The rehabilitative approach to criminal wrongdoing takes one of two principal forms. In its more eclectic form, the rehabilitative approach restricts punishments to what are likely to reform and rehabilitate the offender. The other approach is a more obviously "pure" approach. It does away with punishment and replaces it with a regime of what is most likely to rehabilitate the offender. These approaches to punishment can have the incidental effect of subordinating "respect for innocent persons to the maximizing of good social outcomes such as crime reduction."[36] Punishment has to be balanced with justice for victims, respect for their human dignity, and respect for their human rights.

Some people object to rehabilitation as a theory of punishment because they see part of its aim as bringing benefit to the person being punished without taking due account of those harmed by the wrongdoer's crimes.[37] It has also been criticized for being oppressive in seeking to impose a given set of values on the offender. Both objections have merit.

In former times especially, prisons were intended to be a place for self-reflection, to help people engage with and explore the remorse that it was hoped they would experience. Indeed, the word "penitentiary" is related to the word "penance," and suggests that prison is a place where offenders, on account of their remorse, could do "penance" for their crimes, in the hope that, with the enforced solitude of prison giving time and mental space, prisoners would become morally changed people. (This, of course, in part highlights the absurdity of capital punishment, because, by taking away a person's life, one takes away the possibility of time for reform through self-reflection as well as the opportunity for demonstrating that reform. At best, one can argue that capital punishment is a deterrent, promoting remorse vicariously, and frightening people into understanding what could happen to them if they committed similar crimes.)[38]

The question of how rehabilitation can be recognized and whether it is a process that can ever be thought to be completed is difficult to answer because a claim to be rehabilitated can be spurious, just as a claim to be remorseful can be, as we shall see below. That rehabilitation is an unending process, without fixed points, and somewhat fluid and indeterminate is aptly illustrated in the film *The Shawshank Redemption* (1994, directed by Frank Darabont). Ellis Boyd Redding ("Red,") played by Morgan Freeman,

36. Baker, *Penance*, 311.

37. See also the view of Socrates that punishment should be aimed at improving the wrongdoer's character.

38. See Duff, *Trials*, for a further exploration of how punishment can bring about moral reform. On a Kantian view of capital punishment, see Sorell, *Moral Theory*, 136–43.

has been in prison for a murder committed in his youth. He is called before
a Parole Board for only the third time in the forty years of his imprisonment.
The Board asks him, "Do you feel you've been rehabilitated?" Red replies,
"You know, I don't have any idea what that means." The Board explains they
are asking whether he considers he is "ready to re-join society." In response,
Red says, with great personal honesty and insight, and reflecting the idea
that rehabilitation is an evanescent, tenuous concept:

> "Rehabilitated"? Well now, let me see. You know, I don't have any
> idea what that means. . . . I know what you think it means [that I
> am now ready to re-join society]. To me, it's just a made-up word,
> a politician's word. . . . Rehabilitated? It's just a bullshit word.

Connected with the rehabilitationist approach to punishment is the
recently developed (and still developing) idea of restorative justice.[39] Expressed simply, it is "a process whereby all the parties with a stake in a
particular offence come together to resolve collectively how to deal with
the aftermath of an offence and its implications for the future."[40] Restorative justice coheres with what is widely seen to be an effective way to
resolve the effects of wrongdoing through the making of amends, "moral
reconciliation . . . [and] the subgoals of moral improvement, respectful
communication, and reparation."[41]

Processes of restorative justice offer a forum for wrongdoers to express
their remorse and to make amends for what they have done. In some models of restorative justice, offenders are permitted to suggest what amends
they might make, and even the sentences they should receive. They may
also be permitted face-to-face engagement with their victims. The hoped-
for outcomes are justice, as well as restoration and reconciliation. One of the
theoretical starting points of restorative justice is that all the parties are autonomous, moral persons, with dignity as human beings, and with responsibilities and accountability for their actions and reactions. An especially
attractive feature of restorative justice is that it encourages both victim and
offender to treat themselves and the other person with respect and dignity.
It is offender and victim who are central to the process, and not the state.

39. Some regard restorative justice as an alternative to criminal proceedings; an
increasingly widely accepted view is that it is not, but is a constituent of what Brooks
calls a "unified theory of punishment" (*Punishment*, 123–48), which recognizes multiple goals of punishment (e.g., retribution *and* restoration) through a variety of means.

40. Marshall, quoted in McCold, "Restorative Justice," 20. See Brooks, *Punishment*,
64–85, for a summary of the main approaches to restorative justice.

41. Radzik, *Making Amends*, 153.

Schemes of restorative justice do not require victims to participate if victims do not want to engage with offenders.

Remorseful wrongdoers, that is, those who acknowledge that they are guilty of crimes, who repudiate their past actions, and who wish to make amends, find that models of justice that are restorative in aim integrate the fact of the offender's remorse in most stages of the process, and (unlike in retributive models of justice) not only when it comes to sentencing. This is in part because the responses of offender and victim to the crime are central both to the process and to the outcome of the process. To a much greater extent and more obviously than in models of retributive justice, schemes of justice primarily aimed at restoration enable offenders to demonstrate the integrity of their remorse: they can offer to make restitution, to carry out community service, or to give a public apology, for example. They can also demonstrate that they willingly accept penalties for the wrongdoing. However, in my view, restorative justice is not an alternative to criminal justice but an adjunct to it, to help put right the social and relational consequences of criminal wrongdoing.

Remorse and Deterrence

Another approach to punishment is to look on punishment as being a deterrent to others.[42] This is linked to the utilitarian view of punishment that we have explored above. Punishment that is a deterrent is intended to serve as a warning to and instill fear into others, causing them to experience remorse vicariously, as they imagine how they too might be punished if they offended. Its purpose is also to goad potential wrongdoers into choosing to do right.

If the purpose of punishment is to deter, less severe punishments for people who are remorseful may be a less effective deterrent to others. Wrongdoing, committed for whichever reasons and in respect of which no matter how great the later remorse of the wrongdoer may be, has to be *seen* to be punished if the purpose of deterrence is to be achieved.

Remorse and Mitigation of Punishment

Remorse pays, in the sense that people usually assume that those who show remorse deserve mercy and are in a place to receive mitigation of

42. In "Kant's Theory of Punishment," Byrd argues that Kant recognized deterrence as one of the facets of punishment.

punishment.[43] The more remorseful a wrongdoer, so the thinking goes, the more it is morally indefensible for a victim not to show mercy towards the wrongdoer.

In the case of civil actions in law, damages provide compensation for loss suffered, with the aim of putting the victim in as good a situation as he or she would have been had the wrongful act not been committed. With few exceptions (exemplary damages in Britain are an example of an exception)[44] the amount of the compensation is generally not related to the wrongdoer's moral response to the wrongdoing.

When it comes to the criminal law, the approach is different: a defendant's remorse (or lack of remorse) is sometimes considered when it comes to sentencing.[45] To put it simply, the result can be that the more the evidence of remorse, the less severe the sentence will sometimes be. For example, shortly before I wrote this paragraph, the British press carried a report of a 101-year-old man, thought to be the oldest person convicted of a crime in Britain, who was sent to prison for thirteen years for child sex offences.[46] The convicted man said he was "pretty well immune to feelings" and the judge who heard the case observed that the defendant showed "no remorse whatever." The defendant was jailed for a lengthy term, both because of the seriousness of his offences and his lack of remorse.[47]

According to this way of approaching punishment, remorse is treated as a mitigating factor in punishment. Proponents of the approach argue that, although acts that are against the law should be punished, subsequent morally upright behavior that demonstrates regret and remorse should be rewarded with reduced punishments.

43. For a survey of mitigation, see Scarre, *After Evil*, 139–58.

44. See the report of the Law Commission of England and Wales on Aggravated, Exemplary and Restitutionary Damages (Paper 247, 1997; http://www.lawcom.gov.uk/wp-content/uploads/2015/04/LC247.pdf) and the pre-legislative scrutiny of the House of Commons Justice Committee to the draft Civil Law Reform Bill in 2010 (paragraphs 151–58) (https://www.publications.parliament.uk/pa/cm200910/cmselect/cmjust/300/300i.pdf). The proposed changes to the law were not enacted.

45. For evidence of the mitigating and aggravating effects of remorse on punishment, see Kleinke et al., "Evaluation"; Proeve and Tudor, *Remorse*, 115–57; Robinson et al., "Extralegal Punishment"; Weisman, *Showing Remorse*; and Fine et al., "Can Probation Offenders?" For a critical view of looking at remorse as a consideration when mitigating sentences, see Meyer, "Eternal Remorse" and Vandendriessche, "Should We Punish?"

46. http://www.bbc.co.uk/news/uk-england-38343295 and http://www.independent.co.uk/news/uk/crime/ralph-clarke-britains-oldest-person-to-be-convicted-of-crime-jailed-for-13-years-for-child-sex-a7484171.html.

47. On remorse and punishment, see Smith, *I Was Wrong* and *Justice through Apologies*. Smith offers a taxonomy for evaluating apologies in civil and criminal contexts.

There are at least four reasons why it may be right to take account of remorse to moderate the degree of punishment for doing wrong.[48] First, to experience remorse is to suffer anguish and distress because one knows and feels that one has done wrong. To this extent, remorse is like a self-imposed punishment. Only a reduced judicially imposed punishment may be necessary because the additional self-imposed punishment is taken to make up the difference. Next, genuine remorse may come across as a form of apology, or be accompanied by an apology, and this may have the effect of palpably ameliorating the hurt felt by the victim.[49] In consequence, a court may diminish the severity of a sentence it would otherwise consider appropriate to impose. Third, remorse may also suggest the offender acknowledges and supports the values of the community and is committed again to those values. Less demanding punishment may be considered appropriate because reform, one of the purposes of punishment, appears to have been achieved. Last, in a rehabilitative system of punishment, remorse is one way to demonstrate that a wrongdoer accepts blame, has changed his or her moral attitude and even character, and intends to behave differently in the future. These behavioral changes may diminish the rehabilitative punishment that a court considers necessary.

Research shows that not all expressions of remorse are treated or received equally: a recent study in a jurisdiction in which jurors participate in sentencing has shown that jurors respond differently depending on the way remorse is expressed, with some expressions of remorse seen as less compelling and persuasive than others.[50] The same is likely to be true in many western systems where judges impose sentences for crimes: some groups or types of offenders may be more adept and persuasive than others at expressing remorse in pleas of mitigation.

In addition, from a psychological view, the capacity to show remorse and the desire to make reparation develop early in childhood as part of the process of psychological maturation. Those whose violent, dishonest, and aggressive behavior is not contained may suffer from some types of enduring mental illness, (usually concomitant with certain types of deprivation in childhood) and may lack the capacity to show genuine remorse. There is no "quick fix" with such mental illnesses, and there is likely to be no "fix" quick enough to have taken place between the date of a crime and the time when

---

48. See Henson, *Remorse.*

49. For a theory of punishment grounded on the practice of apology, see Bennett, *The Apology Ritual*; Smith, *Justice through Apologies* and "Dialectical Retributivism."

50. Lo et al., "Does Content Matter?"

a judge decides on sentence.[51] Such people may be less able to show and feel remorse, and to many it seems wrong that their punishments should not be mitigated because of the circumstances of their lives. They are being penalized because they did not have much "moral luck."[52]

Other reasons to criticize the practice of taking account remorse to moderate the degree of punishment for doing wrong include the following. First, it is by no means obvious that it is either just or fair to mitigate punishment after law-breaking. A wrong once done remains a wrong, even if the wrongdoer is subsequently remorseful. The wrongdoer's remorse does not undo the fact of the wrong or its consequences. Second, counter-intuitively and inconsistently with modern practice, since punishment *can* focus attention on the need for and the practice of moral self-restoration, it may not be wise to reduce the severity or duration of a remorseful wrongdoer's punishment, in case a wrongdoer's newly-awakened conscience is dulled, self-reform put off, and the wrongdoer slip back into former ways. Next, according to Freud in *Civilization and Its Discontents*, human beings can feel guilt (one of the constituents of remorse) not only after they have done wrong but also before. In Freud's view, an anticipatory sense of guilt can serve as a check on possible future wrongdoing. James Gilligan cogently asks:

> if a person's conscience and his capacity to identify with another person and feel empathy, sympathy and love for that person, and therefore to feel guilty about his desire to hurt that person, are sufficiently well developed for him to feel remorse afterwards, then how can he bring himself to hurt that person in the first place?[53]

Thus, if a person is so hardened as to disregard anticipatory feelings of guilt, it suggests that expressions of guilt and remorse *after* having done wrong may, on their own, be unpersuasive evidence of a reformed character and pattern of living. Fourth, Alan Thomas thinks it is more rational to look for evidence of guilt in wrongdoers than evidence of remorse.[54] By "guilt," he means evidence that the wrongdoer now accepts and adhered to the moral standards he or she has breached and accepts that the former breach of those standards must receive due punishment. Last, there is no compelling empirical evidence to support the view that evidence of remorse indicates a diminished likelihood of recidivism.[55]

51. See, for example, Sohn, "Defective Capacity," 69–81.
52. Statman, *Moral Luck*, and Williams, *Moral Luck*.
53. Gilligan, "Agenbite," 39.
54. Thomas, "Remorse and Reparation," 131.
55. Proeve and Tudor, *Remorse*, 209 and Lippke, "Ethics," 22.

When it comes to decisions whether to grant a prisoner early release on parole, it is widely believed that a prisoner's remorse is evidence that the prisoner's moral conscience, at least in relation to the crime, is restored to what society thinks it should be, and that prison has therefore "done its job" and the prisoner is fit to be restored to life in the community. (This is so even though, as we have said, there is next to no evidence that people who express remorse will not do wrong again in the future.) What a Parole Board in Britain may take into account is whether a "prisoner has shown by his attitude and behavior in custody that he is willing to address his offending behavior by understanding its causes and its consequences for the victims concerned, and has made positive effort and progress in doing so."[56] In other words, the prisoner must show a change of behavior and a growth in understanding of the causes and consequences of the offending behavior. This is not the same as a prisoner being remorseful, at least in the sense that we are using it in this book.[57]

Spurious Remorse and Punishment

Remorse is easy to counterfeit, and none of us has a window into the inner workings of an offender's conscience to know whether the offender's remorse is genuine or likely to endure.[58] Others have said similar things about other emotions. For example, Bob Monkhouse quipped, "The public love sincerity—if you can fake that, you've got it made."[59] Those who "fake" remorse may well have it made, too. For example, Michel de Montaigne (1532–92) in his essay On Remorse said, "I find no quality so easy to counterfeit as devotion, if men do not conform their manners and life to the profession; its essence is abstruse and occult; the appearances easy and ostentatious." William Miller puts it this way: "Of the big-time moral sentiments, arguably none is easier to fake than remorse . . . ."[60] Rowan Williams

---

56. Parole Board, *Report*, 18.

57. Of more importance in decisions about release on parole is whether a prisoner constitutes a risk to the public: Tidmarsh, "Necessary." On remorse and parole, see also Martel, "Remorse."

58. Murphy, *Punishment*, 148–53. In "Intrusion," 385, Duff calls this an "intrusive interest" in the offender. Counterfeit remorse was recognized in Protestantism in early modern Scotland: see Todd, *Culture*, 160–63. In "Crocodile Tears," ten Brinke et al., identified ways of distinguishing between what they call "genuine remorse" and "fabricated remorse" from the facial expressions of the subjects they observed.

59. http://www.dailymail.co.uk/home/event/article-3100781/Bob-Monkhouse-s-astonishing-joke-book-open-public.html.

60. Miller, *Faking It*, 73.

suggests that moral identity after wrongdoing is too often founded on both a desire to control the narrative of one's past and attempts to market a newly invented identity, rather than on internalizing "what I have been in the eyes of another."[61] Another commentator on moral hypocrisy says:

> What looks like truly moral motivation (moral integrity) often isn't. Instead, it's a subtle form of instrumental moral motivation—motivation to appear moral yet, if possible, avoid the cost of actually being moral. When there's sufficient wiggle room, this moral hypocrisy motive has the virtue of providing us many of the benefits of moral integrity without having to pay the price. We can ride roughshod over our principles, standards, and ideals, yet still see ourselves as persons of character. . . . [T]his goal of moral hypocrisy isn't reached without skill. To gain the full benefits, we must be adept not only at rationalization and deceit of others, but also at self-deception.[62]

In a critical evaluation of court-ordered apologies in the USA, which may include expressions of remorse, Nick Smith on the whole is rightly skeptical of their value because such apologies may be coerced, spurious, and only offered in order to mitigate a penalty.[63] It is also true that unconscious bias may affect the degree of punishment imposed on wrongdoers.[64] There has been little discussion about how to evaluate or prove[65] the integrity of a person's remorse, or the value and weight that may be given to expressions of remorse for sentencing[66] and for parole.[67] The same is true of admissions of guilt, for admissions of guilt may be spurious, often to avoid a greater sentence of punishment, or may be the result of mistaken self-interpretation of negative affect.[68] People are likely to be remorseful, or at least able to trick themselves into thinking they are truly remorseful, if they are about to suffer an unpleasant punishment and if they know that the punishment will be less severe or lengthy (and so less unpleasant) if they

---

61. Williams, *Lost Icons*, 134.

62. Batson, "Getting Cynical," 37.

63. Smith, *Justice through Apologies*.

64. See, for example, Christopher et al., "Protestant Work Ethic."

65. On proving remorse, see Proeve and Tudor, *Remorse*, 93–114.

66. For example, Weisman, "Being and Doing"; Bandes, "Remorse and Criminal Justice" and "Remorse, Demeanor"; Rossmanith, "Affect"; and Oorschot et al., "Remorse."

67. Hola et al., "Does Remorse Count?" for example.

68. Lilienfeld and Fowler, "Self-Report," 110.

convince others that they are truly sorry. Those who are good actors can feign remorse for the same reasons.

The problem of "fake remorse" is particularly obvious with those who suffer from antisocial personality disorders (formerly called "psychopaths").[69] Such people "come on with fake repentance" that evaporates as soon as the goal of escaping punishment is attained.[70] Remitting the measure of punishment due to such people because of their supposed remorse may be to be tricked and manipulated.[71] It has also been shown that the behavior of psychopaths is not changed or improved by punishment and behavior modification techniques.[72] Rather, psychopaths are regarded as not only incurable but also untreatable.

I remain unpersuaded that judges should take much account of offenders' remorse when it comes to sentencing. There is too much the risk that the integrity of offenders' motives will be sullied by the knowledge that expressions of remorse may mitigate their punishments. Even those who voluntarily admit their offending without first having been "caught" for having done wrong may still think, "If I admit to my crime voluntarily, I am likely to receive a mitigated sentence." The heart is deceitful and corrupt, even though we may think it is not, as Jeremiah says (Jer 17:9). I agree with Jeffrie Murphy's conclusion:

> Given that my own nature (alas) tends to be more cynical and suspicious than trusting, my current inclination—although I am still conflicted about this—is *not* to give much weight to expressions of remorse and repentance at the sentencing stage of the criminal process. I simply see too much chance of being made a sucker by fakery.[73]

69. See Cleckley, *The Mask of Sanity*; Hare, *Without Conscience* and *Psychopathy*; in many places in Patrick, *Handbook*, and Prins, *Psychopathy*, for example.

70. Harrington, *Psychopaths*, 15.

71. Grant and Rice, "Treatment."

72. "The prospect of punishment will not keep [such people] from going off the rails again" (Harrington, *Psychopaths*, 16). Smith, *The Psychopath*, 15 has methodological reservations. On 9 April 2019 the Sentencing Council of Britain published guidance to judges for sentencing offenders with mental health conditions and disorders (https://www.sentencingcouncil.org.uk/news/item/proposals-for-sentencing-offenders-with-mental-health-conditions-published/).

73. Murphy, *Punishment*, 161.

Remorse, Punishment, and Apologies

Knowing that wrongdoers are deeply remorseful does not feel as good, some victims say, as "cash in the hand" in compensation for being victims of crimes or knowing that criminals are "behind bars." Others say that what matters more to them than legal redress and punishment for offenders is an acknowledgment of wrongdoing and an apology. As we have seen, truly remorseful people will, among other things, apologize for the wrong they have done. Nick Smith puts it this way:

> Although money can be useful in many ways . . . no amount of cash [can] provide the sorts of meaning that you might receive if the offender apologized, accepted blame, took moral as well as fiscal responsibility for the loss, and then honored a commitment never to cause such blame again.[74]

Christopher Bennett has attempted to address the need for apology in the criminal justice system by suggesting a theory of punishment grounded in the practice of apology. He argues that "we owe it to wrongdoers to blame them and to expect them to apologize."[75] He holds to an underlying assumption that wrongdoing involves "a fundamental failure to respect the demands" of the wrongdoer's community and its relationships. Only when the community blames the wrongdoer and expects a wrongdoer to apologize can the community demonstrate that it "respect[s] the wrongdoer's status as a member of that relationship" and that the wrongdoer has been restored to give the community "appropriate *recognition*."[76]

While Bennett agrees that punishment and retributive attitudes are relevant when we consider moral and legal condemnation, he argues that offenders should be made to do "what we think someone who was sorry enough for their offence would feel it necessary to undertake by making amends."[77] Such amends are not a voluntary act but a requirement that, in his words, is a "ritual." Constantine Sandis has rightly criticized the element of compulsion, arguing that public amends need to be voluntary if they are to be an ethically appropriate response to crime.[78]

Bennett's argument presupposes that community relationships give rise to rights and duties that are quantifiable, and that give rise to the right to punish when those rights and duties have been violated. It seems to me there

74. Smith, *I Was Wrong*, 3.

75. Bennett, *The Apology Ritual*, 8.

76. Bennett, *The Apology Ritual*, 125 (author's italics).

77. Bennett, *The Apology Ritual*, 46.

78. Sandis, "Public Expression."

is a flaw in his argument, as it proceeds from indicative ("there are rights and duties") to an imperative ("those who breach those rights and duties ought to be punished").[79] There is also the more obvious flaw in his argument that there is no way of telling whether an apology is genuine.

Being a Person without Remorse

There are some people with psychiatric disorders that prevent them from appreciating that their behavior is socially and legally deviant. They also sometimes cannot (and so do not) show remorse about doing wrong. In other respects, their intellects are intact. Such people create particular challenges from a legal and philosophical point of view. The pressing question is this: is it ethical to punish such people? On the face of it, it makes no sense to punish people who do not have the capacity for remorse, because no amount of punishment can or will produce genuine remorse or the capacity genuinely to be remorseful in the future. So, for example, those with antisocial personality disorders have "altered brain structure and functioning" that affects sufferers' ability to experience emotions, both their own and others'. The result can be "reduced motivation to behave morally," and to leave the sufferer "less sensitive to the threat of punishment." The cause is "a combination of genetic and environmental factors beyond the individual's control."[80] No amount of punishment can rehabilitate such people into possessing the moral emotions they have not in the past possessed, and which they are not likely to possess in the future.

Without commenting on the measure of punishment for those with psychiatric disorders, Cynthia Ozick writes that a repentant and genuinely remorseful person (that is, someone without an antisocial personality disorder) deserves *greater* punishment than someone who has no moral conscience. This is because the person with the moral conscience knew (or could have known) that what he or she was doing wrong, whereas the person without remorse did not and could not. She implies there is greater mercy for the person who lacks "a moral temperament . . . conscience . . . sensibility . . . humanity" but, of a particular repentant wrongdoer who did not lack those attributes, she writes, "Let him go to hell. Sooner the fly to God than he."[81] She is surely right in logic, but her conclusion belies what many people intuitively feel.

79. This is not a logical flaw if the notions of rights and duties are held to be intrinsically normative: in such a case, they can be construed as implying imperatives.

80. Glenn, "Personality Disorders," 506.

81. Wiesenthal, *The Sunflower*, 218–20.

Also contrary to what many people intuitively feel is the idea of not punishing those with psychiatric disorders that prevent them from appreciating that their behavior is socially and legally deviant. If one wants to argue that they should not be held responsible for what they do because of brain functioning that results from genetic and environmental factors, we could reply that some believe that *all* behavior is the result of brain functioning that results from genetic and environmental factors. We would need to establish criteria of brain functioning that we regard as so deviant as to impair normal decision-making. It is often the case that the more egregious the deficit, the more egregious the deviant behavior, and so the greater the societal clamor for punishment. In such a situation, we will need to come up with ways to restrain and exclude such people from society that do not punish them for what they are constitutionally unable to do. In particular, some with psychiatric disorders may commit crimes (such as murder, torture, rape) that are an egregious assault on the safety and wellbeing of society. Society has a legitimate interest in insisting that such people should be confined to a place of exclusion from others for their safety. The punishment should be neither retributive nor vindictive. It is not that the "punishment should fit the crime"[82] in such cases; it is that the punishment, if it is to be called "punishment," should fit the criminal.

Remorse and the Wider Purposes of the Criminal Law

If we consider that one of the principal purposes of the criminal law is to punish offenders, there is not an obvious place for remorse, as I have suggested. However, the criminal law is about more than punishment, as H. L. A. Hart showed in his famous 1959 address as President of *The Aristotelian Society* and published in the Society's 1959–60 *Proceedings*. Hart suggested, rightly in my view, that punishment is only one element of the complex social and legal organism that we call "the criminal law." Hart argues that one of the purposes of punishment is to bring about beneficial social outcomes, and that to pursue these outcomes, the criminal law must respect the deserts of individuals. This means restricting the imposition of punishments to responsible offenders alone and only according to the seriousness of their offences. In other words, Hart is a qualified retributivist, with consequentialist leanings, seeking to balance what he calls the "General Aim" of the criminal law, which he agrees is retributive, with "Principles

82. Adapted from a song entitled "A More Humane Mikado" by W. S. Gilbert in the comic opera by W. S. Gilbert and A. Sullivan, *The Mikado* (1885).

of Justice," which are the beneficial consequences of the criminal law for the victim and offender and for society generally. Although Hart does not mention a place for remorse or apologies as mitigating factors when it comes to punishment,[83] his notion of "Mitigation" as part of the "Principles of Justice" is broad enough to be adapted to include them. I suspect he avoids discussing whether there should be a place for remorse in sentencing because of the difficulties we have identified in establishing to what extent a person's claim to be remorseful is genuine and to what extent that person's remorse is leading to a re-formed style of life. Unpalatable though the following conclusion may seem to be, I do not see how it can be fair to take account of a criminal's supposed remorse without first having a taxonomy of the characteristics of remorse according to which a judge may measure a defendant's expressions of remorse.[84] A judge would then have an evidenced-based approach to taking account of remorse in sentencing. I suggest that such a taxonomy should include at least the following:

1. The accused to make an unconditional statement of responsibility for the crime, and a description of what the accused understands its impact to be;

2. The accused to give a clear explanation as to why, despite having a "moral compass," the accused chose to ignore the dictates of conscience;

3. The accused to set out what restorative, restitutive, and reparative acts the accused intends to put in place;

4. The accused to set out what networks of support the accused has in place to prevent future offending;

5. The accused to set out the additional networks of support the accused will put in place to prevent future offending;

6. The accused to explain why punishment would be an appropriate response by the court for the wrong done;

7. The accused to suggest what the accused considers an appropriate punishment to be;

8. The accused to agree to accept any punishment imposed by the court, whether or not the plea in mitigation on account of remorse is accepted in whole or in part;

83. Hart, "Prologomenon," 13–16.

84. In "Two Dimensional," Brooks and Reddon have developed the start of what they call "a construct of remorse" to assess the genuineness of remorse in the context of sentencing in criminal cases.

9. The accused to agree to an interview with a suitably qualified officer of the court to test the truthfulness and integrity of the foregoing statements and proposed actions; and

10. In cases where remorse is taken into account in sentencing, the accused to agree to ongoing oversight by a suitably qualified officer of the court after the conclusion of the case.

Chapter 10

Remorse: A Christian Perspective

Ethics

WE HAVE SEEN THAT ethics can be grouped in three ways: the ethics of divinity (ethics derived from God-given standards), the ethics of community (the ethics recognized and followed in particular human communities), and the ethics of autonomy (the ethics resulting from self-directed choices, without the controlling influences of others; these are akin to what Giddens called "the ethics of modernity"). This approach to ethics is based on what is called "the CAD Hypothesis," where "CAD" stands for the initial letters of the words "community," "autonomy," and "divinity." Typically, no more than two of these patterns of ethics will predominate in a society at any one time, and it has been found that, where the ethics of community tend to be strong, the ethics of autonomy are correspondingly weak (and *vice versa*).

We have also looked at the way ethics develop in a society. Jonathan Haidt and Craig Joseph suggest that ethics develop around four "moral domains" (suffering, hierarchies, reciprocity, and purity), with each culture determining particular moral rules around each of the domains.[1] Once a society has developed its normative categories, it will perpetuate its normative categories of behavior through "immersion in custom complexes" and "peer socialization."[2] Haidt and others have increased and adapted the number of the "domains" but the point holds good that normative categories can be the result of "immersion in custom complexes" and "peer socialization."

---

1. Haidt and Joseph, "Intuitive Ethics."
2. Haidt, "The Emotional Dog," 827.

Interpersonal remorse is one kind of response to wrongs done to another person. We have found that interpersonal remorse is an emotion that is typically articulated in societies with an emphasis on the ethics of autonomy. It is an emotion that develops around the moral domains of suffering and reciprocity. Such patterns of behavior are at least in part "phenotypic," that is, behavior arising from personal attributes or character traits that result from a sense of values that do not have their origin in a person's genetic makeup.[3]

Three important points of caution must be raised at this point. First, the research about ethics on which the above remarks are based is inductive, grounded on observed correlations. Correlations do not amount to causation, and we cannot assume that the models explain the existence (or non-existence) of particular norms. Second, the models are based both on modern fieldwork *and* historical records (which obviously are not based on firsthand fieldwork). Despite the value of historical records, they amount only to selective examples of evidence that have survived. We therefore cannot assume that the models that have been developed apply diachronically, although the models seem to provide a helpful way of making sense of the past, as they are consistent with and seem to explain cogently many of the historical data we have. Last, the subject of the research is based on modern presuppositions about concepts such as ethics, morals, virtues, and emotions. We have seen that these terms are not universally known in the material we have been considering, and even when they are known, the terms sometimes have different meanings according to social and historical context. We have seen this particularly clearly with what is meant by the word "emotions," a word that came into widespread use with its contemporary meaning only in the nineteenth century.

Remorse and the Old Testament

In chapter 2 and at other points in this book, we considered some of the difficulties of diachronic studies of remorse. For example, the ways the ancient Israelites thought about what are now called "ethics" and "emotions" are different from the ways ethics and emotions are thought about in contemporary patterns of thought. In the Old Testament, there *is* careful, reflective thinking about (what are now referred to as) ethics and emotions, but not with vocabulary and patterns of thought that correspond with the modern conceptions of these terms. Ancient Israelite thought on emotions especially

---

3. They also fit with what Freud means by "introjection," the process by which a person internalizes, endorses, and then practices a given value.

is different from contemporary traditions of thought about emotions, with points of overlap but not necessarily of equivalence. It is therefore easy to fall into the trap of thinking anachronistically about the way the ancient Israelites regarded ethics and emotions, and (mistakenly) to analyze their thought from within the framework of contemporary approaches.

Among the ancient Israelites, we see patterns of behavior that correspond with remorse as it is now understood, but the remorse is about sin against God. Ancient Israelite thought lacked a framework for articulating an ethic of interpersonal remorse. We explored the reasons why this might be so.

We saw that the CAD hypothesis provides one useful way of explaining the pattern of remorse that we see among the ancient Israelites. Ancient Israelite ethics were the ethics of divinity and the ethics of community; from this we can infer (as indeed is the case) that ethics characteristically associated with autonomy, such as interpersonal remorse, are not likely to be evident to a significant degree. Those whose behavior was like the behavior of the nations that Israel at first dispossessed (and whose successors in a later period surrounded and threatened Israel) not only faced the wrath and judgment of God, as had the surrounding nations, but also put at risk the safety and security of the rest of the community of Israel (e.g., Deut 27–28). Even those who were innocent of doing wrong could express remorse about the sins of others because they knew that *any* sin put the nation in its covenant relationship with God at risk (e.g., 2 Chr 34:14–33). As the book of Judges repeatedly makes clear, when the people were disobedient, they were overrun by their enemies; when they were obedient, they prevailed. What we might today call "remorse" was expressed within the framework of the ethics of divinity and the ethics of community, with individuals' needs and rights (modern concepts that are anachronistic in the period of the ancient Israelites) seen in the setting of the needs and rights of the community. To respond with remorse towards God was to express one's own renewed or continuing commitment to *Israel's* covenant relationship with God.[4]

4. Israelite jurisprudence also disfavored the development of an ethic of interpersonal remorse. When individuals wronged each other, the Levitical law permitted measured retaliation (Exod 21:23–25; Lev 24:20; Deut 19:21), with retaliation based on the idea of the right of reciprocity and seen as restoring the disequilibrium resulting from wrongdoing. See Berlejung, "Sin and Punishment," 280 on "keeping intact the balance of inter-human and human-divine relationships." On literature on retaliation in the Old Testament, see Lee, "Unity," 298, note 1.

Remorse and Greek Culture

At about the same time as the documents of the Old Testament began to
be put in written form, Greek philosophers were reflecting on ethics and
emotions. For the Greeks, there was no god (or gods) who set out what was
right and good to do; there was also no "fall" from a previous state of grace.
Greeks had the written laws of their own cities; there were also "unwritten laws" by which it was assumed that all civilized Greeks were bound.
For example, in the *History of the Peloponnesian War,* Thucydides records
Pericles (c.495–429 BC) saying, "in our public life we are restrained from
lawlessness chiefly though reverent fear, for we render obedience to those in
authority and to the laws."[5] Unlike in the case of the Israelites, none of the
Greek laws had the status of divine commandments. In the absence of a god
who had set out what is right and wrong, the philosophers explored what is
truly good, why people choose to do the right thing and to act virtuously,
and how people develop virtuous character. In other words, knowledge of
truth and ethics come from reason, not revelation.

The view of the Greek philosophers is that a good person would willingly obey written and unwritten laws, but a bad person would not unless,
of course, it was out of fear. They believed that the character of adults, when
it was formed, was fixed; the character of children could be developed so
that children would mature and become adults who would live virtuously.
In their view, adults with a well-trained, virtuous disposition would do good
deeds and so would not do anything about which they should be remorseful,
whereas adults who did wrong acted that way because they lacked a virtuous disposition and, because they lacked a virtuous disposition, would not
feel shame, regret, or remorse. In other words, good people would not feel
remorse because they did not need to, but bad people, when they did wrong,
did not feel remorse because they could not, even though they needed to.

The Greek approach to ethics and morals is therefore different from
the approach of the Jews in the Old Testament. We might describe the
Old Testament as presenting "the carrot or stick" approach:[6] through obedience to God's laws, good behavior and obedience would be rewarded
("the carrot") and bad behavior and disobedience would be punished ("the
stick"). The Greeks asked the question, "How can everyone be trained so as

---

5. Thucydides, *History of the Peloponnesian War* II.xxxvii.3.

6. The "carrot or stick" approach refers to a method of inducing right behavior
through rewards and punishments. It refers to the rider of an animal, such as a mule
or donkey, dangling a carrot in front of the animal to induce it to run forward in a vain
attempt to reach the carrot, or hitting the animal with a stick if the animal refuses to
run forward.

always to have a carrot?" (Here, the carrot is to have virtuous character, to live well, and to behave rightly.)

Of course, good people experienced deep regret for wrongdoing in the pre-Christian period of Greek culture, but only in particular contexts. Aristotle, of course, allowed for acting against one's better judgment and from weakness of will (*akrasia*); in such circumstances, those whose consciences had failed them could regret what they had done. As we saw in chapter 3, people felt regret or remorse either when, like Oedipus, they had committed a wrongful act through ignorance (Oedipus felt remorse) or when, individually or collectively (as in an assembly) people were led astray and would not have acted in the way they had if they had been properly informed (they felt regret). However, since virtuous people would typically not do wrong, remorse and regret are relatively under-explored by Greek philosophers. As we said of the ancient Israelites, so we can say of the ancient Greeks (but for different reasons): ancient Greek thought militated against the development of a framework for articulating an ethic of interpersonal remorse. This is not to say that, on occasions, people were not "remorseful" according to contemporary understanding of interpersonal remorse; rather, it is that there are next to no records of such an emotion.

Remorse and the New Testament

The New Testament includes the history of a Jewish-Christian community that expanded out of its original setting in Palestine, and eventually accommodated and adapted itself to the culture of the Hellenized Roman world.

In some respects, New Testament ethics stand in continuity with Old Testament ethics, and to be remorseful was one way that people still responded when they knew they had sinned against God. In Luke 18:13, for example, the tax collector cried out to *God* for mercy because he knew he was a sinner. John the Baptist urged those who had sinned to repent before *God* and (presumably) to show remorse about their sins (e.g., Matt 3:1–10). Even in the story of Zacchaeus (Luke 19:2–10), though Zacchaeus restores four-fold the amount he had defrauded and also gives half his wealth to the poor, there is nothing explicit about shame, guilt, regret, or interpersonal remorse: rather, the story celebrates Zacchaeus's joy about being a lost sinner who had been saved.[7]

---

7. As for someone having a ground of offence against another person, that other person must seek to be reconciled with the offended person (presumably by repentance and restitution, actions that the New Testament enjoins) but possible psychological concomitants, such as regret or remorse, are not explored (Matt 5:23–24).

As we have seen, the Old Testament approach to ethics tends to be deontic, setting out what are the right things people ought to do. In contrast, Jesus adopted an approach to ethics that we can say bears some resemblance to Aristotelean virtue ethics: he focused both on deontic rules and on an individual's inner motives that are the reasons for his or her behavior. Rather than looking at an action to see if it fulfils a specific rule of the Old Testament, he sometimes also looked at the disposition, motives, and character of the person who carried out the action. We can describe Jesus's approach using the language of Greek philosophy: in a summary of the Old Testament law, he said that virtuous character is the disposition to love God and to love other people as oneself, and that virtuous behavior is the behavior of those who did what they did out of love for God and love for people, treating others as they would want to be treated themselves. To the rich young man, Jesus insisted that keeping to rules and commandments was not what only counted: what also counted was to "go, sell all that you have, and give to the poor" (Mark 10:17–31 // Matt 19:16–22; Luke 18:8–30), presumably because doing these things is the way the young man could express his love for God and for people. Jesus's approach to the interpretation of the Old Testament as a whole also promoted a new approach to ethics, for the implication of what Jesus said about the law (namely, that its purpose could be summed up as being to practice love towards God and towards other people) had the effect of moving attention away from specific rules to the underlying intentions and purposes of the rules.

At this point, the supposed link with Greek thought becomes tenuous at three points at least. First, from the beginning of the Christian tradition, the mark of a virtuous disposition is to acknowledge wrongdoing and to be deeply sorry about it. Repentance for not loving God and other people is a sign of a virtuous disposition, and the evidence of repentance (such as remorse, contrition, confession, reparation, restitution) is a sign of a virtuous character, not a sign of moral weakness. Second, the way a person develops a virtuous disposition is not only (and not even mainly) according to the pattern of the Greeks (through parental teaching, the influences of peers, philosophy, or rhetoric, for example) but principally in response to divine grace. In other words, God is the source of Christian virtue and godly character, with Christians, who are "new creatures" (2 Cor 5:17), working with God (Phil 2:12–13) to be "transformed by the renewal" of their minds, thereby discerning (and so being able to practice) the good, acceptable, and perfect will of God (Rom 12:2). Third, Paul in particular regarded *lypē* (grief or sadness) as integral to a virtuous response to having done wrong. *Lypē* is not regarded as the response of a virtuous person in the contemporary Stoic thought of Paul's day.

There are some clear examples of interpersonal remorse in the New Testament, and we have explored these carefully. We can describe Judas's remorse as "lachrymal" and "illucid" because he was in despair; Peter's remorse is healing and restores his relationship with Jesus. Paul's description of the Corinthians' supposed remorse anticipates the contemporary approach to interpersonal remorse, whereas his description of his own remorse (if he was remorseful) is pragmatic, confused and confusing.

Remorse in the Pre-Modern Period

Interpersonal remorse is almost overlooked in the period after the New Testament. It may be that the examples of Judas and Peter were not regarded as paradigmatic, as they concerned Jesus who came to be regarded as divine, and so examples of remorse towards Jesus were treated as if they were remorse towards God; the examples of remorse in 2 Corinthians are so complex and at times so convoluted that they also were largely overlooked, except, for example, by Aquinas who, as we saw, commends "godly grief" in 2 Cor 7:10. Nevertheless, I have described this period as "The Age of Remorse" and "the Age of Contrition" because it is a period when the Catholic Church developed complex mechanisms and procedures for people to express their contrition about sin against God. Loving God and fearing God were paramount in Christian spirituality, and the other half of what the "law and the prophets" hung on (to love one's neighbor as oneself) was not much explored except as a genus of sin against God. The ethics of divinity in the context of the ethics of the church community prevailed.

There was little immediate change as a result of the Reformation. Even though Aquinas had regarded contrition as a gift of grace and not one of the "passions," Protestantism reacted against the Catholic emphasis on what some regarded as contrition as a form of self-effort. Instead, Protestant theology emphasized the place of faith and grace alone for salvation. The result was to divert the focus of theological attention to salvation *sola fide* and *sola gratia* without (what was believed to be) the self-effort of antecedent contrition and remorse. We have seen that this has set a direction for Protestant theology that even into the twenty-first century has not made much more than passing reference to interpersonal remorse.

Important changes in secular western thought occurred beginning in the period after the Reformation, and we have seen how in this period the ethics of autonomy developed. People began to make meaningful, self-directed choices about how to live, sometimes largely free from the influence of the church. Some nineteenth-century novels explore issues to do with interpersonal remorse, and in *Emotions and the Moral Life*, Robert C. Roberts discusses such novels in relation to remorse. Nevertheless, western churches seem largely to have ignored the new awareness about and understanding of interpersonal remorse.

An example of a Christian theologian in the early period of the changes in western culture who did not identify or explore interpersonal remorse is Bishop Joseph Butler (1692–1752), even though (as we shall shortly see) we might perhaps have expected the focus of his thinking to point him towards developing a theology of interpersonal remorse. His failure to do so may in part be attributable to his view of the central place of the Church of England in English social and political structures. In other words, the place that the Established Church held in the life of the whole community militated against the ethics of autonomy being explored and developed in English theology.

Butler gave two psychologically astute sermons in the Rolls Chapel in 1718 on resentment and on forgiveness.[8] Butler's explorations of topics in the sermons generally show great insight into human emotions, which he variously calls "passions," "natural appetite," "affections," or "emotions of mind." In the sermons, he mentions remorse in Sermon X ("Upon Self Deceit") when referring to David.[9] He said David was guilty of "inhumanity" and showed "not . . . the least remorse or contrition" for engineering the death of Uriah the Hittite, husband to Bathsheba, so that he could marry Bathsheba (2 Sam 11:2–27).

Butler also does not discuss regret or repentance in his published public sermons. He comes tantalizingly close to seeing that there could be a place and opportunity for remorse towards *victims* of wrongdoing but he did not develop an initial observation that could have led him to formulate a theology of interpersonal remorse. Towards the end of Sermon IX, Butler speaks about "[t]he offences of which all are guilty of before God and the injuries which men do to each other": here, Butler links what we might call "remorse towards God for sins" with "remorse towards other human beings for having wronged them." He draws a distinction between the two, saying that God cannot "possibly be affected or moved as we are," and adds that "offences committed by others against ourselves and the manner in which we are apt to be afflicted by them give a real occasion for calling to mind our own sins against God."[10] He does not develop the interpersonal implications about regretting and then putting right wrongdoing, but instead suggests

8. Butler, Sermons VIII and IX respectively in *Fifteen Sermons*.

9. Butler, *Fifteen Sermons*, 114.

10. Butler, *Fifteen Sermons*, 100.

REMORSE: A CHRISTIAN PERSPECTIVE

that being wronged should be a reminder to victims of their own wrong-doing against God. In other words, in his focus on victims, he overlooks wrongdoers and their responsibilities towards their victims.

We have also seen that the liturgies of two modern, mainstream churches, the Catholic Church and the Church of England, pay little attention to the interpersonal effects of wrongdoing and have not developed an obvious theology of interpersonal remorse. The focus of remorse in modern liturgies and traditions is on sin against God.

Remorse, Ethics, and Moral Knowledge

Emotions are not constitutively moral; they are moral if they are responses to moral objects. One can deeply regret dying one's hair blonde: in this example, the deep regret is not about a moral object but a preference of fashion or taste. One can deeply regret lying to a friend: in this case, deep regret concerns a moral object (not telling the truth) and can be described as a "moral emotion."

There is considerable debate about the sources of moral knowledge. Aquinas especially, and the Christian tradition generally, regards moral knowledge as coming from God and sometimes witnessed to human beings through the conscience, which could, at times, be mistaken (e.g., 1 Cor 4:4). Recent contributions to the long-held debate have suggested that moral norms and human emotions are rooted in biological, bodily processes and shaped by natural selection. Some suggest that they are no more than the result of social conditioning. Others says that "prosocial norms" and "self-conscious emotions" can be useful sources of moral knowledge because they concern the conduct of individuals in a communitarian setting. According to such a way of thinking, behavior that is moral is behavior that is socially responsible and linked to the benefit and welfare of society. Jonathan Haidt suggests that these sorts of behaviors are "panhuman products of evolution." I have observed that such an approach to moral knowledge is problematic because there is good evidence to suggest that such behavior is relative and dependent on cultural norms. I have also suggested that the Golden Rule that Jesus enunciated offers a much more cogent and compelling way to derive prosocial norms. Certainly, the medieval Christian approach to the conscience (namely, that the knowledge it gives could be flawed) offers a less dogmatic and more self-reflective and more self-critical approach to the discernment of moral knowledge.

In chapter 7 we highlighted that there remains a lack of consensus about many fundamental questions about emotions. Broadly speaking, debates center on three approaches: emotions as "epiphenomena," that is, the results of bodily changes, emotions as determined through evolutionary development, and emotions as evaluative judgments. No single explanation incorporates all that is observed about emotions. Nico Frijda rightly concludes that the word "emotion" refers "to a loose collection of phenomena," and that emotions "are the outcomes of several sets of processes that are functionally independent, and each can occur in isolation."[11] I also accept the view of Roberts that emotions are concern-based construals with a communicative function, and I regard the construals as the result of cognitions that are shaped by intuitive and reflective appraisals and that result in "action readiness." Remorse is one kind of concern-based construal. What we can also say is that even if remorse consists of some elements of pan-human emotions that have developed through evolutionary adaptation, remorse also consists of elements of other emotions that are not universal. In other words (and our diachronic study of remorse confirms this) interpersonal remorse is not an emotion universally recognized as a discrete emotion, even if many of its elements (such as guilt and regret) appear to be evident in most human societies. Even where remorse is recognized, it takes "local" forms, reflecting idiosyncrasies of its host cultures.

Some important observations also need to be made about current models for understanding emotions, such as remorse. Even if emotions have been determined through evolutionary development and are biological in nature, we still do not know why human beings feel particular emotions or why and how they think that what they feel is significant. We also do not have satisfactory explanations about *what* people will do when they violate moral norms, *when* they will do it, and *why* they will do it. The somatic feedback theory, for example, provides no more than descriptions of what happens. (We can illustrate the point by observing that we can analyze a piece of music scientifically, but the description does not tell us why we like it, for describing something does not explain it.) As for a cognitive basis to emotions, clearly not all emotions have a rational basis, for, as we have seen, we cannot wholly explain from a cognitive viewpoint why a person who knows that household spiders are harmless may still be afraid of a household spider.

As we have also seen, the danger that some modern studies face is the trap of reductionism. A developing view that avoids this pitfall is that the different approaches to understanding emotions are complementary, with no one view being a metanarrative coherently ordering and explaining all the data. According to this view, the right approach to understanding emotions

11. Frijda, "The Evolutionary Emergence," 610, 618.

is by broad, over-arching categories[12] of "complementary" phenomena,[13] with emotions variously described as "an assemblage of processes"[14] and as "multicomponential."[15] Even so, as Roberts observes (and as I said above), though emotions can be studied in a variety of discrete disciplines, each providing answers within that discipline's own framework of understanding, none is able to provide "one category" that explains all that is observed.

It is perhaps not surprising that none of the explanations and descriptions as to the origin, nature, and forms of emotions on their own provides a satisfactory answer. It is perhaps also not surprising that, even when all the explanations and descriptions are put together, they still do not seem to provide a coherent narrative of what we observe and experience. The approach of faith communities perhaps helps at this point. Religious truths such as are reflected in Christianity, for example, usually presuppose that there is more to human identity and experience than is wholly explicable through measurable, physical phenomena. This is not to deny that human identity and experience are *in part* explicable through measurable, physical phenomena, but these do not give the whole picture, as what it means to be a conscious, living, self-aware human being is more than what we can measure. (By saying this, I am not conceding the case for a dualistic approach to human identity; I am saying no more than that we do not appear to be able to measure and thereby explain all that comprises a living, self-aware human being.) What I referred to as "naturalism" in chapter 7 is not the framework for "a theory of everything" when it comes to emotions.[16]

Naturalism also poses a challenge to the idea that people freely make moral choices. In its strongest form, naturalism is the view that all actions and mental processes are causally determined. In chapter 7, we explored more nuanced approaches to naturalism that did not exclude the possibility that a degree of independent choice and of personal responsibility for one's acts, omissions, and reactions is compatible with a qualified approach

---

12. Griffiths, "Modularity."

13. Sander et al., "Appraisal Driven."

14. Frijda, "The Evolutionary Emergence."

15. Sander et al., "Appraisal Driven." See also Nagel, "What Is It Like to Be a Bat?" on reductionism.

16. The phrase "theory of everything" is commonly used by physicists to indicate that, by the theory, there will be one, comprehensive theory that explains all of the known universe. Current models are built on two theories, the theory of general relativity and the quantum field theory, which, though mutually incompatible, have each been rigorously tested and not (yet) disproved. (I am grateful to Simeon Bash for advice on this footnote.)

to naturalism. Such an approach largely accords with the Christian idea of
moral accountability for one's actions and omissions.

The debate that naturalism raises is as old as Jewish and Christian theology, for the Bible as a whole describes God as sovereign, determining causes
and effects in the whole of creation on the one hand, and on the other hand
recognizes that people make choices, and are accountable to God and to other
people for those choices. Despite three millennia of reflection, the antinomy
has not been resolved. The modern debate no more than reflects the antinomy
in secular terms. Both the thesis and the antithesis are, at least to some extent,
true (the degree of "truth" may depend on how they are expressed, as there
are no uncontested statements of the thesis and antithesis), and to ignore one
without the other is to make a mistake: we need to hold on to both.

I suggest that there are at least three bases to Christian ethics that are
relevant to all people, whether they come from a faith tradition or not and
regardless of whether the basis of these norms can be attributed to evolutionary developments. The first is the "Golden Rule" of Matt 7:12 ("whatever
you wish that other would do to you, do also to them"),[17] which Jesus says
sums up the approach of the Old Testament to ethics. The second is the twin
command to love God and other people as oneself (Matt 22:37).[18] Third,
in the post-Easter statement of ethics, another basis to Christian ethics is
the model of the cross described in Phil 2:5–11.[19] The model predicates
that Christian ethics are to be based not on self-interest but (in appropriate circumstances) on regard for the unconditional good of others, even
if this is at great personal cost to one's own wellbeing.[20] Not living with
regard to the unconditional good of others (as qualified above) is, in my
view, the true ground of remorse, so long as remorse is then followed by
repentance, a re-formed pattern of life, and (where appropriate), restitution
and reparations.[21]

17. See also Luke 6:31 ("as you wish that others would do to you, do so to them").
This ties in with Matt 25:31–46, where Jesus also emphasizes the importance of the way
people are treated.

18. These first two reasons are discussed in Rudman, *Concepts*, 263–69 and Gill,
Moral Passion, 183–89.

19. Thus, I stand with Porter in rejecting an apodictic approach to ethics (*Moral
Action*, 5).

20. See Hallett on the place of "other-preference" (*Priorities*, 115) in Christian ethics
(*Priorities*, 114–15, 117) and on the importance of the corporate "solidarity" of humanity as a reason for ethical behavior (*Priorities*, 39–45). Disordered relationships
corrupt human solidarity: remorse and repentance are appropriate ways to put right
the disorder.

21. Compare Cronin, who regards being made in the image of God as giving a "specifically religious justifying reason for acting morally" (*Rights and Christian Ethics*, 233,

Remorse and Language

A recurring theme in this book has been about language for emotions. An obvious, and now well-established, starting point for thinking about language generally is James Barr's observation in *The Semantics of Biblical Language* that linguists must avoid the mistake of taking all of a word's possible associations and assuming that the associations can all be read into each use of the word. Interpretation always has to be context- and situation-specific. Another obvious starting point is that words do not "have" meanings; we "give" them meanings according to context and use. This is why, in this book, we have looked at remorse according to its contexts and have taken both a diachronic and synchronic approach, observing how remorse has been differently understood at various points of its history. We have sought to avoid the mistake Barr warns of and so made it an aim to understand "remorse" and related words in their socio-cultural and historical contexts.

Implicit in our discussion of remorse has been the prototype approach to perceptual and semantic categories developed by Philip Shaver et al., to which I have referred. Adopting the approach, we have, on occasions, treated the word "emotions" as a "superordinate category," with regret (which we have treated as a hyponym for a number of words for emotions) as a "basic category," and remorse (a type of regret) as in a "subordinate category" of words to do with regret. Included in the subordinate category might also be other words for emotions such as contrition, sadness, disappointment, shame, guilt, and so on. This is a helpful way of identifying the interconnectedness of the words for regret and for identifying their points of similarity and difference through shared and excluded components respectively.

Another important development in linguistics is based on Wittgenstein's observation that words do not have "sharp boundaries," but they have "blurred edges" and are "uncircumscribed." James A. Russell has adapted the observation and suggested that words can be considered as "a fuzzy set defined by a class."[22] Combining this approach with the approach of Shaver et al., we can analyze the words in the subordinate category of words that are examples of types of regret and observe that there is "a gradual but specifiable transition from membership to nonmembership" of the class.[23]

253–64). I disagree with his view that "it is necessary to distinguish . . . the secular or humanistic reasons available to all men and women of good will, and the reasons stemming from revelation which are available only to those adhering to a specific religious tradition," although of course I agree that "religious justifying reasons" for moral action "offer a deeper . . . grasp" of the rationale for acting morally (*Rights and Christian Ethics*, 241).

22. Russell, "Circumplex."

23. Russell, "Circumplex," 1165.

A straight-forward inference we can make from this approach to emotions is that certain categories of emotions are not independent of one another but are related to varying extents.

We can also treat *remorse* as itself being in the basic category, with words such as contrition, compunction, guilt, sadness, regret, shame as being in a "fuzzy set" in the subordinate category. What becomes obvious quickly is that it is relatively arbitrary which of the "regret-related" words we put in the basic category; whichever word is in the basic category, the relationships of the words in the subordinate category to one another are still evident. In short, we put in the basic category whichever word that we wish from the "remorse" or "regret" group of words according to our conceptual framework and cognitive structure of language. I have made a judgment that regret is best placed in the basic category, with regret-related words (such as remorse) in the subordinate category. This reflects my preference to move from the general to the more specific. However, it is equally possible to start with a more focused word, such as "remorse," and treat 'remorse" as the hypernym, and then look at and identify more specific words for emotions that are components of remorse.

Types of Remorse

Is it right to regard both interpersonal remorse and remorse towards God as examples of remorse, the only difference being that the subjects of the remorse are different, namely, human beings and God respectively? There are points of similarity between remorse about sin before God and remorse about wronging another person. Remorse in both cases is retrospective, moral, cognitive, and experiential; it can also lead to restoration and repair. The grounds of possible dissimilarity are first, that we cannot assume that interpersonal wrongdoing corresponds with wrongdoing against God (this may be to make a mistake of category), and second, that we cannot assume that remorse felt towards God about sin corresponds with remorse felt towards human beings about offences against those human beings (this may also be a mistake of category). In particular, two of the typical features of lucid, interpersonal remorse that we identified do not apply in the case of remorse towards God: God is in no sense a "victim" of human wrongdoing and it is misplaced to feel "empathy" for the supposed suffering on the part of God as a result of human wrongdoing. In short, remorse towards God about sin is a model for interpersonal remorse, but it is, in many ways, significantly different from interpersonal remorse about wronging a human being.

I next discuss two of the ways of thinking about the differences between remorse towards God about sin and remorse towards other people about wrongdoing. First, one could say the two types of remorse are like intersecting circles in a Venn diagram, with the common elements of remorse (such as remorse as being retrospective, moral, cognitive, experiential, and the precursor to steps to repair the effects of wrongdoing) represented at the intersections of the circles. The two aspects of remorse that are not in the intersection are distinct and not common to both remorse towards God and remorse towards people. This way of thinking about remorse regards both kinds of remorse as part of one "set" ("remorse") that are connected by some common features that are shared by both kinds of remorse, with each kind of remorse having points of dissimilarity with the other as well. This has been the approach of this book.

Another way of thinking about remorse is to regard remorse towards God as deep regret about sin, and to say that such remorse, if it is truly to be remorse, must have deep regret (subject) about sin *against God* (object). So-called "remorse" towards people shares the idea of "deep regret" (subject) but treats the object of remorse to be wrongdoing *against people*, not God. In other words, the object of the remorse is categorically different, and the difference is significant. We could describe interpersonal remorse seen this way as derivative, bearing a "family resemblance" to (Godward) remorse, connected by overlapping similarities but with only one common feature, deep regret. If one takes this approach, interpersonal remorse is akin to Godward remorse, but missing some of the elements of what we might term "authentic remorse." There is not a discrete word in English to describe derivative, interpersonal remorse of this kind.

The church may well have assumed that remorse is best understood in accordance with the second way of thinking about remorse that I have outlined, that is, that remorse is only (or perhaps "primarily") a God-facing emotion. Certainly, this is more-or-less what both the Old Testament and parts of the New Testament seem to assume, and so may well also help to explain why the church has failed for almost two millennia to develop the idea of interpersonal remorse. It has been secular thinkers, in an age of the ethics of autonomy (when belief in God and the authoritative place of biblical ethics were no longer widely held), who rethought remorse as being deep regret (not towards God but) towards other human beings for (not sin against God but) wrongdoing against other people.

Contemporary Approaches to Remorse

In the contemporary period, interpersonal remorse has been recognized to be an emotion in response to violations of ethical norms that result is disruption to relationships. Remorse expresses personal awareness that one's wrongdoing has had personal and social consequences that have brought harm, suffering, or distress to others. Contemporary work on the nature of moral emotions, the sources of moral knowledge, and the role of emotions in making moral judgment, although now set in a secular framework, often bears some resemblance to the Thomist tradition of ethics and is genealogically related to much Christian thinking.[24]

We have identified that the components of authentic interpersonal remorse are empathy for others, and an approach to one's behavior that is self-critical and retrospective and that is based on ethical criteria. We have also explored the different ways that people can be remorseful and drawn widely on the wisdom and insights of those who would not say that they stand in a Christian tradition (and some who say that they do not stand in such a tradition). As Douglas Hicks has argued, we need not be apologetic about drawing on secular wisdom, for "the goal [of formulating modern Christian ethics] is not to be distinctive as much as to be faithful and truthful," though I would argue, as Hicks also does, that Christian ethics does have a distinguishing contribution to make to many modern ethical questions.[25]

Interpersonal remorse can be lucid or "illucid," stronger or weaker, deep or shallow, pathological, or corrupt, or egocentric. It can be a "lachrymal" emotion, expressing one's brokenness arising from guilt and shame about one's wrongdoing and its impact on others. The integrity of one's remorse can be demonstrated by repentance, reparations, and restitution. Remorse is said sometimes to be a form of shock about what one has done, grief both for the harm one has caused and for one's own personal failure, and lament, shame, and guilt for violating the wellbeing of other human beings. It can be an expression of self-blame, disappointment, and even self-disgust; in its morbid forms, its effects can be turned inwards on oneself, leaving remorseful people punishing themselves or yearning for punishment from others.

Remorse is an ambivalent emotion, for one can never truly be sure about the extent to which one's remorse is instrumental, for personal advantage or gain.[26] Remorse is easy to "fake," either deliberately or subconsciously, and

24. Obviously, this does not apply if we regard emotions as evolutionary adaptations.

25. Hicks, *Inequality*, 200.

26. I wonder if Roberts falls into this trap when he suggests that the intention to amend one's life through repentance can be, for the Christian, a response to experiencing

modern psychology has alerted us to the subtlety of defense mechanisms that shield people from psychic pain. Probably the only way to test the integrity of a person's supposed remorse is to measure it against standards of plausibility, coherence, consistency, and long-term patterns of change.

In chapter 9, we looked at the place of remorse in sentencing policy for criminal acts. Remorse is sometimes taken into account when determining a sentence for criminal wrongdoing. We observed the near-impossibility of determining when remorse is genuine, and I suggested some principles that judges might use to discern whether a criminal's supposed remorse is likely to be genuine. The aim of the principles I suggested is to be avoid "being made a sucker by fakery," in Jeffrie Murphy's memorable phrase.

A New Approach to Remorse

Much of what we have considered in this chapter points to the fact that the definition of remorse in the *OED* reflects an approach to remorse based on the ethics of divinity, when people were sure about what was right and wrong and that in each situation there was one course of right action. Remorse was then seen as deep regret about moral wrongdoing, which for many years was taken to be sin against God. It has only been in the last century that remorse as an interpersonal ethic has been clearly recognized, described, and its characteristics set out.

A Christian approach to interpersonal remorse, even if based on biblical principles, does not now necessarily have to assume that to wrong another person is no more than to sin against God "before" another person (as the Prodigal Son said of his own wrongdoing against his father in Luke 15:18, 21). Rather, wrongdoing, even when it is also sin against God, is rightly also regarded as doing wrong to or against another person, in respect of which interpersonal remorse (that is, deep regret or guilt for doing wrong to another person) is an appropriate response. The change that has taken place is that individuals who have been wronged are now regarded as having a legitimate place as the subjects of remorse.

At the center of remorse is also a meta-question about how we approach ethics. Most traditional approaches to ethics are either deontological, emphasizing rules and duties and treating actions as right or wrong regardless of their consequences, or teleological, exploring the consequences of actions and regarding morality as determined by those consequences. Virtue ethics is a third, and concomitant (some might say "different"), approach: it looks at the virtue or moral character of the person who carries out an

---

oneself "as . . . having the prospect of forgiveness" (*Spiritual Emotions*, 107).

action, and asks the question, "What sort of person should I be if I am to live and act in a way that is moral?"[27] The assumption of virtue ethics is that virtuous people will rightly act and so live in moral ways because they have virtues. The emphases of virtue ethics include questions to do with motives and moral character, the role of emotions in the moral life, the sorts of people we should be, and the way we should live.

I remain unconvinced that any one of these three ways of approaching ethics on its own is always necessarily right; a balanced approach is critically to appraise the outcomes of all three approaches to a given moral dilemma. Approaching ethics in this way is much like the way that we concluded in chapter 7 that emotions should be approached, namely, that there is a variety of ways to do so. Likewise, there is a variety of ways of approaching ethics and morality, and no one way is right for every situation and for every perspective of every situation. Ethics and morality, like emotions, are best understood in a multicomponential way.

We have seen that the *OED* indicates that remorse is "deep regret or guilt for doing something morally wrong." It is now time to make three important comments about the definition of remorse.

First, an obvious, and in my view serious, lacuna is not to have included omissions in a gloss on the words "morally wrong." One can be as much remorseful about omissions, as one can about commissions.

Second, it seems to me self-evident that people may be remorseful about not being the sort of virtuous people they think or believe they should be or usually are. An obvious example are those who make morally right decisions but regret having to do what is right or resent the morally right decisions. When such people come to their senses, they may feel "deep regret or guilt" for not being virtuous, notwithstanding that they acted morally. The definition of remorse in the *OED* apparently precludes people from being regarded as remorseful if they have done the right thing and regret or resent it and who later deeply regret their former motives and actions.

Next, and equally importantly, not all moral dilemmas that people face are necessarily capable of being resolved into a choice about doing (or not doing) a single action (or course of actions) that is (or are) morally right, with the assumption that anything else is morally wrong. As we have seen, there may be varieties of actions that are each morally right in different ways; it is a mistake to assume that any one of the actions is necessarily the best or will achieve the most desirable outcome, as moral outcomes sometimes depend on contingencies outside the actor's control

27. The origin of the modern forms of virtue ethics are from Plato and Aristotle and was re-invigorated by Anscombe in "Modern Moral Philosophy" and MacIntyre in *After Virtue*.

or knowledge. One may therefore do one of several possible right things and be remorseful because the outcome of the action one chose to do may be the undesired or unexpected cause of suffering or harm to another person. We may also be remorseful about the outcome of a moral choice we made, if we could have made a different moral choice that, with hindsight, we realize would have had a better outcome.[28] In short, people *may* experience remorse even if they believe that the past actions about which they are remorseful were morally justified.

We may also make what we believe to be the only correct moral choice (which is confirmed in hindsight) but deeply regret the outcome of the choice. For example, a soldier who shoots at point-blank range a young, armed enemy combatant may not have done wrong, for it would be the soldier's life or the enemy combatant's, but the soldier may have such a deep distaste for what she has done and such an overwhelming sense of shame that she feels deep regret but believes she has not done wrong by her actions.

Additionally, sometimes people may be faced with choices all of which will (or may) bring about a degree of harm. As we saw in chapter 1, this is sometimes called "the dilemma of dirty hands." Even though a moral philosopher might say that the right action to take is the one resulting in the least harm, people who take such actions are likely still to be remorseful because they feel compromised and corrupted by what they have done.

Lastly, we may also act in an appropriate way but be the inadvertent and blameless cause of harm to another. It is not that what one does is wrong but that it has consequences that evoke guilt and then remorse. For example, a driver who injures or kills a pedestrian who negligently steps out in front of the driver of the car might feel deep remorse about what he has done, even though he is blameless. Another example might be if I forget a lunch invitation with a friend, and the friend I was meant to eat with took his life later that day because (unknown to me) he had become deeply worried and anxious about a personal matter. In my view, it would not be a sign of neurosis to feel in such a situation guilt and remorse, even though, in most ethical schemes, to forget a social event is not a wrong or moral failure; neither would it be foolish in the circumstances to blame oneself for the unintended consequences of being forgetful. The key factor here has to do the individual's sense of responsibility, which can be over-developed, under-developed, or appropriately balanced. It is therefore appropriate sometimes to feel remorse about actions that are not wrong, but which occur "in situations in which irreparable harm has been done."[29]

28. Williams says this of regret (*Moral Luck*, 28). See also Raz, "Agency."
29. Horne, "Reflections," 23.

Bernard Williams would describe the sort of situations I have described in the paragraph above as "agent regret." "Agent regret" is the sort of regret that people feel when they have brought about, directly or indirectly, an outcome they wish were different. In my view, the "regret" in "agent regret" should be limited to emotions that are typical of regret as we have explained "regret" in this book; to speak of inadvertently contributing to the death of a friend as a species of "regret" seems to me to overlook the profound sorrow, guilt, and shame (emotions that are *not* characteristic only of regret) that one might feel about the unintended consequences of one's actions and omissions.

Though it is right that remorse is a species of regret, its strong, reactive nature also differentiates it from regret, as we saw in chapter 1. I suggest we now use the term *"agent remorse"* for the response of people who cause significant harm to others, and who deeply lament and regret the harm they have caused, even if they may be without fault or moral blame.[30] I disagree with Roberts who says, of those who cause significant harm to others and who are without fault or moral blame, that the appropriate feeling is "intense regret," not remorse; I also disagree that such a reaction can properly be described as a "trivial analog" of remorse.[31]

In view of the foregoing observations, I suggest that a contemporary definition of remorse, informed by a Christian approach to ethics, is:

Deep regret or guilt for an act or omission

1. *That is morally wrong; or*

2. *That results in undesired consequences to or undesirable consequences for another; or*

3. *That a virtuous person would not have done or omitted; or*

4. *That treats another in a way we ourselves would not want to be treated.*

The suggested new definition of remorse includes the explicit addition of a teleological approach to remorse and a place for personal virtue as one of the criteria of what is moral. The definition also implicitly recognizes that remorse can arise if people do not practice one or more of either the injunction to love their neighbor as themselves, the Golden Rule (Matt 7:12; Luke 6:31), or the converse of the Golden Rule (sometimes called 'the Silver Rule"), namely, "Do not do to others as you would not have them to you."

---

30. Compare Philips and Price, "Remorse," and Fulkerson, *No Regrets*, 19 (but not Konstan, *Before Forgiveness*, 9) on whether remorse always presupposes wrongdoing.

31. Roberts, *Moral Life*, 222, 170.

There are some emotions that are like remorse but they do not have all the characteristics of remorse that we have now suggested. What people with such emotions experience bears some resemblance to remorse (such as deep distaste for what one has done or regret for misdeeds, for example) but it is either so alloyed with other emotions or so lacking in some of the other principal characteristics of remorse that the "family resemblance" to authentic remorse is barely seen. I call such emotions "quasi-remorse."[32]

An example of quasi-remorse is, I suggest, collective or corporate remorse. Because remorse is an emotion of the conscience, it is necessarily an individual's emotion, and not a collective or community's emotion because only individuals, and not communities, have consciences.[33] Of course, if enough people in a community are remorseful about the same thing, one might loosely say that the community is "remorseful," but I suspect there may be as many types of remorse as there are remorseful people in the community, and a significant amount of variation in the understanding of each of the individuals in the community as to what may or may not be remorse. I also suspect that part of the confusion about whether Japanese people are or are not remorseful about their imperial past during the Second World War (see chapter 1) is because remorse, as it is understood in the West, is an individual's response in a "guilt culture," and not, in contrast to how it is understood in Japan, a collective response in a "shame culture." The confusion is compounded because the way the Japanese appear to understand the nature of collective remorse is, as we saw, diverse.

Some types of quasi-remorse that do not involve wrongdoing are barely more than regret. Such feelings of regret point to a response that serves to sustain our self-respect as people who care about the outcomes of what we do. Assuming that Paul did not write to the Corinthians in an intemperate or inappropriate way, perhaps this should have been the way Paul referred to his anxiety about the letter he wrote to the Corinthians (2 Cor 7:8–9). Remorse in this situation *is*, in my view, "irrational" and a "trivial analog" of remorse. A better way to describe this sort of emotion is "agent regret."

32. Examples of quasi-remorse bear a weak resemblance to the prototype of remorse, though (as I said) it will bear some "family resemblances" to remorse (see Shaver et al., "Emotion Knowledge," 1062).

33. See Smith on the analytical complexity of collective apologies (*I Was Wrong*, 155–252). He concludes (p. 249), "In the vast majority of cases, victims should seek apologies from those individuals personally responsible for harming them. Collective apologies can supplement this meaning."

Interpersonal Remorse and Christian Theology

There *is* a place for interpersonal remorse in Christian theology, a place that
has been significantly understated and so underdeveloped. The example of
the omission of the Church of England to make an adequate place for interpersonal remorse in the services called "The Reconciliation of a Penitent"
in *Common Worship: Christian Initiation* makes this clear. The Church of
England is not alone among modern churches in failing to make a proper
place for interpersonal remorse.

Interpersonal remorse also has an important place in the day-to-day
discipleship of Christians for at least three reasons.

First, interpersonal remorse can teach people what it means to be "under sin"[34] and point them to respond in repentance. Those who think they are
not wrongdoers should search their consciences; they are likely to discover
they are guilty of wrongdoing. Those who know they have done wrong but
are not remorseful will do well to consider why they are not remorseful. Feelings of remorse, when properly and carefully explored, can tutor people and
expose their capacity for denial and self-deception. There is great wisdom in
Jas 5:16, which suggests that such a process should take place with others,
and not only on one's own, for other people can hold up a mirror to show
what one may not want to (or does not) see.

Next, interpersonal remorse, as a species of regret, is the *sine qua
non* of repentance, and repentance (as I have argued in other places)[35]
is usually the prerequisite of richly textured forgiveness. Repentance and
forgiveness are often found together, and there is no authentic repentance
without emotions such as remorse or regret. As for repentance, it is no
more than an action and cognition if it is without remorse or regret, just
as remorse or regret without repentance is no more than emotion. Repentance and remorse go together and, when they are together, they constitute one of the ways to love God with both actions and emotions, that is,
with one's heart, soul, strength, and mind.[36]

Last, the contemporary approach to remorse rightly recognizes the
obscenity of wronging people without properly engaging with the effects
of wrongdoing on those people. Without wanting to assume that what is
in a biblical account about an incident is all that there is to know about the
incident, I find something deeply unsettling about the account of David's

34. Rom 3:10, and see vv. 11–18, 23.

35. E.g., Bash, *Forgiveness and Christian Ethics, Just Forgiveness,* and *Forgiveness: A
Theology.*

36. This reflects the way that "faith without works is dead" (Jas 2:14, 17) and that
works without faith is equally moribund (Rom 3:20).

response to having committed adultery with Bathsheba and to having engineered the death of Uriah, her husband: he appears to regard what he did as sin against God, and against God alone (Ps 51:4). Three people at least (Bathsheba, Uriah, and Joab, the army commander who colluded with David's intention to get Uriah killed in war) were affected by David's action, and David also wronged them.[37] However, in giving a proper place to people as the subjects of remorse, there is a danger that we make people the equivalent of gods. The apostle Paul warns of the danger of worshipping and serving "the creature rather than the creator" in Rom 1:25 (and see vv. 18–32). We do well to remember that in wronging other people we also wrong the God in whose image people are made. To be remorseful with this in mind can also help us to understand better what it means to sin against God and so to look to God for the grace of forgiveness.

Christian Moral Justifications of Remorse

We have seen in chapter 7 that thoughts (cognitions) give form and content to emotions. We have also seen that appraisal is the process of thought that results in an individual construing and evaluating the significance of a situation.

I suggest that there are at least six important ways that the Christian gospel—that is, "the priority of God's action"[38] in its broadest sense—informs the framework and content of what Magda Arnold calls "intuitive appraisal" and "reflective appraisal." The framework of appraisal is not based on prescriptive rules, natural law, or church traditions;[39] rather, it is an existential response to God and to the gospel. The gospel understood this way thereby provides what in another context Gordon Graham calls "theologically interpreted conceptions";[40] it also provides the theological underpinning of the emotional response called "remorse." In other words, and as Graham observes (in a different context, too), such an approach discloses "an identifiable Christian ethic."[41] The first five of the six ways are, to varying extents, relatively well-known among the starting points

37. David also had seven wives at this time (Ahinoam, Abigail, Maacah, Haggith, Abital, Eglah [2 Sam 3:2–5], and Michael), who would have been indirectly affected by his actions (2 Sam 3:14–15).

38. Fergusson, *Community*, xi.

39. Compare Cahill, *Global Justice*, 281.

40. Graham, *Evil*, 24.

41. Graham, *Evil*, 73.

for Christian ethics, though their importance for remorse has been little considered. They are as follows.

First, remorse is an emotion that celebrates that people have been "made in the image of God" and, because God's handiwork, they are those for whom Christ has died. For these reasons, people are to be treated with dignity and respect, and not wronged.[42] If they have been wronged, remorse is an appropriate response, because the image of God in them has been dishonored.

Second, remorse is also an emotion that evidences that we love our neighbors as ourselves and treat others in ways that we ourselves would like to be treated. In other words, to be remorseful is to practice principles that are at the center of Christian ethics, albeit because one recognizes that one has previously failed to live up to those principles.

Next, lucid remorse is an emotion that points people to repentance, and so to putting right (as best they can and if they can) what they have done, through making reparations and restitution.

In addition, at the heart of the gospel is the notion of a loving God who takes initiative with humanity and invites humanity to seek reconciliation with God. This model of initiative-taking to seek restored relationships with one another is central to the gospel, just as the call to seek restored relationships with God is central to the task of those who proclaim the gospel (2 Cor 5:18–20).[43] Remorse and repentance are the starting points if human beings are to seek reconciliation with God *and* with one another,[44] with interpersonal reconciliation to *precede* reconciliation with God (Matt 5:23–24).

Fifth, remorse and then repentance are the essential groundwork and precondition of richly textured forgiveness. It is only a slight exaggeration to say that there is "no forgiveness without repentance": certainly, the normal and typical pattern of forgiveness in the New Testament is that acceptance of personal responsibility for wrongdoing (evidenced not only cognitively but also emotionally, such as by remorse) followed by repentance (and so reparation and restitution) precede forgiveness or at least are integral to the process of being forgiven. Remorse prepares the way for repentance, and so for forgiveness and reconciliation.

---

42. The concept is explored at length in Rudman, *Concepts,* 130–41 in the context of the Trinity; see also Cronin, *Rights and Christian Ethics,* 233.

43. See Martin, *Reconciliation* and Bash, *Ambassadors for Christ.*

44. We see this clearly in the Parable of the Prodigal Son (Luke 15:11–32).

There remains a sixth reason why remorse models essential aspects of the Christian gospel. This reason, and its rationale, have been little explored as moral justification for ethical behavior.

Some of the ways human identity is understood in the New Testament is about with whom or with what one is "interrelated,"[45] about in whom or in what one shares or participates, and about with whom or with what one identifies. In other words, people share in the identity of those or what they follow and imitate, or the examples they practice.

Several different models are used to explore and explain this approach to identity. For example, Paul refers to humanity as being "in Adam" or as being "in Christ" according to what they believe and do. The way a person lives, as well as in what or whom they believe, indicate whether they are "in Adam" or "in Christ."[46] In another example, Paul regards those who eat food that has been offered to idols as being "participants with demons" (2 Cor 10:20) and those who consume the Eucharistic elements as "participants" in the body and blood of Christ (2 Cor 10:16).[47] A different model is that salvation is for those who participate in the resurrection of Christ through faith,[48] because, since Christ participated in the identity of humanity, humanity may, by faith and obedience, participate in the identity of the risen Son of God. The point is, as Morna D. Hooker explains (borrowing from Irenaeus's thought), that Christ became what we are (fully human) so that in him we may become as he is (raised to new life for eternity).[49] We see this process of "interchange" (as Hooker calls it) or of reciprocity at work in this way: those who are "in Christ" will also experience Christ[50] and the Holy Spirit in *them*.[51]

Given these varieties of metaphors, one of the ways Paul expresses the rationale of Christian ethics is that it is incongruent, even absurd, for Christians to live out their freedom as if they do not participate in the life and example of Christ.[52] In consequence, in relation to interpersonal conduct,

45. The word in this context is Davison's (*Participation*, 367) and see his comments generally on participation in the New Testament (*Participation*, 271–75).

46. 1 Cor 15:22; 2 Cor 5:17; Rom 16:7; Gal 1:22, for example. Paul also uses a variety of other metaphors to describe this too, e.g., Rom 6:3–10. On Adam and union with Christ see Macaskill, *Union*, 128–43.

47. On can also "share" *in* the sufferings of Christ (Phil 3:10; 2 Cor 1 in Davison, *Participation*, 220–21); see also Col 1:24.

48. Sanders, *Paul*.

49. Hooker, *From Adam to Christ*, 13–102.

50. Eph 3:17; Col 1:27.

51. Rom 8:9; 1 Cor 3:16; 12:13; and 2 Tim 1:14.

52. Rudman summarizes this elegantly in *Concepts*, 7.

we can ask these questions: in whose example is one participating and with whose example is one identifying? Is it with the example and way of life that Jesus exemplified, or is it with humanity's patterns of behavior and being that Jesus sought to change through his teachings? More specifically, when one wrongs another human being, is one identifying with Jesus, or is one modelling, albeit inadvertently, something akin to the chicanery, injustice, and violation of those who perpetrated Jesus's arrest, trial, and death?

A distinctively Christian, theological approach to remorse suggests that a person who knowingly wrongs another is, in some measure, modelling, identifying with, and practicing deviant and abusive behavior, just as those who brutalized Jesus did. To state what Jesus said in Matt 25:31–46, but this time of those who do wrong: "As you did it to one of the least of these, you did it to me." According to this way of thought, doing wrong violates and demeans not only another person who is made in the image of God *but also Christ in them*, who is their hope of glory (Col 1:27).[53]

Remorse and repentance can reshape and perhaps even re-constitute aspects of human identity. They are ways wrongdoers can re-align themselves to practice the truth of the gospel, affirm they are sinners in need of the grace of forgiveness, and participate in identity-re-forming and identity-re-shaping grace. To be remorseful and repentant about interpersonal wrongs leads to life-giving grace and to relationships, and so to communities, that model the gospel ethics of mercy, love, forgiveness, and reconciliation. Remorse about interpersonal wrongs is therefore a compelling Christian emotion and ethic, and we neglect it at our peril. It is, as we saw at the start of this book, one of "eternity's emissaries" that leads to "purity of heart"[54] and so to blessing and the way to "see God" (Matt 5:8).

53. See also Hallett, *Priorities*, 46–48 on this pericope in the context of almsgiving.
54. Kierkegaard, *Purity*, 11.

Bibliography

Achino-Loeb, Maria-Luisa. "Agency in Emotions. Notes on Three Perspectives from an Anthropologist's Eye." *Theory & Psychology* 14(4) (2004) 554–61.

Adolphs, Ralph, and David J. Anderson. *The Neuroscience of Emotion: A New Synthesis*. Princeton, NJ: Princeton University Press, 2018.

Adolphs, Ralph, and Daniel Andler. "Investigating Emotions as Functional States Distinct from Feelings." *Emotion Review* 10(3) (2018) 191–201.

Al-Rawi, F. N. H., and A. R. George. "Back to the Cedar Forest: The Beginning and End of Tablet V of the Standard Babylonian Epic of Gilgameš." In *The Epic of Gilgamesh: A New Translation, Analogues, Criticism*, translated and edited by Benjamin R. Foster, 69–90. New York: Norton, 2011.

Anderson, Gary A. *Sin: A History*. New Haven: Yale University Press, 2009.

Annas, Julia. *Hellenistic Philosophy of Mind*. Berkeley, CA: University of California Press, 1992.

Anscombe, G. E. M. "Modern Moral Philosophy." *Philosophy* 33(124) (1958) 1–19.

Aquinas, Thomas. *Summa Theologiae. Latin Text and English Translation, Introduction, Notes, Appendices and Glossaries* by Eric D'Arcy. Volume 19, The Emotions, 1a2ae. 22–30. Cambridge: Cambridge University Press, 2006.

———. *Summa Theologiae. Latin Text and English Translation, Introduction, Notes, Appendices and Glossaries* by Eric D'Arcy. Volume 20, Pleasure, 1a2ae. 31–39. Cambridge: Cambridge University Press, 2006.

———. *Summa Theologiae. Latin Text and English Translation, Introduction, Notes, Appendices and Glossaries* by John Patrick Reid. Volume 21, Fear and Anger, 1a2ae. 40–48. Cambridge: Cambridge University Press, 2006.

———. *Summa Theologiae. Latin Text and English Translation, Introduction, Notes, Appendices and Glossaries* by Reginald Masterson and T. C. O'Brien. Volume 60, Penance. 3a. 84–90. Cambridge: Cambridge University Press, 2006.

Arendt, Hannah. *The Human Condition*. Chicago: University of Chicago Press, 1958.

Aristophanes. *Wasps*. Edited with introduction and commentary by Zachary P. Biles and S. Douglas Olson. Oxford: Oxford University Press, 2015.

Aristotle. *Art of Rhetoric.* Translated by John Henry Freese. LCL 193. Cambridge: Harvard University Press, 2014.

————. *De Anima.* Translated by J. A. Smith. In *The Basic Works of Aristotle,* edited by Richard McKeon, 534–603. New York: Random House, 1941.

————. *Nicomachean Ethics.* Translated by H. Rackham. LCL 73. Cambridge: Harvard University Press, 2014.

Arnold, Bill T. *Genesis.* Cambridge: Cambridge University Press, 2009.

Arnold, Magda B. *Emotion and Personality,* Volume 1. New York: Columbia University Press, 1960.

Asmis, Elizabeth. "Psychagogia in Plato's *Phaedrus.*" *Illinois Classical Studies* 11(1/2) (1986) 153–72.

Augustine. *The Works of St Augustine: A Translation for the 21st Century.* Books 6 and 7. *The City of God.* Translated by William Babcock. Hyde Park, NY: New City, 2012–13.

Augustine. *City of God.* Books 8–11, with an English translation by David S. Wiesen. LCL 413. Cambridge: Harvard University Press, 1966.

Augustine. *City of God.* Books 12–15, with an English translation by Philip Levine. LCL 414. Cambridge: Harvard University Press, 1968.

Aune, David Charles. "Passions in the Pauline Epistles: The Current State of Research." In *Passions and Moral Progress in Greco-Roman Thought,* edited by John T. Fitzgerald, 221–37. London: Routledge, 2008.

Aus, Roger David. *Simon Peter's Denial and Jesus' Commissioning Him as His Successor in John 21:15–19.* Studies in their Judaic Background (Studies in Judaism). Lanham, MD: University Press of America, 2013.

Ayer, A. J. *Language, Truth, and Logic.* New York: Dover, 1952.

Babcock, William. *The Works of Saint Augustine. A Translation for the 21st Century. The City of God (De Civitate Dei) I/6. Introduction and Translation by William Babcock, and notes by Boniface Ramsey (General Editor).* Hyde Park, NY: New City, 2012.

————. *The Works of Saint Augustine. A Translation for the 21st Century. The City of God (De Civitate Dei) I/7. Introduction and Translation by William Babcock, and notes by Boniface Ramsey (General Editor).* Hyde Park, NY: New City 2013.

Bagaric, Mirko, and Kumar Amarasekara. "Feeling Sorry?—Tell Someone Who Cares: The Irrelevance of Remorse in Sentencing." *The Howard Journal of Crime and Justice* 40(4) (2001) 364–76.

Bagnoli, Carla, ed. *Morality and the Emotions.* Oxford: Oxford University Press, 2011.

————. "Value in the Guise of Regret." *Philosophical Explorations* 3(2) (2000) 169–87.

Baird, Abigail A. "Adolescent Moral Reasoning: The Integration of Emotion and Cognition." In *Moral Psychology. Volume 3. The Neuroscience of Morality: Emotion, Brain Disorders, and Development,* edited by Walter Sinnott-Armstrong, 323–41 Cambridge: MIT Press, 2008.

Baker, Brenda M. "Penance as Model for Punishment." *Social Theory and Practice* 18(3) (1992) 311–32.

Bandes, Susan A. "Remorse and Criminal Justice." *Emotion Review* 8(1) (2016) 14–19.

————. "Remorse, Demeanor, and the Consequences of Misinterpretation. The Limits of Law as a Window into the Soul." *Journal of Religion, Law and State* 3(2) (2014) 170–99.

Barnum-Roberts, Brooke Natalie. "Apologizing without Regret." *Ratio: An International Journal of Analytic Philosophy* 24(1) (2011) 17–27.

Barr, James. *Fundamentalism*. London: SCM, 1977.

———. *The Semantics of Biblical Language*. London: SCM, 1961.

Barrett, Charles Kingsley. *The Second Epistle to the Corinthians*. Black's New Testament Commentaries. London: A & C Black, 1973.

Barton, John. "The Basis of Ethics in the Hebrew Bible." *Semeia: An Experimental Journal for Biblical Criticism* 66(4) (1994) 11–22.

———. *Ethics in Ancient Israel*. Oxford: Oxford University Press, 2014.

———. "Understanding Old Testament Ethics." *Journal for the Study of the Old Testament* 9 (1978) 44–64.

———. *Understanding Old Testament Ethics*. Louisville, KY: Westminster John Knox, 2003.

Barrett, Lisa Feldman. *How Emotions Are Made. The Secret Life of the Brain*. London: Macmillan, 2017.

Bash, Anthony. *Ambassadors for Christ: An Exploration of Ambassadorial Communication in the New Testament*. WUNT 2.92. Tübingen: Mohr-Siebeck, 1997.

———. *Forgiveness: A Theology*. Eugene, OR: Cascade, 2015.

———. *Forgiveness and Christian Ethics*. Cambridge: Cambridge University Press, 2007.

———. *Just Forgiveness, Exploring the Bible, Weighing the Issues*. London: SPCK, 2011.

Bassett, Rodney L., et al., "Feeling Bad: Different Colors of Remorse." *Journal of Psychology and Christianity* 30(1) (2011) 51–69.

Bassham, Gregory, ed. *The Ultimate Harry Potter and Philosophy: Hogwarts for Muggles*. Hoboken, NJ: Wiley, 2010.

Batson, Daniel C. "Getting Cynical about Character: A Social-Psychological Perspective." In *Moral Psychology. Volume 5. Virtue and Character*, edited by Walter Sinnott-Armstrong and Christian B. Miller, 11–44. Cambridge: MIT Press, 2017.

Battistella, Edwin L. *Sorry About That. The Language of Public Apology*. Oxford: Oxford University Press, 2014.

Battle, Michael Jesse. *Reconciliation: The Ubuntu Theology of Desmond Tutu*. Cleveland, OH: Pilgrim, 1997.

Baumeister, Roy F. "Constructing a Scientific Theory of Free Will." In *Moral Psychology. Volume 4. Free Will and Moral Responsibility*, edited by Walter Sinnott-Armstrong, 235–55. Cambridge: MIT Press, 2014.

Baumeister, Roy F., et al. "Guilt: An Interpersonal Approach." *Psychological Bulletin* 115 (1994) 243–67.

———. "Interpersonal Aspects of Guilt: Evidence from Narrative Studies." In *Self-Conscious Emotions: The Psychology of Shame, Guilt, Embarrassment, and Pride*, edited by June Price Tangney and Kurt W. Fischer, 255–73. New York: Guilford, 1995.

Bebbington, David, and David Ceri Jones. *Evangelicalism and Fundamentalism in the United Kingdom in the Twentieth Century*. Oxford: Oxford University Press, 2013.

Bebbington, David W. *Holiness in Nineteenth Century England*. Carlisle, UK: Paternoster, 2000.

———. *The Nonconformist Conscience. Chapel and Politics 1870–1914*. London: Allen & Unwin, 1982.

————. *Victorian Nonconformity.* Bangor: Headstart History, 1992.

Bedford, Errol. "Emotions and Statements about Them." *Proceedings of the Aristotelian Society* 57 (1956–57) 281–304.

Ben-Ze'ev, Aaron. "Emotions and Morality." *Journal of Value Enquiry* 31(2) (1997) 195–212.

Benn, Piers. "Forgiveness and Loyalty." *Philosophy* 71 (1996) 369–83.

Bennett, Christopher. *The Apology Ritual: A Philosophical Theory of Punishment.* Cambridge: Cambridge University Press, 2008.

Bennett, Jonathan. "The Conscience of Huckleberry Finn." *Philosophy* 49 (1974) 123–34.

Benson, George. "Death and Dying: A Psychoanalytic Perspective." *The Journal of Pastoral Care* 26(2) (1972) 77–85.

Berkouwer, G. C. *Sin.* Translated from the Dutch by Philip C. Holtrop. Grand Rapids: Eerdmans, 1971.

Berlejung, Angelika. "Sin and Punishment: The Ethics of Divine Justice and Retribution in Ancient Near East and Old Testament Texts." *Interpretation: A Journal of Bible and Theology* 69(3) (2015) 272–87.

Betzler, Monika. "Sources of Practical Conflicts and Reasons for Regret." In *Practical Conflicts: New Philosophical Essays,* edited by Peter Baumann and Monika Betzler, 197–222. Cambridge: Cambridge University Press, 2004.

————. Review of R. Jay Wallace, *The View From Here: On Affirmation, Attachment, and the Limits of Regret. Ethics* 125(2) (2015) 614–21.

Biggar, Nigel. "Evolutionary Biology, 'Enlightened' Anthropological Narratives, and Social Morality: A View from Christian Ethics." *Studies in Christian Ethics* 26(2) (2013) 152–57.

Birch, Bruce C. "Divine Character and the Formation of Moral Community in the Book of Exodus." In *The Bible in Ethics. The Second Sheffield Colloquium,* edited by John W. Rogerson, Margaret Davies, and Mark Daniel Carroll R., 118–35. Sheffield, UK: Sheffield Academic, 1995.

————. *Let Justice Roll Down: The Old Testament, Ethics, and Christian Life.* Louisville, KY: Westminster/John Knox, 1991.

Bittner, Rüdiger. "Is It Reasonable to Regret Things One Did?" *Journal of Philosophy* 89(5) (1992) 262–73.

Blank, Ksana. *Dostoevsky's Dialectics and the Problem of Sin.* Evanston, IL: Northwestern University Press, 2010.

Blume, Lawrence E., and Steven N. Durlauf. *The Economy as an Evolving Complex System III—Current Perspectives and Future Directions.* Oxford: Oxford University Press, 2006.

Bockmuehl, Markus. *Simon Peter in Scripture and Memory: The New Testament Apostle in the Early Church.* Grand Rapids: Baker Academic, 2012.

Boone, Mark J. "Love and Emotional Fit: What Does Christian Theology Tell Us about Unfitting Emotions?" *Heythrop Journal* 49 (2018) 1–10.

Bovens, Luc. "Apologies." *Proceedings of the Aristotelian Society* 108.1.3 (2008) 219–39.

Braithwaite, John. "Survey Article: Repentance Rituals and Restorative Justice." *The Journal of Political Philosophy* 8(1) (2000) 115–31.

Brooks, John H., and John R. Reddon. "The Two Dimensional Nature of Remorse." *Journal of Offender Rehabilitation* 38(2) (2003) 1–15.

Brooks, Thom. *Punishment.* Abingdon, UK: Routledge, 2012.

Brothers, Barbara Jo. "Remorse and Regeneration." *The Psychotherapy Patient* 5(1 and 2) (1988) 47–62.

Brown, Raymond E. *The Death of the Messiah: From Gethsemane to the Grave. A Commentary on the Passion Narratives in the Four Gospels.* 2 volumes. New Haven, CT: Yale University Press, 1994.

Brueggemann, Walter. *Genesis.* Interpretation: A Bible Commentary for Teaching and Preaching. Atlanta: John Knox, 1982.

Buber, Martin. "Guilt and Guilt Feelings." In *Conscience: Theological and Psychological Perspectives*, edited by C. Ellis Nelson, 224–37. New York: Newman, 1973.

Burton, Neel. *Heaven and Hell: The Psychology of the Emotions.* Exeter, UK: Acheron, 2015.

Buss, David M. *The Handbook of Evolutionary Psychology.* 2 Volumes. 2nd ed. Hoboken, NJ: Wiley, 2016.

Butler, Joseph. *Fifteen Sermons Preached at the Rolls Chapel. To Which are Added Six Sermons Preached on Public Occasions. By Joseph Butler, LL D, late Lord Bishop of Bristol.* New edition, corrected. London: C. and R. Ware, T. Longman, and J. Johnson, 1774.

Byrd, Sharon. "Kant's Theory of Punishment: Deterrence in Its Threat, Retribution in Its Execution." *Law and Philosophy* 8(2) (1989) 151–200.

Cahill, Lisa Sowle. *Global Justice, Christology, and Christian Ethics.* Cambridge: Cambridge University Press, 2013.

Cairns, Douglas, L. "Representations of Remorse and Reparation in Classical Greece." In *Remorse and Reparation*, edited by Murray Cox, 171–78. London: Jessica Kingsley, 1999.

Cairns, Douglas L., and Laurel Fulkerson, eds. *Emotions between Greece and Rome.* London Institute of Classical Studies, School of Advanced Study, University of London, 2015.

Calhoun, Laurie. "At What Price Repentance? Reflections on Kubrick's 'A Clockwork Orange.'" *Journal of Thought* 36(1) (2001) 17–34.

Cameron, William Bruce. *Informal Sociology: A Causal Introduction to Sociological Thinking.* New York: Random House, 1963.

Campbell, Tom. *Seven Theories of Human Society.* Oxford: Clarendon, 1981.

Campos, Joseph J., et al. "A Functionalist Perspective on the Nature of Emotion." In *The Development of Emotion Regulation: Biological and Behavioral Considerations*, edited by Nathan A. Fox, 284–303. Monographs of the Society for Research in Child Development 59(2/3). Chicago: University of Chicago Press, 1994.

Camras, Linda. "A Review of *Emotion: A Psychoevolutionary Synthesis* by Robert Plutchik." In *The American Journal of Psychology* 9(4) (1980) 751–53.

Cane, Anthony. *The Place of Judas Iscariot in Christology.* Aldershot, UK: Ashgate, 2005.

Cannon, Walter Bradford. *Bodily Changes in Pain, Hunger, Fear, and Rage. An Account of Recent Researches into the Function of Emotional Excitement.* New York: Appleton, 1915.

Caplovitz Barrett, Karen. "A Functionalist Approach to Shame and Guilt." In *Self-Conscious Emotions: The Psychology of Shame, Guilt, Embarrassment, and Pride*, edited by June Price Tangney and Kurt W. Fischer, 25–63. New York: Guilford, 1995.

Carlsmith, J. Merrill, and Alan E. Gross. "Some Effects of Guilt on Compliance." *Journal of Personality and Social Psychology* 11(3) (1969) 232–39.

Carroll, John. *The Wreck of Western Culture: Humanism Revisited.* Melbourne, Australia: Scribe, 2004.

Cassidy, Richard J. *Four Times Peter: Portrayals of Peter in the Four Gospels and at Philippi.* Collegeville, MI: Glazier, 2007.

Cates, Diana Fritz. "Conceiving Emotions: Martha Nussbaum's 'Upheavals of Thought.'" *Journal of Religious Ethics* 31(2) (2003) 325–41.

Cave, Sydney. *Redemption: Hindu and Christian.* London: Humphrey Milford, Oxford University Press, 1919.

Cerney, Mary S. "'If Only'. Remorse in Grief Therapy." *The Psychotherapy Patient* 5(1 and 2) (1988) 235–48.

Chaniotis, Angelos, and Ducrey, Pierre, eds. *Unveiling Emotions II. Emotions in Greece and Rome: Texts, Images, and Material Culture.* Stuttgart: Franz Steiner Verlag, 2013.

Chaniotis, Angelos. "Approaching Emotions in Greek and Roman History and Culture. An Introduction." In *Unveiling Emotions II. Emotions in Greece and Rome: Texts, Images, and Material* Culture, edited by Angelos Chaniotis and Pierre Ducrey, 9–14. Stuttgart: Franz Steiner Verlag, 2013.

———. "Constructing the Fear of Gods: Epigraphic Evidence from Sanctuaries of Greece and Asia Minor." In *Unveiling Emotions. Sources and Methods for the Study of Emotions in the Greek* World, edited by Angelos Chaniotis, 205–34. Stuttgart: Franz Steiner, 2012.

———. "Moving Stones: The Study of Emotions I. Greek Inscriptions." In *Unveiling Emotions. Sources and Methods for the Study of Emotions in the Greek World,* edited by Angelos Chaniotis, 91–129. Stuttgart: Franz Steiner, 2012.

———. "The Social Construction of Emotion: The View from Ancient Greece." *Current Opinion in Social Sciences* 24 (2018) 56–61.

———. "Unveiling Emotions in the Greek World: Introduction." In *Unveiling Emotions: Sources and Methods for the Study of Emotions in the Greek* World, edited by Angelos Chaniotis, 11–36. Stuttgart: Franz Steiner, 2012.

Chapman, Alister. "Evangelical or Fundamentalist? The Case of John Stott." In *Evangelicalism and Fundamentalism in the United Kingdom in the Twentieth Century,* edited by David Bebbington and David Ceri Jones, 193–208. Oxford: Oxford University Press, 2013.

Chase, F. H. "Note on ΠΡΗΝΗΣ ΓΕΝΟΜΕΝΟΣ in Acts 1.18." *Journal of Theological Studies* OS 13(50) (1911) 78–85. (The author of the article was the Bishop of Ely and so the article appears under the name "F. H. Ely.")

Chaucer, Geoffrey. *The Canterbury Tales.* Edited with an introduction and notes by Jill Mann. London: Penguin, 2005.

———. *Troilus and Criseyde,* by A. C. Spearing. London: Arnold, 1976.

Cherry, Stephen. "Uses and Abuses of Self-Forgiveness." In *Forgiveness in Practice,* edited by Stephen Hance, 69–81. London: Jessica Kingsley, 2019.

Chomsky, Noam. "Review of B. F. Skinner's 'Verbal Behavior.'" *Language* 35(1) (1959) 26–38.

Christopher, Andrew N., et al. "The Protestant Work Ethic: Expectancy, Violations, and Criminal Sentencing." *Journal of Applied Social Psychology* 33(3) (2003) 522–35.

Clark, Jason A. "Relations of Homology between Higher Cognitive Emotions and Basic Emotions." *Biology and Philosophy* 25(1) (2010) 75–94.

Clark, Stephen R. L. *Biology and Christian Ethics*. Cambridge: Cambridge University Press, 2000.

Cleckley, Hervey. *The Mask of Sanity: An Attempt to Clarify Some Issues about the So-Called Psychopathic Personality.* 5th ed. St Louis, MO: Hare, 1976.

Coates, Justin D., and Neal A. Tognazzini, eds. *Blame: Its Nature and Norms*. Oxford: Oxford University Press, 2013.

Collins, Adela Yarbro. "Psychological Hermeneutics Now and Suggestions for Future Work: A Review of *Psychological Hermeneutics of Biblical Themes and Texts*." *Pastoral Psychology* 64(4) (2015) 493–97.

———. *The Religion of Protestants: The Church in English Society 1559–1625*. Oxford: Clarendon, 1982.

Cornelius, Randolph R. "Magda Arnold's Thomistic Theory of Emotion, the Self-Ideal, and the Moral Dimension of Appraisal." *Cognition and Emotion* 20(7) (2006) 976–1000.

Cose, Ellis. *Bone to Pick: Of Forgiveness, Reconciliation, Reparation, and Revenge*. New York: Washington Square, 2004.

Cosmides, Leda, and John Tooby. "Evolutionary Psychology and the Emotions." In *Handbook of Emotions*, edited by Michael Lewis and Jeannette M. Haviland-Jones, 91–115. 2nd ed. New York: Guilford, 2000.

Cover, Robin C. "Sin, Sinners." In *ABD* 6:31–40.

Cowley, Christopher. "Regret, Remorse and the Twilight Perspective." *International Journal of Philosophical Studies* 25(5) (2017) 624–34.

Cox, Murray, ed. *Remorse and Reparation*. London: Jessica Kingsley, 1999.

Cronin, Kieran. *Rights and Christian Ethics*. Cambridge: Cambridge University Press, 1992.

Cuneo, Terence, and Russ Shafer-Landau. "The Moral Fixed Points: New Directions for Moral Nonnaturalism." *Philosophical Studies* 171(3) (2014) 399–443.

D'Arms, Justin, and Daniel Jacobson. "The Moralistic Fallacy: On the 'Appropriateness' of Emotions." *Philosophy and Phenomenological Review* 61(1) (2000) 65–90.

Dahl, Elizabeth S. "Is Japan Facing up to Its Past? The Case of Japan and Its Neighbors." In *The Age of Apology: Facing up to the Past*, edited by Mark Gibney, Rhoda E. Howard-Hassman, Jean-Marc Coicand, and Niklaus Steiner, 241–55. Philadelphia: University of Pennsylvania Press, 2008.

Damasio, Antonio. *Descartes's Error: Emotion, Reason, and the Human Brain*. New York: Putnam, 1994.

Damon, William, and Anne Colby. *The Power of Ideals: The Real Story of Moral Choice*. Oxford: Oxford University Press, 2015.

Damrau, Peter. "Tears That Make the Heart Shine? 'Godly Sadness' in Pietism." In *Sadness and Melancholy in German-Language Literature and Culture,* edited by Mary Cosgrove and Anna Richards, 19–34. Volume 6 of *Edinburgh German Yearbook*. Rochester, NY: Camden House, 2012.

Darwin, Charles. *The Descent of Man, and Selection in Relation to Sex*. With an Introduction by James Moore and Adrian Desmond. London: Penguin, 2004.

———. *The Expression of the Emotions in Man and Animals*. With an Introduction, Afterword and Commentaries by Paul Ekman. 3rd ed. London: Harper Collins, 1998.

———. *On The Origin of Species by Means of Natural Selection, or The Preservation of Favoured Races in the Struggle for Life*. London: John Murray, 1859.

Davies, Eryl W. "Ethics of the Hebrew Bible: The Problem of Methodology." *Semeia: An Experimental Journal for Biblical Criticism* 66(4) (1994) 43–52.

———. "Walking in God's Ways: The Concept of *Imitatio Dei* in the Old Testament." In *In Search of True Wisdom: Essays in Old Testament Interpretation in Honour of Ronald E. Clements*, edited by Edward Ball, 99–115. Journal for the Study of the Old Testament Supplement Series 300. Sheffield, UK: Sheffield Academic, 1999.

Davies, Philip R. "Ethics and the Old Testament." In *The Bible in Ethics: The Second Sheffield Colloquium*, edited by John W. Rogerson, Margaret Davies, and M. Daniel Carroll R., 164–73. Sheffield, UK: Sheffield Academic, 1995.

Davis, Paul. "On Apologies." *Journal of Applied Philosophy* 19(2) (2002) 169–73.

Davison, Andrew. *Participation in God: A Study on Christian Doctrine and Metaphysics.* Cambridge: Cambridge University Press, 2019.

Davison, Ian Michael. "Regret as Autobiographical Memory." PhD diss., University of Durham, 2010.

De Waal, Frans. *Good-Natured: The Origins and Right and Wrong in Humans and Other Animals.* Cambridge: Harvard University Press, 1996.

———. *Primates and Philosophers: How Morality Evolved.* Edited and introduced by Josiah Ober and Stephen Macedo. Princeton, NJ: Princeton University Press, 2006.

Deberri, Edward P., and James E. Hug. *Catholic Social Teaching: Our Best Kept Secret.* 4th rev. and exp. ed. New York: Orbis, 2003.

Decety, Jean, and Thalia Wheatley, eds. *The Moral Brain: A Multidisciplinary Approach.* Cambridge: MIT Press., 2015.

Deigh, John, ed. *On Emotions: Philosophical Essays.* Oxford: Oxford University Press, 2013.

Deigh, John. "Cognitivism in the Theory of Emotions." *Ethics* 104(4) (1994) 824–54.

———. "Concepts of Emotions in Modern Philosophy and Psychology." In *The Oxford Handbook of Philosophy of Emotion*, edited by Peter Goldie, 17–40. Oxford: Oxford University Press, 2010.

———. "Reactive Attitudes Revisited." In *Morality and the Emotions*, edited by Carla Bagnoli, 197–216. Oxford: Oxford University Press, 2011.

———. *The Sources of Moral Agency.* Cambridge: Cambridge University Press, 1996.

Delasanta, Rodney. "Penance and Poetry in the Canterbury Tales." *Publications of the Modern Language Association of America* 93(2) (1978) 240–47.

Descartes, René. *Meditations on First Philosophy: With Selections from the Objections and Replies.* 1641. Cambridge: Cambridge University Press, 2017.

———. "Passions of the Soul." In *The Philosophical Writings of Descartes.* Translated by John Cottingham, Robert Stoothoff, and Dugald Murdoch. Cambridge: Cambridge University Press, 1984.

Dewey, John. "The Theory of Emotion." *Psychological Review* 2(1) (1985) 13–32.

Dhareshwar, Vivek. "Valorizing the Present: Orientalism, Postcoloniality and the Human Sciences." *Cultural Dynamics* 10(2) (1998) 211–31.

Dickens, Charles. *Oliver Twist.* Edited by Kathleen Tillotson. With an introduction and notes by Stephen Gill. Oxford: Oxford University Press, 2008.

Diogenes Laertius. *Lives of Eminent Philosophers.* Translated by R. D. Hicks. Volume II, Books 6–10. LCL 185. London: Heinemann, 1925.

Dostoyevsky, Fyodor. *Crime and Punishment.* Translated by David Magarshack. Harmondsworth, UK: Penguin, 1952.

Dow, Jamie. *Passions and Persuasion in Aristotle's* Rhetoric. Oxford: Oxford University Press, 2015.

———. "A Supposed Contradiction about Emotion-Based Arousal in Aristotle's *Rhetoric.*" *Phronesis* 52(4) (2007) 382–402.

Dryden, John. "Passions, Affections, and Emotions: Methodological Difficulties in Reconstructing Aquinas' Philosophical Psychology." *Literature Compass* 13(6) (2016) 343–50.

DSM-5. American Psychiatric Association: *Diagnostic and Statistical Manual of Mental Disorders, Fifth Edition.* Arlington, VA.: American Psychiatric Association, 2013.

Dublin, James E. "Remorse as Mental Dyspepsia." *The Psychotherapy Patient* 5(1 and 2) (1998) 161–74.

Duff, R. A. "The Intrusion of Mercy." *Ohio State Journal of Criminal Law* 4(2) (2007) 361–87.

———. *Trials and Punishments.* Cambridge: Cambridge University Press, 1986.

Duffy, Korrina A., and Tanya L. Chartrand. "From Mimicry to Morality: The Role of Prosociality." In *Moral Psychology. Volume 5. Virtue and Character,* edited by Walter Sinnott-Armstrong and Christian B. Miller, 439–64. Cambridge: MIT Press, 2017.

Dunbar, Robin I. M., and Louise Barrett. *The Oxford Handbook of Evolutionary Psychology.* Oxford: Oxford University Press, 2007.

Ehrman, Bart D. *The Apostolic Fathers.* Edited and translated by Bart D. Ehrman. 2 vols. LCL 24 and 25. Cambridge: Harvard University Press, 2003.

———. *The Lost Gospel of Judas Iscariot: A New Look at Betrayer and Betrayed.* Oxford: Oxford University Press, 2006.

Eidelman, Nechama Levy. "Sorry, I Apologize." *The Psychotherapy Patient* 5(1 and 2) (1988) 175–89.

Eisenberg, Nancy. "Empathy and Sympathy." In *Handbook of Emotions,* edited by Michael Lewis and Jeannette M. Haviland-Jones, 677–91. 2nd ed. New York: Guilford, 2000.

Ekman, Paul, and Daniel Cordaro. "What Is Meant by Calling Emotions Basic?" *Emotion Review* 3(4) (2011) 364–70.

Ekman, Paul. "An Argument for Basic Emotions." In *Cognition and Emotion* 6.3–4 (1992) 169–200.

———. "Basic Emotions." In *Handbook of Cognition and Emotion,* edited by Tim Dalgleish and Mick J. Power, 45–60. Chichester, UK: Wiley, 1999.

———. "Biological and Cultural Contributions to Body and Facial Movement." In *The Anthropology of the Body,* edited by John Blacking, 39–84. London: Academic, 1977.

Elliott, Mark W. "The Bible in Protestantism from 1750–2000." In *The Bible From 1750 to the Present,* edited by John Riches, 563–86. Cambridge: Cambridge University Press, 2015.

Elpidorou, Andreas, and Lauren Freeman. "The Phenomenology and Science of Emotions: An Introduction." *Phenomenology and the Cognitive Sciences* 13(4) (2014) 507–11.

Elshtain, Jean Bethke. "Politics and Forgiveness: The Clinton Case." In *Judgment Day at the Whitehouse: A Critical Declaration Exploring Moral Issues and the Political Use and Abuse of Religion,* edited by Gabriele Fackre, 11–17. Grand Rapids: Eerdmans, 2011.

Enoch, David. "Being Responsible, Taking Responsibility, and Penumbral Agency." In *Luck, Value, and Commitment: Themes from the Ethics of Bernard* Williams, edited by Ulrike Heuer and Gerald Lang, 95–132. Oxford: Oxford University Press, 2012.

Epictetus. *Epictetus: Discourses: Book I. Translation with an Introduction and Commentary by Robin F. Dobbin.* Oxford: Clarendon, 1998.

Etzioni, Amitai, and David E. Carney, eds. *Repentance: A Comparative Perspective.* Lanham, NY, Boulder: Rowman and Littlefield, 1997.

Evans, Christopher F. *Saint Luke.* 2nd ed. London, SCM, 2008.

Evans, Dylan. *Emotion: A Very Short Introduction.* Oxford: Oxford University Press, 2001.

Feinberg, Joel. "The Expressive Function of Punishment." *The Monist* 49(3) (1965) 397–423.

Fergusson, David. *Community, Liberalism and Christian Ethics.* Cambridge: Cambridge University Press, 1998.

Fernández-Dols, José-Miguel, *et al.*, eds. *The Science of Facial Expression.* New York: Oxford University Press, 2017.

Fine, Adam, et al. "Can Probation Offenders Identify Remorse among Male Adolescent Offenders?" *American Psychological Association* 19(2) (2016) 754–62.

Fingarette, Herbert. "Punishment and Suffering." *Proceedings and Address of the American Philosophical Association* 50(6) (1977) 499–525.

Fischer, Kurt W., and June Price Tangney. "Self-Conscious Emotions and Affect Revolution: Framework and Overview." In *Self-Conscious Emotions: The Psychology of Shame, Guilt, Embarrassment, and Pride*, edited by June Price Tangney and Kurt W. Fischer, 3–22. New York: Guilford, 1995.

Fitzgerald, John T., ed. *Passions and Moral Progress in Greco-Roman Thought.* London: Routledge, 2008.

Fitzgerald, John T. "The Passions and Moral Progress: An Introduction." In *Passions and Moral Progress in Greco-Roman Thought* edited by John T. Fitzgerald, 1–25. London: Routledge, 2008.

Fortenbaugh, William Wall. *Aristotle on Emotion. A Contribution to Philosophical Psychology, Rhetoric, Poetics and Ethics.* London: Duckworth, 1975.

Foster, Benjamin R., ed. *Before the Muses: An Anthology of Akkadian Literature.* 3rd ed. Bethesda, MD: CDL, 2005.

Fredriksen, Paula. *Sin: The Early History of an Idea.* Princeton, NJ: Princeton University Press, 2012.

French, Peter A. "Self-Blaming, Repentance, and Atonement." *Journal of Value Inquiry* 48(4) (2014) 587–602.

Freud, Anna. *The Ego and the Mechanisms of Defence.* Rev. ed. London: Karnac, 1993.

Freud, Sigmund. *Civilisation and Its Discontents.* In *The Standard Edition of the Complete Psychological Works of Sigmund Freud*, edited and translated by J. Strachey, 59–148. Volume XXI. London: Hogarth Press and The Institute of Psycho-Analysis, 1961.

———. "Five Lectures on Psycho-Analysis." In *The Standard Edition of the Complete Psychological Works of Sigmund Freud*, edited and translated by J. Strachey, 3–182. Volume XI. London: Hogarth Press and The Institute of Psycho-Analysis, 1990.

———. "New Introductory Lectures on Psycho-Analysis." In *The Standard Edition of the Complete Psychological Works of Sigmund Freud*, edited and translated by J. Strachey, 3–182. Volume XXII. London: Hogarth Press and The Institute of Psycho-Analysis, 1964.

———. "Obsessive Actions and Religious Practices." In *The Standard Edition of the Complete Psychological Works of Sigmund Freud*, edited and translated by J. Strachey, 115–28. Volume IX. London: Hogarth Press and The Institute of Psycho-Analysis, 1959.

———. "On Narcissism.: An Introduction." In *The Standard Edition of the Complete Psychological Works of Sigmund Freud*, edited and translated by J. Strachey, 67–104. Volume XIV. London: Hogarth Press and The Institute of Psycho-Analysis, 1957.

Frevert, Ute. "The History of Emotions." In *Handbook of Emotions*, edited by Lisa Feldman Barrett, Michael Lewis, and Jeanette M. Haviland-Jones, 49–65. 4th ed. London: Guilford, 2016.

Fridlund, Alan J. *Human Facial Expression: An Evolutionary View*. New York: Academic, 2014.

Friedman, Bruce H. "Feelings and the Body: The Jamesian Perspective on Automatic Specificity of Emotion." *Biological Psychology* 84(3) (2010) 383–93.

Frijda, Nico H. "Emotion Regulation and Free Will." In *Decomposing the Will*, edited by Andy Clark et al., 199–220. Oxford: Oxford University Press, 2013.

———. *The Emotions*. Cambridge: Cambridge University Press, 1986.

———. "The Evolutionary Emergence of What We Call 'Emotions.'" *Cognition and Emotion* 30(4) (2016) 609–20.

———. "The Laws of Emotion." *American Psychologist* 43 (1988) 349–58.

———. "The Place of Appraisal in Emotion." *Cognition and Emotion* 7(3–4) (1993) 357–87.

———. "The Psychologists' Point of View." In *Handbook of Emotions*, edited by Michael Lewis and Jeannette M. Haviland-Jones, 59–74. 2nd ed. New York: Guildford, 2000.

Frijda, Nico H., and W. G. Parrott. "Basic-Emotions or Ur-Emotions." *Emotion Review* 3 (2011) 406–15.

Fritz Cates, Diana. *Aquinas on the Emotions: A Religious-Ethical Enquiry*. Washington, DC: Georgetown University Press, 2009.

Fulkerson, Laurel. "Helen as Vixen, Helen as Victim: Remorse and the Opacity of Female Desire." In *Gender and Emotion in Classical Antiquity*, edited by Dana LaCourse Munteanu, 113–33. London, Bloomsbury: 2011.

———. "*Metameleia* and Friends. Remorse and Repentance in Fifth- and Fourth-Century Athenian Oratory." *Phoenix* 58(3/4) (2004) 241–59.

———. *No Regrets. Remorse in Classical Antiquity*. Oxford: Oxford University Press, 2013.

Gaita, Raimond. *A Common Humanity: Thinking about Love and Truth and Justice*. 2nd ed. Abingdon, UK: Routledge, 2000.

———. "Ethical Individuality." In *Value and Understanding: Essays for Peter Winch*, edited by Raimond Gaita, 118–48. London: Routledge, 1990.

———. *Good and Evil: An Absolute Conception*. 2nd ed. London: Routledge, 2004.

Garrison, Elise P. "Attitudes towards Suicide in Ancient Greece." *Transactions of the American Philological Association* 121 (1991) 1–34.

Gascoigne, Robert. *The Public Forum and Christian Ethics*. Cambridge: Cambridge University Press, 1995.

Gazzaniga, Michael S. "Mental Life and Responsibility in Real Time with a Determined Brain." In *Moral Psychology. Volume 4. Free Will and Moral Responsibility*, edited by Walter Sinnott-Armstrong, 59–74. Cambridge: MIT Press, 2014.

Gendron, Maria, et al. "Perceptions of Emotion from Facial Expressions Are Not Culturally Universal: Evidence from a Remote Culture." *Emotion* 14(2) (2014) 251–62.

Gibney, Mark, et al., eds. *The Age of Apology: Facing up to the Past*. Philadelphia: University of Pennsylvania Press, 2008.

Giddens, Anthony. *Modernity and Self-Identity: Self and Society in the Late Modern Age*. Stanford, CA: Stanford University Press, 1991.

Gilbert, Paul. "Vain Regrets." *International Journal of Philosophical Studies* 25(5) (2017) 635–45.

Gill, Robin. *Moral Passion and Christian Ethics*. Cambridge: Cambridge University Press, 2017.

Gilligan, James. "The Agenbite of Inwit, or, The Varieties of Moral Experience." In *Remorse and Reparation*, edited by Murray Cox, 33–47. London: Jessica Kingsley, 1999.

Gilovich, Thomas, and Victoria Husted Medvec. "The Experience of Regret: What, When and Why." *Psychological Review* 102(2) (1995) 379–95.

Ginzberg, Louis. *Legends of the Jews*. Translated from the German Manuscript by Henrietta Szold and Paul Radin. Volume 1. Philadelphia: Jewish Publication Society, 2003.

Gladd, Clarence E. "Paul and Philodemus: Adaptability in Epicurean and Early Christian Psychagogy." Supplements to *Novum Testamentum*, Volume 81. Leiden: Brill, 1995.

Glendon, Mary Ann. "Public Acts of Contrition in the Age of Spin Control." www.vatican.va/jubilee_2000/magazine/documents/ju_mag_01071997_p-26_en.html, c. 2000.

Glenn. Andrea L. "Personality Disorders and Character." In *Moral Psychology. Volume 5. Virtue and Character*, edited by Walter Sinnott-Armstrong and Christian B. Miller, 497–519. Cambridge: MIT Press, 2017.

Goldie, Peter. *The Emotions: A Philosophical Exploration*. Oxford: Clarendon, 2000.

Goodwin, Geoffrey P. "Prosociality Is Not Morality." In *Moral Psychology. Volume 5. Virtue and Character*, edited by Walter Sinnott-Armstrong and Christian B. Miller, 465–75. Cambridge: MIT Press, 2017.

Gorgias of Leontini. *Encomium of Helen*. Edited with introduction, notes, and translation by D. M. MacDowell. Bristol, UK: Bristol Classical, 1982.

Graham, Gordon. *Evil and Christian Ethics*. Cambridge: Cambridge University Press, 2001

Graham, Jesse, et al. "Moral Foundations Theory: The Pragmatic Validity of Moral Pluralism." *Advances in Experimental Social Psychology* 47 (2013) 55–130.

Graham, Jesse, et al. "Mapping the Moral Domain." *Journal of Personality and Social Psychology* 101(2) (2011) 366–85.

Grant, Harris, and Marnie Rice. "Treatment of Psychopathy: A Review of Empirical Findings." In *Handbook of Psychopathy*, edited by Christopher J. Patrick, 555–72. 1st ed. New York: Guilford, 2006.

Graver, Margaret R. *Stoicism and Emotion*. Chicago: University of Chicago Press, 2007.

Greenberg, George, and Mary FitzPatrick. "Regret as an Essential Ingredient in Psychotherapy." *The Psychotherapy Patient* 5(1 and 2) (1988) 35–46.

Greene, Joshua. *Moral Tribes: Emotion, Reason, and the Gap between Us and Them.* New York: Penguin, 2013.

Greenspan, Patricia S. "Learning Emotions and Ethics." In *The Oxford Handbook of Philosophy of Emotion*, edited by Peter Goldie, 539–59. Oxford: Oxford University Press, 2010.

———. *Practical Guilt: Moral Dilemmas, Emotions, and Social Norms.* New York: Oxford University Press, 1995.

Greenstein, Edward L. "Wisdom in Ugaritic." In *Language and Nature. Papers Presented to John Huehnergard on the Occasion of his Sixtieth* Birthday, edited by Rebecca Hasselbach and Naʿama Pat-El, 69–89. Chicago: University of Chicago Press, 2012.

Gregory of Nyssa. *The Soul and the Resurrection.* Translated from the Greek by Catharine P. Roth. Crestwood, NY: St Vladimir's Seminary, 1993.

Griffiths, Paul E. "Modularity and the Psychoevolutionary Theory of Emotion." In *Philosophy and the Emotions: A Reader*, edited by Stephen Leighton, 256–75. Peterborough, Canada: Broadview, 2003.

———. *What Emotions Really Are: The Problem of Psychological Categories.* Chicago: Chicago University Press, 1997.

Griffiths, Paul E., and Andrea Scarantino. "Emotions in the Wild: The Situated Perspective on Emotion." In *Cambridge Handbook of Situated Cognition*, edited by Philip Robbins and Murat Aydede, 437–53. Cambridge: Cambridge University Press, 2008.

Grinker, Roy Richard. *Korea and Its Futures: Unification and the Unfinished War.* New York: St Martin's, 1998.

Grisez, Germain, and Russell Shaw. "Conscience: Knowledge and Moral Truth." In *Conscience*, edited by Charles E. Curran, 39–50. Mahwah, NJ: Paulist, 2004.

Griswold, Charles L. *Forgiveness: A Philosophical Exploration.* Cambridge: Cambridge University Press, 2007.

Gula, Richard M. "The Moral Conscience." In *Conscience*, edited by Charles E. Curran, 51–62. Mahwah, NJ: Paulist, 2004.

Gundry, Robert H. *Peter: False Disciple and Apostate according to Saint Matthew.* Grand Rapids: Eerdmans, 2015.

Gusdorf, Georges. *Mémoire et Personne.* Volume 2. Paris: Presses Universitaires de France, 1951.

Gutiérrez, Gustavo. *The Power of the Poor in History.* Translated by Robert R. Barr. London: SCM, 1983.

Haas, Peter J. "The Quest for Hebrew Bible Ethics: A Jewish Response." *Semeia: An Experimental Journal for Biblical Criticism* 66(4) (1994) 151–59.

Haidt, Jonathan, and Craig Joseph. "Intuitive Ethics: How Innately Prepared Intuitions Generate Culturally Variable Virtues." *Daedalus* 133(4) (2004) 55–66.

Haidt, Jonathan, and Fredrik Björklund. "Social Intuitionists Answer Six Questions about Moral Psychology." In *Moral Psychology. Volume 2. The Evolution of Morality: The Cognitive Science of Morality*, edited by Walter Sinnott-Armstrong, 181–217. Cambridge: MIT Press, 2008.

Haidt, Jonathan, and Selin Kesebir. "Morality." In *Handbook of Social Psychology,* Volume 1, edited by Susan T. Fiske et al., 797–832. 5th ed. Hoboken, NJ: Wiley, 2010.

Haidt, Jonathan. "The Emotional Dog and Its Rational Tail: A Social Intuitionist Approach to Moral Judgment." *Psychological Review* 108.4 (2001) 814–34.

———. *The Happiness Hypothesis.* New York: Basic, 2008.

———. "The Moral Emotions." In *Handbook of Affective Sciences,* edited by Richard J. Davidson et al., 852–70. Oxford: Oxford University Press, 2003.

———. "The New Synthesis in Moral Psychology." *Science* 316 (5827) (2007) 998–1002, 18 May 2007.

———. *The Righteous Mind: Why Good People Are Divided by Politics and Religion.* New York: Vintage, 2013.

Hallett, Garth L. *Priorities and Christian Ethics.* Cambridge: Cambridge University Press, 1998.

Halton, Charles, and Saana Svärd. *Women's Writing of Ancient Mesopotamia: An Anthology of Earliest Female Authors.* Cambridge: Cambridge University Press, 2017.

Hamann, Stephan. "Integrating Perspectives on Affective Neuroscience: Introduction to the Special Section on the Brain and Emotion." *Emotion Review* 10(3) (2018) 187–90.

Hamilton, Victor P. *The Book of Genesis. Chapters 18–50.* Grand Rapids: Eerdmans, 1995.

Hampton, Jean. "Correcting Harms Versus Righting Wrongs: The Goal of Retribution." *UCLA Law Review* 39 (1991–92) 1659–1702.

Hanna, Nathan. "The Passions of Punishment." *Pacific Philosophical Quarterly,* 90(2) (2009) 232–50.

Harcourt, Edward. "Aristotle, Plato, and the Anti-Psychiatrists: Comment on Irwin." In *The Oxford Handbook of Philosophy and Psychiatry,* edited by K. W. M. Fulford et al., 47–52. Oxford: Oxford University Press, 2013.

Hare, Robert D. *Psychopathy Checklist—Revised.* Toronto: Multi-Health System, 2003.

———. *Without Conscience: The Disturbing World of the Psychopaths among Us.* New York: Guilford, 1991.

Harkness, Sarah K., and Steven Hitlin. "Morality and Emotions." In *Handbook of the Sociology of Emotions: Volume II,* edited by Jan E. Stets and Jonathan H. Turner, 451–71. Dordrecht: Springer, 2014.

Harman, Gilbert. "Guilt-Free Morality." In *Oxford Studies in Metaethics,* Volume 4, edited by Russ Shafer-Landau, 203–14. Oxford: Oxford University Press, 2009.

Harré, Rom, ed. *The Social Construction of Emotions.* Oxford: Blackwell, 1986.

Harrington, Alan. *Psychopaths . . . .* London: IF Books, 1972.

Harris, Mary B., et al. "The Effects of Confession on Altruism." *The Journal of Social Psychology* 96(2) (1975) 187–92.

Hart, H. L. A. "Prolegomenon to the Principles of Punishment." *Proceedings of the Aristotelian Society* 60 (1959–60) 1–26.

Hauck, Paul A. "The Remorseful Patient." *The Psychotherapy Patient* 5(1 and 2) (1988) 13–18.

Hawk, L. Daniel. *Joshua.* Collegeville, MN: Glazier, 2000.

Heelas, Paul. "Emotion Talk across Cultures." In *The Emotions. Social, Cultural and Biological Dimensions*, edited by Rom Harré and W. Gerrod Parrott, 171–99. London: Sage, 1996.

Helmreich, Jeffrey S. "The Apologetic Stance." *Philosophy and Public Affairs* 43.2 (2015) 75–108.

Hengel, Martin. *Saint Peter: The Underestimated Apostle*. Translated by Thomas H. Trapp. Grand Rapids: Eerdmans, 2010.

Henson, Jamie. "Remorse and the Courts: A Defence of Remorse-Based Sentencing." PhD diss., the University of Manchester, 2018.

Herman, Barbara. *The Practice of Moral Judgment*. Cambridge: Harvard University Press, 1993.

Hicks, Douglas A. *Inequality and Christian Ethics*. Cambridge: Cambridge University Press, 2000.

Himes, Kenneth R., ed. *Modern Catholic Social Teaching: Commentaries and Interpretations*. Washington DC: Georgetown University Press 2005.

Hola, Barbora, et al. "Does Remorse Count? ICTY Convicts' Reflections on Their Crimes in Early Release Decisions." *International Criminal Justice Review* 28(4) (2018) 349–71.

Holmes, Janice. "Methodists and Holiness." In *The Oxford History of Protestant Dissenting Traditions: The Nineteenth* Century, edited by Timothy Larsen and Michael Ledger-Lomas, III, 124–49. Oxford: Oxford University Press, 2017.

Hooker, Morna D. *From Adam to Christ: Essays on Paul*. Cambridge: Cambridge University Press, 1990.

Horne, Andrew S. "Reflections on Remorse in Forensic Psychiatry." In *Remorse and Reparation*, edited by Murray Cox, 21–31. London: Jessica Kingsley, 1999.

Hume, David. "A Dissertation of the Passions." In *British Philosophy 1600–1990: Past Masters*. http: //pm.nlx.com/xtf/view?docId=britphil/britphil.44. xml;chunk.id=div.britphil.v40.1;toc.depth=2;toc.id=div.britphil.v40.1;hit. rank=0;brand=default, 1757.

———. *An Enquiry Concerning the Principles of Morals*. Edited by Tom L. Beauchamp. Oxford: Oxford University Press, 1998.

———. *A Treatise of Human Nature*. Edited with an analytical index by Lewis Amherst Selby-Bigge. Edited by Peter Harold Nidditch. 2nd ed., revised. Oxford: Clarendon, 1978.

ICD-10. *The ICD-10 Classification of Mental and Behavioral Disorders: Clinical Descriptions and Diagnostic Guidelines*. Geneva: World Health Organization, 1992.

Irwin, Terence. "Mental Health as Moral Virtue: Some Ancient Arguments." In *The Oxford Handbook of Philosophy and Psychiatry*, edited by K. W. M. Fulford et al. 37–46. Oxford: Oxford University Press, 2013.

Jacobson, Daniel. "Moral Dumfounding and Moral Stupefaction." In *Oxford Studies in Normative Ethics,* Volume 2, edited by Mark Timmons, 289–316. Oxford: Oxford University Press, 2012.

James, William. *The Principles of Psychology*. 2 vols. New York: Dover, 1950.

———. "What Is an Emotion?" In *The Heart of William James*, edited with an introduction by Robert D. Richardson, 2–19. Harvard, MA: Harvard University Press, 2010.

Jankélévitch, Vladimir. "La Mauvaise Conscience." In *Revue néo-scolastique de philosophie.* 37ᵉ année, Deuxième série, no. 44 (1934) 432–33.

———. *L'Imprescritible: Pardonner? Dans l'honneur et la dignité.* Paris: Seuil, 1986.

———. *Le Paradoxe de la Morale.* Paris: Éditions du Seuil, 1981.

Jasper, James M. "What the Devil are Emotions?" In *Qualitative Sociology* 25(1) (2002) 145–48.

Jeffrey, Renee. "When Is an Apology Not an Apology? Contrition Chic and Japan's (Un)Apologetic Politics." *Australian Journal of International Affairs* 65(5) (2011) 607–17.

Jensen, Lene Arnett. "The Cultural Development of Three Fundamental Moral Ethics: Autonomy, Community, and Divinity." *Zygon* 46(1) (2011) 150–67.

Jenson, Matt. *The Gravity of Sin: Augustine, Luther, and Barth on* homo incurvatus in se. London: T. & T. Clark, 2006.

Jeschke, Marlin. *Discipling in the Church: Recovering a Ministry of the Gospel.* Scottsdale, PA: Herald, 1988.

Jones, Owen D. "Laws, Emotions, and Behavioral Biology." *Jurimetrics* 39(3) (1999) 283–89.

Jones, Richard. "Anatomy of a Modern Apology: How Stars Say Sorry—and Why It Makes Us Angry." https: //www.telegraph.co.uk/men/thinking-man/anatomy-modern-apology-stars-say-sorry-makes-us-angry/, 2018.

Josephus, Flavius. *The Jewish War, Volume III: Books 5–7.* Translated by H. St. J. Thackeray. LCL 210. Cambridge: Harvard University Press, 1928.

Joyce, Richard. "What Neuroscience Can (and Cannot) Contribute to Metaethics." In *Moral Psychology. Volume 3. The Neuroscience of Morality: Emotion, Brain Disorders, and Development,* edited by Walter Sinnott-Armstrong, 371–94. Cambridge: MIT Press, 2008.

Jurasinski, Stefan. *The Old English Penitentials and Anglo-Saxon Law."* Cambridge: Cambridge University Press, 2015.

Kaiser Jr., Walter C. *Toward Old Testament Ethics.* Grand Rapids: Zondervan, 1983.

Kalbian, Aline H. "The Catholic Church's Public Confession: Theological and Ethical Implications." *Annual of the Society of Christian Ethics* 21 (2001) 175–89.

Kant, Immanuel. *Anthropology from a Pragmatic Point of View.* Translated and edited by Robert B. Louden. Cambridge: Cambridge University Press, 2006.

———. *Groundwork of the Metaphysics of Morals.* Translated by Mary J. Gregor. Cambridge: Cambridge University Press, 1998.

———. *The Philosophy of Law: An Exposition of the Fundamental Principles of Jurisprudence as the Science of Right.* Translated by W. Hastie. Edinburgh: T. & T. Clark, 1887.

———. *Practical Philosophy.* Edited by Mary J. Gregor, with an introduction by Allen W. Wood. Cambridge: Cambridge University Press, 1996.

Kaster, Robert A. *Emotion, Restraint, and Community in Ancient Rome.* Oxford: Oxford University Press, 2005.

Katz, Irwin, et al. "Ambivalence, Guilt, and the Scapegoating of Minority Group Victims." *Journal of Experimental Social Psychology* 9(5) (1973) 423–36.

Kazen, Thomas. *Emotions in Biblical Law: A Cognitive Science Approach.* Sheffield, UK: Sheffield Phoenix, 2011.

Kelley, Andrew. "Jankélévitch and Gusdorf on Forgiveness of Oneself." *Sophia* 52(1) (2013) 159–84.

Keltner, Dacher, et al. "Social Functionalism and the Evolution of Emotions." In *Evolution and Social Psychology*, edited by Mark Schaller, et al., 115–42. New York: Psychology, 2006.

Kennett, Jeanette, and Cordelia Fine. "Internalism and the Evidence from Psychopaths and 'Acquired Sociopaths.'" In *Moral Psychology. Volume 3. The Neuroscience of Morality: Emotion, Brain Disorders, and Development*, edited by Walter Sinnott-Armstrong, 173–90. Cambridge: MIT Press, 2008.

Kenny, Anthony. *Action, Emotion and Will*. London: Routledge and Kegan Paul, 1963.

Kent, John. "The Transition to Modernity." In *Companion Encyclopedia of Theology*, edited by Peter Byrne and Leslie Houlden, 251–71. London: Routledge, 1995.

Kierkegaard, Søren. *Purity of Heart Is to Will One Thing*. Radford, VA: Wilder, 2008.

———. *Upbuilding Discourses in Various Spirits*. Edited and translated with introduction and notes by Howard V. Hong and Edna H. Hong. Kierkegaard's Writings: XV. Princeton, NJ: Princeton University Press, 1993.

Kim, Andrew. *An Introduction to Catholic Ethics Since Vatican II*. Cambridge: Cambridge University Press, 2015.

King, Peter. "Aquinas on the Emotions." In *The Oxford Handbook of Aquinas*, edited by Brian Davis and Eleonore Stump, 209–26. Oxford: Oxford University Press, 2012.

———. "Emotions in Medieval Thought." In *The Oxford Handbook to Philosophy of Emotion*, edited by Peter Goldie, 167–88. Oxford: Oxford University Press, 2010.

Kirk, Kenneth E. *Conscience and Its Problems: An Introduction to Casuistry*. London: Longmans, Green, 1927.

Kleinke, Chris L., et al. "Evaluation of a Rapist as a Function of Expressed Intent and Remorse." *The Journal of Social Psychology* 132(4) (1992) 525–37.

Kloos, John. "Constructionism and Its Critics." In *The Oxford Handbook of Religion and Emotion*, edited by John Corrigan, 474–89. Oxford: Oxford University Press, 2008.

Kloppenborg, John S. "James 1:2–15 and Hellenistic Psychagogy." *Novum Testamentum* 52.1 (2010) 37–71.

Kolnai, Aurel. "Forgiveness." In *Utopian Mind and Other Papers: A Critical Study in Moral and Political Philosophy*, edited by Francis Dunlop, 211–24. London: Athlone, 1995.

Konstan, David. "Assuaging Rage: Remorse, Repentance, and Forgiveness in the Classical World." In *Ancient Forgiveness: Classical Judaic and Christian*, edited by Charles L. Griswold and David Konstan, 17–30. Cambridge: Cambridge University Press, 2012.

———. *Before Forgiveness: The Origins of a Moral Idea*. Cambridge: Cambridge University Press, 2010.

———. "Emotions and Morality: The View from Classical Antiquity." *Topoi* 34(2) (2015) 401–7.

———. *The Emotions of the Ancient Greeks: Studies in Aristotle and Classical Literature*. Toronto: University of Toronto Press, 2006.

Koppel, Stephen, and Mark R. Fondacaro. "The Retribution Heuristic." In *The Routledge Handbook of Criminal Justice Ethics*, edited by Jonathan Jacobs and Jonathan Jackson, 191–202. London: Routledge, 2017.

Krentz, Edgar M. "ΠΑΘΗ and ΑΠΑΘΕΙΑ in Early Roman Empire Stoics." In *Passions and Moral Progress in Greco-Roman Thought*, edited by John T. Fitzgerald, 122–35. London: Routledge, 2008.

Kugel, James L. "Testaments of the Twelve Patriarchs." In *Outside the Bible: Ancient Jewish Writings Related to Scripture*, edited by Louis H. Feldman, et al., 1697–1855. Philadelphia: Jewish Publication Society, 2013.

Kurzban, Robert, and Peter deScioli. "Morality." In *The Handbook of Evolutionary Psychology*, edited by David M. Dunbar, 770–87. 2 vols. 2nd ed. Hoboken, NJ: Wiley, 2016.

Lambert, David A. *How Repentance Became Biblical: Judaism, Christianity, and the Interpretation of Scripture*. Oxford: Oxford University Press, 2016.

———. "Mourning over Sin/Affliction and the Problem of 'Emotion' as a Category in the Hebrew Bible." In *Mixed Feelings and Vexed Passions: Exploring Emotions in Biblical Literature*, edited by F. Scott Spencer, 139–60. Atlanta: SBL, 2017.

Landman, Janet. *Regret: The Persistence of the Possible*. Oxford: Oxford University Press, 1993.

Larsen, Timothy, and Mark A. Noll. *The Oxford History of Protestant Dissenting Traditions: The Long Eighteenth Century, c.1689–c.1828*. Volume II. Edited by Andrew C. Thompson. Oxford: Oxford University Press, 2018.

Layton, Richard A. "*Propatheia*: Origen and Didymus on the Origin of the Passions." *Vigiliae Christianae* 54(3) (2000) 262–82.

Lazare, Aaron. *On Apology*. Oxford: Oxford University Press, 2004.

Lazarus, Richard S. "Appraisal: The Minimal Cognitive Prerequisites of Emotion." In *What Is an Emotion? Classic and Contemporary Readings*, edited by Robert C. Solomon, 125–30. Oxford: Oxford University Press, 2003.

———. "Cognition and Motivation in Emotion." *American Psychologist* 46 (1991) 362–67.

———. *Emotions and Adaptation*. Oxford: Oxford University Press, 1994.

———. *Psychological Stress and the Coping Process*. New York: McGraw-Hill, 1966.

Lee, Bernon P. "Unity in Diversity: The Literary Function of the Formula of Retaliation in Leviticus 24.15–22." *Journal for the Study of the Old Testament* 38.3 (2014) 297–313.

Letter, P. de. "Two Concepts of Attrition and Contrition." *Theological Studies* 11 (1950) 3–33.

Levenson, Alan T. *Joseph. Portraits through the Ages*. Philadelphia: Jewish Publication Society, 2016.

Lévinas, Emmanuel. *Otherwise than Being, or Beyond Essence*. Translated by Alphonso Lingis. Dordrecht: Kluwer Academic, 1991.

Levine, Michelle J. *Nahmanides on Genesis: The Art of Biblical Portraiture*. Atlanta: SBL, 2009.

Levine, Philip. *Augustine: City of God*. Translated by Philip Levine. Volume IV, Books 12–15. LCL 414. Cambridge: Harvard University Press, 2014.

Levy, Robert I. *Tahitians: Mind and Experience in the Society Islands*. Chicago: University of Chicago Press, 1973.

Lewis, C. S. *A Grief Observed*. Grand Rapids: Zondervan, 2001.

Lewis, Michael. "Self-Conscious Emotions: Embarrassment, Pride, Shame, Guilt, and Hubris." In *Handbook of Emotions*, edited by Lisa Feldman Barrett et al., 792–814. 4th ed. London: Guilford, 2016.

Libet, Benjamin. "Unconscious Cerebral Initiative and the Role of Conscious Will in Voluntary Action." *Behavioral and Brain Sciences* 8(4) (1985) 529–66.

Lilienfeld, Scott O., and Katherine A. Fowler. "The Self-Report Assessment of Psychopathy: Problems, Pitfalls, and Promises." In *Handbook of Psychopathy*, edited by Christopher J. Patrick, 107–32. New York: Guilford, 2006.

Lippke, Richard L. "The Ethics of Recidivist Premiums." In *The Routledge Handbook of Criminal Justice Ethics*, edited by Jonathan Jacobs and Jonathan Jackson, 17–27. London: Routledge, 2017.

Lively, Kathryn J., and Emi A. Weed. "The Sociology of Emotion." In *Handbook of Emotions*, edited by Lisa Feldman Barrett et al., 66–81. 4th ed. London: Guilford, 2016.

Lo, Lap Yan, et al. "Does Content Matter? The Effect of Remorseful Tone on Length of Prison Sentence." *Asian Journal of Social Psychology* 19(2) (2016) 170–77.

Locke, John. *An Essay Concerning Human Understanding*. Edited by Lewis Amherst Selby-Bigge and P. H. Nidditch. 2nd ed. Oxford: Oxford University Press, 1988.

Lomax, Eric. *The Railway Man*. London: Vintage, 1996.

Lombardo, Nicholas E. *The Logic of Desire: Aquinas on Emotion*, Washington DC: Catholic University of America Press, 2011.

Lord, Andy. "Emergent and Adaptive Spiritualities in the Twentieth Century." In *The Oxford History of Protestant Dissenting Traditions*. Volume V. *The Twentieth Century: Themes and Variations in a Global Context*, edited by Mark P. Hutchinson, 224–57. Oxford: Oxford University Press, 2018.

Luardi, Katherine Jackson, and Anne T. Thayer, eds. *Penitence in the Age of Reformations*. St Andrews Studies in Reformation History. Abingdon, UK: Routledge, 2017.

Luc, Alex. לֵב. In *NIDOTTE* 2:749–54.

Lucretius Carus. *On the Nature of Things*. With an English translation by W. H. D. Rouse. Revised by Martin F. Smith. LCL 181. Cambridge: Harvard University Press, 2014.

Lutz, Catherine A. *Unnatural Emotions: Everyday Sentiments on a Micronesian Atoll and Their Challenges to Western Theory*. Chicago: University of Chicago Press, 1988.

Lyons, William E. *Emotion*. New York: Cambridge University Press, 1980.

Macaskill, Grant. *Union with Christ in the New Testament*. Oxford: Oxford University Press, 2014.

Maccoby, Hyam. *Judas Iscariot and the Myth of Jewish Evil*. New York: Free Press— Maxwell Macmillan, 1992.

Macfarlane, Alan. *The Origins of English Individualism: The Family, Property and Social Transition*. Oxford: Blackwell, 1978.

Machan, Tibor R. "Why Moral Judgments Can Be Objective." *Social Philosophy and Policy* 25(1) (2008) 100–125.

MacIntyre, Alasdair. *After Virtue: A Study in Moral Theory*. 3rd ed. London: Bloomsbury, 2007.

Mackie, John L. *Ethics: Inventing Right and Wrong*. Harmondsworth, UK: Penguin, 1977.

Madigan, Kevin. *Medieval Christianity: A New History*. New Haven, CT: Yale University Press, 2015.

———. *The Passions of Christ in High Medieval Thought: An Essay on Christological Development*. Cambridge: Cambridge University Press, 2007.

Malherbe, Abraham. "Hellenistic Moralists and the New Testament." *Aufstieg und Niedergang der römischen Welt*, 2.26.1 (1992) 267–333.

Malina, Bruce J. "Understanding New Testament Persons." In *Social Sciences and the New Testament*, edited by Richard L. Rohrbaugh, 41–61. Grand Rapids: Baker Academic, 2010.

Marcus, Joel. *Mark 8–16. A New Translation with Introduction and Commentary.* The Anchor Yale Bible. New Haven, CT: Yale University Press, 2009.

Marks, Joel. "A Theory of Emotions." *Philosophical Studies* 42(3) (1982) 227–42.

Marks, Malcolm J. "Remorse, Revenge, and Forgiveness." *The Psychotherapy Patient* 5(1 and 2) (1988) 317–30.

Martel, Joane. "Remorse and the Production of Truth." *Punishment and Society* 12(4) (2010) 414–37.

Martin, Adrienne M. "Owning Up and Lowering Down: The Power of Apology." *The Journal of Philosophy* 107.10 (2010) 534–53.

Martin, Ralph P. *Reconciliation: A Study of Paul's Theology.* Atlanta: John Knox, 1980.

Maslow, Abraham H. *Motivation and Personality.* New York: Harper & Row, 1954.

McCold, Paul. "Restorative Justice: Variations on a Theme." In *Restorative Justice for Juveniles*, edited by Lode Walgrave, 19–53. Leuven: Leuven University Press, 1998.

McConnell, Terence. "Moral Dilemmas." In *The Stanford Encyclopedia of Philosophy* (Fall 2018 edition), edited by Edward N. Zalta. https://plato.stanford.edu/archives/fall2018/entries/moral-dilemmas/.

McGrath, Alister E. "The Transition to Modernity." In *Companion Encyclopedia of Theology*, edited by Peter Byrne and Leslie Houlden, 230–50. London: Routledge, 1995.

McGrath, Joanna Collicutt. "Post-Traumatic Growth and the Origins of Early Christianity." *Mental Health, Religion & Culture* 9(3) (2006) 291–306.

McIlvenna, Una. "Punishment." In *Early Modern Emotions. An Introduction,* edited by Susan Broomhill, 195–98. London: Routledge, 2017.

McQueen, Paddy. "When Should We Regret?" *International Journal of Philosophical Studies* 25(5) (2017) 608–23.

Meeks, Wayne A. *The Moral World of the First Christians.* Philadelphia: Westminster, 1986.

Meyer, Linda Ross. "Eternal Remorse." In *Towards a Critique of Guilt: Perspectives from Law and the Humanities*, edited by Matthew Anderson, 141–60. Studies in Law, Politics, and Society, Volume 36. Bingley, UK: Emerald, 2005.

Meyer, Susan Sauvé, and Adrienne M Martin. "Emotion and the Emotions." In *The Oxford Handbook of the History of Ethics*, edited by Roger Crisp, 638–71. Oxford: Oxford University Press, 2013.

Miller, William Ian. *Faking It.* Cambridge, Cambridge University Press, 2003.

Miner, Robert. *Thomas Aquinas on the Passions: A Study of* Summa Theologiae *1a2ae 22–48.* Cambridge: Cambridge University Press, 2009.

Mirguet, Françoise. "What Is an 'Emotion' in the Hebrew Bible? An Experience That Exceeds Most Contemporary Concepts." *Biblical Interpretation* 24(4–5) (2016) 442–65.

Moberly, R. Walter L. *Old Testament Theology: Reading the Hebrew Bible as Christian Scripture.* Grand Rapids: Baker Academic, 2013.

Moll, Jorge, et al. "The Cognitive Neuroscience of Moral Emotions." In *Moral Psychology. Volume 3. The Neuroscience of Morality: Emotion, Brain Disorders, and Development*, edited by Walter Sinnott-Armstrong, 1–17. Cambridge: MIT Press, 2008.

Montaigne, Michel de. *Essays*. Translated by Charles Cotton. Published in Project Gutenberg's, *The Essays of Montaigne, Complete, by Michel de Montaigne*. 17 September 2006 (ebook no. 3600), 1877.

Moore, Michael. "The Moral Worth of Retribution." In *Responsibility, Character, and the Emotions: New Essays in Moral* Psychology, edited by Ferdinand Shoeman, 179–219. Cambridge: Cambridge University Press, 1987.

———. *Placing Blame: A General Theory of the Criminal Law*. Oxford: Clarendon, 1997.

Moore, Thomas. "Re-Morse: An Initiatory Disturbance of the Soul." *The Psychotherapy Patient* 5(1 and 2) (1988) 83–94.

Morris, Herbert. "The Decline of Guilt." *Ethics* 99(1) (1988) 62–76.

———. *On Guilt and Innocence*. Berkeley, CA: University of California Press, 1976.

Mortensen, Beth. *Saint Thomas Aquinas: Commentary on the Sentences of Peter Lombard, Book IV, Distinctions 14–25*. Translated by Beth Mortensen. Volume 8. Latin/English Edition of the Works of St. Thomas Aquinas. Green Bay, WI: Aquinas Institute, 2017.

Moulton, J. H. *A Grammar of New Testament Greek*. Accidence and Word-Formation with an Appendix on Semitisms in the New Testament. Volume II, J. H. Moulton and W. F. Howard. Edinburgh: T. & T. Clark, 1996.

Moxnes, Havor. "Honor and Shame." In *Social Sciences and the New Testament*, edited by Richard L. Rohrbaugh, 19–40. Grand Rapids: Baker Academic, 2010.

Murdoch, Iris. *The Sovereignty of Good*. London: Routledge, 1970.

Murphy, Jeffrie G. "Christian Love and Criminal Punishment." In *Agape, Justice, and Law: How Might Christian Love Shaped Law?* edited by Robert C. Cochran Jr. and Zachary R. Calo, 151–65. Cambridge: Cambridge University Press, 2017.

———. "Last Words on Retribution." In *The Routledge Handbook of Criminal Justice Ethics*, edited by Jonathan Jacobs and Jonathan Jackson, 28–41. London: Routledge, 2017.

———. *Punishment and the Moral Emotions: Essays in Law, Morality, and Religion*. Oxford: Oxford University Press, 2012.

Murphy, Jeffrie G., and Jean Hampton. *Forgiveness and Mercy*. Cambridge: Cambridge University Press, 1988.

Nagase, Takashi. *Crosses and Tigers*. Translated by Takashi Nagase and Watase Masaru. Bangkok: Allied Printers, 1990.

Nagel, Thomas. "Freedom." In *Free Will*, edited by Gary Watson, 229–56. 2nd ed. Oxford: Oxford University Press, 2003.

———. *Mortal Questions*. New York: Cambridge University Press, 1993.

———. "What Is It Like to Be a Bat?" *Philosophical Review* 83(4) (1974) 435–56.

Nahmias, Eddy. "Is Free Will and Illusion? Confronting Challenges from the Modern Mind Sciences." In *Moral Psychology. Volume 4. Free Will and Moral Responsibility*, edited by Walter Sinnott-Armstrong, 1–25. Cambridge: MIT Press, 2014.

Nandé, Jackie A. קדוש. In *NIDOTTE* 3:883.

Nellisen, Rob M. A. "Guilt-Induced Self-Punishment as a Sign of Remorse." *Social Psychological and Personality Science* 3(2) (2012) 139–44.

Nelson, Derek R. *Sin: A Guide for the Perplexed*. London: T. & T. Clark, 2011.

Nesse, Randolph. "Evolutionary Explanations of Emotions." *Human Nature* 1.3 (1990) 261–89.

Nielsen, Kai. "There Is No Dilemma of Dirty Hands: Response to Stephen de Wijze." *South African Journal of Philosophy* 15(4) (1996) 155–59.

Nietzsche, Friedrich. *Beyond Good and Evil: Prelude to a Philosophy of the Future.* Translated by R. J. Hollingdale, with an introduction by Michael Tanner. London: Penguin, 2003.

———. *On the Genealogy of Morals: A Polemic: By Way of Clarification and Supplement to My Last Book, "Beyond Good and Evil."* Translated with an Introduction and Notes by Douglas Smith. Oxford: Oxford University Press, 2008.

Nobles, Melissa. *The Politics of Official Apologies.* Cambridge: Cambridge University Press, 2008.

North, Joanna. "The 'Ideal' of Forgiveness: A Philosopher's Exploration." In *Exploring Forgiveness*, edited by Robert D. Enright and Joanna North, 15–34. Madison, WI: University of Wisconsin Press, 1998.

Nussbaum, Martha C. *Anger and Forgiveness: Resentment, Generosity, Justice.* Oxford: Oxford University Press, 2016.

———. *The Therapy of Desire: Theory and Practice in Hellenistic Ethics.* Princeton, NJ: Princeton University Press, 1994.

———. *Upheavals of Thought: The Intelligence of Emotions.* Cambridge: Cambridge University Press, 2001.

O'Connell, Robert H. *The Rhetoric of the Book of Judges.* Leiden: Brill, 1996.

O'Keefe, Tim. *Epicureanism.* Durham: Acumen, 2010.

Olick, Jeffrey K. *The Politics of Regret: On Collective Memory and Historical Responsibility.* London: Routledge, 2007.

Olson, Dennis. "Emotion, Repentance, and the Question of the 'Inner Life' of Biblical Israelites: A Case Study in Hosea 6:1–3." In *Mixed Feelings and Vexed Passions: Exploring Emotions in Biblical Literature*, edited by F. Scott Spencer, 161–76. Atlanta: SBL, 2017.

Oorschot, Irene van, et al. "Remorse in Context(s): A Qualitative Exploration of the Negotiation of Remorse and its Consequences." *Social and Legal Studies* 26(3) (2017) 359–77.

Packer, James I. *A Quest for Godliness: The Puritan Vision of the Christian Life.* Wheaton, IL: Crossway, 1990.

Paffenroth, Kim. *Judas: Images of a Lost Disciple.* Louisville, KY: Westminster John Knox, 2001.

Paris, Peter J. "An Ethicist's Concerns about Biblical Ethics." *Semeia* 66(4) (1994) 173–79.

Parker, Simon B., ed. *Ugaritic Narrative Poetry.* SBL Writings from the Ancient World Series, Volume 9. Atlanta: Scholars, 1997.

Parole Board. *Report of the Parole Board for 1996/7.* London: The Stationery Office, 1996/7.

Parsons, Richard D. "Forgiving-Not-Forgetting." *The Psychotherapy Patient* 5(1 and 2) (1988) 259–73.

Pasnau, Robert. *Thomas Aquinas on Human Nature: A Philosophical Study of Summa Theologiae, 1a75–89.* Cambridge: Cambridge University Press, 2002.

Patera, Maria. "Reflections on the Discourse of Fear in Greek Sources." In *Unveiling Emotions II. Emotions in Greece and Rome: Texts, Images, and Material Culture*, edited by Angelos Chaniotis and Pierre Ducrey, 109–34. Stuttgart, Franz Steiner, 2013.

Patrick, Christopher J., ed. *Handbook of Psychopathy*. New York: Guilford, 2006.

Pattison, Steven. *The Challenge of Practical Theology: Selected Essays*. London: Jessica Kingsley, 2007.

Peijnenburg, Jeanne. "Is What Is Done Done? On Regret and Remorse." *Journal of Mind and Behavior* 26(4) (2005) 219–27.

Peristiany, J. G., ed. *Honor and Shame: The Values of Mediterranean Society*. Chicago: Chicago University Press, 1966.

Perkins, Pheme. *Peter: Apostle for the Whole Church*. Minneapolis, MN: Fortress, 2000.

Philips, D. Z., and H. S. Price. "Remorse without Repudiation." *Analysis* 28(1) (1967) 18–20.

Philo. *On the Virtues*. Translated by F. H. Colson. LCL 341. Cambridge: Harvard University Press, 1939.

Pieper, Josef. *The Concept of Sin*. Translated from the German by Edward T. Oakes. South Bend, IN: St Augustine, 2001.

Pierce, C. A. *Conscience in the New Testament*. London: SCM, 1955.

Pizarro, David, et al. "On Disgust and Moral Judgment." *Emotion Review* 3(3) (2011) 267–68.

Plamper, Jan. *The History of Emotions: An Introduction*. Translated by Keith Tribe. Oxford: Oxford University Press, 2015.

Plato. *Gorgias*. With an English Translation by W. R. M. Lamb. LCL 166. London: Heinemann, 1925.

———. *Phaedrus*. Edited and translated by Chris Emlyn-Jones and William Preddy. LCL 36. Cambridge MA: Harvard University Press, 1971.

———. *Republic*. Edited and translated by Christopher Emlyn-Jones and William Preddy. 2 vols. LCL 237, 276. Cambridge: Harvard University Press, 2013.

———. *Timaeus*. With an English Translation by R. G. Bury. LCL 234. London: Heinemann, 1929.

Pleins, J. Davis. *The Social Visions of the Hebrew Bible: A Theological Introduction*. Louisville, KY: Westminster John Knox, 2000.

Plutarch. *Moralia*. With an English translation by F. C. Babbitt et al. London: Heinemann, 1927.

Plutchik, Robert. *Emotion: A Psychoevolutionary Synthesis*. New York: Harper & Row, 1979.

Pope, Stephen J. *Human Evolution and Christian Ethics*. Cambridge: Cambridge University Press, 2007.

Porter, Jean. *Moral Action and Christian Ethics*. Cambridge: Cambridge University Press, 1995.

Postles, David. "Penance and the Market Place: A Reformation Dialogue with the Medieval Church (c.1250–1600)." *Journal of Ecclesiastical History* 54(3) (2003) 441–68.

Pouncey, Claire. "Inappropriate Regret." *Philosophy, Psychiatry, & Psychology* 16(3) (2009) 233–34.

Prins, Herschel. *Psychopathy: An Introduction*. Hook, UK: Waterside, 2013.

Prinz, Jesse J. "Against Empathy." *Southern Journal of Philosophy* 49(1) (2011) 214–33.

———. *The Emotional Construction of Morals*. Oxford: Oxford University Press, 2007.

———. *Gut Reactions: A Perceptual Theory of Emotion*. Oxford: Oxford University Press, 2004.

————. "Is Morality Innate?" In *Moral Psychology. Volume 1. The Evolution of Morality: Adaptations and Innateness,* edited by Walter Sinnott-Armstrong, 367–406. Cambridge: MIT Press, 2008.

————. "The Moral Emotions." In *The Oxford Handbook of Philosophy of Emotion,* edited by Peter Goldie, 519–38. Oxford: Oxford University Press, 2010.

Prinz, Jesse J., and Shaun Nichols. "Moral Emotions." In *The Moral Psychology Handbook,* edited by John M. Doris and the Moral Psychology Research Group, 111–46. Oxford: Oxford University Press, 2010.

Proeve, Michael, and Steven Tudor. *Remorse: Psychological and Jurisprudential Perspectives.* Farnham, UK: Ashgate, 2010.

Pugh, Jonathan, and Thomas Douglas. "Neurointerventions as Criminal Rehabilitation: An Ethical Review." In *The Routledge Handbook of Criminal Justice Ethics,* edited by Jonathan Jacobs and Jonathan Jackson, 95–109. London: Routledge, 2017

Pugh, Jonathan, and Hannah Maslen. "'Drugs That Make You Feel Bad'? Remorse-Based Mitigation and Neurointerventions." *Criminal Law and Philosophy* 11(3) (2017) 499–522.

Rabbås, Øyvind, et al., eds. *The Quest for the Good Life: Ancient Philosophers on Happiness.* Oxford: Oxford University Press, 2015.

Radzik, Linda. *Making Amends: Atonement in Morality, Law, and Politics.* Oxford: Oxford University Press, 2009.

Rawls, John. *A Brief Enquiry into the Meaning of Sin and Faith, with 'On my Religion'.* Edited by Thomas Nagel, with Commentaries by Joshua Cohen and Thomas Nagel, and by Robert Merrihew Adams. Cambridge: Harvard University Press, 2009.

————. *A Theory of Justice.* Oxford: Clarendon, 1972.

Raz, Joe. "Agency and Luck." In *Luck, Value, and Commitment: Themes from the Ethics of Bernard Williams,* edited by Ulrike Heuer and Gerald Lang, 133–62. Oxford: Oxford University Press, 2012.

Renteln, Alison Dundes. "Apologies: A Cross-Cultural Analysis." In *The Age of Apology. Facing Up to the Past,* edited by Mark Gibney et al., 61–76. Philadelphia: University of Pennsylvania Press, 2008.

Roberts, Robert C. *Emotions: An Essay in Aid of Moral Psychology.* Cambridge: Cambridge University Press, 2003.

————. *Emotions and the Moral Life.* Cambridge: Cambridge University Press, 2013.

————. "Emotions as Access to Religious Truths." *Faith and Philosophy: Journal of the Society of Christian Philosophers* 9(1) (1992) 83–92.

————. "Forgivingness." *American Philosophical Quarterly* 32 (1995) 289–36.

————. *Spiritual Emotions: A Psychology of Christian Virtues.* Grand Rapids: Eerdmans, 2007.

Roberts, Rodney C. "Another Look at a Moral Statute of Limitations on Injustice." *The Journal of Ethics* 11.2 (2007) 177–92.

————. "Justice and Rectification: A Taxonomy of Justice." In *Injustice and Rectification,* edited by Rodney C. Roberts, 7–28. New York: Lang, 2002.

————. "The Morality of a Moral Statute of Limitations on Injustice." *The Journal of Ethics* 7.1 (2003) 115–38.

Robinson, Jenefer. "Emotion: Biological Fact or Social Construction?" In *Thinking about Feeling: Contemporary Philosophers on Emotions,* edited by Robert C. Solomon, 28–43. Oxford: Oxford University Press, 2004.

Robinson, Paul H., et al. "Extralegal Punishment Factors: A Study of Forgiveness, Hardship, Good Deeds, Apology, Remorse, and Other Such Discretionary Factors in Assessing Criminal Punishment." *Vanderbilt Law Review* 737(3) (2012) 737–826.

Rodd, Cyril S. *Glimpses of a Strange Land: Studies in Old Testament Ethics.* Edinburgh: T. & T. Clark, 2001.

Roeser, Sabine. "Reid and Moral Emotions." *The Journal of Scottish Philosophy* 7(2) (2009) 177–92.

Rogerson, John W. "Discourse Ethics and Biblical Ethics." In *The Bible in Ethics: The Second Sheffield Colloquium,* edited by John W. Rogerson et al., 17–26. Sheffield, UK: Sheffield Academic, 1995.

———. "Old Testament Ethics." In *Text in Context: Essays by Members of the Society for Old Testament* Study, edited by A. D. H. Mayes, 116–37. Oxford: Oxford University Press, 2000.

———. *Theory and Practice in Old Testament Ethics: Edited and with an Introduction by M. Daniel Carroll R.* London: T. & T. Clark, 2004.

Rolls, Edmund T. *Emotion Explained.* Oxford: Oxford University Press, 2005.

Rorty, Amélie Oksenberg. "Agent Regret." In *Explaining Emotions,* edited by Amélie Oksenberg Rorty, 489–506. Berkeley CA: University of California Press, 1980.

Roseman, Ira J. "Cognitive Determinants of Emotion: A Structural Theory." In *Review of Personality and Social Psychology,* edited by Philip Shaver, 11–36. Emotions, Relationships, and Health, Volume 5. London: Sage, 1984.

Rosner, Fred. "Suicide in Biblical, Talmudic and Rabbinic Writings." *Tradition: A Journal of Orthodox Jewish Thought* 11(2) (1970) 25–40.

Rossmanith, Kate. "Affect and the Judicial Assessment of Offenders: Feeling and Judging Remorse." *Body & Society* 21(2) (2015) 167–93.

Rosthal, Robert. "Moral Weakness and Remorse." *Mind,* New Series, 76(304) (1967) 576–79.

Rousseau, Jean-Jacques. *Discourse on the Origin of Inequality.* Edited by Greg Boroson. Mineola, NY: Dover, 2004.

———. *Emile.* Edited by Peter Jimack. London: Grant & Cutler, 1983.

Rowland, Christopher. "Liberationist Readings of the Bible." In *The Bible From 1750 to the Present,* edited by John Riches, 249–60. Cambridge: Cambridge University Press, 2015.

Rozin, Paul, et al. "Disgust." In *Handbook of Emotions,* edited by Lisa Feldman Barrett, Michael Lewis, and Jeanette M. Haviland-Jones, 815–34. 4th ed. London: Guilford, 2016.

Rozin, Paul, et al. "The CAD Triad Hypothesis: A Mapping between Three Moral Emotions (Contempt, Anger, Disgust) and Three Moral Codes (Community, Autonomy, Divinity)." *Journal of Personality and Social Psychology* 76.4 (1999) 574–86.

Rudman, Stanley. *Concepts of Persons and Christian Ethics.* Cambridge: Cambridge University Press, 1997.

Russell, Henry M. W. "Beyond the Will: Humiliation as Christian Necessity in *Crime and Punishment.*" In *Dostoevsky and the Christian Tradition,* edited by George Pattison and Diane Oenning Thompson, 226–36. Cambridge: Cambridge University Press, 2001.

Russell, James A. "A Circumplex Model of Affect." *Journal of Personality and Social Psychology* 39(6) (1980) 1161–78.

———. "Core Affect and the Psychological Construction of Emotion." *Psychological Review* 110(1) (2003) 145–72.

———. "Culture and the Categorization of Emotions." *Psychological Bulletin* 110 (1991) 426–50.

Rybarczyk, Edmund J. "New Churches: Pentecostals and the Bible." In *The Bible from 1750 to the Present,* edited by John Riches, 587–605. Cambridge: Cambridge University Press, 2015.

Ryrie, Alec. *Being Protestant in Reformation Britain.* Oxford: Oxford University Press, 2013.

Sabini, John, and Maury Silver. "Why Emotional Names and Experiences Don't Neatly Pair." *Psychological Enquiry* Volume 16(1) (2005) 1–10.

Sander, David, et al. "An Appraisal-Driven Componential Approach to the Emotional Brain." *Emotion Review* 10(3) (2018) 219–31.

Sanders, E. P. *Paul and Palestinian Judaism.* London: SCM, 1977.

Sanders, Ed, and Matthew Johncock, eds. *Emotion and Persuasion in Classical Antiquity.* Stuttgart: Franz Steiner Verlag, 2016.

Sanders, Ed. "Beyond the Usual Suspects: Literary Sources and the Historian of Emotions." In *Unveiling Emotions: Sources and Methods for the Study of Emotions in the Greek World,* edited by Angelos Chaniotis, 151–73. Stuttgart, Franz Steiner, 2012.

Sandis, Constantine. "The Public Expression of Penitence." *Teorema* 31(2) (2012) 141–52.

Scarantino, Andrea. "The Motivational Theory of Emotions." In *Moral Psychology and Human Agency: Philosophical Essays on the Science of Ethics,* edited by Justin D'Arms and Daniel Jacobson, 156–85. Oxford: Oxford University Press, 2014.

———. "The Philosophy of Emotions and Its Impact on Affective Science." In *Handbook of Emotions,* edited by Lisa Feldman Barrett, et al., 3–48. 4th ed. London: Guilford, 2016.

Scarre, Geoffrey F. *After Evil. Responding to Wrongdoing.* Aldershot, UK: Ashgate, 2004.

———. "The 'Constitutive Thought' of Regret." *International Journal of Philosophical Studies* 25(5) (2017) 569–85.

———. "On Taking Back Forgiveness." *Ethical Theory and Moral Practice* 19(4) (2016) 931–44.

Schachter, Stanley, and Jerome E. Singer. "Cognitive, Social, and Physiological Determinants of Emotional States." *Psychological Review* 69(5) (1962) 379–99.

Scheid, Don E. "Kant's Retributivism." *Ethics* 93(2) (1983) 262–82.

Scherer, Klaus R. "Appraisal Considered as a Process of Multilevel Sequencing." In *Appraisal Processes in Emotion: Theory, Methods, Research,* edited by Klaus R. Scherer et al., 92–120. Oxford: Oxford University Press, 2001.

———. "What Are Emotions? And How Can They Be Measured?" *Social Science Information* 44(4) (2005) 695–729.

Scherer, Klaus R., et al., eds. *Appraisal Processes in Emotion: Theory, Methods, Research.* Oxford: Oxford University Press, 2001.

Schlimm, Matthew Richard. *From Fratricide to Forgiveness: The Language and Ethics of Anger in Genesis.* Winona Lake, IN: Eisenbrauns, 2011.

Schopenhauer, Arthur. *On the Basis of Morality*. Translated by E. F. J. Payne and with an introduction by David E Cartwright. Providence RI: Berghahn, 1995.

Schrock, Douglas, and Brian Knop. "Gender and Emotions." In *Handbook of the Sociology of Emotions: Volume II*, edited by Jan E. Stets and Jonathan H. Turner, 411–28. Dordrecht: Springer, 2014.

Schweiker, William. *Responsibility and Christian Ethics*. Cambridge: Cambridge University Press, 1995.

Scrutton, Anastasia. "Emotion in Augustine of Hippo and Thomas Aquinas: A Way Forward for the Impassibility Debate?" *International Journal of Systematic Theology* 7(2) (2005) 169–77.

Sell, Alan P. F., ed. *Protestant Nonconformist Texts*. 4 vols. Aldershot, UK: Ashgate, 2007.

Sentencing Council. *Sentencing Children and Young People. Definitive Guidance.* (No publication details in the Guidance.) 2017.

Shabad, Peter. "Remorse. The Echo of Inner Truth." *The Psychotherapy Patient* 5(1 and 2) (1988) 113–33.

Shafer-Landau, Russ. *The Fundamentals of Ethics*. Oxford: Oxford University Press, 2010.

———. *Moral Realism: A Defence*. Oxford: Oxford University Press, 2003.

Shaffer, Jerome. "Mental Events and the Brain." *Journal of Philosophy* 60(6) (1963) 160–66.

Shafranske, Edward P. "The Significance of Remorse in Psychotherapy." *The Psychotherapy Patient* 5(1 and 2) (1988) 19–33.

Shaver, Philip, et al. "Emotion Knowledge: Further Explorations of a Prototype Approach." *Journal of Personality and Social Psychology* 52(6) (1987) 1061–86.

Shaw, Jeanne. "The Usefulness of Remorse." *The Psychotherapy Patient* 5(1 and 2) (1988) 77–82.

Sher, George. *Desert*. Princeton, NJ: Princeton University Press, 1987.

———. *In Praise of Blame*. New York: Oxford University Press, 2005.

Sherman, Nancy. "The Place of Emotions in Kantian Morality." In *Kant on Emotion and Morality*, edited by Alix Cohen, 11–32. London: Palgrave Macmillan, 2014.

Shweder, Richard A. *Thinking Through Cultures: Expeditions in Cultural Psychology*. Cambridge: Harvard University Press, 1991.

Shweder, Richard A., and Robert A. Levine, eds. *Cultural Theory: Essays on Mind, Self, and Emotion*. Cambridge: Cambridge University Press, 1984.

Shweder, Richard A., et al. "The 'Big Three' of Morality (Autonomy, Community, Divinity) and the 'Big Three' Explanations of Suffering." In *Morality and Health: Interdisciplinary Perspectives*, edited by Allan M. Brandt and Paul Rozin, 119–69. London: Routledge, 1997.

Sihvola, J., and T. Engberg-Pedersen, eds. *The Emotions in Hellenistic Philosophy*. Dordrecht: Kluwer, 1998.

Silk, Joan M. "Empathy, Sympathy, and Prosocial Preference in Primates." In *The Oxford Handbook of Evolutionary Psychology*, edited by Robin I. M. Dunbar and Louise Barrett, 115–25. Oxford: Oxford University Press, 2009.

Singer, Peter. "Sidgwick and Reflective Equilibrium." *The Monist* 58(3) (1974) 490–517.

Singer, Peter N. "A New Distress: Galen's Ethics in Περι Ἀλυπιας and Beyond." In *Galen's Treatise Περι Ἀλυπιας (De Indolentia) in Context. A Tale of Resilience*, edited by Caroline Petit, 180–98. Leiden: Brill, 2019.

Sinnott-Armstrong, Walter. "Framing Moral Intuitions." In *Moral Psychology. Volume 2. The Evolution of Morality: The Cognitive Science of Morality*, edited by Walter Sinnott-Armstrong, 47–76. Cambridge: MIT Press, 2008.

Sinnott-Armstrong, Walter, ed. *Moral Psychology. Volume 1. The Evolution of Morality: Adaptations and Innateness*. Cambridge: MIT Press, 2008.

———. *Moral Psychology. Volume 3. The Neuroscience of Morality: Emotion, Brain Disorders, and Development*. Cambridge: MIT Press, 2008.

———. *Moral Psychology. Volume 4. Free Will and Moral Responsibility*. Cambridge: MIT Press, 2014.

Skinner, B. F. *Verbal Behavior*. New York: Appleton-Century-Crofts, 1957.

Smit, Harry. *The Social Evolution of Human Nature: From Biology to Language*. Cambridge: Cambridge University Press, 2014.

Smith, Adam. *The Theory of Moral Sentiments*. Edited by Knud Haakonssen. Cambridge: Cambridge University Press, 2002.

Smith, Angela M. "Guilty Thoughts." In *Morality and the Emotions*, edited by Carla Bagnoli, 233–56. Oxford: Oxford University Press, 2011.

Smith, Nick. "The Categorical Apology." *Journal of Social Philosophy* 36.4 (2005) 473–96.

———. "Dialectical Retributivism: Why Apologetic Offenders Deserve Reduction in Punishment Even under Retributive Theories." *Philosophia: Philosophical Quarterly of Israel* 44(2) (2016) 343–60.

———. *I was Wrong: The Meanings of Apologies*. Cambridge: Cambridge University Press, 2008.

———. *Justice through Apologies: Remorse, Reform, and Punishment*. Cambridge: Cambridge University Press, 2014.

Smith, Robert J. *The Psychopath in Society*. New York: Academic, 1978.

Soggin, J. Alberto. *Joshua: A Commentary*. London: SCM Press, 1972.

———. *Judges: A Commentary*. London: SCM Press, 1982.

Sohn, Leslie. "A Defective Capacity to Feel Sorrow." In *Remorse and Reparation*, edited by Murray Cox, 69–81. London: Jessica Kingsley, 1999.

Solomon, Robert C. "On Emotions as Judgments." In *Philosophy and the Emotions: A Reader*, edited by Stephen Leighton, 165–77. Peterborough, Canada: Broadview, 2003.

———. *The Passions: The Myth and Nature of Human Emotions*. 2nd ed, New York: Hackett, 1993.

———. "The Philosophy of Emotions." In *Handbook of Emotions*, edited by Michael Lewis and Jeannette M. Haviland-Jones, 3–15. 2nd ed. London: Guilford, 2000.

———. *What Is an Emotion? Classic and Contemporary Readings*. 2nd ed. Oxford: Oxford University Press, 2003.

Sommers, Tamler. "The Three Rs: Retribution, Revenge and Reparation." *Philosophia: Philosophical Quarterly of Israel* 44(2) (2016) 327–42.

Sophocles. Edited and Translated by Hugh Lloyd-Jones. In Two Volumes. LCL 20 and 21. Cambridge: Harvard University Press, 1994.

Sorabji, Richard. *Emotion as Peace of Mind: From Stoic Agitation to Christian Temptation*. Oxford: Oxford University Press, 2000.

———. "Emotions and the Psychotherapy of the Ancients." In *Philosophical Psychology. Psychology, Emotions, and Freedom*, edited by Craig Steven Titus, 176–95. Arlington, VA: The Institute for the Psychological Sciences, 2009.

————. "Is Stoic Philosophy Helpful as Psychotherapy?" In *Aristotle and After*, edited by Richard Sorabji, 197–209. London: Institute of Classical Studies, School of Advanced Study, University of London, 1997.

————. *Moral Conscience Through the Ages: Fifth Century BCE to the Present*. Oxford: Oxford University Press, 2014.

Sorell, Tom. *Moral Theory and Capital Punishment*. Oxford: Blackwell, 1987

Sorensen, Roy. "Rewarding Regret." *Ethics: An International Journal of Social, Political, and Legal Philosophy* 108.3 (1998) 528–37.

Spencer, F. Scott., ed. *Mixed Feelings and Vexed Passions: Exploring Emotions in Biblical Literature*. Atlanta: SBL, 2017.

Sperling, S. David. "Blood." In *ABD* 1:761–63.

Speziale-Bagliacca, Roberto. *Guilt. Revenge, Remorse and Responsibility after Freud*. Translated by Ian Harvey. Forward by Frank Kermode. Edited by Susan Budd. London: Routledge, 2013.

Spinoza, Benedict de. *Spinoza: Ethics*. Edited and Translated by G. H. R. Parkinson. Oxford: Oxford University Press, 2000.

Statman, Daniel, ed. *Moral Luck*. Albany, NY: State University of New York Press, 1993.

Staub, Ervin. *The Psychology and Evil: Why Children, Adults and Groups Help and Harm Others*. Cambridge: Cambridge University Press, 2003.

Stearns, Peter N. "History of Emotions: Issues and Change and Impact." In *Handbook of Emotions*, edited by Michael Lewis and Jeannette M. Haviland-Jones, 16–29. 2nd ed. New York: Guilford, 2000.

Stern, E. Mark. "The Psychotherapy of Remorse." *The Psychotherapy Patient* 5(1 and 2) (1988) 1–11.

————. "Remorse: Restructure and Restitution (A Preface)." *The Psychotherapy Patient* 5(1 and 2) (1988) xiii–xiv.

Stern, E. Mark, ed. *Psychotherapy and the Remorseful Patient*. New York: Haworth, 1988.

Strawson, Peter F. *Freedom and Resentment and Other Essays*. London: Methuen, 1974.

Street, Sharon. "A Darwinian Dilemma for Realist Theories of Value." *Philosophical Studies* 127(1) (2006) 109–66.

Striker, Gisela. "*Ataraxia*: Happiness as Tranquility." *The Monist* 73(1) (1990) 97–110.

Sturdevant, Jason S. "Incarnation as Psychagogy: The Purpose of the World's Descent in John's Gospel." *Novum Testamentum* 56(1) (2014) 24–44.

Sumney, J. L. "Paul's Use of Παθος in His Argument against the Opponents of 2 Corinthians." In *Paul and Pathos*, edited by T. H. Olbricht and J. L. Sumney, 147–60. Atlanta: Society of Biblical Literature, 2001.

Swinburne, Richard. *Responsibility and Atonement*. Oxford: Clarendon, 1989.

Switzer, David K. "The Remorseful Patient: Perspectives of a Pastoral Counselor." *The Psychotherapy Patient* 5(1 and 2) (1988) 275–90.

Szablowinski, Zenon. "Apology with and without a Request for Forgiveness." *The Heythrop Journal* 53(5) (2012) 731–41.

Tallon, Andrew. "Christianity." In *The Oxford Handbook of Religion and Emotion*, edited by John Corrigan, 111–24. Oxford: Oxford University Press, 2008.

Tamiolaki, Melina. "Emotions and Historical Representation in Xenophon's *Hellenika*." In *Unveiling Emotions II. Emotions in Greece and Rome: Texts, Images, and Material Culture*, edited by Angelos Chaniotis and Pierre Ducrey, 15–52. Stuttgart, Franz Steiner, 2013.

Tangney, June Price. "Shame and Guilt in Interpersonal Relationships." In *Self-Conscious Emotions: The Psychology of Shame, Guilt, Embarrassment, and Pride*, edited by June Price Tangney and Kurt W. Fischer, 114–39. New York: Guilford, 1995.

Tangney, June Price, and Ronda L. Dearing. *Shame and Guilt*. New York: Guilford, 2004.

Tangney, June Price, et al., "Moral Emotions and Moral Behavior." *Annual Review of Psychology* 58 (2007) 345–72.

Tappolet, Christine. "Values and Emotions: Neo-Sentimentalism's Prospects." In *Morality and the Emotions*, edited by Carla Bagnoli, 17–34. Oxford: Oxford University Press, 2011.

Tasioulas, John. "Punishment and Repentance." *Philosophy. The Journal of the Royal Institute of Philosophy* 81(2) (2006) 279–322.

Tavuchis, Nicholas. *Mea Culpa: A Sociology of Apology and Reconciliation*. Stanford, CA: Stanford University Press, 1991.

Taylor, Gabriele. "Guilt and Remorse." In *The Emotions: Social, Cultural and Biological Dimensions*, edited by Rom Harré and W. Gerrod Parrott, 57–74. London: Sage, 1996.

———. *Pride, Shame, and Guilt: Emotions of Self-Assessment*. Oxford: Clarendon, 1985.

Taylor, Jacqueline. "Moral Sentiment and the Sources of Moral Identity." In *Morality and the Emotions*, edited by Carla Bagnoli, 257–74. Oxford: Oxford University Press, 2011.

Teichman, Jenny. "Punishment and Remorse." *Philosophy* 48(186) (1973) 335–46.

ten Brinke, Leanne, et al. "Crocodile Tears: Facial, Verbal and Body Language Behaviors Associated with Genuine and Fabricated Remorse." *Law and Human Behavior* 36(1) (2012) 51–59.

Thagard, Paul, and Tracy Finn. "Conscience: What Is Moral Intuition?" In *Morality and the Emotions*, edited by Carla Bagnoli, 150–69. Oxford: Oxford University Press, 2011.

Thalberg, Irving. "Remorse." *Mind*, New Series, 72 (288) (1963) 545–55.

———. "Rosthal's Notion of Remorse and Irrevocability." *Mind*, New Series, 77 (306) (1968) 288–89.

Thatcher, Adrian. *Living Together and Christian Ethics*. Cambridge: Cambridge University Press, 2002

Thayer, Anne T. *Penitence, Preaching and the Coming of the Reformation*. Abingdon, UK: Routledge, 2017.

Thom, Johan C. "The Passions in Neopythagorean Writings." In *Passions and Moral Progress in Greco-Roman Thought*, edited by John T. Fitzgerald, 67–78. London: Routledge, 2008.

Thomas, Alan. "Remorse and Reparation: A Philosophical Analysis." In *Remorse and Reparation*, edited by Murray Cox, 127–33. London: Jessica Kingsley, 1999.

Thrall, Margaret E. *A Critical and Exegetical Commentary on The Second Epistle to the Corinthians*. Volume 1: Introduction and Commentary on II Corinthians I–VII. Edinburgh: T. & T. Clark, 1994.

Thucydides. *History of the Peloponnesian War*. Translated by Charles Forster Smith. LCL 108–10 and 169. London: Heinemann. 1920.

Tiberius, Valerie. "Does Virtue Make Us Feel Happy? A New Theory for an Old Question." In *Moral Psychology. Volume 5. Virtue and Character*, edited by Walter Sinnott-Armstrong and Christian B. Miller, 547–77. Cambridge: MIT Press, 2017.

———. *Moral Psychology: A Contemporary Introduction*. London: Routledge, 2015.

Tidmarsh, David. "Necessary But Not Sufficient: The Personal View of a Psychiatric Member of the Parole Board." In *Remorse and Reparation*, edited by Murray Cox, 49–62. London: Jessica Kingsley, 1999.

Todd, Margo. *The Culture of Protestantism in Early Modern Scotland*. New Haven: Yale University Press, 2002.

Tudor, Steven. *Compassion and Remorse: Acknowledging the Suffering Other*. Morality and the Meaning of Life 11. Leuven: Peeters, 2001.

Vaillant, George E. "Where Do We Go from Here?" *Journal of Personality* 66(6) (1998) 1147–57.

Van De Wiele, Tarah. "Book Review: John Barton, *Ethics in Ancient Israel*." In *Studies in Christian Ethics* 30(1) (2017) 105–7.

Van Pelt, M. V., et al. רוח. In *NIDOTTE* 3:1073–78.

Van Straalen, Humber. "Remorse and Virtue Ethics." In *Aristotle on Emotion in Law and Politics*, edited by E. (Liesbeth) A. Huppes-Cluysnenaerham, 277–95 Switzerland: Springer, 2018.

Vandendriessche, Tine. "Should We Punish a Remorseful Offender? Punishment within a Theory of Symbolic Restoration." *South African Journal of Philosophy* 33(2) (2014) 113–19.

Vegge, Ivar. *2 Corinthians—A Letter about Reconciliation: A Psychagogical, Epistolographical and Rhetorical Analysis*. WUNT 2.239. Tübingen: Mohr Siebeck, 2008.

Vellacott, P. H. "The Guilt of Oedipus" *Greece and Rome* 11(2) (1964) 7–48.

Wall, R. W. "Conscience." In *ABD* 1:1128–30.

Wallace-Hadrill, Andrew, ed. *Patronage in Ancient Society*. London: Routledge, 1989.

Wallace, R. Jay. *Responsibility and the Moral Sentiments*. Cambridge: Harvard University Press, 1994.

———. *The View from Here: On Affirmation, Attachment, and the Limits of Regret*. Oxford: Oxford University Press, 2013.

Walzer, Michael. "Political Action: The Problem of Dirty Hands." *Philosophy & Public Affairs* 2(2) (1973) 160–80.

Watson, Gary, ed. *Free Will*. 2nd ed. Oxford: Oxford University Press, 2003.

Weisman, Richard. "Being and Doing: The Judicial Use of Remorse to Construct Character and Community." *Social & Legal Studies* 18(1) (2009) 47–69.

———. *Showing Remorse: Law and the Social Control of Emotion*. Farnham, UK: Ashgate, 2014.

Welborn, L. L. "Paul and Pain: Paul's Emotional Therapy in 2 Corinthians 1.1—2.13; 7.5–16 in the Context of Ancient Psychagogic Literature." *New Testament Studies* 57(4) (2011) 547–70.

———. "Paul's Appeal to the Emotions in 2 Corinthians 1.1—2.13; 7:5–16." *Journal for the Study of the New Testament* 82 (2001) 31–60.

Westermann, Claus. *Genesis 37–50. A Commentary*. Translated by John J. Scullion. Minneapolis, MN: Augsburg, 1986.

Wierzbicka, Anna. *Emotions across Languages and Cultures: Diversity and Universals*. Cambridge: Cambridge University Press, 1999.

———. "Everyday Conceptions of Emotion: A Semantic Perspective." In *Everyday Conceptions of Emotion: An Introduction to the Psychology, Anthropology and Linguistics of Emotion*, edited by James A. Rusell et al., 17–47. Dordrecht: Kluwer Academic, 1995.

Wiesenthal, Simon. *The Sunflower: On the Possibilities and Limits of Forgiveness. With a Symposium edited by Harry James Cargas and Bonny V. Fetterman.* Rev. and exp. ed. New York: Schocken, 1997.

Williams, Bernard. *Moral Luck: Philosophical Papers 1973–80.* Cambridge: Cambridge University Press, 1981

———. "Postscript." In *Moral Luck*, edited by Daniel Statman, 251–58. Albany, NY: State University of New York Press, 1993.

———. *Problems of the Self: Philosophical Papers 1956–1972.* Cambridge, Cambridge University Press, 1973.

———. *Shame and Necessity.* Berkeley, CA: California University Press, 1993

Williams, Rowan. *Lost Icons. Reflections on Cultural Bereavement.* London: Continuum, 2003.

Willis, Robert J. "The Prisoner of Death." *The Psychotherapy Patient* 5(1 and 2) (1988) 301–15.

Wilson, Edward O. *Sociobiology: The New Synthesis.* Cambridge: Harvard University Press, 1975.

Wilson, Robert R. "Sources and Methods in the Study of Ancient Israelite Ethics." *Semeia: An Experimental Journal for Biblical Criticism* 66(4) (1994) 55–63.

Winston, David. "Judaism and Hellenism: Hidden Tensions in Philo's Thought." *Studia Philonica Annual* 2 (1990) 1–19.

———. "Philo's Doctrine of Repentance." In *The School of Moses. Studies in Philo and Hellenistic Religion: In Memory of Horst R. Moehring*, edited by J. P. Kennedy, 29–40. Atlanta: Scholars, 1995.

Wittgenstein, Ludwig. *Philosophical Investigations.* Translated by G. E. M. Anscombe. 2nd ed. Oxford: Blackwell, 1968.

Wreen, Michael. "Mackie on the Objectivity of Values." *Dialectica: International Review of Philosophy and Knowledge* 39(2) (1985) 147–56.

Wright, Christopher J. H. *Deuteronomy.* Peabody, MA: Hendrickson, 1996.

———. *Old Testament Ethics for the People of God.* Leicester, UK: Inter-Varsity, 2004.

Xenophon. *Hellenica.* With an English Translation by Carleton L. Brownson. LCL 88 and 89. London: Heinemann, 1920.

Yoder, John Howard. *The Politics of Jesus.* Grand Rapids: Eerdmans, 1972.

Zahavi, Dan, and Søren Overgaard. "Empathy without Isomorphism: A Phenomenological Account." In *Empathy: From Bench to Bedside*, edited by Jean Decety, 3–20. Cambridge: MIT Press, 2012.

Zeelenberg, Marcel. "Regret." In *Encyclopedia of the Mind*, Volume 2, edited by H. Pashler, 639–41. New York: Sage. 2013.

———. "The Use of Crying Over Spilled Milk: A Note on the Rationality and Functionality of Regret." *Philosophical Psychology* 12.3 (1999) 325–40.

Zehr, Howard. *Changing Lenses: A New Focus for Crime and Justice.* Scottdale, PA: Herald, 1990.

WEBSITES

http://d.lib.rochester.edu/teams/text/morey-prik-of-conscience-introduction   - (accessed on 16 March 2018).

http://essays.quotidiana.org/montaigne/repentance/ (accessed on 27 September 2006; accessed on 27 December 2017).

http://www.bbc.co.uk/news/uk-england-38343295 (accessed on 20 December 2016).

http://www.bbc.co.uk/news/world-us-canada-38447542 (accessed on 28 December 2016).

http://www.independent.co.uk/news/uk/crime/ralph-clarke-britains-oldest-person-to-be-convicted-of-crime-jailed-for-13-years-for-child-sex-a7484171.html (accessed on 20 December 2016).

http://www.lawcom.gov.uk/wp-content/uploads/2015/04/LC247.pdf (accessed on 21 December 2016).

http: //www.newadvent.org/cathen/11618b.htm (accessed on 20 December 1917).

http: //www.vatican.va/archive/ENG0015/_INDEX.HTM (accessed on 10 April 2019).

https: //scotsthesaurus.org (accessed on 12 April 2018).

https://www.bbc.com/ideas/videos/which-language-has-400-words-for-snow/po63vmwx (accessed on 12 April 2018).

https://www.gov.uk/government/news/prime-minister-outlines-plan-for-reform-of-prisons (accessed on 3 April 2019).

https://www.nytimes.com/2015/09/17/arts/television/steve-rannazzisi-comedian-who-told-of-9-11-escape-admits-he-lied.html (accessed on 27 March 2018).

https://www.publications.parliament.uk/pa/cm200910/cmselect/cmjust/300/300i.pdf (accessed on 21 December 2016).

https://www.sentencingcouncil.org.uk/news/item/proposals-for-sentencing-offenders-with-mental-health-conditions-published/ (accessed on 10 April 2019).

https://www.telegraph.co.uk/men/thinking-man/anatomy-modern-apology-stars-say-sorry-makes-us-angry/ (accessed on 3 March 2019).

https://archive.org/stream/danmichelsayenbo1michgoog/danmichelsayenbo1michgoog_djvu.txt (accessed on 16 March 2018).

https://mwc-cmm.org/content/walking-conflict-and-reconciliation (accessed on 27 May 2019).

https://uwaterloo.ca/grebel/publications/conrad-grebel-review/issues/winter-2016/complication-mennonite-peace-tradition-wilhelm-mannhardts (accessed on 17 November 2019).

https://www.churchofengland.org/more/media-centre/news/working-party-report-ministry-confession (accessed on 27 May 2019).

Author Index

Subject Index

Scripture Index

Genesis

Exodus

Leviticus

Numbers

Matthew (continued)

21:29, 32	49
22:5	49
22:16	49
22:34–40	162
22:37	212
23	166
23:24	129
25:31–46	212, 226
26:4–16	64
26:24	67
26:31–35	68
26:37	78
26:50	69
26:69–75	68
26:75	68
27:3–5	66
27:3–4	65, 75
27:3	49, 65, 68, 75
27:4	65–66
27:7	65–66

Mark

4:37	69
4:38	49
10:17–31	206
14:10–11	64
14:27–31	68
14:34	78
14:66–72	68
14:72	68
16:7	70

Luke

6:31	212, 220
10:34–35	49
10:40	49
15:11–32	70, 224
15:16	71
15:17	70
15:18, 21	70, 217

15:19	71
18:8–30	206
18:13	205
19:2–10	205
22:3–6	64
22:3	64
22:31–34	68
22:62	68

John

6:70–71	64
8:10–11	185
8:11	185
10:13	49
12:6	49
13:2	64
13:27	64
13:36–38	68
18:3–12	65
18:15–28	68
18:15–18	69
18:25–27	68–69
21:15–19	70

Acts

1:16–20	66
1:18	65
5:34	79
7:58—8:1	71
8:3	71
9:1–18	71
9:1–2, 13, 26	71
9:26–27	16
18:17	49
22:3	79
22:6–16	71
22:19	71
22:20	71
23:1	156
24:16	156
26:12–18	71
28:6	50

1 Timothy

1:12–14	122
1:13–15	71
1:13	16
3:5	49
4:2	124
4:14	49

2 Timothy

1:14	225

Hebrews

2:3	49
7:21	49

8:9	49

James

2:8	162
2:14, 17	222
5:16	222

1 Peter

5:7	49

2 Peter

1:12	49
3:16	159